The
Fisherman's
Field Guide

The

Fisherman's

Field Guide

to the
Freshwater
and
Saltwater Gamefish
of North America
by
Robert Elman

A Ridge Press Book

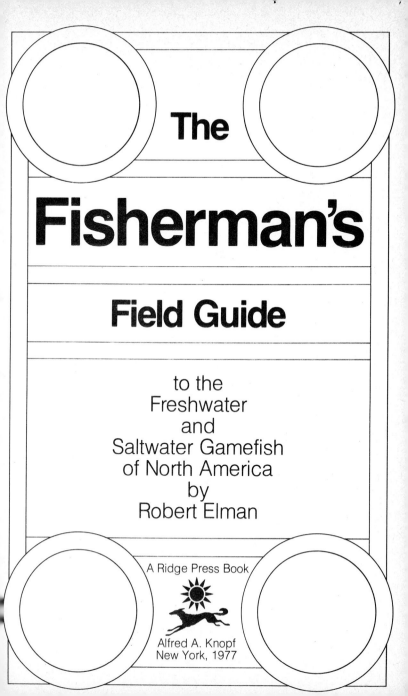

Alfred A. Knopf
New York, 1977

Editor-in-Chief: Jerry Mason
Editor: Adolph Suehsdorf
Art Director: Harry Brocke
Associate Editor: Ronne Peltzman
Associate Editor: Joan Fisher
Art Associate: Nancy Mack
Art Production: Doris Mullane
Picture Editor: Marion Geisinger

This is a Borzoi Book
Published by Alfred A. Knopf, Inc.

Published in the United States by Alfred A. Knopf, Inc.,
New York, and simultaneously in Canada by Random House of
Canada Limited, Toronto.
Prepared and produced by The Ridge Press.
Distributed by Random House, Inc., New York.

Library of Congress Catalog Card Number: 77-74978
ISBN: 0-394-41399-7

Manufactured in Italy by Mondadori Editore, Verona.

To Ellen—
my favorite partner in fishing as in all else

Photo Credits

Abbreviations

BC—Bruce Coleman
EAB—Erwin A. Bauer
SCA—Stuart C. Apte
SL—Sea Library

Front Cover

Top left: SCA; top rt: Hanson Carroll; btm left: Hanson Carroll; btm rt: Bill Browning.

Back Cover

Top left: SCA; top rt: Peter Lake (SL); btm left: J. C. Hookelheim (SL); btm rt: EAB.

Freshwater and Anadromous Game

18: EAB; 19 (top): Leonard Lee Rue III; (btm): Stouffer Productions (BC); 20: Leonard Lee Rue III; 24: EAB; 27: Leonard Lee Rue III; 29: EAB; 33 (top): Leonard Lee Rue III; (btm): SCA; 34-35 (top & btm left): EAB; (btm rt): Tom Brakefield; 36 (top): Bill Browning; (btm): Hanson Carroll; 37 (top): Everette Short; (btm): Peter & Stephen Maslowski; 38 (top): EAB; (btm): Everette Short; 39 (top): EAB; (btm): Tom Brakefield; 40 (top): Peter & Stephen Maslowski; (btm): J. C. Hookelheim (SL); 42, 44-45, 49: EAB; 52: Tom Brakefield; 55: Thomas D. Fegely; 56-57, 59 (top & btm): EAB; 63: Tom Brakefield; 65 (left & rt): Peter & Stephen Maslowski; 67: EAB; 69: Arkansas Game & Fish Commission; 71, 73: Tom Brakefield; 74: Thomas D. Fegely; 76 (top): Thomas D. Fegely; (btm): Tom Brakefield; 77: Everette Short; 81: Peter & Stephen Maslowski; 82: Thomas D. Fegely; 88-89: Henry E. Bradshaw; 91: Arkansas Game & Fish Commission; 93 (top): Leonard Lee Rue (BC); (btm): Henry E. Bradshaw; 96: EAB; 99: California Dept. of Fish & Game; 102: Thomas D. Fegely; 103, 105: EAB; 110-11: Thomas D. Fegely; 113 (top): BC; (btm): Tom Brakefield; 114: Thomas D. Fegely; 116, 119, 123, 125, 127: EAB; 129: Jane Burton (BC); 133 (top & btm), 134, 137, 139: EAB; 142: BC; 143: Thomas D. Fegely; 149: Leonard Lee Rue III; 153: EAB; 157, 159: SCA; 164: Milton Rosko, Jr.; 166: Leonard Lee Rue; 171, 174: EAB; 176: Doug Wilson; 181: SCA; 184: Bill Browning; 185 (top): Leonard Lee Rue III; (btm): BC; 186 (top): Joe Van Wormer; (btm): EAB; 187: SCA; 188-89 (top & btm rt): Jeffrey O. Foott; (btm left): SCA; 190 (top): Jeffrey O. Foott; (btm): EAB; 191: EAB; 192 (top): Henry E. Bradshaw; (btm): BC; 194, 195: Henry E. Bradshaw; 197: Charles F. Waterman; 201: Milton Rosko, Jr.; 205: Thomas D. Fegely; 209 (top & btm): Tom Brakefield; 210-11 (top left & rt): EAB; (btm): Karl H. Maslowski; 212: EAB; 213 (top): EAB; (btm): Hanson Carroll; 214 (top): EAB; (btm): Hanson Carroll; 215, 216 (top & btm): EAB; 219: Michael P. Gadomski (BC); 220: Thomas D. Fegely; 222: Collection of Robert Elman; 223: J. C. Hookelheim (SL); 224: California Dept. of Fish & Game; 227: Arkansas Game & Fish Commission; 229 (top): Leonard Lee Rue (BC); (btm): Albert Squillace; 235, 239, 247, 248: EAB; 253: U.S. Fish & Wildlife Service; 254: EAB; 259: Tom Brakefield; 261: Bill Browning; 264: EAB; 267: U.S. Dept. of the Interior, Bureau of Sport Fisheries & Wildlife; 269, 271, 274, 277: EAB; 280: Bill Browning;

283, 285: EAB; 288: Montana Dept. of Fish & Game; 291: Leonard Lee Rue III; 294: Peter & Stephen Maslowski; 299: EAB; 301: State of Alaska; 306, 309: J. C. Hookelheim (SL); 313 (top): Tom Brakefield; (btm): EAB; 314 (top): S. Keiser (SL); (btm): Jeffrey O. Foott (BC); 315 (top): Milton Rosko, Jr.; (btm): Steve Ferber; 316 (top): EAB; (btm): James Tallon; 317: EAB; 318 (top): Bill Browning; (btm): Allan Power (BC); 319: EAB; 321 (top): EAB; (btm): Carl Roessler (SL); 322: Thomas D. Fegely.

Saltwater and Brackish-water Game

324-25 (top): EAB; (btm left): Robert Elman; (btm rt): SCA; 326: N.C. Wildlife; 331: SCA; 333: SL; 335: EAB; 337 (top): Everette Short; (btm): James Tallon; 338-39 (top): Jen & Des Bartlett (BC); (btm left): Tom Brakefield; (btm rt): BC; 340 (top): Jeffrey O. Foott (BC); (btm): Robert B. Evans (SL); 341 (top): SCA; (btm): Jeffrey O. Foott (BC); 342: James Tallon; 343 (top & btm): EAB; 344 (top): J. C. Hookelheim (Marineland of the Pacific); (btm): Al Giddings (SL); 346: Steve Ferber; 349: Milton Rosko, Jr.; 353: J. C. Hookelheim (SL); 358: Charles F. Waterman; 360: J. C. Hookelheim (SL); 361: Everette Short; 367, 373: Al Ristori; 375: James Tallon; 379: EAB; 382: Milton Rosko, Jr.; 386 (top): EAB; (btm): Tom Brakefield; 390, 393: J. C. Hookelheim (SL); 394: Milton Love (SL); 397: EAB; 400 (top & btm): BC; 402: SCA; 405: Al Ristori; 406: R. Robert Abrams (BC); 408: BC; 409: SCA; 410: Charles H. Turner (California Dept. of Fish & Game); 413: Charles F. Waterman; 416: J. C. Hookelheim (SL); 418: Everette Short; 419: Florida News Bureau; 421: SCA; 425: BC; 427: Tom Brakefield; 430: EAB; 432: SCA; 435: Des Bartlett (BC); 437: Carl Roessler (SL); 439: EAB; 441: National Oceanic & Atmospheric Administration; 445: BC; 449, 452: SCA; 454: Milton Rosko, Jr.; 457: Doug Wilson; 460: BC; 464, 468: Milton Rosko, Jr.; 473: Timothy O'Keefe (BC); 474: Florida News Bureau; 477: Milton Rosko, Jr.; 480: Wallace Hughes; 483: EAB; 485: Daniel W. Gottshall (SL); 486: Doug Wilson; 489 (top): Peter A. Luke (SL); (btm): Naval Photographic Center; 490 (top): Steve Ferber; (btm): Tom Brakefield; 491: EAB; 492 (top): Tom Brakefield; (btm left & rt): SCA; 493 (top & btm): EAB; 494-95 (top left): Tom Brakefield; (top rt & btm): EAB; 496 (top & btm rt): Daniel W. Gottshall (SL); (btm left): SCA; 501, 503, 505: EAB; 508, 511: Milton Rosko, Jr.; 514: Al Ristori; 518: Charles F. Waterman.

Contents

Introduction

Many years ago my father said something to the effect that one of the joys of fishing is being alone, another is being with good companions, and a third is just being there. By "being there" he meant being immersed in nature, cleansed of the trappings and tensions of modern life, able to concentrate on more important things like the sound of lapping water, the color of the sky, or the sail-topped shape and lemony fragrance of a grayling.

Apart from those three joys, he believed the greatest attraction of angling to be based on intense curiosity about the way fish live and behave down there under a surface that hides so much from human eyes. Catching fish consistently brought him a feeling of satisfaction because it meant he had learned something (though never enough) about that way of life.

Those were the important things, and not a matter of besting a creature with a small brain and a lack of sophistication about human duplicity. I agree with him. Certainly he wanted to bring home fish, and so do I—a stringer of panfish or, in the case of bigger game, an impressive trophy. Doing so, after all, will not make me what is derisively known as a meat-fisherman or game hog as long as I do it by sporting means and within legal limits, as well as the moral and esthetic limits a good fisherman imposes on himself. A stringerful or a bragging-size trophy has little to do with objectionable types of bragging. It is a symbol that something has been learned, and it is also a means of providing oneself with savory and wholesome food.

I believe that most fishermen—certainly all those who are entitled to call themselves sportsmen—share this attitude. Admittedly, there have been occasions when anglers, individually or collectively, failed in their responsibility to their quarry. Sport fishermen probably devastated the weakfish populations more severely than did commercial fishermen before the long decline of that species. Other factors were involved, but the fact remains that the weakfish revived only after years of lightened fishing pressure. In the main, however, anglers are motivated by an enlightened love of the sport, not by the market-trawler's greed. When they say they want to know more about fishing, they do not mean they just want information on the latest tackle or gadgets. They also want to know how a fish is born; how it lives as a larva, juvenile, and adult; how it feeds, escapes enemies, reproduces, and reacts to everything in its watery world. And they want to know about the other denizens of the aquatic ecosystems and their fascinating interactions.

In part, this is the kind of information I have tried to give in this book. Aside from the inherent value of knowledge, such information has applied value, in that the more an angler knows about the habits and habitat of his game, the better he can meet the conditions imposed by a given time, place, water and weather conditions, and type of fish; in other words, the more fish he will catch, whether or not he feels compelled to release most of them.

Obviously, an angler wants to be able to identify unfamiliar species and to know where he can fish for them with reasonable hope of success. I have therefore provided a section on game identification and location of fishing regions in the entry for each species. That, I suppose, is the essence of any field guide, but this guide is meant to go further. I have also devoted copious space, in the final section of each entry, to fish habitat and feeding behavior—the factors on which angling tactics hinge —and have offered suggestions regarding baits and lures, tackle, methods of presentation, preferred depths, temperatures, bottom structure, vegetation, and anything else related to successful fishing tactics.

Much but not all of this lore is based on my experience. I doubt that anyone has fished for and caught every species enumerated in this book. If someone has, he must be exceptionally old, well-traveled, and wealthy. There are, however, authorities who have fished for most or all of the major varieties and many of the minor ones. In appropriate instances, I have relied on their advice or printed works. They are fishermen whose collective expertise is enormous. With regard to scientific data, I have relied on still other authorities in the field of ichthyology and related biological studies. A few of them—Edward C. Migdalski, to cite one example—are sportsmen as well as scientists, and their reference works have therefore been of double value. In the course of writing this guide, I consulted hundreds of books, articles, monographs, and other sources, and if I were to acknowledge the help of so many angling writers individually, the list would read like a roll call of candidates for a Fishing Writers' Hall of Fame. The list would also be somewhat bewildering, as it would have to include other kinds of writers—from Lord Byron to Dickens, to cite two examples this time—who have contributed mostly forgotten bits and scraps to angling lore. The Dolly Varden's name is taken from a Dickensian character, and a poem of Byron's reminded me to devote careful attention (as he did) to the description of a dolphin's eerily changing colors when the fish is taken from the water. I do not mean to slight the angling writers by omitting a book-length bibliography. Where I have relied heavily on details supplied by them or their works—as in the case of Stanley Babson on a couple of bonefishing techniques, or Ernest Schwiebert, Vincent Marinaro, and others on the characteristics of certain types of trout streams—I have mentioned their names in the text.

I have also tried to make my information up-to-date, not only in the matter of recent trends in fish populations, the establishment of various game species in new waters, and the development of new lures and tackle, but also in the matter of biology, wildlife management, and technical nomenclature. Observations regarding spawning, feeding habits, temperature preferences, and migrations are based on the latest available scientific findings. Many orders, families, and genera of fishes are still being classified, with the result that their scientific designations occasionally change. I have used the most recent ones. I have also provided regional vernacular names as well as the most widely accepted common name of each species, because one region's bluegill is another region's bream.

The metric system of weights and measures is gradually overshadowing the old English-American system of pounds and ounces, yards, feet and inches. But most American anglers find metric nomenclature and figures confusing, even though tackle specifications are beginning to appear in metrics. In the text, for the sake of clarity to the majority of readers, I have used the traditional American system. In the tables of fresh- and saltwater world records, I have added the metric conversions.

A final problem in making the information current involved record trophies. Every year (I am almost tempted to say every month) some old record is broken, a new one set. I have not included records in the various tackle-strength categories, as they are too numerous and changeable to be useful in a book of this sort. I have included—both in the text and in charts for quick reference—the all-tackle world records for major American gamefish. Even these tend to change quickly for some species, but they give a fairly reliable indication of the size required to establish a record. In the case of the brown trout, a new record was set while I was finishing work on the book. I managed to change the text accordingly, but because the record is still under review as I complete these final lines of introduction, the new listing is omitted from the official tables. For the compilation of those tables I wish to thank *Field & Stream* (keeper of freshwater records) and the International Game Fish Association (keeper of saltwater records). For the eventual breaking of some of those records, I count on my readers. Whether they happen to be seeking records or just a nice stringer of fish, I hope they will find this book helpful as well as entertaining.

Robert Elman
June 30, 1977

FRESHWATER RECORD FISH CAUGHT BY ROD AND REEL

World Records—North American Game Species

SPECIES		Weight		Length & Girth				
Common Name	Scientific Name	Lbs.-Oz.	Kilograms	Inches	Centimeters	Where	When	Angler
Bass, Largemouth	*Micropterus salmoides*	22-4	10.09	32½x28½	82.55x72.39	Montgomery Lake, Ga.	6/ 2/1932	George W. Perry
Bass, Redeye	*Micropterus coosae*	7-8	3.40	23x18	58.42x45.72	Lazer Creek, Ga.	4/ 9/1975	Jimmy L. Rogers
Bass, Rock	*Ambloplites rupestis*	3	1.36	13½x10¾	34.29x27.31	York River, Ontario	8/ 1/1974	Peter Gulgin
Bass, Smallmouth	*Micropterus dolomieui*	11-15	5.40	27x21⅔	68.58x55.04	Dale Hollow Lake, Ky.	7/ 9/1955	David L. Hayes
Bass, Spotted	*Micropterus punctulatus spp*	8-10½	3.92	23½x19⅞	59.69x50.50	Smith Lake, Alabama	2/25/1972	Billy Henderson
Bass, White	*Morone chrysops*	5-5	2.41	19½x17	49.53x43.18	Ferguson Lake, Calif.	3/ 8/1972	Norman W. Mize
Bass, Yellow	*Morone mississippiensis*	2-2	.96	14x13	35.56x33.02	Lake Monona, Wis.	1/18/1972	James Thrun
Bluegill	*Lepomis macrochirus*	4-12	2.15	15x18¼	38.10x46.36	Ketona Lake, Alabama	4/ 9/1950	T. S. Hudson
Bullhead, Black	*Ictalurus melas*	8	3.63	24x17¾	60.96x45.09	Lake Waccabuc, N.Y.	8/ 1/1951	Kani Evans
Carp	*Cyprinus carpio*	55-5	25.08	42x31	106.68x78.74	Clearwater Lake, Minn.	7/10/1952	Frank J. Ledwein
Catfish, Blue	*Ictalurus furcatus*	97	44.00	57x37	144.78x93.98	Missouri River, S.D.	9/16/1959	Edward B. Elliott
Catfish, Channel	*Ictalurus punctatus*	58	26.31	47¼x29⅛	120.02x73.98	Santee-Cooper Res., S.C.	7/ 7/1964	W. B. Whaley
Catfish, Flathead	*Pylodictis olivaris*	79-8	36.06	44x27	111.76x68.58	White River, Indiana	8/13/1966	Glenn T. Simpson
Catfish, White	*Ictalurus catus*	10-5	4.67	25x17½	63.50x44.45	Raritan R., N.J.	6/23/1976	Lewis W. Lomerson
Char, Arctic	*Salvelinus alpinus*	29-11	13.47	39¾x26	100.97x66.04	Arctic R., N.W.T.	8/21/1968	Jeanne P. Branson
Crappie, Black	*Pomoxis nigromaculatus*	5	2.27	19¼ x18⅝	48.90x47.32	Santee-Cooper Res., S.C.	3/15/1957	Paul E. Foust
Crappie, White	*Pomoxis annularis*	5-3	2.35	21x19	53.34x48.26	Enid Dam, Miss.	7/31/1957	Fred L. Bright
Dolly Varden	*Salvelinus malma*	32	14.51	40½x29¾	102.87x75.57	L. Pend Oreille, Idaho	10/27/1949	N. L. Higgins
Drum, Freshwater	*Aplodinotus grunniens*	54-8	24.72	31½x29	80.01x73.66	Nickajack Lake, Tenn.	4/20/1972	Benny E. Hull
Gar, Alligator	*Lepisosteus spatula*	279	126.55	93	236.22	Rio Grande River, Texas	12/ 2/1951	Bill Valverde
Gar, Longnose	*Lepisosteus osseus*	50-5	22.82	72¼x22¼	183.52x56.52	Trinity River, Texas	7/30/1954	Townsend Miller
Grayling, American	*Thymallus arcticus*	5-15	2.69	29⅞ x15⅛	75.90x38.42	Katseyedie R., N.W.T.	8/16/1967	Jeanne P. Branson
Kokanee	*Oncorhynchus nerka*	6-9¾	3.00	24½x14½	62.23x36.83	Priest L., Idaho	6/ 9/1975	Jerry Verge
Muskellunge	*Esox masquinongy*	69-15	31.72	64½x31¾	163.83x80.65	St. Lawrence River, N.Y.	9/22/1957	Arthur Lawton

Species	Scientific name	Weight (lb-oz)	Weight (kg)	Length × Girth (in)	Length × Girth (cm)	Location	Date	Angler
Perch, White	*Morone americanus*	4-12	2.15	19½x13	49.53x33.02	Messalonskee Lake, Me.	6/ 4/1949	Mrs. Earl Small
Perch, Yellow	*Perca flavescens*	4-3½	1.91			Bordentown, N.J.	5/ /1865	Dr. C. C. Abbot
Pickerel, Chain	*Esox niger*	9-6	4.25	31x14	78.74x35.56	Homerville, Georgia	2/17/1961	Baxley McQuaig, Jr.
Pike, Northern	*Esox lucius*	46-2	20.92	52½x25	133.35x63.50	Sacandaga Res., N.Y.	9/15/1940	Peter Dubuc
Salmon, Atlantic	*Salmo salar*	79-2	35.89			Tana River, Norway	1928	Henrik Henriksen
Salmon, Chinook	*Oncorhynchus tshawytscha*	92	41.73	58½x36	148.59x91.44	Skeena River, B.C.	7/19/1959	Heinz Wichman
Salmon, Chum	*Oncorhynchus keta*	24-4	11.00	40½x22⅞	102.87x58.12	Margarita Bay, Alaska	8/19/1974	Richard Coleman
Salmon, Landlocked	*Salmo salar*	22-8	10.21	36	91.44	Sebago Lake, Maine	8/ 1/1907	Edward Blakely
Salmon, Coho	*Oncorhynchus kisutch*	31	14.06			Cowichan Bay, B.C.	10/11/1947	Mrs. Lee Hallberg
Sauger	*Stizostedion canadense*	8-12	3.97	28x15	71.12x38.10	Lake Sakakawea, N.D.	10/ 6/1971	Mike Fischer
Shad, American	*Alosa sapidissima*	9-2	4.14	25x17½	63.50x44.45	Enfield, Connecticut	4/28/1973	Edward P. Nelson
Sturgeon, White	*Acipenser transmontanus*	360	163.30	111x86	281.94x218.44	Snake River, Idaho	4/24/1956	Willard Cravens
Sunfish, Green	*Lepomis cyanellus*	2-2	.96	14¾x14	37.47x35.56	Stockton Lake, Missouri	6/18/1971	Paul M. Diley
Sunfish, Redear	*Lepomis microlophus*	4-8	2.04	16¼'x17¾	41.28x45.09	Chase City, Virginia	6/19/1970	Maurice E. Ball
Trout, Brook	*Salvelinus fontinalis*	14-8	6.58	31½	80.01	Nipigon River, Ontario	7/ /1916	Dr. W. J. Cook
Trout, Brown	*Salmo trutta*	Record being reviewed						
Trout, Cutthroat	*Salmo clarki*	41	18.60	39	99.06	Pyramid Lake, Nevada	12/ /1925	John Skimmerhorn
Trout, Golden	*Salmo aguabonita*	11	4.99	28x16	71.12x40.64	Cook's Lake, Wyoming	8/ 5/1948	Chas. S. Reed
Trout, Lake	*Salvelinus namaycush*	65	29.48	52x38	132.08x96.52	Great Bear L., N.W.T.	8/ 8/1970	Larry Daunis
Trout, Rainbow, Stlhd. or Kamloops	*Salmo gairdneri*	42-2	19.10	43x23½	109.22x59.69	Bell Island, Alaska	6/22/1970	David Robert White
Trout, Sunapee	*Salvelinus aureolus*	11-8	5.22	33x17¼	83.82x43.82	Lake Sunapee, N.H.	8/ 1/1954	Ernest Theoharis
Trout, Tiger	*Brown X Brook*	10	4.54	27x16¾	68.58x42.55	Deerskin River, Wis.	5/23/1974	Charles J. Mattek
Walleye	*Stizostedion vitreum*	25	11.34	41x29	104.14x73.66	Old Hickory Lake, Tenn.	8/ 1/1960	Mabry Harper
Warmouth	*Lepomis gulosus*	2	.91	12x12½	30.48x31.75	Sylvania, Ga.	5/ 4/1974	Carlton Robbins
Whitefish, Lake	*Coregonus clupeaformis*	13	5.90	32¼x19	81.92x48.26	Great Bear L., N.W.T.	7/14/1974	Robert L. Stintsman
Whitefish, Mountain	*Prosopium williamsoni*	5	2.27	19x14	48.26x35.56	Athabasca R., Alberta	6/ 3/1963	Orville Welch

Records compiled by Field & Stream

SALTWATER RECORD FISH CAUGHT BY ROD AND REEL

World Records—North American Game Species

SPECIES		Weight		Length & Girth				
Common Name	**Scientific Name**	**Lbs.-Oz.**	**Kilograms**	**Inches**	**Centimeters**	**Where**	**When**	**Angler**
Albacore	*Thunnus alalunga*	74-13	33.93	50x34¾	127x88.27	Canary Islands	10/28/1973	Olof Idegren
Amberjack, Greater	*Seriola dumerili*	149	67.59	71x41¾	180.34x106.05	Bermuda	6/21/1954	Peter Simons
Barracuda, Great	*Sphyraena barracuda*	83	37.65	72¼x29	183.52x73.66	Lagos, Nigeria	1/13/1952	K. J. W. Hackett
Bass, Black Sea	*Centropristis striata*	8	3.63	22x19	55.88x48.26	Nantucket Sound, Mass.	5/13/1951	H. R. Rider
Bass, Giant Sea	*Stereolepis gigas*	563-8	255.60	89x72	226.06x182.88	Anacapa Island, Calif.	8/20/1968	James D. McAdam, Jr.
Bass, Striped	*Morone saxatilis*	72	32.66	54½x31	138.43x78.74	Cuttyhunk, Mass.	10/10/1969	Edward J. Kirker
Bluefish	*Pomatomus saltatrix*	31-12	14.40	47x23	119.38x58.42	Hatteras Inlet, N.C.	1/30/1972	James M. Hussey
Bonefish	*Albula vulpes*	19	8.62	39⅝x17	100.66x43.18	Zululand, So. Africa	5/26/1962	Brian W. Batchelor
Cobia	*Rachycentron canadum*	110-5	50.04	63x34	160.02x86.36	Mombasa, Kenya	9/ 8/1954	Eric Tinworth
Cod	*Gadus morhua*	98-12	44.79	63x41	160.02x104.14	Isle of Shoals, N.H.	6/ 8/1969	Alphonse J. Bielevich
Dolphin	*Coryphaena hippurus*	85	38.56	69x37½	175.26x95.25	Spanish Wells, Bahamas	5/29/1968	Richard Seymour
Drum, Black	*Pogonias cromis*	113-1	51.28	53⅛x43½	134.94x110.49	Lewes, Del.	9/15/1975	Gerald M. Townsend
Drum, Red	*Sciaenops ocellata*	90	40.82	55½x38¼	140.97x97.16	Rodanthe, N.C.	11/ 7/1973	Elvin Hooper
Flounder	*Paralichthys spp.*	30-12	13.95	38½x30½	97.79x77.47	Vina del Mar, Chile	11/ 1/1971	Agusto Nunez Moreno
Jewfish	*Epinephelus itajara*	680	308.45	85½x66	217.17x167.64	Fernandina Beach, Fla.	5/20/1961	Lynn Joyner
Mackerel, King	*Scomberomorus cavalla*	90	40.82	71x30	180.34x76.20	Key West, Fla.	2/16/1976	Norton I. Thomton
Marlin, Atlantic Blue	*Makaira nigricans*	1142	518.01	166x80	421.64x203.20	Nags Head, N.C.	7/26/1974	Jack Herrington
Marlin, Black	*Makaira indica*	1560	707.62	174x81	441.96x205.74	Cabo Blanco, Peru	8/ 4/1953	A. C. Glassell, Jr.
Marlin, Pacific Blue	*Makaira nigricans*	1153	523.00	176x73	447.04x185.42	Ritidian Point, Guam	8/21/1969	Greg D. Perez
Marlin, Striped	*Tetrapturus audax*	415	188.24	132x52	335.28x132.08	Cape Brett, N.Z.	3/31/1964	B. C. Bain
Marlin, White	*Tetrapturus albidus*	174-3	79.01	104⅓x35½	265.00x90.17	Vitoria, Brazil	11/ 1/1975	Otavio Canha Reboucas
Permit	*Trachinotus falcatus*	50-8	22.91	44¾x33¾	113.67x85.73	Key West, Fla.	3/15/1971	Marshall E. Earnest
Pollock	*Pollachius virens*	46-7	21.07	50½x30	128.27x76.20	Brielle, N.J.	5/26/1975	John Tomes Holton
Roosterfish	*Nematistius pectoralis*	114	51.71	64x33	162.56x83.82	LaPaz, Mexico	6/ 1/1960	Abe Sackheim
Runner, Rainbow	*Elagatis bipinnulata*	33-10	15.25	55¼x22½	140.34x57.15	Clarion Is., Mexico	3/14/1976	Ralph A. Mikkelsen

Sailfish, Atlantic	*Istiophorus platypterus*		128-1	58.09	106¼x34¼	269.88x87.00	Luando, Angola	3/27/1974	Harm Steyn
Sailfish, Pacific	*Istiophorus platypterus*		221	100.25	129	327.66	Galapagos Islands	2/12/1947	Carl W. Stewart
Seabass, White	*Cynoscion nobilis*		83-12	37.99	65½x34	166.37x86.36	San Felipe, Mexico	3/31/1953	L. C. Baumgardner
Seatrout, Spotted	*Cynoscion nebulosis*	TIE	15-3	6.89	34½x20½	87.63x52.07	Fort Pierce, Fla.	1/13/1949	C. W. Hubbard
			15-6	6.98	33x23¾	83.82x60.33	Jensen Beach, Fla.	5/ 4/1969	Michael J. Foremny
Shark, Blue	*Prionace glauca*	TIE	410	185.98	138x52	350.52x132.08	Rockport, Mass.	9/ 1/1960	Richard C. Webster
			410	185.98	134x52½	340.36x133.35	Rockport, Mass.	8/17/1967	Martha C. Webster
Shark, Hammerhead	*Sphyrnidae*		703	318.88	172x63	436.88x160.02	Jacksonville, Fla.	7/ 5/1975	H. B. "Blackie" Reasor
Shark, Porbeagle	*Lamna nasus*		430	195.05	96x63	243.84x160.02	Channel Islands, England	6/29/1969	Desmond Bougourd
Shark, Shortfin Mako	*Isurus oxyrinchus*		1061	481.27	146x79½	370.84x201.93	Mayor Island, N.Z.	2/17/1970	James B. Penwarden
Shark, Thresher	*Alopias vulpinus*		739	335.21	106x68	269.24x172.72	Tutukaka, N.Z.	2/17/1975	Brian Galvin
Shark, Tiger	*Galeocerdo cuvieri*		1780	807.41	166½x103	422.91x261.62	Cherry Grove, S.C.	6/14/1964	Walter Maxwell
Shark, White	*Carcharodon carcharias*		2664	1208.39	202x114	513.08x289.56	Ceduna, So. Australia	4/21/1959	Alfred Dean
Snook (Robalo)	*Centropomus undecimalis*		52-6	23.76	49½x26	125.73x66.04	LaPaz, Mexico	1/ 9/1963	Jane Haywood
Swordfish	*Xiphias gladius*		1182	536.16	179¼x78	455.30x198.12	Iquique, Chile	5/ 7/1953	L. Marron
Tarpon	*Megalops atlantica*		283	128.37	86³/₅	219.96	Lake Maracaibo, Ven.	3/19/1956	M. Salazar
Tautog	*Tautoga onitis*		21-6	9.70	31½x23½	80.01x59.69	Cape May, N.J.	6/12/1954	R. N. Sheafer
Tuna, Atlantic Bigeye	*Thunnus obesus*		335-1	151.98	100¾x60¼	255.91x153.04	Canary Islands	7/11/1975	Wilhelm Rapp
Tuna, Blackfin	*Thunnus atlanticus*	TIE	38	17.24	39¼x28¾	99.70x73.03	Bermuda	6/26/1970	Archie L. Dickens
			38	17.24	41x28	104.14x71.12	Islamorada, Fla.	5/22/1973	Elizabeth Jean Wade
Tuna, Bluefin	*Thunnus thynnus*		1120	508.03	122x85½	309.88x217.17	Prince Edward Island	10/19/1973	Lee Coffin
Tuna, Pacific Bigeye	*Thunnus obesus*		435	197.32	93x63½	236.22x161.29	Cabo Blanco, Peru	4/17/1957	Dr. Russel V. A. Lee
Tuna, Skipjack	*Euthynnus pelamis*	TIE	39-15	18.11	39x28	99.06x71.12	Walker Cay, Bahamas	1/21/1952	F. Drowley
			40	18.14	38¾x27½	98.43x69.85	Mauritius	4/19/1971	J. R. P. Caboche, Jr.
Tuna, Yellowfin	*Thunnus albacares*		308	139.71	84x57	213.36x144.78	San Benedicto Is., Mex.	1/18/1973	Harold J. Tolson
Tunny, Little	*Euthynnus alletteratus*		27	12.25	39x22	99.06x55.88	Key Largo, Fla.	4/20/1976	William E. Allison
Wahoo	*Acanthocybium solanderi*		149	67.59	79¾x37½	202.57x95.25	Cat Cay, Bahamas	6/15/1962	John Pirovano
Weakfish	*Cynoscion regalis*		19-8	8.85	37x25¾	93.98x65.41	Trinidad, West Indies	4/13/1962	Dennis B. Hall
Yellowtail	*Seriola dorsalis*		111	50.35	62x38	157.48x96.52	Bay of Islands, N.Z.	6/11/1961	A. F. Plim

Records compiled by the International Game Fish Association

Freshwater
and
Anadromous
Game

◀ Fly-rodder netting brown trout. ▲ Northern pike. ▼ Pacific salmon leaping falls.

American Grayling *(Thymallus arcticus)*
COMMON & REGIONAL NAMES: *grayling, arctic grayling, Alaska grayling*

GAME IDENTIFICATION & LOCATION OF FISHING REGIONS: On some cold, clear river in Alaska or northern Canada, the main channel deepens and swerves through a pool where minuscule shrimp scurry, where several varieties of duns hatch, and where other ephemera, flotsam on the current, bob and flutter into the eddies after their brief imago stage has flickered away. A fisherman gingerly steps downstream toward the pool's edge. Here the water becomes too deep for wading and he peers ahead, hoping his polarized sunglasses will help him penetrate the surface reflections. He thinks—or wants to think—he can discern several slim shadows hovering near the bottom, perhaps seven or eight feet deep. He backs off, then casts across and down, letting a Dark Hendrickson dry fly fall gently to the surface a yard or so upstream of the nearest shadow. He uses a long, delicate, tapered leader, but even this light tippet may alarm a grayling if the fish detects it before seeing the fly.

He keeps his line slack, letting the fly drift naturally on the current. It passes above one of the shadows and sweeps toward his side of the river as the line begins finally to go taut. Just before the fly skims over, another shadow turns, rises in a long arc, follows the fly for a moment, puckers the surface, but fails to snatch the offering. The fish has not quite been persuaded, but neither has it been seriously alarmed. A grayling is more inquisitive than a trout and not as easily put down.

The angler tries again, and again, and at last switches from the Hendrickson to an Adams Spentwing. It is of little consequence that the Hendrickson mimics an *Ephemerella subvaria,* a mayfly dun that does not inhabit this particular water. Neither does the impressionistic Adams represent a species prevalent here (or anywhere), but both artificials are sufficiently like local ephemeroptera. A switch from one somber pattern to another sometimes fools grayling that have become suspicious of a repeatedly presented fly.

This time a fish clears the surface in a porpoise roll and sucks in the fly on the way down. The angler, controlling his impulse, waits a split second for the grayling's small jaws to

Angler examining dorsal fin of male grayling.

mantle the lure, and then he sets the hook. Experience has disabused him of the fiction, recurrent in angling literature ever since Izaak Walton popularized it, that a grayling "has so tender a mouth, that he is oftener lost after an angler has hooked him, than any other fish." The mouth is not a whit too tender to hold a barb. The difficulty is the smallness of the gape. The hook must be appropriately small and, even then, if set an instant too soon its point will barely have passed the lip and will easily pull away; the fish must have that instant to drink it in.

The fish arches into the air, spraying droplets as dramatically as a trout or char—it is, after all, a fellow member of the salmon family—then dives for the bottom and runs. It does not leap as many times as a trout might, nor can it battle as long or brilliantly, but a 2-pound American grayling is very game for its size and very beautiful when at last it is laid gently on the gravel. Even its odor is a pleasant surprise; when first taken from the water it smells faintly like thyme, the herb for which its genus was named.

No other salmonid has this refreshing fragrance, and none duplicates the grayling's high, sweeping sail of dorsal fin, which always has at least seventeen rays. The fin indicates sex as well as genus. On a female, its forward portion is higher than the rear, while the male's dorsal rises toward the rear and tends to be larger than the female's in proportion to body size.

At least four species and several more subspecies of grayling are scattered over the world. The American grayling, though it occurs in Siberia, too, and is closely related to the European grayling, is the lone representative of the genus in the Western Hemisphere. Its coloration varies, but as a rule the dorsal fin is gray or purplish with irregular rows of bluish spots, some of which may be outlined in red. Often this fin has a vague pink or whitish edging. The other fins and the forked tail are dark, usually a murky yellow-green, and sometimes the pectoral fins are vaguely striped along their rays with pink and black. The upper body is gray, silver, bronze, or brown, darkening on the back. The sides are silvery and the forward parts randomly marked with black or purplish spots, some of which may be delicately rimmed with green. Like many other bright and handsome fish, a grayling quickly fades after death. In life it gleams with iridescent tones that shift with the light—glints of brass and gold, rose and lilac.

It is a freshwater fish of cold, clear, arctic and alpine rivers and oligotrophic lakes, that is, lakes whose depths hold abundant oxygen throughout the summer. Alaska has some of the finest fishing. The big Alaskan rivers tend to be too silty, but the tributaries—and the big-river stretches where those tributaries empty—are clear and fast enough to provide ideal habitat.

In the southwestern part of the state, the Ugashik Lakes near Bristol Bay are known for large grayling, and the fishing is excellent in many of the western rivers: the Brooks, Kuskokwim, Holitna, Hoholitna, Stony, Aniak, and others. Some of these waters are equally renowned for rainbows, Dolly Vardens, pike, salmon, and lake trout. To the east, in the Yukon-Tanana drainage, there are famous grayling streams like the Nation, the Charley, the upper reaches of the Kandik, the Tatonduk, Chantanika, Fortymile River, Clear Creek, and Birch Creek.

The streams of the Yukon Territory also hold many grayling, as do Great Bear Lake, Great Slave Lake, and numerous other waters in the western half of the Northwest Territories. There is good grayling fishing in parts of upper British Columbia, but it is better in the lakes of Alberta and Saskatchewan. Among the famous ones are the Careen in Saskatchewan, the Athabasca on the Alberta-Saskatchewan border, and the Reindeer on the Saskatchewan-Manitoba border.

The retreat of the great glaciers left isolated populations of grayling in lakes and streams of the Rocky Mountains and in Michigan. A small subspecies was plentiful on the Michigan peninsula until late in the nineteenth century, when it was extirpated by a combination of intensive commercial fishing, unregulated sport fishing, and a severe alteration of water conditions caused by deforestation. Isolated stocks in the Big Hole and Green River watersheds of Montana and Wyoming fared better. Small but fishable populations of the Montana race *(T. montanus)* remain in those states and in Utah's Uinta Mountains, where they were introduced in 1899.

FISH HABITAT & FEEDING BEHAVIOR—ANGLING TACTICS: In a frigid, relatively sterile northern habitat, the growth rate is slow even for a fish like the grayling, which continues to feed actively on bitter winter days. It may attain a length of 4 inches in its first year, 6 or 8 in its second, but then its growth decelerates. In the

big lakes of the Northwest Territories, biologists have found that a 2-pound grayling is usually nine years old, and anywhere in its range a 3-pound grayling is almost certainly more than seven years old. Below the Canadian border, a grayling more than half that size is rare. In the North, slow growth is offset by long life. The food is sufficient, water conditions right, disturbance and predation moderate despite enemies like the large and voracious inconnu, or sheefish, a game species that feeds avidly on small grayling. Three-pound grayling are fairly common in the North. Fish measuring over 20 inches and weighing 5 pounds have been caught on Great Slave Lake. The world record, just an ounce under 6 pounds, was a male taken from the Katseyedie River in the Northwest Territories. Whereas a trophy bass is usually a female, a trophy grayling is more often a male.

Most salmonids, including the European grayling, deposit their eggs in redds, but the American grayling spawns without

Arctic grayling resting near bottom.

a nest. Breeding takes place from March until June in small, fast, gravelly streams. The male establishes a territory and, when repelling other males, erects his imposing dorsal fin as a threat gesture.

The female may produce only a couple of thousand eggs and seldom more than about thirteen thousand. Some of the mature fish, three years old or more, fail to spawn in a given year in any locality, for an individual grayling breeds but once in two or three years. By comparison with other fish, the species is not prolific; if it were, the cold northern habitat might not provide enough food.

Nearly three weeks elapse before the eggs develop into troutlike fry with large yolk sacs. As soon as the sacs are absorbed, the young must begin to cruise in search of prey. The adults also spend much time cruising rather than lying in wait for food, and on a summer morning or evening the fishing is often best around rocky points or near shorelines, where they hunt. During the greater part of the day, however, most of the grayling stay in deeper water. Unlike trout, they move and hold in schools. A common prospecting method is to drift or paddle along, perhaps twenty yards from shore, watching for submarine shadows and for the dimpling of the surface when grayling rise to gulp an insect or some other bit of food. Although they may forage anywhere, they often establish favorite resting and feeding spots. A typical holding area is a deep pocket or a channel where the current is eddied by a boulder, sunken log, or other obstacle. A fisherman crossing a deep pool in a canoe might look down and see a whole school, perhaps a couple of dozen grayling, lying over the bottom. Oddly, they do not take quick alarm at the approach of a boat or a wading angler, yet the leader an angler uses must be almost a gossamer and must exert no drag on a drifting fly or the grayling will shy from it.

An angler who neglects to examine the stomach contents of his catch may assume that grayling feed chiefly if not entirely on mayflies, stoneflies, caddisflies, and similar insects. The assumption is logical since the species readily takes nymphs and wet flies and will hungrily rise to a dry fly. In fact, a grayling often turns, moves back toward a drifting fly, and lunges for it with lupine rapacity. If the northern waters produced continually sufficient insect life, perhaps such prey would be the grayling's mainstay. Actually, small freshwater shrimps and scuds are the staples, and a grayling reacts to insect food almost as a child reacts to candy—or as a gourmet fisherman reacts to the delicately flavored white flesh of a grayling poached with white wine and herbs.

An examination of stomach contents can produce more surprises than just a paucity of insect foods. Anglers have reported finding blueberries and blueberry stains in the stomachs of grayling when the fruits were ripening and dropping. A typical grayling may station itself just off the bottom, several yards below a boulder, log, or other eddying object, to await what nature offers. When some morsel—often invisible to the angler—drifts near, the fish swims up to meet it but hesitates, facing upstream, finning backward for several feet to inspect the food before taking it in a rush and swimming back to the lie. Watching this procedure, an angler cannot always deduce what morsels will tempt the fish; sometimes experimentation is needed.

Although the American species is less selective than the European grayling, on occasion it can become touchy about accepting flies. A hundred miles north of the Arctic Circle one recent September day, a veteran angler fished the clear pools of a stream that was about to ice up. Unable to raise a single grayling on free-drifted dries or wets, he began to experiment. At that time and place, as he soon discovered, the grayling would take any dark nymph—would take it, that is, when the free drift was enhanced by a little subtle twitching action.

To tempt a grayling it is not necessary to match the fly pattern to any local insect hatch, but it is important to choose dark or dull flies. A Quill Gordon, a Hendrickson, or a March Brown may be very successful, but not because these patterns imitate species of mayflies with some degree of realism. Equal success is possible with a Dark Cahill's much vaguer suggestion of a mayfly, or with an Adams, which might be described as an impressionistic rendering of a caddis possessing mayfly characteristics. A stonefly imitation will also bring strikes, as will quite nondescript patterns like the Brown Hackle and Gray Hackle. Flies suggesting the various ephemera are generally tied on hooks ranging from size 10 down to 14 for this kind of fishing.

There are times when grayling seem to be interested almost exclusively in very small terrestrial insects, perhaps having

had their appetites spurred by a windfall. At these times the most consistent action is to be had with an ant, midge, or gnat imitation tied on a very small hook—no. 18 or 20.

Grayling can also be caught with bait such as salmon roe on a small egg hook. However, users of spinning tackle generally do at least as well with lures—small, light spinners or the smallest of wobbling spoons. The red-and-white candy-striped standby will attract grayling, just as it attracts other game species, and a brass, gold, or silver finish also works well. To most anglers, however, a major element in the mystique of grayling fishing is the deft presentation of a dry fly.

String of grayling caught on Alaskan stream.

Black Bass *(Micropterus)*

GENERAL DESCRIPTION & DISTRIBUTION: In the Pocono Mountains there is a sprawling impoundment, fed by a creek, several smaller streams and springs, and the mountain runoff that percolates down through granite boulders along much of the shoreline. Walleyes and a few rainbows cruise the depths or rest among treetops five fathoms down, or still deeper amid the algae-covered ruins of a submerged village. Occasionally, in twenty-foot water over a weedy bar, a small muskellunge delights or panics a trolling angler. Near the stream mouths are brook trout and brown trout, and in the shallows of the islands and the shoreline points and coves are pickerel, yellow perch, assorted minnows that will never grow longer than 3 inches or so, 3-inch fingerlings that will reach 3 feet if they survive the constant predation of their elders, and sunfishes—redears, pumpkinseeds, rock bass.

At one time or another, two enormously more impressive members of the sunfish family prowl these waters from the grassy shoals to the underwater valleys. Thick-tailed, deep-bodied, powerful, with glistening blackish-green backs and darkly splotched olive or bronze sides, they are the most famous species of the black bass genus—the largemouth and the smallmouth. In waters like this, both the geographic ranges and the habitats of the largemouth and smallmouth overlap.

Cloistered in the mixed timber nearby are several small natural lakes that hold bass, but some of the local anglers like to fish the impoundment often, even now while it is slowly recovering from disastrous storms. Several winters ago, deep snow covered the ice and impeded photosynthesis by the aquatic plants; some fish simply died in the prolonged cold, while many more perished for lack of oxygen. Then there was a high runoff and a spring storm that washed away or silted over the spawning nests. Last year hardly more than two out of ten bass caught here were legal "keepers"—9 inches long or better. But barrel-bellied lunkers had survived to spawn again, and the ratio is improving. Although bass grow slowly in northerly waters, in six years there will be 3-pound smallmouths once again, and there will be largemouths a foot and a half long, weighing 7 pounds or more.

In the cool early morning one of the shrewd local anglers regularly canoes the shallows. Even in the shade of bluffs and

Angler removing hook from lip of smallmouth bass.

trees there is plenty of room for the leisurely backcasts of his 8½-foot fly rod as he twitches bass bugs over the surface. Just before dusk he puts on waders, awkwardly hitches into the leg straps of a big nylon-covered rubber doughnut—a "waterwalker"—and floats and foot-paddles about near the creek mouth, where clear water riffles over gravel and tumbles into the reservoir. Even in midsummer the water there is cool and well oxygenated. Near it is a patch of swaying pickerelweed. Little baitfish dart through the fringes, every minute of their lives a simultaneous foraging and escape from predators that include hordes of sunnies as well as bass and the other large gamefish. Here the smallmouth bass and the largemouth share a single transitional domain.

Encumbered by his float and unabashedly clumsy with loose coils of line, the angler now abandons his fly rod for a light spinning rod with monofilament testing 6 pounds. He will cast spinners and spinner-flies, bugs and plugs, plastic worms and occasionally real ones. The weeds claim many, and his inner-tube float—more often seen in the weedy, shallow lakes of the South than on northern reservoirs—may elicit smiles from anglers comfortably chaired atop big bass boats. Whether from angler's obstinacy or frequent success, he persists.

At moderate speed he retrieves a green-and-silver, slab-sided, big-lipped floating-diving plug that is abruptly yanked by a pumpkinseed no more than twice the size of the lure. He releases the sunny, fortunately snagged on only one hook, thinks about the small unfortunate hoptoad in a little bait box clipped to his vest, and switches instead to another artificial, a buckhair grasshopper trailing behind a transparent plastic casting bubble. After a dozen casts, as the hopper lies motionless on the water while the angler thinks about switching again, the surface swirls, the lure disappears with a plopping sound, and the rod bows. He takes in the slack fast, feeling the positive tugs, and sets the hook hard. The fish comes out once, in a low arc that reminds him of small brook trout, then sounds toward deeper water.

A smallmouth is his guess. They seem to jump less in lakes than in rivers. A largemouth probably would stay in the shallows, jumping more, head-wagging to throw the hook, twisting through weeds and around snags that wrap up line.

Mingling pleasure and shame, he plays the bass a few seconds longer than necessary before raising the rod up high, and with his other hand he lifts the fish by its lower lip. Wriggling and spraying droplets from its wide, flapping tail, it has a rich brownish-bronze gleam in the evening sun. On its sides are dark, ragged olive spots and vertical bars, but they almost run together like the lateral bar on a largemouth, and coloration varies somewhat among individuals as well as regionally. Though he already knows his catch is a smallmouth, he enjoys examining it for the other distinguishing characteristics—less because he needs confirmation than because each fish is strange and beautiful.

The upper jaw of this one extends to a point just below the rear rim of its dark, unmoving eye: fairly long for the maxillary of a smallmouth, short for a largemouth. Still, there can be no doubt, for the spiny forward portion of the dorsal fin is connected to the rear portion with only a dip in the membrane, not a complete notch as on a largemouth. Moreover, the scales overlap the base of the soft portion. They are absent near the posterior dorsal of a largemouth.

Though black bass can tolerate slight salinity and are sometimes found in estuaries, they are freshwater fishes, unrelated to the true basses (Serranidae). They are the largest of the sunfishes (Centrarchidae). There are six species totaling eleven forms, or varieties, if the largest of all, the Florida largemouth, is counted as a subspecies. Some taxonomists have been reluctant to grant separate status to the Florida bass (which might more accurately be named the southern bass, as it is common from lower Kentucky to Florida). Apart from its great size and weight—often more than 10 pounds, sometimes twice that—it differs from the northern race only in having more scales in the lateral line and more rows of scales above and below it. Among the other species, too, racial differences are subtle, consisting chiefly of variations in scale count and coloration. There are, in addition to the northern and Florida largemouth, a northern smallmouth and a Neosho smallmouth (the latter having very limited distribution); and there are northern, Alabama, and Wichita spotted bass (sometimes called Kentucky bass), a Guadalupe bass, a Suwannee bass, and the Apalachicola and Alabama races of redeye bass. The largemouth and smallmouth are by far the most important species to the angler, and also the most widely distributed. The spotted bass is next in importance, followed at a considerable distance by the redeye, Guadalupe, and Suwannee, all three of which are small in size as well as distribution.

All black bass have dark backs, often black or blackish-green, with green, olive, or bronze sides barred or raggedly spotted and fading to white on the belly; and all are chunky, with relatively large dorsal and anal fins and a wide, moderately bifurcated tail. The less important varieties have jaws like that of the smallmouth and markings approaching those of either the largemouth or smallmouth. Under their specific headings, more detailed descriptions will be given for field identification.

Black bass, indigenous to North America, originally existed in the eastern, southern, and midwestern portions of the United States. The northernmost species is the smallmouth, whose natural range extends into lower Canada. Both the largemouth and smallmouth have now been established throughout the country and in Europe, Africa, and Latin America. Details of North American range—the location of good fishing regions—will be given for each species.

GENERAL LIFE CYCLE & ANGLING STRATEGIES: Spawning usually begins when the water temperature climbs above 60°. In the North this is usually in May or early June; in the deep South it often starts in February, and there are places where largemouth spawning activity may occur in every month of the year. The fisherman's quarry, like the hunter's, is most easily duped at breeding time, and there is danger of overharvesting where spawning is concentrated during a short period; this is why the bass season is closed until July in some states. However, there are regions where carefully controlled fishing of the spawning beds does not reduce the population sufficiently to be injurious. Up in New Brunswick, for example, spawning season is the best time of all for catching smallmouths—and most of the bass taken at that time are released. When in the shallows to breed, they are not only hungry but aggressively protective of their eggs, and they are extremely susceptible to such surface lures as hair-bodied frogs and bugs.

The smallmouth bass prefers water that is intermediate between the cold of a typical mountain trout stream and the relative warmth of a largemouth river or lake. Its spawning grounds and habitat therefore overlap those of other fishes. Oddly, it favors clear water for reproduction even though high visibility would

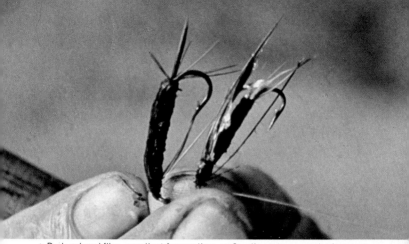

▲ Dark-colored flies, excellent for grayling. ▼ Grayling taken on spinning gear.

▲ Fly fishermen floating the Snake River. ▼ Largemouth trying to throw plug.

▼ Redeye bass (top) and northern largemouth.

▲ Montana bass fishing. ▼ Largemouth hooked on plug.

▲ California largemouth. ▼ Bluegill.

▲ Head of muskellunge. ▼ Catfish in shallows.

▲ Anglers netting big musky.　▼ Bill of longnose gar.

▲ White crappie. ▼ Paddlefish.

seem to make the nest more vulnerable to predation and excessive solar heating. In clear water a nesting site is likely to be fairly far from shore and sometimes at a depth of more than twenty feet, while in turbid water it may be at a depth of only three feet. When the water temperature induces the necessary hormonal increase, a male smallmouth searches out a suitable gravel bed and fans a clearing with his tail, much as a trout prepares its redd. The nest may be hardly more than a foot across or nearly three feet.

After sweeping it clear he selects a ripe female. She is apt to be bigger than he is; real trophy bass, regardless of species or race, are invariably females. But she lets herself be herded to the nest by the aggressive male, and he will threaten any rival male she attracts. She deposits a couple of hundred eggs, often more. She produces thousands, sometimes as many as seven thousand per pound of her own weight, but they do not all ripen at once. When ready she will mate again. The male drives her from the nest and quickly returns with a second ripe female and often a third.

He releases his milt and guards the fertilized eggs from hungry panfish, insects, and crawfish. Nature's efficient economies frequently appear ironic to the observant angler, who notes that these small creatures nourish themselves and grow in size and abundance by preying on the bass eggs and hatchlings, seemingly in order to be available when the bass grow large enough to become their predators instead of their prey. All varieties of black bass feed on whatever insects come their way, and actively hunt small panfish. Crawfish—either real ones (hooked through the tail to keep them alive and active) or man's impressionistic imitations, but especially "softshell" crawfish caught while molting—are excellent bass attractors.

So, too, are those tough-shelled, multisegmented, wicked-jawed, fish-eating stream dwellers, the hellgrammites—larvae of the fishflies and the larger dobsonflies. Adults of some species are more than 3 inches long, and the males have huge but harmless mandibles (used in the mating ritual) which make them look sinister as they flutter and bump about a camp lantern. At rest, the wings are held flat like those of a stonefly, rather than mayfly-high. They are clear on some species, marked with gray or black on others; one large variety has white-banded black wings. The jaws of a 1- or 2-inch hellgrammite are not harmless;

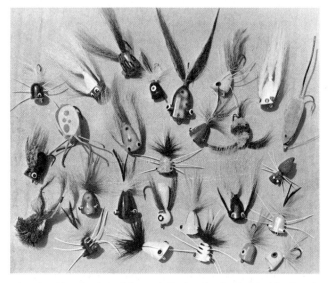

when hooking the insect through the hard collar behind the head, care must be taken to avoid a painful bite. Some of us, when we were boys, used to turn up stream rocks and catch scurrying hellgrammites with a small net. In some states they can be legally sold as bait, although aquatic insects are now widely protected. The old-fashioned way to fish a hellgrammite is on a light leader under a small bobber (and when fishing with a baitcasting rod and braided linen line, one midwestern angling writer sometimes still uses one of the 3-foot gut leaders from the tackle box his father left to him, simply because monofilament has neither character nor nostalgia). Artificial hellgrammites can be cast, trolled, or drifted from a baitcasting, spinning, or fly rod. Curiously, impressionistic ones seem to bring more strikes than do precise imitations.

Smallmouth eggs may hatch after just a couple of days in warm water, but cooler temperatures can prolong incubation for eight or nine days. The tiny fry, jet-black, golden-eyed, and as front-heavy as tadpoles until they have absorbed their yolk sacs, wriggle up from the nest but remain close for several hours.

Bass bugs—a few of the many available types.

Though the guardian male seems unaware of their presence, he will attack any conquerable predator that comes near. Soon the young depart, but remain schooled until they are about half an inch long. Any that linger at the nest will probably be driven away by the male. Nesting can be considered successful if many of the eggs hatch and a few survive to maturity.

When the yolk sac is absorbed the fry begin to feed on nymphs and other small insects, as well as on tiny crustaceans. Growth does not stop with sexual maturity, but the speed of growth depends on latitude (which governs the growing season), water temperature and oxygen content, and food. In a good river a 9-inch bass may be two years old, while in a poor river a bass of the same size may be twice as old. Rich water can produce 18-inch smallmouths in seven or eight years, and the trophy catches are at least that old—proof of longevity and a good survival rate for mature black bass.

This is not to imply there are no enemies other than larger carnivores. If neither turtle nor snake nor fish nor bird, neither otter nor raccoon nor man kills a small bass, it may yet be weakened though not killed by parasites. A common one is the yellow grub *(Clinostomum marginatum)* sometimes found by anglers in the meat and gill covers. Great blue herons and snails together are the vectors. As the heron spears a darting fingerling, the parasite's eggs fall from the bird's throat. The larvae infest snails, wherein they mature and produce another generation; those propagated in the snails attach themselves to bass and burrow in. The grubs are not lethal to the host and they are harmless to man, but the angler is rare who will eat a grubby fish. More destructive is the bass tapeworm *(Proteocephalus amblo-plites)*. It is no danger to a fisherman who eats an infested bass and, indeed, he is usually unaware of having done so because the tapeworm resides in the intestine or gonads and is removed unseen when the fish is eviscerated. Largemouths as well as smallmouths ingest tapeworms but only smallmouths are seriously affected; infestations reduce their reproductive capacity so severely that they have been almost exterminated in some lakes.

As smallmouths approach maturity they acquire a prefer-ence for the kinds of food trout favor. (To a degree, this is also true of largemouths, but the bigger fish, like the biggest bulldog-jawed trout, prefer larger prey.) Mature smallmouths will root

along a river bottom as grazing carp do, but not for the same purpose. Carp are almost vegetarians. An angler who examines the stomach contents of a river smallmouth that seemed to be bottom-rooting will usually find that it was pursuing nymphs. Traditional wet and dry bass flies (mostly the offspring of old salmon patterns) have pretty much given way to bulky, easily cast, hackleless bass bugs—"bugs" that represent a frog or mouse or nothing in particular as often as they do a moth or bee—and these are perhaps even more effective for largemouths than small-mouths. Whether with flies or bugs, it is lazily pleasant as well as productive to drift a canoe down a smallmouth river like the Delaware in Pennsylvania or the James in lower Missouri, or along one of the chained lakes in upper New England and lower Canada.

The largemouth's life cycle is not much different from the smallmouth's, except that the bigger species thrives in warmer, slower, weedier water. Anglers tend to think of the largemouth as purely a lake fish and the smallmouth as a river fish, despite the fact that monstrous largemouths are taken from big, sluggish rivers in the deep South, while the heaviest smallmouths gener-ally are caught in impoundments. If sand or gravel is available nearby (black bass make no lengthy migrations) a male large-

mouth will sweep a nest in it, perhaps half a foot deep and a foot and a half or so wide. But spawning grounds in lakes are just as likely to be at weed edges or openings on a clay or silt bottom if it is not too softly muddy. It is in shallow water, usually no more than a yard deep and a few yards from shore. Several females may spawn in a single nest, or a female may deposit a few hundred eggs, depart, and return later to deposit more. The females seem to be more enticed than bullied toward the nest, and a nest utilized by several of them may hold thousands of eggs while others contain only a few hundred.

The young usually hatch in five to ten days—depending on temperature, as with smallmouths. The male has remained on guard, turning with ferocious speed on any predator that approaches. Soon, however, he scatters the fry and, being both hungry and cannibalistic, may gobble a few in the process. They regroup into schools and remain together until more than an inch long. (Mature bass often form feeding schools, too, invariably with others of approximately the same size; when an angler casts into a boil of little shad trying to flee a school of bass he knows, upon catching a 2-pounder, that anything else he catches there and then is likely to be the same size.)

Wading the weedy shallows for Florida largemouths.

Largemouth fry are yellowish, translucent, and marked with a lateral black stripe. By the time their yolk sacs are absorbed, they have begun feeding on minuscule fairy shrimp, the somewhat clamlike crustaceans known as ostracods, and other drifting or weakly swimming organisms in the freshwater plankton. But they very soon begin to hunt larger prey, including insects and even small fish before the bass themselves are 2 inches long. A 6-inch bass, like other sunfish, will sometimes strike a plug half its own size. A yearling largemouth in northern waters is unlikely to be more than 4 inches long, and it will probably be three years old before it becomes a keeper. It is not likely to reach a length of 18 inches until it is seven or eight years old, and it will not grow much bigger. In the North a 5-pound bass is an excellent catch, and 10-pounders are scarce. Yet a Florida largemouth—partly as a result of its rich, warm environment, partly as a result of its genetic background—may easily reach twice the northern maximum. (Until recent years, the bass in California lakes and impoundments were descendants of transplanted northern stock, but record-book fish are now being taken on the West Coast because of an infusion of the southern variety. In some of those waters, as well as in the mid-Southeast, there are also "intergrade" largemouths where the northern and southern races interbreed.)

GENERAL GAME BEHAVIOR & FISH HABITAT: The behavior, metabolism, and even the very survival of many fishes depend not only on food but on the combined and interrelated effects of light penetration, temperature, and dissolved oxygen content in the water. Because of the effects of temperature on metabolism and feeding behavior, for example, a bass in relatively cold water may respond to a slowly retrieved lure or a bait that can be worked even more slowly, whereas in warmer water a fast-moving lure is generally more deadly (except for a surface-disturbing lure that entices by resting and moving sporadically in imitation of distressed prey). Black bass are among those species which are quite sensitive to light, temperature, and oxygen. The complexity of their requirements cannot be fully revealed by the more or less horizontal, or traditionally two-dimensional, generalizations about overlapping habitats: that smallmouths prefer clear, cool water moving over gravel, and are therefore found in rivers and relatively infertile northern lakes or impoundments; that large-mouths favor relatively warmer, weedier, stiller, and even some-what turbid lake waters or very slow rivers; and that spotted bass are intermediate in their preferences.

The partial truth of these generalizations should be en-hanced by a grasp of the vertical changes in habitat within a single body of water—that is, the thermal stratification that occurs in many areas. Water's molecular density is governed by tempera-ture, and it is heaviest at 39.2° F. Warm water is lighter than cold water, though ice is light enough to float. In autumn the cooling air lowers the temperature of a top layer of water, especially in the easily altered shallows. This water sinks, while the warmer water rises, cools, and again sinks, a phenomenon known as the fall turnover. During late summer the bass in stratified water normally prowl the shallows only to pursue baitfish during the cool, dim evening and early-morning hours. At other times of day they tend to hover in a deeper stratum, where the water retains more oxy-gen, where the temperature does not slow their metabolism, and where the sun's strong rays do not penetrate. The pupils of a fish's eyes do not expand and contract like those of mammals; bass see best in dim light and there is experimental evidence that they feel discomfort or actual pain in strong sun. With autumn's decreasing light penetration and thermal turnover they are drawn to the shallows.

As the weather continues to cool, the turnover puts an end to thermal stratification, producing a uniform water temperature of about 39°, except at the surface, where it can freeze in the cold air. In northern waters many gamefish, including smallmouth bass, could winter more actively by keeping to the 39° bottom waters if decreasing photosynthesis did not lower the oxygen in the depths. Instead, they must rise to the cold upper level, close to the ice, where there is more oxygen but where the temperature slows their metabolism until they become lethargic and may virtually stop feeding. All the same, good ice fishing may be provided by other species that are more tolerant of low oxygen content and low temperatures.

The "spring turnover" is not actually a turnover. Since the warming surface water is lighter than the water beneath it, there is no significant sinking or circulating. The deeper waters warm and form strata, instead, by conduction—the simple transfer of heat from molecule to molecule. Because heat rises, the spring warming takes much longer than the fall cooling and turnover. In shallow, turbid water and in the warm South a uniform temperature may soon be reached. The keys to locating bass in such unstratified ponds and lakes are weeds, brush, boulders, submerged trees, bars, drop-offs, and other underwater obstacles or topographical irregularities that provide cover and food for baitfish. Shaded points and covers will also attract both prey and predators. The outlets of streams—providing cool, oxygenated water and pouring forth fry as well as the foods to sustain fry—will also attract the bass.

But in clear northern lakes and reservoirs, particularly those at least thirty feet deep, summer brings stratification because the top water heats up much faster than the depths, and heat transfer may become almost negligible. The bottom of a very deep lake may remain a constant 39°. Three thermal layers form: the sun-saturated, warm *epilimnion* at the top; the transitional *thermocline* beneath it; and the cold *hypolimnion* at the bottom.

Bass and many other gamefish are most abundant and active within the thermocline. This is the ideal habitat, the zone where, as a rule but not always, the fishing is best. It can be defined as the layer of temperature between 55° and 70° or so. It averages about seven to ten feet in thickness (with wide variations) and most often is found at a depth of ten to thirty feet, but since it is affected by cold springs, feeder streams, wind, air temperature, lake eutrophication, bottom contours, and so on, the strata undulate. A thermocline may be thin or thick, near the surface or fifty feet down. Among bass, the old lunkers seem to be most sensitive to strong sun and are therefore likeliest to be near the bottom of the thermocline, except in morning and evening or on overcast days.

Many fishermen carry water-temperature gauges. It is no longer unusual to see an angler in a gadget-laden boat drop an electrically wired thermometer over the side and push a button to read the dial for temperature at various depths. On the side of the instrument may be a label stating preferred temperatures for various game species—about 63°–68° for smallmouths, 65°–70° for spotted bass, 65°–75° for largemouths—temperatures well within the thermocline. The same angler may then use a somewhat similiar instrument to probe various depths for oxygen

content, the ideal being between about 5 and 12 parts per million
—again, readings that usually occur within the thermocline. A
reading of 9 ppm or more indicates excellent water for largemouths; spotted bass require a little less and smallmouths still
less.

Having satisfied himself as to temperature and oxygen
content, the electronically armed angler may turn to a third
sorcerer's box to read the sonar dial of his fish-finding depth-
sounder. A band of light indicates the depth under his boat. Close
to the band may appear a series of blips indicating tree limbs;

Playing a bass seduced by plastic worm.

narrower blips indicating brush; thin, pale signals for the swaying weeds; clear, narrow lines above and below the bottom band to indicate a rocky bed; multiple lines of varying thickness revealing the rough incline of a bar, a drop-off, or some large submerged object; and moving blips at other depths to betray the fish themselves. Even without the moving flashes to indicate a few fish or a school, the angler knows he is over promising terrain, for black bass seek both cover and prey near or amid such bottom obstacles.

There are bass aficionados who would feel ill-equipped without these instruments, and their success proves the deadly efficiency of technology. But there are also those of us who feel that electronic gadgetry gives man an unsporting advantage over his game and blocks off a more personal, more satisfying study of nature. Anglers of this conviction seldom employ any tool of detection more sophisticated than a mercury-bulb water thermometer. Unencumbered by technological cargo, we would rather "read" the water and the shorelines for ourselves, in the old-fashioned way, perhaps taking a few less fish but ultimately perhaps knowing more about them and their hidden world. To us the gadgetry is to fishing equipment as bass tournaments are to fishing methods and mystique. A tournament is a very effective contest, a proof of skill and tackle quality, but it is not the leisurely, solitary, quiet communion with nature that is the essence—the sport—of angling.

Some angling writers have insisted that temperature has little to do with the thermocline's productivity, for a fish is a cold-blooded animal whose body temperature approximates that of the immediate environment. One might doubt that such a creature ever feels uncomfortably hot or cold. But laboratory experiments have proved that cold-blooded animals do indeed have temperature preferences, or ranges of tolerance, and of course temperature affects their metabolism. It even affects their ability to withstand illness or injury. Nonetheless, experienced bass fishermen know that too much reliance can be placed on the thermocline. Sometimes, even in stratified water, no lure is more effective than a plastic worm or eel, with a full quarter-ounce sinker to keep it wriggling along the bottom. The cold of the hypolimnion slows the metabolism and reactions of a bass, but does not necessarily make it too sluggish to strike. In a relatively young lake that has not much eutrophied, or in northern lakes that simply have little aquatic vegetation, there is not enough decaying matter to reduce the oxygen content severely on the bottom. This is also true of clear though fertile lakes in the late spring, when the lower strata have warmed up somewhat and still have enough oxygen to attract the fish. Where there is no decaying vegetation, cool water retains more oxygen than warm water. Occasionally lower depths actually contain more dissolved oxygen than the thermocline; they also contain food and, of course, admit minimal light.

The thermocline is least important in the morning and evening, when bass often stalk the shallows as their feeding cycle reaches its greatest intensity. This intensity can continue almost undiminished through the dark hours, making for excitingly productive night fishing. On their way to and from the morning and evening hunting grounds, black bass tend to follow routes, actually miniature migration paths, along the sides of drop-offs and the ridges formed where shoreline points dip into the water. Here, too, they find an abundance of foods, just as they do around assorted underwater obstacles and the somewhat roiled mouths of streams, and thus provide good fishing both above and below the theoretical zone of preference. As a final qualification to the Rule of the Thermocline, an angler must keep in mind the hungering watchfulness of all predatory fish. They will pursue a passing school of bait, and an angler will do better to cast into a commotion of shad than to ignore such activity while probing for a supposedly preferred thermal zone.

Guadalupe Bass *(Micropterus treculi)*
COMMON & REGIONAL NAMES: *bass, black bass, Texas bass, river bass*

GAME IDENTIFICATION & LOCATION OF FISHING REGIONS:
The little Guadalupe—a chunky, greenish-bronze, white-bellied fish seldom more than a foot long—has a broken lateral band of irregular vertical bars, more pronounced than those of the smallmouth, larger and darker than those of the spotted bass. Like the spotted variety, it has a prominent opercular spot (a dark marking at the rear of the gill cover) and basicaudal spot where the lateral

markings reach the tail. With age, however, the basicaudal spot fades. Also like the spotted bass, and unlike its other relatives, it has glossohyal teeth—a patch of bristles on the tongue. Its mouth usually extends to a point below the center of the eye, more or less like all black bass except the largemouth. Of all its kin, it looks most like the Alabama spotted bass, but since it does not share its waters with that fish there can be no confusion. If the rather similar Suwannee bass should find its way into the fringes of the Guadalupe's range, an angler can easily identify it by the bluish cast that extends along a Suwannee's underside from the jaw almost to the belly.

There are trout-eating (as well as trout-fishing) purists who insist that only their favorite salmonids are worth eating and that, among all other fish, black bass in particular are rank and oily. These anglers are closely related to the gustatory provincials who, never having eaten a northern pike, spread the false gospel that pike are inedible. All black bass, including the little Guadalupe, are excellent panfish. If skinned rather than scaled, a sautéed bass fillet of any kind is tasty. However, the Guadalupe is not sufficiently important as game to have been transplanted from its original realm, and its distribution is restricted to Texas.

FISH HABITAT: The Guadalupe bass is essentially a stream dweller, found in the Guadalupe, San Antonio, and Colorado rivers of south-central Texas, and in the offshoots and tributaries of these drainages. A baitcasting rod, even a very light one, seems unnecessarily heavy and stiff for so small a fish, but a fly rod or light spinning rig will easily cast appropriately small bugs, spin-

Guadalupe bass.

ners, and other lures, and will accentuate the scrappiness of panfish like this one. An on-the-spot study of stream fauna might help an angler decide on bait (as will an exchange of ideas with local fishermen), but it should be remembered that all bass, everywhere, can be drawn to a hook by a minnow, crawfish, salamander, frog of appropriate size, terrestrial insect, or night-crawler (slightly elevated by the title nightwalker in some regions). Since this Texas bass occupies a river system, somewhat like the stream habitat of the smallmouth and even more like that of the Wichita River strain of spotted bass, the Guadalupe species will succumb to the same angling methods and tactics as the small-mouth and spotted varieties (which see).

Largemouth Bass *(Micropterus salmoides)*
COMMON & REGIONAL NAMES: *bass, black bass, green bass, Oswego bass, mossback, bigmouth bass, green trout, trout (in Florida), lineside*

GAME IDENTIFICATION & LOCATION OF FISHING REGIONS:
Although a largemouth's maxillary plate usually extends aft of the eye, jaw length is not an invariably reliable way to distinguish the species from the smallmouth and other relatives. The most easily recognized mark of distinction is the almost complete separation of the forward spiny rays and rear soft rays of the largemouth's big dorsal fin. No other species of black bass has such a pro-nounced dip in the connective membrane of the fin. Another unique characteristic is the absence of scales overlapping the base of the soft portion.

Coloration varies, but a largemouth bass is usually dark green or blackish along the back and upper sides, and has a dark, irregular, sometimes broken horizontal band from the rear of the gill cover to the tail, separating the upper and lower portion of the side. Above this band, the dark color of the back pales to olive or bronze, and below the band it fades into the whitish belly. A trophy bass is always an old one, and often the upper body of such a fish has darkened until the markings are blended and obscured.

In fertile waters, although an eight- or nine-year-old northern largemouth may weigh nearly 10 pounds, a 3-pounder is a better-than-average catch. An angler journeying southward will encounter progressively larger fish. This is partly a matter of genetics and partly a result of longer growing seasons.

The world's record—22 pounds, 4 ounces—has stood since 1932. That largemouth was caught by George Perry in Montgomery Lake, Georgia. Although it has often been cited in angling literature as a northern largemouth, it came from an area where the northern commonly intergrades with the Florida, or southern, subspecies (*M. s. floridanus*). Florida's shallow, weedy lakes produce 15- to 18-pound bass with some regularity. Apart from size, the only discernible difference between the northern and Florida races lies in scale count, which is not always definitive. A northern largemouth *usually* has sixty-one to sixty-five scales along the lateral line, eight rows above it, fifteen to seventeen below it, and ten or eleven on the cheek. A Florida largemouth is more likely to have sixty-nine to seventy-three scales along the lateral line, eight or nine rows above it, seventeen or eighteen below it, and eleven to thirteen on the cheek.

An intensive stocking program, begun in 1959 in a chain of lakes near San Diego, introduced the Florida largemouth to hospitable California waters. (Until then, California's largemouth bass had been of the northern strain.) The result has been a doubling of the average weight of bass taken in those waters. At this writing the California record stands at 20 pounds, 15 ounces —a mammoth boated by Dave Zimmerlee in 1973 on Lake Miramar. The fish was caught one summer afternoon when Zimmerlee, who had boated only a few small ones that day, actually saw it loafing near the surface. Using a big treble hook, he dangled a nightcrawler in front of the bass, which had dropped down perhaps five feet when his skiff approached. His inexpensive spin-casting (closed-face) reel—an unfortunate choice in waters holding big bass—broke as he played the fish, and he had to handline it to the boat.

Zimmerlee's record may be beaten as this is written or soon afterward. Larger fish have been sighted in the same waters, and a few have been conservatively estimated to weigh at least 24 pounds. Their phenomenal size is not due entirely to genetics and environment. It is also a result of careful, somewhat restrictive management by fishery biologists and administrators. The San Diego lakes are closed to fishing for up to half the year, and during

the open season there are several rest days per week when no fishing is allowed. Moreover, night fishing is prohibited, and the record books of other states indicate that many of the real lunker largemouths are taken at night. The older bass are particularly inclined to stay deep and inactive while light remains strong; they wait until it weakens before coming up to the shallows to feed. The fishing regulations on these California lakes increase the seasonal holdover—the survival rate—of bass as they approach trophy size.

Originally, largemouth bass ranged from southeastern Canada and the Great Lakes region down through the Mississippi valley to Mexico, eastward through Florida, and in the seaboard states up into Maryland. During the 1800's they were introduced to the Columbia River system and other parts of the West, and then into New England. They have now been well established in all the contiguous states. In addition to the Florida lakes and rivers and the California lakes and impoundments, some of the celebrated largemouth waters are in the Great Lakes region, the Santee-Cooper and other southeastern impoundments, as well as some in Texas, Oklahoma, and Oregon, and even some of the small lakes in Rocky Mountain states where a nonresident angler

Largemouth bass.

would be more expectant of western trout than eastern bass.

The fish thrive not only in rivers, lakes, and reservoirs, but in farm ponds (or "tanks," as they are called in parts of the Southwest) and industrial ponds such as flooded quarries and strip mines. Such ponds may cover only an acre or fifty times that. Effective fishing on the larger ones usually resembles lake or reservoir fishing, often requiring a boat to reach some of the best spots. The small ones usually can be "prospected" from shore, waded, or crossed with the aid of a "waterwalker" float. Such waters are, of course, stocked. If a pond is overcrowded with bass (or any competitive species) the fish will tend to be stunted as a result of lack of space and food. Obviously, big bass will also be scarce in a pond that is fished too hard, or "fished out," as the popular expression goes. But most farm ponds are shallow,

weedy, and fertile enough for bass to flourish under sensible management. They also thrive in some of the quarry and mine ponds, but those waters are more often deep, clear, scantily weeded, steep-sided, and lacking in such underwater cover as stumps, boulders, and drop-offs. This makes for a kind of paradox, with the big bass wary and difficult to catch but most often taken very close to the shoreline.

The importance of ponds has been vividly demonstrated in Ohio, where an angler named Roy Landsberger broke the state largemouth record in the spring of 1976 with a fish measuring more than 25 inches long and weighing 13 pounds, 2 ounces. This northern largemouth was caught on a surface plug in a farm pond, and Ohio's previous record largemouth came from a strip-mine pond.

Bass jumping, shortly after being hooked.

FISH HABITAT & FEEDING BEHAVIOR—ANGLING TACTICS: It has been said that bass tend to school with companions of about the same age and size. This is true of largemouths until they grow beyond medium size, after which any schooling is loose and ephemeral. All the same, even the biggest largemouth never outgrows a preference for relatively shallow, weedy water. A ponderously powerful, bucket-mouthed old female (sometimes called a "hawg" or "sow") spends a hot summer afternoon lurking deep not because she finds more food in the depths but only to get oxygen and avoid excessive heat and light. She is not then feeding very actively, though she can be pried out of her torpor by the smell of a nightcrawler, or the smell and sight of a minnow, crawfish, frog, or salamander, or the sight alone of an artificial bait such as a deep-running plug or wobbling spoon.

But her active feeding, and therefore the best fishing, will usually take place in water less than twenty feet deep, near debris, topographic irregularities, rooted vegetation, or similar cover. There is significance in the popularity of weedless hooks and lures, and the equal popularity of fishing-camp art that features stumps, water lilies, and evening shadows.

If a thermocline exists at all in these relatively shallow regions it will be quite low. There is no need for a sophisticated water-temperature gauge here, but a simple water thermometer can be of help. It is usually mounted on a metal plate, has a water-holding cup around its bulb, and is tied to a line knotted to show depths at intervals of, say, five or ten feet. The angler drops it to what he hopes is the depth of the thermocline, holds it there a minute, then brings it up. Since the water-holding cup prevents the mercury from climbing rapidly after retrieval, it gives a fairly accurate reading.

On overcast days or when the shadows lengthen, a sow largemouth is apt to abandon the bottom of the thermocline to search the weeds for prey. She is a voracious meat-eater and not very selective. At one time or another she has probably pursued every conceivable kind of prey, from water rats or mice flooded out of burrows to frogs, ducklings, fallen terrestrial insects, crustaceans, and baitfish of all available species—including small members of her own. This explains the effectiveness of a wide variety of surface lures, including popping plugs, assorted spinning lures, hair-bodied mice, frogs, insects, and the like, realistic

Top: Largemouth caught on bottom-fished worm.
Bottom: Largemouth taken on deep-running lure.

plastic frogs, and fluffy bass bugs ranging from the imitative to the nonobjective.

A way of fishing such lures that combines chicanery, suspense, and productiveness is to drop one gently on the water or else on a stump, rock, or lily pad from which it can be hopped into the water, and then retrieve it slowly, allowing it to rest now and then before twitching it as if it were an injured creature struggling over the surface. Conversely, the deep-working plugs, spoons, spinners, spinner-flies, and other such lures often work best when trolled or reeled in rather fast to impart plenty of action, in imitation of a fleeing fish. An exception is the plastic worm or eel, which can be bumped along the bottom slowly to catch the attention of a cruising bass.

Live bait, too, is most enticing when it moves naturally. A minnow will swim if hooked forward of the tail or lightly through the back. A crawfish will crawl if tied on or hooked through the tail from underneath. A salamander, one of the deadliest largemouth baits, will remain active if hooked through the lips from the bottom, the way a frog is used.

To a hungry bass, the passing flash of a silver spinner probably looks like a shiner, dace, or other baitfish, and a glint of gold may resemble a small yellow perch, darter, or similar prey. But it is very doubtful that a largemouth smashes a plug because it is painted the green of a longnose dace, the blue and crimson of a red shiner, or the pinkish-gray of a crawfish. Laboratory experiments and the study of comparative anatomy have proved that most fish perceive colors pretty much as humans do, and some species are attracted by colors resembling common prey. Shallow-water fish are quite sensitive to colors, yet black bass do not seem to associate those colors with desired foods.

There is, after all, nothing in fresh water that approximates the stark red and white of some of the most popular and effective old standby plugs and spoons. No prey glows with the fluorescent red-orange that adorns so many jigs and small, fat-bodied, long-lipped, deep-diving plugs—a color that surged in popularity in 1975 and 1976 and was probably considered revolutionary by anglers who had not been born when luminous paint first appeared on plugs after the First World War. Even the traditional and deadly pork rind is now sold not only in its natural white state but dyed lime-green and cut to the shape of a frog. It is also dyed a brilliant luminous yellow and sometimes cut in a twister-tail shape that resembles a popular, luminously bright jig. The shape (like the trailing plastic skirt on some surface plugs) adds flutter, which combines with bright color to capture the attention of passing fish.

Purple is another unnatural color, yet it is used successfully on soft-bodied artificials ranging from plastic frogs to plastic worms and eels.

Light or bright colors seem to work best in clear water or on sunny days. Some anglers theorize that deep purple or black attracts bass in murky waters or dim light because a fish approaches the lure from below and sees it in sharp contrast to the light of the sky. This hardly explains the deadly attraction of a black plug at night or a purple worm wriggling over bottom debris behind a slip sinker.

A fish's eye, like the human retina, contains two receptor mechanisms: rod cells and cone cells. The cones register color, but only when the illumination is brighter than about one foot-candle. When less light penetrates, the rods—impervious to color, capable of registering only black and white, but perhaps thirty times more light-sensitive than the cones—become the image receptors. Water filters out the wavelengths of certain colors, thereby changing or diminishing them, and dimming light accentuates the process. In good light, red stands out sharply, contrasting with other hues and strongly stimulating a bass's optical nerves. The classic red-and-white combination works very well while there is sufficient light to show the red and reflect against the white. But red is the first color to be filtered out. Even in clear water, it becomes black at a depth of twenty feet or so. The shorter wavelengths of yellow penetrate to greater depths, and although a bottom-fished yellow lure may lose much of its brightness it will remain more clearly visible than red. Blues and greens penetrate most deeply, yet these colors may escape the notice of a fish in very deep water, where the entire background takes on a blue-green hue. In turbid water, on darkly overcast days, or at night, the fish perceive no colors but they seem to be as sensitive as an owl or a cat to faint reflections. It is then that a dark lure—whether black or deep purple hardly matters—may catch the slightest reflection and stimulate a bass to turn on it with startled ferocity.

Redeye Bass *(Micropterus coosae)*
COMMON & REGIONAL NAMES: *bass, black bass, shoal bass, Chipola bass*

GAME IDENTIFICATION & LOCATION OF FISHING REGIONS:
Except for the red cast of its iris, the redeye closely resembles the smallmouth (which see). It has the same bronze body coloration and dark, irregular vertical bars running down its sides. When fairly young it is easily distinguished by its dull red fins, and it remains quickly identifiable even when the markings fade somewhat with age. One of the two regional strains of redeye, the Alabama River form, is a relatively gaudy bass with bluish spots or shadings on its black, and reddish dorsal, caudal, pectoral, and anal fins. Less colorful is the Apalachicola River form, sometimes called the Flint River smallmouth after Georgia's Flint River. It lacks the blue shadings, and its pectoral and anal fins are whitish, but it has a prominent dark spot at the base of the tail and another, smaller one at the rear of the gill cover.

Both types tend to be small. A ten-year-old may be no more than 10 inches long. The average weight of mature specimens is slightly less than a pound, but anglers have occasionally caught redeyes weighing more than six times that much, and a big redeye has the same battling ability as a smallmouth of comparable size. It is, in addition, a tasty panfish, and is therefore highly regarded by many anglers in its limited area of distribution.

The redeye is strictly a southeastern fish, inhabiting streams and ponds along the upland drainages of a number of river systems: the Conasauga in Tennessee, the Alabama and Chattahoochee in Alabama, the Savannah in Georgia, and the Chipola in Florida.

FISH HABITAT: Redeyes are caught in ponds as well as streams, although they will not spawn in ponds as smallmouths often do. They share the feeding characteristics of smallmouths, trout, and other species that like flowing water; that is, a large percentage of their feeding is on insects snapped or sucked from the surface. This means the angler can do well by adopting trout tactics: presenting dry flies that mimic locally common insects. Redeyes will also take the other artificial lures often used for smallmouths: bass bugs, spoons and spinners, spinner-flies, deer-hair floaters,

bicolored bucktails, streamers, and the like. Among natural baits, the hellgrammite is probably the most eagerly taken.

The most promising habitat in a redeye river is a pool with a current strong enough to feel or one of the deeper pockets in a riffle. Redeyes are often leery of unfamiliar objects—a sinker, a big hook, a swivel, a visibly thick leader. Very light terminal tackle is therefore recommended. A fly rod or light spinning outfit will facilitate deception and then give full realization of the redeye's scrappiness.

Smallmouth Bass *(Micropterus dolomieui)*
COMMON & REGIONAL NAMES: *bass, black bass, bronzeback*

GAME IDENTIFICATION & LOCATION OF FISHING REGIONS: A smallmouth bass, though it rarely attains the weight of an old largemouth, can be an even more formidable opponent for an angler. Deep waters seem to divert it somewhat from aerial combat to the tactic of sounding, and warm waters seem to soften its resistance. But if hooked in cool waters—and especially in a stream—a 3-pound smallmouth can be a wilder fighter than a 5-pound largemouth. It may jerk and wag and yank savagely, peel away with startling speed on a short, early run, then leap from the water with the spectacular agility of a trout, arching, skittering, flipping, sometimes literally dancing across the surface on its tail. Like the largemouth, it well may take line under a boat and around a snag or jagged boulder, as if it had the reasoning ability to try to escape by breaking off.

Redeye bass.

A bass, pike, or almost any powerful gamefish will occasionally befuddle an angler by quitting the fight and swimming toward him, apparently exhausted or in shock. Then, as the disconcerted angler fumbles and works to take up slack, a sudden, powerful surge may bow his rod tip right into the water. If the game is a smallmouth, overconfidence or carelessness can quickly snatch defeat from victory.

Although the record books show smallmouth catches of over 11 pounds, the average size is only a pound or two, and anything much over four is a memorable trophy. An immature specimen can be identified by its tail, which has an orange cast at the base, a blackish band behind that, and whitish edging at the tips. As these colors are lost, the tail matches the body color—bronze or brownish, sometimes with a slightly green or gray tone, fading to a white belly. The sides are marked with vertical bars or splotches, sometimes of a dark olive hue, sometimes grayer or even blackish, and sometimes quite faint. The jaw usually extends to a point no farther rearward than the eye; the dorsal spines and soft fin rays are separated by only a shallow notch in the membrane; and scales overlap the base of the soft rays. These characteristics distinguish a smallmouth from a largemouth bass of comparable size. There are subtle differences between the northern, or common, smallmouth and a subspecies known as the Neosho River smallmouth *(M. d. velox)*. The latter has somewhat more uniform coloration than the northern type, a more protruding lower jaw, a rather pronounced dark spot on the rear of the gill cover, and no scales on the caudal membrane. Sometimes this form can be hard to tell from a spotted bass, especially since it may have a weakly developed glossohyal patch—tooth bristles on the tongue that mark the spotted and Guadalupe bass.

The Neosho smallmouth likes swift water, and it was probably this fast, tough variety that originally brought fame to the Ozark bass rivers. However, it interbreeds with the common smallmouth, and its preferred habitat has been reduced by the building of big impoundments on the Neosho, so it has become a scarce subspecies. It is found in the Neosho and a number of tributaries of the Arkansas flowing through the lower Midwest.

Originally, the primary range of the common smallmouth was not much larger. It was centered on the drainage systems of the Ohio River and Lake Ontario. As railroads were extended

westward and southward, smallmouths were introduced into new waters along their courses. Today the primary range stretches from Quebec to Minnesota in the North, down to Alabama in the Southeast, and across the East and Midwest into Oklahoma and Kansas. In addition, the species has been established in many other states, as far west as California. There is good smallmouth fishing in countless streams, lakes, and impoundments, but some of the best is still found in old, traditional spots, from the Ozark rivers to the Potomac basin and up into Maine's Belgrade Lakes.

FISH HABITAT & FEEDING BEHAVIOR—ANGLING TACTICS:

There are cool, fast streams where the strike of a smallmouth may surprise an angler expecting trout, and there are relatively warm lakes where a smallmouth may steal a deep-running plug being trailed warily by a largemouth. It is a prolific fish and a voracious one, a difficult competitor for trout and landlocked salmon in some waters. A few of the New England salmon lakes have become primarily bass lakes in the generations since the early transplantations. If not for the fierce competition of the largemouth, the smallmouth could probably thrive on a mud bottom, and certainly it flourishes in rocky-bottomed reservoirs, where, in fact, it reaches its largest size. The record smallmouths generally come not from such famous rivers as the Rappahannock, the Delaware, the Susquehanna, or Wisconsin's St. Croix, but from the TVA reservoirs in Kentucky, Tennessee, and Alabama. In such waters a big specimen is inclined to stay deep even when cruising about after forage fish, and is most inclined to hit a slow-moving bait or lure.

Smallmouth (left) and largemouth bass.

In rivers, whether the smallmouths happen to be rooting for nymphs and crawfish, chasing fingerlings from top to bottom, or rising to snatch insects, they offer the angler a peculiar luxury, for they do not demand that he make his offerings at dawn or in the late evening. They may continue to feed actively at midmorning and through the afternoon even during midsummer, and in low, clear rivers may become progressively greedier in late summer, when the lake fish are least active. They do, however, seem to be greediest in the morning and at night. In the darkness they are especially vulnerable to surface lures. Lakes, too, offer their best surface fishing in early morning or again in the evening, when smallmouths probe the shallows for prey.

On lakes, surface lures may also be effective at any time over reefs and shoals where smallmouths will interrupt their crawfish-hunting and rise a few feet to snatch prey passing overhead. But over drop-offs, submerged stony points, and gravel clearings between weed beds, deeply worked baits, spoons, or plugs will more frequently attract the attention of foraging bass.

In rivers, smallmouths prefer pools, relatively quiet pockets, and channel edges near riffles. They will not fight a very strong current to stay for long in fast water the way some trout do, but will seek food-collecting spots such as ledges, rocks, logs, banks, and the foamy edges at the heads of pools. These spots offer cover as well as food. A bass, like a trout, may be hiding behind a boulder, in a crevice, or under a slanting log or undercut bank. Much as smallmouths like rocks and gravel, they are somewhat selective about the type of rocks they seek. Smooth boulders, flat bedrock, sand, and well-rounded gravel hold less food than do the rough slabs and gravel, grassy banks, and irregularities cut by the current—the places where bass forage. On both lakes and rivers the lee sides of bars seem particularly productive on windy days or just after a wind has died.

In many streams the best smallmouth fishing occurs in spring and fall when the water is beginning to clear and go down. The banks may then be most productive in early morning. As the day warms the bass will be hungrier and more abundant in mild eddies and pockets, having followed the movement of oxygenated water and current-borne food. At evening the banks may again attract bass, as may the shallow tails of pools. When the water is subsiding but still high, fairly large plugs and bugs work well,

Jumping smallmouth, trying to throw hook.

but in low, clear water it is better to rely on flies, spinner-flies, and small spinners. Under these conditions the big, noisy surface-disturbers that often cause a largemouth to charge will more likely alarm than attract a smallmouth. A gently worked grasshopper, cricket, beetle, caterpillar, or other terrestrial will beguile a smallmouth at these times. So will an artificial minnow. Maribous, Muddlers, and Woolly Worms are deservedly acclaimed smallmouth flies. Streamers are deadly, whether cast or trolled.

But a fly must be presented lightly, and drifted or twitched with restraint. A floating bucktail, squirreltail, or hair-bodied frog, mouse, or similar concoction can be quieted by coating it with line dressing. Any of these offerings should either be drifted down naturally or, on still water, allowed to rest motionless for a while and then moved slowly, with long pauses and occasional twitches.

In his *New Standard Fishing Encyclopedia,* the celebrated angling writer A. J. McClane cites an Iowa survey which revealed early fall to be the best season in that region for natural baits. (In smallmouth waters these would include nightcrawlers, minnows, small stonecats, crawfish, hellgrammites, and small frogs

and salamanders.) Spinner-flies were found to be most productive in June, hair-bodied floaters in July, plugs and hair-bodied floaters in August. All of us who have wandered from our native smallmouth waters to distant and unfamiliar lakes and streams have noted that the richest habitat—the smallmouth haunts—seem to shift, along with food preferences, as the season progresses. There is no real migration, just a drifting to slightly deeper or shallower waters, or even into sloughs, in search of food, oxygen, cool water, and cover.

Unfortunately from the angler's point of view, the shift differs from stream to stream and lake to lake, without any easily seen pattern. The fisherman must do some slow, cautious prospecting based on his knowledge of preferred water and bottom types. He must cast gently, with finesse, and let his offering drift or retrieve it slowly. He should do some wading, even when nominally engaged in floating a river. And he should remember that smallmouths are more wary than largemouths; the impatience that rejects a likely-looking pocket after three or four casts, or prompts half a dozen fast casts and retrieves, is the impatience that leaves the bass there for the angler who casts sparingly but keeps at it for a while, then rests the spot, then tries again before moving on.

Spotted Bass (Micropterus punctulatus)
COMMON & REGIONAL NAMES: bass, black bass, Kentucky bass, Kentucky spotted bass

GAME IDENTIFICATION & LOCATION OF FISHING REGIONS: A talented but erratic nineteenth-century naturalist, Constantine Rafinesque, described the spotted bass as a distinct species when he studied the fishes of the Ohio River. Fishermen also recognized it as differing from the largemouth and smallmouth. But Rafinesque had a mania for discovering and naming new species on the basis of scanty evidence, and in his *Ichthyologia Ohiensis* he naively included ten fictitious ones, invented and foisted on him by a prankish acquaintance, John James Audubon. As a result, taxonomists ignored Rafinesque's legitimate discovery of the spotted bass until 1927, when at last it was granted its separate classification.

When immature this fish has an orange, black, and white tail like that of a juvenile smallmouth, and body coloration resembling a young largemouth's, except that it has belly spots and a pronounced dark spot at the base of the tail. When mature it looks even more like a hybrid: dark olive on the back, lighter olive or bronze on the sides, with numerous dark spots that tend to be more or less diamond-shaped. These diamonds usually are somewhat elongated vertically, but midway down the sides a series of them forms a horizontal band rather like that of a largemouth. However, the jaw does not extend rearward of the eye, although it often reaches a point below the rear edge of the eye. The spotted bass also differs from the largemouth in having only a shallow notch rather than a virtual separation between the spiny and soft portions of the dorsal fin. It has no true vertical side bars, as the smallmouth usually does, and is likely to have spotting below the lateral line, which is lacking on both the largemouth and smallmouth. An angler who is in doubt can run his finger over the tongue of his catch; if he feels glossohyal teeth the fish is a spotted bass. The Guadalupe bass also has glossohyal teeth, but its limited distribution and differences in markings should prevent confusion.

The foregoing description applies most closely to the northern, or common, spotted bass. There are two additional races: the Alabama spotted bass *(M. p. henshalli)* and Wichita

Spotted bass.

spotted bass *(M. p. wichitae).* The former inhabits the Alabama River system in Alabama, Mississippi, and Georgia. It tends to have a more pronounced opercular and basicaudal spot than the northern variety, a slightly higher scale count, and perhaps slightly more weight. Both the Alabama and Wichita subspecies lack scales on the caudal membrane, which the northern spotted bass does have. The Wichita race is limited to the waters of the Wichita Mountains in Oklahoma. Spotted bass range through the Ohio-Mississippi drainage from Ohio down to the Gulf, eastward to the Florida panhandle and westward into Texas, Oklahoma, and Kansas. They seldom attain the size of a smallmouth, although specimens weighing over 4 pounds are occasionally caught.

FISH HABITAT: The spotted bass is usually described as occupying a habitat more or less intermediate between that of the smallmouth and largemouth. Though the generalization is accurate, the species has a paradoxical ability to tolerate more turbidity than either of its more celebrated relatives. In the northern part of its range it occupies the stream waters that are least attractive to the smallmouth and largemouth. Whereas the smallmouth seeks riffled water or pools with some current, and the largemouth is likelier to hover in weedy coves, the northern spotted bass is most common in the deepest, stillest pools, often where silting is pronounced. For reasons neither biologists nor anglers have been able to unravel, the preferred habitat in the South is almost opposite. There the spotted bass outdoes the smallmouth in seeking cool, gravel-bottom streams and deep, clear lakes.

Spotted bass run upstream into shallow waters to spawn. They sweep rather small redds in the gravel, but apart from the size and location of the nests their breeding habits resemble those of largemouths. When young they feed chiefly on tiny crustaceans and on the larvae of the same midges that infest most trout streams—to the great annoyance of anglers so harassed by gnats and no-see-ums that they almost forget the great dependence of gamefish on this source of nourishment. (Occasionally, in fact, they seem to forget that artificial midges tied on, say, no. 16 hooks are excellent flies on slow streams.) Reaching maturity and a length of a little over half a foot at about the same time, spotted bass then begin to feed more heavily on large insects, crawfish, minnows, frogs, and the other foods sought by small-mouths. Important game in the waters of their range, they are caught by means of the same baits, lures, and tactics that take smallmouths.

Suwannee Bass *(Micropterus notius)*
COMMON & REGIONAL NAMES: *bass, black bass, Suwannee smallmouth*

GAME IDENTIFICATION & LOCATION OF FISHING REGIONS:
The little Suwannee is so unimportant to anglers and so limited in range that it was not recognized as a distinct species until 1941. This is rather strange in view of its unique marking—a blue tinge under the mouth and extending back to the whitish belly. The body coloration is the bronze of a smallmouth with the dark splotches of a spotted bass. Suwannee bass of 2½ pounds have been caught, but the species rarely weighs a pound or reaches a foot in length. This is a stream bass, the only one that can tolerate the acid, relatively infertile waters of the Suwannee River. It has also been found in other Florida rivers—the Santa Fe and the Withlacoochee.

FISH HABITAT: The Suwannee bass ignores the weeds, brush, logs, boulders, riffles, and pools that attract other members of its family. It prefers to hover in the middle of the stream, intercepting whatever foods come to it there. It can be taken with the same tackle, offerings, and methods used for smallmouth and spotted bass. Since it is drawn to relatively deep midstream habitat, low water forces numbers of Suwannee bass to gather in small areas, and the fishing is best when they are thus concentrated.

Suwannee bass.

Bluegill *(Lepomis macrochirus)*

COMMON & REGIONAL NAMES: *bream, brim, sun perch, blue sunfish, robin, copperbelly*

GAME IDENTIFICATION & LOCATION OF FISHING REGIONS:
The bluegill, like the black bass, is a sunfish that merits a section of its own in an angling guide, for the fisherman holds it in greater esteem than the smaller sunnies. It vies with the yellow perch and the several most popular catfishes as America's most sought-after panfish. Indeed, its fighting power and occasional elusiveness place it almost in the category of gamefish. At least one eminent angling writer has declared that no freshwater species exceeds it "in ounce-for-ounce fighting ability or succulent flavor" and that more Americans therefore seek the bluegill than any other fish, including the glamorous game varieties. Many of us, reflecting on the succulence of trout, salmon, perch, bullheads, and other favorites, might dispute the claim regarding flavor. We would readily concede, however, that the bluegill, yellow perch, and catfish are to the angler what the rabbit and squirrel are to the hunter.

The bluegill's amiable qualities and adaptability have led to its extensive introduction into farm ponds and other easily fished waters. Originally its range extended from the Minnesota lakes eastward to Lake Champlain and down into the deep South where, depending on locality, it is better known as bream or "brim." (It is a true sunfish, all the same, and not a member of the Cyprinidae, or minnow family of the European bream and the carp.) Bluegill or bream, it now thrives almost everywhere in the United States.

Short-bodied, deep-bellied, it has the saucerlike contours that typify its family. Though its colors tend to vary more than those of other sunfishes, it can be distinguished from close relatives by several features: a long, broad, black gill flap (sometimes called an "ear") on the rear end of the bluish gill cover; a long, pointed pectoral fin; and a dark or black blotch on the rear of the dorsal fin. An immature bluegill is generally a pale, silvery fish—and may remain so in a sterile quarry pond. As it matures, six to eight irregular vertical chains or bars usually appear, dark or greenish-gray against a body ranging from yellowish to dark grayish-blue. The striping fades and the body darkens as the fish

grows old. On a spawning female, the forward part of the belly sometimes turns yellow. An adult male often has a purple luster and a coppery or dark olive back, and sometimes a facial tinge that leads anglers to speak of "copperheads" instead of bluegills. More common regional names are "copperbelly" and "robin"—references to the bright orange or red that appears on the underparts of many spawning males.

In northern lakes, spawning begins in late May, peaks in June, and continues into early August. In warmer southern waters the males may begin congregating on the beds by March or even earlier—before February ends in Florida—and spawning activity may peak at intervals, beginning in April and not subsiding completely until September.

In warm waters characterized by a long spawning and growing period, if there are few predators the bluegills are likely to be extremely numerous but stunted by excessive competition for food. This situation is most common on small lakes or ponds

Bluegill fishermen using "brim poles."

covering only a few hundred acres or sometimes less than fifty. Such waters may swarm with 3- to 5-inch bluegills but very few larger ones. Many of these are mature fish, perhaps three years old or more. Cold northern waters also retard the growth rate. A Vermont bluegill may require seven or eight summers to attain a length of 9 inches, whereas a Florida bluegill may be half that size at the end of its first summer if predatory fish such as bass are numerous enough to prevent overpopulation.

It is chiefly in the South, where the growth rate is fast, that anglers catch the big bluegills known as "bulls" or "plate-size" bream. A half-pound bluegill is a good catch. Even in the South an angler is unlikely to catch many 1-pound bream in a season. Yet once in a great while someone takes a 15-inch specimen that weighs more than 4 pounds and fights with the sudden, surprising lunges if never the acrobatics of a smallmouth.

FISH HABITAT & FEEDING BEHAVIOR—ANGLING TACTICS: The bluegill is much like the largemouth bass in its choice of habitat. Though it thrives in slow streams, particularly in the South, it is most common in fertile lakes and ponds, where it occupies areas that are weedy but not choked with weeds.

Large bluegill.

Spawning occurs near the shoreline. Small bluegills tend to nest in water no deeper than a couple of feet and sometimes only half a foot deep, while the largest ones congregate a little farther out, where the bottom may be six or eight feet down or even deeper and the weed or grass patches are interspersed with sand, clay, or fine gravel that can be fanned easily into nests and will not smother the eggs in silt. The bulls arrive first on the beds, usually when the water reaches a temperature of about 67°, and spawning activity intensifies as the temperature rises. There are many lakes and streams where spring-cooled stretches remain in the 70's while the shallows nearby reach the 80's, and it is in the warmer water that the fish gather in greatest numbers.

The bulls fan out shallow depressions a foot or a foot and a half across—pale discs and ovals that an angler can easily spot in fairly clear water. Some bluegills seem to avoid very clear water for spawning, and all of them avoid water too murky for them to see both prospective mates and predators. They also avoid constantly shaded areas, for the eggs require some daily sunlight to incubate. Good beds are protected from strong currents or silt, sheltered by barriers of weeds, brush, snags, or stumps.

A female, probably attracted by the spawning colors of the bulls, flits over the beds, selects a nest, lays her eggs, and departs. The male hovers there, remaining on guard for the two to five days of incubation and an additional few days after hatching. There is an old fishing adage that the beds are most active at the full of the moon, and this has been confirmed by the observations of biologists. The best time to fish for spawning bluegills is within five days of the full moon.

The bluegill is not one of those species that require protection while breeding. It is so prolific and has such a protracted spawning period that no harm is done by fishing the bream beds. An average mature female deposits eighteen thousand eggs annually (and sometimes more than twice that number), producing more than seventy thousand in her lifetime. Even if many of the eggs fail to hatch and relatively few of the hatchlings survive, there is rarely any cause for concern about the bluegill population where the waters are clean and fertile and there is a balance between predators and prey.

Bluegills bite most greedily, fight best, and taste best during the early part of the spawning season, before breeding

activity has drained some of their energy, but they can be taken long after the reproductive urge has waned—even through the ice on northern waters, where fishermen turn their augers over weed beds and lower jigs or grubs. After spawning, the small bluegills mostly remain schooled near shore, but the larger ones go deeper, some of them prowling in loose schools, some scattering but schooling again perhaps a month later. Whereas the warmest waters provide the best bluegill fishing during the spawning frenzy of spring and early summer, the cool depths attract big bluegills as they attract bass during the heat of midsummer, and an angler seeking either of these species may be pleasantly surprised by the other.

It is also true that bluegills, like bass, are inclined to feed very actively in the first couple of hours after dawn and the last couple of hours before darkness (and throughout the day if there is a dull overcast). As dusk deepens, however, their behavior diverges significantly from that of bass and most other fish. Night fishing is not for the light-tackle devotee who typically pursues the bluegill. The species does not feed nocturnally.

More than half of the bluegill's diet consists of insects, and the remainder consists chiefly of small crustaceans and assorted worms, supplemented by very little vegetable matter. It is no surprise, then, that as spawning begins in the spring the effective lures include trout flies—wets, dries, and nymphs. Nymphs continue to take fish throughout the summer. At nearly any time,

Left: Fisherman with nice bluegill.
Above left: Angler pointing out bream's long gill flap.
Above right: Redear sunfish.

bluegills can be found around slopes, submerged humps, points, and weedy flats where aquatic larvae usually abound.

Earthworms may be the most traditionally revered bait, and they are certainly attractive to bluegills, but recent experiments indicate that they are not quite the deadliest of easily available bream baits. White grubs probably are, and they can be real or artificial. In a study of bluegill ecology and behavior, conducted by *Sports Afield* magazine on Florida's Silver River, the most effective rig was a lead-bodied Skunk Nymph on a no. 8 hook, tipped with a triangular sliver of white plastic worm to suggest a grub; this lure, which took an average of more than twenty-six spawning bream per hour of angling, appears to be particularly attractive to bluegills rooting along the bottom as smallmouths do for nymphs and other prey.

The next most effective lure was a very small bluegill spoon, silver on one side and either white or yellow on the other, molded on a no. 10 or no. 12 hook, tailed with a wisp of yellow or white feathers, and enhanced, like the Skunk Nymph, with a sliver of white plastic worm behind the barb.

After these two highly recommended lures came live freshwater shrimp and live crickets. These minuscule shrimp reside along the weedy edges of streams and lakes. They can be collected with a small, fine-mesh net, then strained into a bait box through a piece of heavy-gauge screening to remove weeds, pebbles, and other debris. When threaded over the barb of a no. 6 hook, they are even more productive than live grubs for the angler who will take the time and effort to gather them.

Catching (or buying) crickets or grasshoppers is easier, of course. A light, long-shanked no. 8 hook will hold a cricket for at least a short while, although such flimsy baits preclude energetic casting even with a light spinning rod and plastic casting bubble. Some anglers prefer to hook a cricket through its collar, others thread the hook through the body and out the thorax or tie the insect to the shank. Either way, it can be fished with or without a bobber, about a foot below a small split-shot sinker. Real grubs, though they performed less effectively than artificials in the Florida study, are in deservedly good repute throughout the country as bait for bluegills and other panfish. Grubs such as gallworms and mealworms stay on a thin-wire hook surprisingly well and can be fished like crickets.

There are those of us who will never outgrow the drowsy pleasure of recapturing the pollen-dusty, heat-shimmering summers of our childhood by strolling through goldenrod patches to gather bait grubs. The galls, bulging out on the stalks, are easily cut off and tossed into a bucket for temporary storage. Later they can be split to extract the grubs, which are dumped into a small holder such as a plastic film container or pharmacist's tablet container. If mixed in roughly equal measure with dry farina and stored in a freezer, the grubs are ready for use throughout the year.

Also effective is an inch or so of pork rind, which is probably perceived as a grub by hungry bluegills. As for the ubiquitous earthworm, it can be a nightcrawler or the smaller garden worm known in many areas as a redworm. Some anglers simply gob the worm onto a no. 8 snelled hook below a foot of light monofilament leader; 4-pound test is more than sturdy enough, and since bluegills can be more skittish than smallmouths on occasion, it may be well to keep snaps and swivels away from the bait. On the other hand, the fish are attracted to metallic glints that flicker through the water as prey might. Between the line and monofilament leader, many anglers swivel a small spoon—or, better yet, a double spinner with its silver blades in tandem to draw the quarry's attention to the worm.

There is a widespread belief that gobbing a worm reduces its effectiveness—as perhaps it does, slightly—and that the bait should merely be hooked once through the collar (which is a component of the creature's reproductive mechanism). This light hooking allows for natural movement and shape, but since panfish are small-mouthed, often hesitant nibblers, it can lead to short strikes and a frequent loss of bait. An improvement is to run a long-shanked no. 6 hook through the worm's "nose" and out behind the collar so that a substantial length of the bait covers the hook and leaves little more than the point and barb protruding.

When fishing a worm without a spinner or similar attractor, a good method is to use a sinker and two leaders. The leader with the hook and worm is just a short dropper—6 inches or so attached to the end of the line. A second leader of twice that length is snapped or blood-knotted to the same point, and it carries a small dipsey sinker—a teardrop of lead with a threading eye at the top. The weight gently drags or bumps along the bottom while the worm undulates a little higher, moving at a creep.

With these or other baits—leeches, live nymphs, catalpa worms, very small minnows—the angler can use a small weight to help cast and sink the terminal rig, which is then twitched, just lightly and occasionally. Artificials can also be jigged over the bottom. A small bass bug with a split shot will attract big bluegills, as will small spinners, spinner-flies, and jigs. A baitcasting rod, unless it is exceptionally light, seems somewhat indelicate for bluegills, but a fly rod can be used, or a spinning outfit with a small casting bubble. The lighter the rod and line, the more exciting will be the playing of a bluegill as it jolts and runs from side to side.

Both baits and lures should be fished very slowly, the more so if the water is cool—below about 70°. When using a trout nymph, the tactic is to let it settle and then twitch it gently. Dry flies should be dead-drifted in classic trouting manner. Such concoctions as a black gnat, an Adams, or one of the bivisibles tied on a no. 10 or no. 12 hook will serve well. Popping bugs work best over the spawning shallows or in the dim light of morning or evening. They should be retrieved slowly, with rests and small twitches. But it is well to remember that such lures have limitations, for the bulls among the bluegills feed chiefly in the middle depths or along the bottom, and when darkness comes even the hungriest will cease foraging as abruptly as if some biological generator had been switched off.

Carp *(Cyprinus carpio)*
COMMON & REGIONAL NAMES: *sewer bass*

GAME IDENTIFICATION & LOCATION OF FISHING REGIONS:
Floating the Susquehanna, a fisherman kneads a wad of cornmeal dough onto a no. 4 sproat—a straight-pointed hook with a parabolic bend. He lets it go to the bottom, pulled by a sliding sinker with a ring that is stopped by the swivel above a long, fine leader, a minor variation on the surfcaster's fishfinder rig. When the weight touches bottom he fingers a little more line out, allowing it to run through the sinker ring so that the doughball sways freely with the current just above the riverbed. He slips a small split twig onto the monofilament just beyond his rod tip,

and he watches it as he would a bobber, waiting for a dip or twitch.

For his purposes the Susquehanna might be many another sluggish river or some fertile lake or pond. Though his quarry is most common in the East, it has established itself almost everywhere across the temperate zone of North America. It is a heavy bronze or brownish or olive-gold fish with a yellowish underside and the extended, flexible snout of a bottom-grubbing sucker. On each side of the jaw is a pair of fleshy barbels, a small one backed by a larger one, and both equipped, like the "horns" or "whiskers" of a catfish, with sensitive taste buds and olfactory nerves.

As it roots along the bottom, clouding the water with silt and tattered algae, it smells the doughball. Tentatively, the fish sucks in the bait, mouths it, feels the hard, pointed wire, and is in the act of spitting it out when the angler sees the split twig shiver subtly. He has felt nothing but instantly he sets the hook. Some minutes later, after a bulldogging tug of war, he lifts an 8-pound carp into his skiff. It is a rough fish, as the biologists say, a trash

Head of carp. Note bottom-feeding mouth structure.

fish to the majority of anglers, a "sewer bass" whose invasion of American waters has been detrimental to many game species, yet it is also one of the most cautious fishes, tricky to hook, a hardy fighter, and a source of tasty meat when skinned and trimmed of its tough areas of dark muscle. Carp in aspic is a deservedly famous European dish.

Taxonomically the carp is a giant minnow. It has a blunt tail, an elliptical body about a third as deep as it is long, and sometimes a high, bulging back almost like that of the sucker *Ictiobus*, commonly called the buffalo. Above the belly, each big, coarse scale has a dark spot at the base and a dark border that forms diagonal crossing and parallel lines with adjacent scales, as if the bronze armor were cross-stitched. Wild carp are fully scaled. Among commercially reared strains there are unscaled "leather carp" and partially scaled "mirror carp"—genetic varia-

Carp sucking food off bottom.

tions incidentally produced by selective breeding for such characteristics as large size, fast growth, resistance to cold, and so on.

Young carp grow rapidly, gaining about a pound a year in the wild. Those inhabiting the middle latitudes become sexually mature after three to five years, and then their growth rate slows down. Popular writings tend to exaggerate their longevity, but they do survive conditions of habitat that would kill most species, and often live more than twenty years in the wild and over twice that long in captivity. Adult size varies with climate and the availability of browse. In American rivers and lakes, carp usually range from 5 to 15 pounds. A 20-pounder is uncommon but not a rarity. The largest yet taken by rod on this continent was a 55-pound, 5-ounce specimen heaved from Clearwater Lake in Minnesota. Sixty-pound carp have been caught in Great Britain. The heaviest fully authenticated record was a South African fish caught by netting; it weighed 83½ pounds. In Germany, however, there are old reports of a carp weighing 140 pounds.

For many centuries carp have been husbanded as food fish in Asian rice paddies, where they root and loosen the soil, thus increasing the grain yield. They must have been brought to Europe by about 350 B.C., for Aristotle mentioned their presence, but their spread from the Mediterranean countries was slow. The first record of stocked carp in Britain was a reference in 1462 and the first British angling reference was by the great lady versifier and essayist of field sports, Dame Juliana Berners, in 1496. During the next two centuries or so the emigrant fish were established in Scandinavia and Russia. There is evidence that in 1830 a few may have been released in the Hudson River near Newburgh, New York, and a few more in California waters in 1870. The first successful (one might also say calamitous) American stocking was conducted in 1876 by the United States Fish Commission. Baltimore breeding ponds received 345 adult carp, some of which were sent to the nation's capital the following year. They multiplied rapidly, as did votes for the politicians who subsequently used refrigerated railroad cars to ship hundreds of thousands as gifts to their congressional districts. In some waters they were stocked indiscriminately; in others they were spread by floods, broken dams, and the like.

Today they are present throughout the country and abundant in many states. They thrive in muddier, warmer, less oxygenated, more eutrophied water than can be tolerated by game species, and in a polluted river or aging lake they may be the best if not the only available catch. But it is also true that they speed the demise of an aging lake and its native species. They require less oxygen than bass, trout, or pike, and together with other rough fish such as gar, bullheads, and dogfish, they crowd the water and consume much of the remaining oxygen. Their rooting can ruin spawning beds and destroy aquatic vegetation. It can also silt the water severely enough to impede the respiratory gill action of gamefish. The oxygen-generating photosynthesis of plants dwindles as the sun goes down, and on a hot, still night when no breeze stirs the surface to provide at least minimal aeration, the carp browse contentedly while their neighbors die of suffocation.

The checks and balances of European habitat—sufficient predators but fewer consumers of oxygen, appropriate water temperatures, flow rates, nutrients—have permitted the carp to attain abundance and great size without devastating other species. There it is prized as both game and food. Indeed, many English anglers are carp specialists who use a long, light rod (rather like a salmon spinning rod) and a surprisingly large, leaderless hook dangled interminably in chummed "swims" where carp are known to feed. Most American specialists (who are neither so numerous nor so devoted) use medium spinning equipment or a spin-casting reel—the closed-face, thumb-controlled variation on the fixed-spool design of the spinning reel. In the spring, when big carp are ravenous after their hibernation, some of these anglers use stout braided line. Generally, however, they favor monofilament of 8- or 10-pound test, as the English do, for the wild carp is a suspicious creature and in spite of its detestable traits and lowly reputation it will challenge the stratagems of an average fisherman.

FISH HABITAT & FEEDING BEHAVIOR—ANGLING TACTICS: In the spring, as the water warms to about 60°, a "buck" carp sprouts tiny tubercles about his head and gills. He rubs these stimulating growths against receptive females during a spawning period which, in temperate regions, may last from late April until June or may be retarded a month by cold water.

A male and female pair off in the manner of pike and breed

in the weedy shallows. As they rub and roll and bump, leaping and splashing, they lose their usual caution. These frenzied carp are not particularly interested in food but are frequently speared or taken by archers using specially rigged bows and arrows with line running from the arrow to a spool on the bow.

No nest is cleared. The small grayish eggs are merely cast, immediately fertilized, and abandoned. Masses of them adhere to vegetation and debris, and in four to eight days they hatch fry a quarter-inch long. A healthy female carp usually casts about 150,000 eggs per pound of her body weight—millions of potential progeny—so predation of the fry is bound to leave plenty of survivors. The hatchlings sink and hold themselves on the bottom or against plants by means of an adhesive organ, but a day later wriggle to the top and gulp air for their swim bladders. When their yolk sacs are absorbed, they begin to suck in algae and plankton.

Carp are neither scavengers, as is sometimes alleged, nor strict vegetarians, as supposed by many fishermen. They have also been charged with raiding the nests of gamefish, as bluegills and some other species do; actually, though they may inadvertently destroy nests, they are not roe-eaters. They subsist chiefly on vegetation but also eat small crustaceans, mollusks, snail eggs, nematode worms, protozoa, and insect larvae—especially midges. They succumb to a wider array of baits than is generally realized, and if found in relatively clear water in the spring they can even be taken on artificial flies—midges and nymphs fished just over the bottom. At this time of heavy insect hatches the carp may be a trifle less cautious than usual because the winter fast has absorbed much of the weight accumulated in autumn, another time of greedy foraging. Cold makes many freshwater fishes torpid but none more so than the carp, which actually hibernates through the coldest part of winter in iced-over waters.

After spawning, both males and females scatter into somewhat deeper water but will gather into schools where the browse is good. Very fond of fungi, they are sometimes caught around mossy boulders or gravel where other vegetation is sparse. One of the many effective baits is a bit of moss scraped from a submerged stone and balled onto the barb of a thin-wire hook. They will even assemble beneath shoreline berry trees whose fruits drop into the water. When feeding at the surface on insects, mosquito eggs, floating berries, or other flotsam, they can be seen rolling and heard sucking in morsels with a kissing or slurping sound. More often they root along the bottom, their leathery protrusile mouths sucking in food-rich mud. The species has no true teeth but its pharyngeal bone is equipped with two rows of "throat teeth" that help send fodder to the stomach. The nutritive ingredients are then digested and the mud expelled.

Some anglers make no effort to set the hook since the initial tug of the fish is so light that timing is an art, and a carp will occasionally hook itself or swallow the bait without feeling a well-covered hook. Anglers of the hook-setting persuasion use a nibble-detecting contrivance such as a split twig on the line or a light quill, cork, or plastic bobber. The fisherman must strike the instant the bobber dips; if he is not too late and the hook is still in the carp's mouth, the battle is joined. There are also anglers who forgo any sinker—even a tiny split shot or wraparound strip— so sensitive is the carp to any drag on a bait. But often a slip sinker is the only means of putting the bait where the fish will smell it.

In some waters the carp will gobble a small bit of worm almost as readily as a catfish will if the bait covers the barb and bend of the hook. Carp will also take cheese or the cheese-based type of commercial catfish bait. Most anglers press it onto a small or medium sproat hook, but some of us have more faith in the small treble catfish hook (about no. 10) that has a wire coiled around the shank. The coil holds dough or cheese securely, and it can be molded into a teardrop that covers the entire hook.

Other good baits include canned peas or corn strung onto the hook, a bit of half-cooked potato, kneaded bread, a lump of shrimp or fish, even pieces of soap, gumdrops, or marshmallow. Recognizing the carp's exquisite sense of smell and taste, some fishermen treasure bait recipes involving such flavorings as sugar, vanilla, milk, egg, or cinnamon. One of the best is corn-meal mixed with enough corn syrup to make a dough and then boiled until rubbery. A ball of the concoction can be carried in a rag or jar, and baits pinched off as needed. On a dark, rainy day when the water is murky and the fish cannot see clearly enough to be spooked by the slightest alien movement, an inveterate carp fisherman is likely to be experimenting. He may be sharing his sandwich with the fish or sowing the waters over sand and gravel clearings with crumbs and cooked vegetables—chumming for carp.

Catfish *(Ictalurus)*

COMMON & REGIONAL NAMES: *cat.* (In addition to many local names for various species, the name *horned pout,* or *hornpout,* is commonly applied to the bullhead varieties, especially the black bullhead. The name *mud cat* is also applied to at least four species that thrive in turbid waters.)

GAME IDENTIFICATION & LOCATION OF FISHING REGIONS: Catfish and catfishermen appear in a wide array of types and sizes. On an eastern or midwestern pond, a catfisherman may be a boy using a cane pole and a canful of worms to catch a stringer of horned pout while he dreams of hooking one that will weigh more than a pound. On the same water in the evening, a somewhat more sophisticated catfisherman may be casting small spinners or flies to sunfish, which he cleans on the spot so he can bait a hook with a gob of entrails and dream of taking a horned pout that will weigh more than 2 pounds. On the churning waters below a southern dam, a catfisherman may be using a stiff-action baitcasting rod or a medium saltwater spinning rod to bounce large baits over the bottom while he dreams of a 20-pound blue or channel cat or an occasional flathead of comparable size. For that matter he may wade or float a river and try plugs or spoons or even streamers for the big channel species. Or he may be a meat-fisherman who uses a handline or setline or jugline and dreams of 50- and 60-pound blues. Or, anywhere in the United States, he may be a visitor to a farm pond or fish-for-a-fee lake, using almost any kind of tackle and dreaming of small to medium cats of whatever sort he finds—bullheads or whites, blues or channel cats.

In recent years Asiatic walking catfish and South American armored catfish have invaded Florida waters after escaping from the holding ponds of exotic-fish dealers. Both interlopers are competitive with native fauna, neither is worth the trouble of cleaning it when caught, and the Asiatic type has sharp, poison-dispensing dorsal spines that can inflict severe pain. Efforts to eradicate these pest species have been unsuccessful, but the alien fish have not—so far—spread very widely because they require a high water temperature. Whether a gradual genetic adaptation will allow them to spread into cooler habitats is un-known.

Far more congenial to the angler are North America's indigenous cats, which belong to two families, the large freshwater group *(Ictaluridae)* and a less important marine group *(Ariidae)*.

Marine catfish lack the nasal barbels of freshwater species and therefore have only six "whiskers" rather than eight. Two species are occasionally caught by southern anglers fishing the bottom in rivers and estuaries as well as in Atlantic coastal waters. One is the gafftopsail catfish *(Bagre marinus)*, whose common name is derived from its long, pointed, triangular dorsal fin. A blue-and-silver fish, it sometimes measures 2 feet in length and weighs up to about 6 pounds. The maxillary barbels trailing from its jaws are long and fleshy, and the upper lobe of its deeply forked tail is longer than the lower one. The other species is the sea catfish, or hardhead *(Arius felis)*. Slightly smaller than the gafftopsail, it is blue- or gray-backed, sometimes with greenish tinges, paling on the sides and belly. Either breed of cat should be handled with care. The sharp first spine on the dorsal fin of any bullhead can puncture a finger but that of a marine catfish can produce much greater pain. Like the leading spine on the walking

catfish and on the very small freshwater cats known as madtoms (which, incidentally, are good bass and walleye bait), it has a venom sac at its base and inflicts a wound like a severe bee sting.

The world's many species of catfish—fifteen distinct families of them—include climbing, parasitic, electric, and blind types. Some are tiny, others weigh hundreds of pounds. Some have stringent habitat requirements, but all can breathe air and many are extremely adaptable. North America's twenty-eight freshwater species vary in size from the inch-long least madtom to the ponderous blue catfish, which may weigh over 100 pounds. Those of greatest angling interest are a half-dozen of the bullheads and four other species that grow to more impressive size. All are native to the East, Midwest, and South, but some, because they are so popular for sport and food and so easily reared in farm ponds, have been successfully introduced throughout the United States. Fingerlings become harvestable 1-pound fish in about four months, and catfish "farming" yields up to a ton per acre. Channel, blue, and white cats (in that order) are most popular—the country's most important commercially reared fish—but bullheads are also very popular.

Catfishing in midwestern river.

All but the "armored" Latin American species are scaleless, and all the North American freshwater species have eight barbels—the "whiskers" and "horns" that characterize the family. Four of these appendages hang from the chin, one trails from each side of the jaw, and two nasal barbels grow from the upper part of the snout. Many species, and particularly the bullheads, feed chiefly at night or prefer turbid water in which to hide from predators. They must therefore depend on senses other than sight to locate food. Although some of them (notably the channel cat and blue cat, which will readily hit moving lures and live baits) are to some extent "sight-feeders," their barbels and even their skin surfaces are equipped with a keen sense of smell and taste as well as touch. Therein lies the efficacy of homemade and commercial "stink baits" (which need not have an obnoxious stench to attract catfish).

A large bullhead can be distinguished from a small member of some other species by its caudal fin—the tail—which is square, rounded, or only slightly forked. Of the bigger varieties sought by anglers, only the flathead has a rounded tail, and it can be distinguished by its pancake cranium and by its very big, fat adipose fin—a fleshy posterior dorsal fin. Of the madtoms, which also have rounded tails, only the one known as the stonecat (*Noturus flavus*) grows large enough to be mistaken for a bullhead, and it has a very long adipose fin. On most species, this fin is relatively small.

The brown bullhead (*Ictalurus nebulosus*) may be the most important of the bullhead group from the angler's point of view. It is widely abundant, scrappy, and attracted to a large assortment of baits. A 9-inch brown bullhead can offer a brief but sporting tussle on ultralight tackle, and there are occasional 16-inch specimens that weigh about 3 pounds. The species is indigenous to the eastern third of the country, from Maine to the Great Lakes and the Mississippi and down into Florida and Mexico. It has been introduced to other waters across the continent. All the cats exhibit local color variations, and some change colors slightly with age, but this one is usually mottled brown or yellow-brown with dark barbels and a pale belly.

If children, novices, casual fishermen, and farm-pond owners are counted among the nation's sportsmen, the black bullhead (*I. melas*) vies with the brown in importance. The black is the one most commonly known as a horned pout. It is native to the entire East and Midwest, from New England to the Dakotas and down to the Gulf, and like the brown bullhead it has been widely transplanted. It has a black back, black or dark gray sides, and a pale belly. Stockier but shorter than the brown bullhead, it seldom weighs more than 2 pounds, the average being a pound or less. In 1976 an unofficial world record may have been set when three young boys—Randy Pike, Mark Potvin, and Len Stoessel—together fought and landed a big catfish on the Shawsheen River, a tributary of the Merrimack in Massachusetts. They put the fish in a bucket of water and carried it to the offices of the Lawrence *Eagle Tribune* to be photographed, weighed, and measured. Owing to its size, the fish was at first assumed to be a channel cat rather than a horned pout. However, it had an unforked tail and the barbels were black (those of a channel cat are pale or mottled). The fish had a length of 23½ inches, a girth of 14½ inches, and a weight of 7½ pounds—2 pounds more than the accepted world-record horned pout. Unfortunately, before any state biologist or other qualified expert could examine it to verify the species, the children carried their catch back to the Shawsheen and released it.

Comparable in size to the average black—under a pound, though occasionally twice that—is the flat bullhead *(I. platycephalus)*, which ranges from Virginia into Georgia. It is a brown or mottled yellowish species with black edging on the dorsal and anal fins and on the slightly forked tail. It looks like the brown

Blue catfish.

or yellow bullhead except that it has a flattened head and a black splotch over the base of the dorsal fin. Equally limited in distribution is the green bullhead (*I. brunneus*), which is found from North Carolina to Florida. The scientific designation refers to the immature phase, which is brownish; adults are olive on the back and sides, paling below. Mature specimens generally weigh no more than 4 ounces, but there have been catches of about 1½ pounds. The spotted bullhead (*I. serracanthus*) of Georgia, Alabama, and Florida attains the same size as the green. It is gray-black with pale spots. Chiefly a predator of mollusks, it is sometimes called the snailcat.

The yellow bullhead (*I. natalis*) is often mistaken for the brown, as it grows to about the same size and is caught in many of the same regions. Its flesh is not very firm and savory, however, and it is not as commonly stocked in farm ponds. It is found from North Dakota to New York and southward to Florida and the Gulf. The dominant hue is yellowish-olive, sometimes almost black on top, with pale chin barbels and a belly coloration varying from bright yellow to the dull cream of the brown bullhead's underparts. Its numbers undulate cyclically and it seems to be most plentiful at all times in the southern part of its range.

Catfish in general and bullheads in particular are derided by the elitists among American anglers, good sport and good eating notwithstanding. There is no aura of glamour or nobility about bullheads; they are to the larger cats as bluegills are to black bass or as pickerel are to muskies. The giant of the catfish family is the blue cat (*I. furcatus*), though it is occasionally rivaled by an old channel cat. Most of the blue catfish taken on rod and reel weigh between 2 and 15 pounds, but a few 50-pounders are caught and blues weighing nearly 120 have been recorded. Native to the big rivers from Minnesota to Ohio and down into Mexico, the species has been established in many eastern streams and, despite its preference for swifter, clearer waters than the haunts of its smaller relatives, is successfully raised in farm ponds everywhere. It has a thick but deeply forked tail and a pale blue or blue-gray back and upper sides. The color usually turns silvery before fading out on the belly.

The natural distribution of the channel catfish (*I. punctatus*) extends farther west and north than the ranges of most cats—from the region of the Great Lakes northwest to the Saskatchewan

Top: Channel catfish.
Bottom: Fly-rodder taking cat from shallow canal.

River and south to the Gulf and into Mexico. Now established throughout the United States, it generally attains its greatest size in southern and midwestern waters. This is a fork-tailed fish, bluish-gray or olive above, white below, with small black speckles scattered over the body; the depth of color and degree of speckling vary sharply from one region to another and even among individual fish in a single stretch of river. At spawning time the males darken until they are almost blue-black. A foot-long channel cat may weigh only a pound, while a 2½-foot catch may weigh close to 15 if taken in the summer in food-rich water. Anglers occasionally take much larger ones, and commercial fishing methods have harvested 60-pound channel cats.

The flathead catfish *(Pylodictus olivarus)* generally attains only a modest weight, perhaps 4 pounds, but has been known to weigh 100. It is a mottled brown fish with a white belly, square tail, big, fleshy adipose fin, and long, wide, flattened head. It inhabits the big rivers of the Mississippi valley, from the northernmost tier of states to the Gulf and into Mexico.

The white catfish *(I. catus)*, originally caught in streams, ponds, sloughs, and bayous from Chesapeake Bay to Texas, has now been introduced throughout the country. It is a trim and rather handsome cat with a forked tail, bluish and silver upper parts, a white belly, and sometimes dark mottling on the sides. Most of those hooked measure from a little under a foot to a foot and a half long and weigh up to 3 pounds or a trifle more. White cats have a tolerance for mildly brackish waters, and sometimes they descend rivers into the upper parts of estuaries where anglers may boat a mixed bag of such widely diversified species as striped bass, largemouth bass, snapper bluefish, white perch, and white cats. This species has also gained popularity on northeastern lakes, for it is a less nocturnal feeder than the native brown bullhead and frequently grows to a larger size.

FISH HABITAT & FEEDING BEHAVIOR—ANGLING TACTICS:
The spotted bullhead spawns from December into July, the green bullhead from February into July, and both may breed sporadically throughout the year. In general, however, catfish spawn in May and June, when the water reaches a temperature of about 70°, and nesting activity peaks as the water warms to 80° or so. The breeding habits of the various species are roughly similar,

with several exceptions: the channel cat and, to a lesser extent, the white cat migrate into streams, where they nest under banks, logs, and stones or sometimes inside hollow logs or holes in the bank, and the male alone stands guard over eggs and fry; the male channel cat, in fact, is very aggressive in chasing the female off. Yellow bullheads, though they do not migrate, sometimes nest in burrows, and the male guards the fry. All cats prefer a spawning bed sheltered by rocks, debris, logs, weeds, or submerged brush, and when commercially reared they take advantage of such nesting boxes as milk cans. In the wild, most species clear a shallow, sheltered redd where the female deposits gelatinous clusters of eggs. Like most fish, they are prolific; a ripe channel cat, for instance, carries three or four thousand eggs per pound of her body weight. They hatch in a week or less in warm waters, a bit longer in cool northern habitat.

Among most of the American species, the female participates at least briefly in the guarding of eggs and hatchlings. Some varieties are extraordinarily solicitous of their young. Brown bullheads have been observed grooming their eggs and fry by gently mouthing them and then blowing them back into the nest. Usually the adults linger for several days, until the young absorb their yolk sacs and are swimming actively and feeding. Sometimes a parent will remain on guard until the fry are about an inch long.

The occasional removal of a parent will not significantly reduce the stock, however, and fishing is good around spawning cover. For that matter, catfish will take baits eagerly before spawning begins. Bullheads are the earliest to start gorging themselves in the spring. Right after ice-out on northern lakes and ponds, they avidly take nightcrawlers fished on the bottom along the shorelines. Fishing for the bigger cats is best in summer, when the water has warmed, but is a year-round sport in many southern regions.

Predators include fry-devouring insects such as backswimmers (which may partially account for the occasional effectiveness of small bass bugs and similar surface lures in catching the larger varieties, particularly the channel cat). Fingerlings that attain a length of about 2 inches have an excellent chance of escaping insect predation but continue to be an important food for panfish and gamefish, especially bass. All the same, a great many mature. In eutrophic or crowded waters they may consume

oxygen as well as food needed by game species, but where the ecosystem is well balanced they can be beneficial both as a food source and as environmental cleansers. All are more or less omnivorous and some, chiefly the bullheads, perform scavenging service.

Bullheads are the most nocturnal feeders—and they can provide an almost frenzied session of night fishing with natural baits—but all catfish rely almost as heavily as bullheads on their olfactory sense to locate food. Most anglers know that fish are alarmed by the odor of perspiration; fewer are aware of the strange

Brace of very big flathead catfish.

fact that catfish are attracted to human saliva. Perhaps it holds the odor of foods enjoyed by man and catfish alike. Whatever the reason, there is a basis for the old superstition some of us honor about spitting on a bait for luck. In experiments conducted by Utah fishery biologists, the scent most attractive to catfish was that of worms, the mainstay of freshwater bait-fishing. The second most attractive was liver, a widely effective bait that is less familiar to anglers other than the muskellunge fishermen who occasionally switch from big lures to blood baits. The third most enticing was human saliva.

Perhaps even less familiar is the fact that some catfish will strike artificial lures, and with fair frequency if the lures are rubbed with saliva or, better still, daubed with sticky cheese, dough, or a chum of meaty or fishy paste, or dipped into one of the clinging commercial catfish scents. Bullheads will take wet flies, deeply and slowly retrieved spinners, and small jigs. Blue cats, which hunt more by sight than other catfish, will grab at a jig, plug, spoon, streamer, or bucktail, but there is no denying that they are more easily caught on natural baits. Channel cats will hit jigs, deep-running plugs and spoons, and even popping bugs, but small streamers are more effective. Best of all among the artificials—since channel cats prowl the bottom for insect life—are big fuzzy nymphs such as the Woolly Worm.

Fly fishing for channel cats is an art for anglers bored with the dangling of heavy-weighted naturals. A streamer or nymph must be cast upstream or above food-collecting eddies and pools —ideally, the kind of spot that looks like a trout lie—and drifted down right over the bottom. If the lure is not lead-bodied, it must be sunk by a small split shot or thin lead strip wrapped on the tippet. A cat will not slam the offering like a bass or pike; it will take it in gently, again showing an unexpected emulation of trout. However, the cat has a keener sense of smell and taste than a trout, and is inclined to spit out a mistake very quickly (although, unlike a cautious trout, it will not be "put down" for hours by the mistake but will investigate it again on the next presentation). Hooking a channel cat on a nymph requires unhesitating judgment and a kind of compromise. A light tap by the fish may call for a split second of delay and a little slack while the cat decides whether to engulf the fly; but if the cat takes it, the hook must be set instantly, before it can be spit out.

This is quite different from bobber-and-sinker fishing for the smaller varieties. Bullheads may peck away at a worm for several seconds or even minutes, repeatedly but lightly tugging the bobber down. When they are feeding in this tentative way, even a sharp little size 8 or 10 hook will often come away fishless if an attempt is made to set it before the cat at least moves away with it, giving the bobber a long, strong pull below the surface. A common catfishing error is to use too large a hook; nothing bigger than a size 8 is needed for bullheads, and a 6 is big enough for white cats. With cheese and other soft baits, many anglers use a treble catfish hook with a wire coiled around the shank to hold the material. Even the large species require a hook no bigger than 1/0 or 2/0 as a general rule.

Productive natural baits for catfish include nightcrawlers, fish entrails, minnows, grasshoppers, shrimp, crawfish, clams, mussels, doughballs, beef, chicken, pork, all kinds of liver, strong cheese, meat-and-cheese pastes (sometimes with a cotton binder), fish chunks or strips, commercial preparations (often cheese base permeated with fish or meat), even stronger-smelling homemade and ripened concoctions, and, for the big species, whole smelt, skipjack herring, gizzard or threadfin shad, suckers, and the like.

The habitat, preferred foods, and foraging behavior of the cats furnish an obvious key to baits and angling methods. All cats feed chiefly on the bottom, but in different kinds of water. Even the bullheads, which will nibble at any scrap of flesh, exhibit definite preferences in foods and foraging haunts. The little black bullhead moves through shallow, silty water over soft mud, chiefly seeking small fish, insects, and mollusks. Insect larvae and mollusks also provide the bulk of the diet for the brown bullhead, but this species likes somewhat deeper, weedy lakes and slow rivers, and it will prowl over mud, sand, or gravel. The spotted bullhead, or snail cat, and the flat bullhead both have a fondness for mollusks and both can be caught with clams on mud or sand bottoms of lakes and streams. The green bullhead prefers faster current over gravel or rock—in river channels and pools and below dams—where it consumes small fish and bits of vegetation as well as insects and snails. The yellow bullhead seeks the same kind of slow, shallow, soft-bottomed waters that hold the black, but is even more omnivorous and more of a scavenger.

The white catfish is another unselective feeder with a preference for slow or still waters. However, it may hunt by sight somewhat more than the bullheads, for it displays a strong attraction to live baits. Since it can thrive in mild salinity, it is caught in tidal creeks and bayous as well as fresh ponds and streams.

The flathead catfish is one of the species sometimes called mud cats. The description in this case is inappropriate. On occasion it lies still in the shallows to ambush prey but it favors deep, slow, hard-bottomed pools in big rivers. Though omnivorous, it seems to prefer fish and crustaceans. Whole or cut fish or crawfish will therefore be a choice bait. Flatheads are generally caught on baitcasting or spinning tackle but, like blues and channel cats, they are also taken on trotlines by those less interested in sport than in meat. And, like channel cats, they are occasionally caught by "jugging." In sporting quality, this technique is a slight cut above trotlining. A chunk of meat or fish (as much as a pound where big channel cats may lurk) is impaled on a large saltwater hook that trails on several yards of heavy line or cord attached to a big corked jug. The fisherman follows the floating jug in a boat, and in the case of channel cats he may shoot white water with this queer rig.

More conventional anglers sometimes catch big flatheads as well as channel cats and blue cats in the foamy waters below big southern dams such as Tennessee's Pickwick. Some use a treble hook, some prefer a big single hook, and some attach several single hooks in tandem, but the rule is to use a heavy

White catfish.

sinker (4 to 8 ounces) to bounce a large bait over the bottom, where the cats are feeding on small fish that have tumbled down a spillway or ground through a turbine and been injured or killed. In calmer waters or for medium-sized cats, line testing 15 pounds or so is adequate, but saltwater gear and line testing as much as 100 pounds will be seen often in boiling tailwaters, for the sinker and bait alone are heavy, and there is a good chance of hooking a very large fish.

The channel cat prefers lakes or big rivers with sand, gravel, or boulders. Neither this species nor the flathead can long tolerate the really fast waters that regularly hold blue catfish, but both will buck a heavy current if it carries a feast of prey, as it does below dams and in the bows and cauldrons of rivers. The channel cat is fond of insects and crustaceans as well as fish, but probably the best bait for a lunker channel cat is a strip of fish belly.

The prize of the lot is, of course, the blue cat. The sporting record dates back to 1957, when Edward B. Elliott took a 97-pound blue catfish from the Missouri River in South Dakota. A larger one has been handlined below Kentucky Lake Dam, and a 117-pound specimen has been captured on a trotline in Missouri's Osage River. Like the channel cat, this species prefers rock, gravel, or sand bottoms, but it wants them under clearer, swifter water. Sometimes it feeds in rapids. It finds crawfish scuttling among the stones and under submerged branches, but it must also capture fish as they move past in heavy current. For this reason it must depend on sight more heavily than other catfish, yet many anglers have found it to be a bit less inclined than the channel cat to attack lures. Perhaps the movement of a lure in very fast water is not realistic enough. In any case, the blue cat comes most eagerly to large baits, including whole fish. They need not be alive, and they need not always be lowered to the very bottom; if they are ignored down there, it may be wise to raise them to the middle depths.

To experienced catfishermen, almost all the cats are a culinary as well as a sporting pleasure, yet anglers accustomed to other fare often perceive a catfish as a scaleless, slimy, bewhisk-ered, and somewhat daunting oddity. Probably the least tasty of the commonly caught species are the brown and yellow bull-heads, and even these can be quite appetizing. The other bullheads have whiter, firmer flesh, as do the larger species—the most delicious of all. Contrary to almost universal belief, it is not necessary to skin a small catfish. The slime, a protective secretion, can be rubbed off under running water, and some of the skin may come with it. If not, no matter; unless the fish is breaded, the skin can be crisped off by frying the meat. A medium or large catfish must, however, be skinned. After cleaning and beheading it, this is most easily done by peeling the skin away, using pliers to grip it securely. If the fish is too big or slippery for easy handling, a nail through the base of the tail will hold it to a board. Some insist on filleting even a small bullhead, for most of the flesh is far forward, around the "shoulders," but it can be deep-fried or sautéed whole. Medium-sized cats are often but not always filleted. The really big ones can be conventionally filleted or cross-sectioned into steaks in the manner of salmon. Fried, sautéed, baked, or broiled, they achieve a nobility on the table not often ascribed to them in life.

Crappie *(Pomoxis)*
COMMON & REGIONAL NAMES: *croppie, speckled perch, bridge perch, bachelor perch, bachelor, papermouth, tinmouth.* (The black crappie is also known as the *calico bass.*)

GAME IDENTIFICATION & LOCATION OF FISHING REGIONS:
The black crappie *(Pomoxis nigromaculatus)* and the white crappie *(P. annularis)* are closely related members of the sunfish family, but like those other magnificent sunfish, the black bass and the bluegill, they merit a more detailed examination than that accorded the smaller sunnies. Perhaps neither of the crappies is quite as tasty as a bluegill, or quite as game, but both the black and white varieties often outweigh the bluegill, can be caught in even larger numbers when schooling, and are now established in almost as many waters across the country. Moreover, they are of tactical interest to the angler. Strictly carnivorous, they have a reputation for being catchable only with live minnows, yet they show a contrary predilection at times for hitting small jigs, spinners, streamers, and other artificials.

Both varieties have a wide tail and a wide, long dorsal and anal fin, and both have the flattened shape typical of their family.

The black crappie, however, has a higher-arching back than the white. Where crowded or impoverished habitat has not caused stunting, white crappies may average just a trifle larger than the blacks, but both are relatively slow-growing and short-lived; a foot-long crappie, as a rule, is at least four years old and unlikely to live more than another year or two. Most weigh less than a pound. Nevertheless, quite a few weighing 2 or 3 pounds are caught. The record black crappie was a 5-pound fish taken in South Carolina's Santee-Cooper reservoir system; the record white, heavier by just 3 ounces, was caught at Enid Dam, Mississippi.

Crappies have dark or blackish mottling over the caudal, dorsal, and anal fins, and these markings tend to form bars across the dark fin rays, producing a vaguely crosshatched effect. Usually, but not invariably, the black crappie is considerably darker than the white. Its back is black, gray-black, or olive, with a few lighter scales, grading to silver or yellowish-silver sides. Dark spots and streaks scattered over the body have given it the

common name calico bass. The white crappie has silver sides, usually washed with pale yellow or olive. It, too, has dark or blackish markings, but not in a calico scattering; the spots are grouped to form eight or nine (or, less often, seven) vertical bars. The back is dark, usually olive-green. This species is the only sunfish with six spines in the dorsal fin and six in the anal fin. When an angler catches a dark crappie whose species is uncertain, he can identify it by counting the stiff dorsal spines; if it has seven or eight, it has to be the black variety.

Originally the black crappie ranged across lower Canada from Manitoba through Quebec and across the United States from the eastern part of the Dakotas to western Pennsylvania and down to the Gulf. It was also found close to the Atlantic seaboard, from Florida into the Carolinas. It has now been introduced in New England, British Columbia, and a number of western states.

The natural distribution of the white crappie is more southerly—from Nebraska to Lake Ontario, down the Ohio and Mississippi drainages to the Gulf, and in the same lower-seaboard states that have always held black crappies. Both species were brought to California waters before the turn of the century. Today there is fine crappie fishing in lakes and reservoirs as far west as New Mexico, California, and Oregon.

Left: Black crappie, or calico bass.
Above: Membranous jaw structure from which crappie gets the name papermouth.

FISH HABITAT & FEEDING BEHAVIOR—ANGLING TACTICS:
The pursuit of the crappie is a cyclic affair—feast or famine. In a good year, when the fish have ample food, normal spring temperatures and water levels, a healthy protective screen of weeds or brush in the spawning shallows, and no unusual influx of larger predaceous species, the result is a large and hardy population of young—a "dominant brood." Two years later the dominant brood will be mature, ready to reproduce. That spring and the next, and perhaps for another year, fishermen will catch plenty of big crappies. However, the mature fish will be preying indiscriminately on fry and fingerlings, including their own young. During this period the dominant brood is slowly reduced by predation, aging, fishing pressure, and diverse natural causes. After two or three years of excellent fishing, there are two or three lean years. By then, of course, with the attrition of cannibalism and the lessening of competition, another dominant brood has been made possible. The cycle repeats itself, as the two or three poor seasons are followed by a resurgence of good fishing.

Competition affects size as well as numbers. A fairly new impoundment, like a young lake, may produce 2-pound crappies in fair quantity and even a few 4-pound catches, but the growth rate of the young slows down as the waters become crowded. Thus the average size of mature fish is diminished. A year-old black crappie may be about 3 inches long in typical habitat; during its second year it may grow another 8 inches or not even half that. A half-pound ripe female usually holds at least twenty thousand eggs and sometimes closer to fifty thousand. The white species produces fewer eggs but is very hardy, may have a longer spawning period in some of its southern habitat, and is less stringent in its habitat requirements than the black. Consequently it is more prolific and its growth rate is even more variable, more subject to the stunting effect of competition.

The two varieties prefer quiet waters and may share the same ecosystem, especially where man has introduced one or both. But the white crappie, a particularly abundant fish in southern impoundments, likes its rivers and lakes a bit silty, while the black prefers clearer, cooler, but weedier habitat. The black fares best over hard bottoms; the white may feed *near* the bottom but is not a true bottom-forager and seems to be about equally content (and abundant) over a hard or muddy bed.

Stringer of fat whites taken in autumn.

Angling becomes very good in late autumn, when the crappies are fattening themselves for winter, but it is even better in the spring, just before and during the spawning period, which peaks in late April and May and in some waters may last into early summer. Crappies are strongly colonial spawners, crowding a great many saucerlike nests into good cover in the shallows. The nests are cleared amid protective vegetation, those of black crappies mostly at depths of three to six feet, those of white crappies sometimes at depths up to eight feet. Either type may be locally known as the bachelor or bachelor perch, for the male alone performs guard duty. The fry of many fish rely heavily on vegetation for sustenance, but crappies are almost totally carnivorous from the first. The young eat plankton as well as aquatic insects until they grow large enough to hunt well. Then their diet consists chiefly of fish, supplemented by mollusks, crustaceans, and insects. While it is true that any sunfish may bite at a worm, the best of all natural crappie baits is a small live minnow, no

more than 2 inches long. But with regard to artificial lures, regional feeding habits (or more probably food availability) can differ sufficiently to influence the angler's choice. In northern waters many insects are eaten. In southern lakes and impoundments the extreme abundance of the gizzard shad leads to a proportionate abundance of white crappies, and the crappies there rely on this little shad for more than half of their total food consumption.

A small minnow can be hooked through the lips and drifted or still-fished under a bobber, or it can be slowly trolled. Crappies gather into large schools before spawning, and a good way to locate a school is to troll a spinner-fly, a streamer, or a pork-rind strip fluttering behind a spinner, in waters up to about fifteen feet deep; an even better way where minnows are plentiful is to troll one behind a small attention-getting spinner. Springtime trollers in the South sometimes use long cane poles to put their baits under or near the brushy creek banks. A good alternative to the minnow for this technique is a little bucktail that will not continually catch in the brush.

After spawning, crappies move into deeper water, returning in good numbers only to feed during early morning and at dusk. Their retreat is not governed simply by the completion of breeding. In part it is probably a basslike reaction to heat and light. In greater part, it is probably triggered by the lowering of the water level, which may occur as early as mid-June, and which forces the baitfish farther out from the shoreline. The crappies follow their prey to deeper thickets of weeds, brush, or similar cover. Now again, a good way to locate schools is to troll with a minnow or pork rind behind a very small spinner. Another very effective arrangement for summer trolling consists of two or three jigs on droppers above a small spoon.

At this time the crappies may be in twenty-five or thirty feet of water. Ideal "crappie beds" are thickets or piles of brush, from fifty to a hundred yards offshore. Where no such cover exists, anglers or fishery biologists sometimes lower and anchor mats or piles of brush, thus building crappie homes. Willow is excellent for the purpose because it will take root—one reason it is so popular among trout fishermen who practice stream improvement. In addition to brushy patches, good prospecting spots are those with fallen trees, undercut banks, weeds, and lilies. A live minnow on a size 6 hook can be hovered just off the bottom or just above or around the cover patches. A small, light, bright jig— the sort known as a shad dart to anglers who delight in the runs of American shad—will also draw crappies from deep cover. It can be a plastic twister or a tuft of hair or marabou behind a lead head. For trolling it works very effectively on one of those "safety-pin" spinners with the blade on one prong and the jig on the other. The appeal of jigs and small minnows is no summertime infatuation; both are used to catch crappies through the ice.

Whether cast or trolled, a crappie lure usually has to be worked near the bottom, slowly but with pronounced action. In this situation one does not want the kind of plug that requires a fast retrieve to give it life. The small, deep-running, wobbling plugs with built-in action—the various models now popularly called "crankbaits"—will attract crappies, and so will light, bright spoons. Although, generally speaking, jigs are the most promising lures, one of the most consistently productive arrangements in northern waters is the spinner-fly combination; a silver blade ahead of red or white seems to be the favorite, and a few beads between the blade and the fly will not only enhance the attraction but add a little casting weight. Minnow-mimicking streamers will also bring strikes; the color of choice is white or yellow with a silver-tinsel body. Although no hook can be truly snagproof and at the same time efficient at gripping a fish, some small spoons and other lures have prongs that make them reasonably weedless. And streamers can be made relatively weedless by tying them on keel hooks. Why this is not done more often is one of the minor mysteries of fishing. Where insect feeding is heavy, fat wet flies can sometimes outperform streamers. These panfish seem to be most strongly attracted to the widely flared hair-wing patterns.

Many crappie fishermen regard surface lures as useless decorations, but most will concede the existence of an exception to the rule. On occasion, especially near dusk, crappies are seen feeding on the surface. They will not be going about it as strenuously as bluegills but will make rings on the surface. Cast a small popping bug or a fluffy dry fly to these rings and a crappie may abruptly prove how worthy an adversary it can be on a light fly rod. At such times a small Flatfish plug may be equally remunerative but it is lacking in stylish appeal to the fly fisherman.

A cautionary observation is in order with regard to the hooking and playing of a crappie. The genus is colloquially called a papermouth for the same reason that the rugged weakfish is called a weakfish: it has a fragile mouth from which a barb can easily tear free. Actually, the mouth of a weakfish is not as papery as it is reputed to be, but that of a crappie is. If the fish does not obligingly hook itself, the hook must be set gently, and there can be no subsequent horsing. A good crappie fisherman is a gentleman of finesse, at least when playing his fish.

Gar *(Lepisosteus)*
COMMON & REGIONAL NAMES: *garpike, garfish, freshwater needlefish*

GAME IDENTIFICATION & LOCATION OF FISHING REGIONS:
Lolling just below the surface like dark, thin sticks that have been in the water almost long enough to sink, gars infest many lakes, sloughs, bayous, and sluggish rivers in the South and Midwest. Occasionally they raise their narrow, toothy snouts above the water, gulping air. They are a primitive family of creatures whose inefficient gills are supplemented by modified swim bladders that double as lungs, taking in oxygen directly. Their breathing mechanism enables them to thrive in stagnant waters fit only for themselves and such fellow pariahs as carp. In some ecosystems they help to control other coarse fish but in many areas they are destructive pests, competing with and preying on the young of gamefish and panfish. Their roe is poisonous to man and their flesh provides mediocre food at best. Yet there are anglers who spend summers trying to take the almost unhookable smaller varieties on needle-sharp hooks and tufts of tooth-snagging nylon, and some who specialize in dangling fish-baited treble hooks before the saurian snouts of monstrous alligator gar.

When hooked, a big gar will run, sulk, roll, and jump, showing good form for a fish never classified as game. It should be dispatched before boating it, as its bellicosity will not quickly subside when it is taken from the water and its teeth can be murderous. A yard-long gar can be clubbed, but the inexpensive pistols known as kit guns are common equipment among anglers who seek alligator gar.

The five American species are the alligator gar *(Lepisos-teus spatula),* Florida gar *(L. platyrhincus),* longnose gar *(L. osseus),* shortnose gar *(L. platostomus),* and spotted gar *(L. oculatus).* The Florida, shortnose, and spotted varieties are usually less than a yard long, with narrow, streamlined bodies rather like that of a northern pike. The longnose quite often reaches a length of 5 feet but seldom weighs much more than a 3-foot pike because its body is even more snakelike and a bit of the overall length is composed of narrow, beaky snout. The giant of the clan is the alligator. Among the freshwater fishes of the United States, it is outweighed only by the western sturgeons. The largest alligator gar on record was a 10-foot behemoth weigh-ing 302 pounds. Catches weighing 200 pounds are very uncom-mon but 100-pound specimens are not. The largest ever taken on rod and reel was a 7-foot, 9-inch monster hauled in from the Rio Grande in Texas in 1951. It weighed 279 pounds. A closely related sixth species, the giant gar *(L. tristoechius),* attains comparable proportions but is found only in Mexican, Cuban, and Central American waters.

All gars inhabit still, shallow waters and slow-moving rivers. The alligator gar ranges from northeastern Mexico up through the Mississippi River basin to the area of St. Louis and up the Ohio to Louisville, Kentucky. Its best-known lairs are the indolent meanders of the Trinity River and Rio Grande in Texas, the Atchafalaya in Louisiana, and the White in Arkansas. For many years the White River was renowned for huge and abundant gar, but cool water flowing from upstream dams has adversely af-fected gar fishing there and on portions of other rivers.

Size will easily distinguish an old alligator gar from its relatives, while a young one can be identified by double rows of large upper teeth. Other gars have only a single row on each side. The body of an alligator is long and slender, and the snout is comparable to that of a shortnose gar—long and narrow but less so in relation to body size than the snouts of other gars. The color is usually greenish-brown or olive, mottled near the head and fading toward the underside, with big black spots on the fins and rear portion of the body. All gars have hard, shiny, diamond-shaped scales, rounded, somewhat fanned-out tails, and rounded fins, with the dorsal fin located far back, more or less opposite the anal fin.

The Florida gar is distributed from South Carolina down through Florida and is so abundant in Florida canals like the Tamiami that removal programs have sometimes been necessary. It is a gregarious fish, perhaps a trifle more so than other gars; where one is lurking or feeding, there will usually be at least one or two others and often eight or nine. The species is generally olive-green on the back, bronze on the sides, yellowish or whitish below, with a relatively broad snout and big dark spots on the body, fins, and top of the head. It resembles the spotted gar so closely that identification can be difficult. If the distance from the front of the eye to the rear of the gill cover is less than two-thirds as long as the snout, the fish is of the Florida rather than the spotted breed.

The spotted gar, which ranges from Texas to Florida in the South and up the Mississippi and Ohio drainages to Minnesota and Ohio in the North, has a much broader snout than the longnose and a deeper, thicker body than either the longnose or

shortnose. Its fins and tail are densely spotted and blotched, sometimes even more than those of the Florida gar. Its range is large but its numbers are small.

Most plentiful and widely distributed is the longnose, whose slim snout stretches forward like an exaggerated beak, about eighteen times longer than the width of its narrowest part. It inhabits the Mississippi and neighboring systems from northern Mexico into Montana, and eastward into the Great Lakes (except for Lake Superior) as well as Quebec's St. Lawrence watershed. Its fins and tail are reddish, its back dark gray, sometimes with olive or bluish shadings, paling to white below, and there are black spots along the lateral line near the tail, on the tail itself, and on the dorsal fin. An average mature longnose measures 3 feet from snout to tail—about the maximum size of the Florida, spotted, and shortnose varieties. A 5-footer is occasionally caught, but the species is so slim-bodied that it rarely outweighs its smaller relatives by much.

Longnose gar.

The shortnose is found in the Mississippi and Ohio drainages from Texas northward to Minnesota and South Dakota, but is not very abundant in the upper part of its range. It, too, has a cylindrical, attenuated body, but is a trifle stockier than the longnose, and the beak is only five or six times as long as the width of its narrowest part. The young have short jaws and a black side-stripe. Adults are brownish, bronze, or yellowish with a white belly. There are black spots near and on the tail and on the dorsal and anal fins.

FISH HABITAT & FEEDING BEHAVIOR—ANGLING TACTICS:
The American gars have roughly similar life histories. They spawn in shallow backwaters, usually in May and June though breeding lasts through July in Florida. The thousands of green eggs, adhering to weeds and debris, hatch in six to eight days. The longnose can take faster current than other gars and is sometimes caught while feeding in a moderate flow rather than in still or very sluggish water, but otherwise its way of life resembles that of other gars. Its young feed on plankton and insect larvae for a few days but very soon snap up passing minnows. Like the adults, they spend long periods basking at or near the surface, moving only to catch food or rise for a gulp of air. Growing rapidly at first, many gars are nearly 2 feet long by the end of their first year even though males require three or four years to mature and females require six.

Gars feed chiefly on fish, but in some areas this diet is heavily enriched by other prey. Florida gar, for instance, consume plenty of freshwater shrimp plus smaller quantities of other crustaceans and insects. A gar will hit a plug, spoon, or anything else that looks like a fish, and might even mouth a fly tied to imitate a shrimp or scud, but artificial lures seldom hook a gar's bone-hard snout. One exception is a peculiar homemade lure—a tattered streamer or tuft of nylon, sometimes draped over a sharp hook and sometimes used without any hook. When a gar mouths the offering, its teeth catch in the material and it is, in a manner of speaking, hooked. This device, cast at surfacing gar, is not infallible but it works often enough with the smaller varieties of gar.

Among baits, the most effective is a dead minnow, still or drifting just under the surface. A few specialists fashion noose-

Top: Alligator gar.
Bottom: Angler boating longnose gar.

type wire snares with a minnow dangling in the center of the loop; when the gar pokes into it and the rod is yanked as if to set a hook, the snare tightens around the gar's snout. Most minnow fishermen, however, simply impale the bait on a sharp hook and then wait while a gar mouths it, makes an initial run, stops, and works it far back into the mouth. Then the hook is set hard, suddenly, and sometimes successfully. A short wire leader is used because a gar's teeth will sever anything else.

Another specialized method has evolved in waters frequented by the enormous alligator gar. Here the favorite bait is "gaspergou"—freshwater drum—usually obtained from commercial trapnetters or seiners. It works best when scaled and cut into half-pound chunks. Marine gear is the general rule: a big revolving-spool reel with heavy line on a boat rod or big saltwater casting rod, 4 feet or more of steel-wire leader on a sturdy swivel, and a size 7/0 or even larger treble hook. A bobber is attached at the swivel. A gar tends to mouth the big chunk of bait for a while and then run with it, sometimes sixty or seventy yards, after which the fish may circle or just lie and gnaw for a little longer. Baits are frequently stolen, but if the gar is not alarmed before finally working the bait into its gullet and slowly moving off, it is time to take up any slack and set the hook hard. The ensuing contest is long, violent, and sometimes punctuated by eerie grunts and gasps as a jumping alligator gar expels and inhales air.

Shortnose gar.

Muskellunge (Esox masquinongy)

COMMON & REGIONAL NAMES: *maskinonge, musky, muska-longe, 'lunge, pike, great pike, blue pike, jack.* (Canadian laws and publications designate this fish as *maskinonge.* The many variations of the name are believed to be derived from the Ojibway *mas-kinononge—mas,* meaning "ugly," and *kinononge,* meaning "fish.")

GAME IDENTIFICATION & LOCATION OF FISHING REGIONS:
The Ojibways had little use for it. They called it ugly and spurned its meat when fatter fish were available. Yet epicures have compared it with salmon. Anglers curse its unpredictable behavior, its slippery, flailing intractability and dangerous fangs when it is brought to the boat, and the long, frequent periods of somnolence when it cannot be tempted, goaded, or cajoled into touching a lure or bait. Yet those who have caught a musky can understand why some fishermen become musky addicts, gambling a whole season of frustration against the hope of taking a few, or perhaps just one or two.

The high odds may be part of the attraction, but only a small part. The excellence of the meat (Ojibway tastes notwithstanding) and the anticipation of an impressive wall trophy are additional incentives, but these, too, are minor factors. A chillingly serpentine quality can be discerned in this carnivore as it eyes potential prey long and indolently, then contracts its slender body into a lazy S before striking. And there is something both serpentine and feline about its habit of gorging itself and then lying inactive for many days. Aptly, striped specimens are often called tiger muskies and spotted ones are sometimes called leopard muskies. Certainly, the fascination of hunting such a creature—and "hunting" is the word for this pursuit—must intensify the musky addiction. But the strongest attractions are the battling ability of the quarry and the dismaying size it often attains. It vies with the salmon as monarch of freshwater gamefish.

If a lure is used, the joust begins with a slashing strike, and as soon as the musky relaxes the vise-grip of its jaws, the hook must be set—fast, hard, and several times. When a musky takes live bait, there may be many minutes of suspense, because the hook can be set with assurance only after the fish has moved some distance with its victim, felt it, tasted it, played with it,

savored it, juggled it into swallowing position, and at last engulfed it. This prelude is of uncertain duration and ends without warning. Then the angler gains a sudden intimate knowledge of the musky's awesome endurance, jarring rushes, dogged resistance, changes of direction, line-straining maneuvers under or around snags, long runs, spectacular jumps and rolls. And when the fight seems to be nearly won and the fish is close to the boat, it often erupts in a final desperate climax of leaping and rolling. It fights like a big northern pike but with greater élan. It is, after all, the largest and strongest species of pike.

Musky, doing one of the things it does best.

It is a lithe, sinewy adversary, six times as long as the depth of its body, built for sudden attack. It is also a very fast-growing fish, but there are great regional variations in size and rate of growth. In less than a year, a 2½-pound specimen tagged in Dale Hollow Lake, Tennessee, grew to more than 7 pounds, yet a 30-inch, 5-pound southern musky is considered fairly large and the legal keeping size in Tennessee is only 25 inches. The legal length in Canada is 30 inches; there and in the northern United States, most of the muskies gaffed or netted probably weigh between 10 and 30 pounds. A ten-year-old musky in the St. Lawrence River (where climate and water levels are usually ideal and food is extremely plentiful) may weigh 20 pounds, and the following year it may weigh 26. The archives of the state of Michigan contain a description of a mammoth musky caught in 1919. It was 7 feet, 4 inches long and weighed 110 pounds. Caught on Intermediate Lake in Antrim County, it was photographically authenticated; however, the angler's name is unknown, as are details regarding the catch, and it is not accepted as an official record. The world's record muskellunge was caught by Len Hartman on the New York side of the St. Lawrence in 1957. Taken in September, a prime musky-fishing month, it weighed just an ounce under 70 pounds.

Most muskies weighing 20 pounds or more come from lakes. Stream fishing can be exciting in terms of strike frequency and numbers caught, but most of these fish weigh less than 5 pounds except in big rivers like the St. Lawrence and a few other notable waterways—Michigan's St. Clair, Ohio's Muskingum, and the larger rivers in Pennsylvania, West Virginia, Kentucky, and Tennessee. The species range through the lakes and rivers of seven major drainages: the St. Lawrence, the Great Lakes, James Bay, the southwestern extremities of Hudson Bay, the upper Mississippi, the Ohio, and the TVA system. Thus it can be caught as far north as Lake Abitibi below James Bay, on the Quebec-Ontario border; west to Lake of the Woods on the Ontario-Manitoba-Minnesota border; down into Minnesota, Wisconsin, and upper Michigan; in the Great Lakes Basin; in the lakes and tributaries of the St. Lawrence system; and in the Ohio system from New York and Pennsylvania down into the TVA waters of Tennessee, North Carolina, and Georgia. Justly famous musky habitats include New York's Black Lake, Chautauqua Lake, and the St. Lawrence; Quebec's Thousand Islands, Nicolet River, and

Pigeon Lake; Ontario's Lake of the Woods, Little Vermillion, and Eagle Lake; Michigan's Grand Traverse Bay and St. Clair River; Wisconsin's Chippewa Flowage, Flambeau Flowage, Lake Court Oreilles, and Mentowish; Minnesota's Big Mantrap, Lake Belle Taine, Winnibigoshish, and Leech Lake; Ohio's Rocky Fork Lake and Muskingum River; Pennsylvania's Shenango River, Conneaut Lake, and Pymatuning Reservoir (all on or near the Ohio border), the Allegheny at Tionesta Reservoir, and Presque Isle Bay; West Virginia's Little Kanawha, Hughes, and Pocatelico rivers; Kentucky's Green River, Barren River, Tigart Creek, and the Ohio; and Tennessee's Crab Orchard Creek and Obed River.

Occasional crosses between muskellunge and northern pike tend to produce infertile offspring. These hybrids look like muskies but exhibit northern-pike characteristics with strong appeal to anglers—an eagerness to feed more regularly than muskies and a relative gullibility concerning lures. Though they do not grow as large as the North Country muskies, they furnish plenty of sport. Hatchery hybrids have therefore been introduced to many waters in the musky states. They often have narrow striping and are popularly known as tiger muskies, a name also given to one of the three recognized subspecies of purebred muskellunge. The true tiger *(E. m. immaculatus)* is also known as the northern, or Mississippi, musky. It is usually bluish-gray with an olive tinge and with faint rows of spots that sometimes form tiger stripes. This race is found chiefly in Minnesota, Wisconsin, and northwestern Michigan. The Great Lakes musky *(E. m. masquinongy)* usually has spotted or unmarked sides; it occurs throughout the Great Lakes Basin. The Ohio, or Chautauqua, musky *(E. m. ohioensis)* is also known as the barred musky. It generally has a bronze back and silvery bronze sides, with dark spots forming bars.

There are color variations from region to region and even among individuals in the same water. Generally speaking, the muskellunge is a green, brownish-green, or greenish-gray fish with a dark back, dark mottling on the fins and forked tail, a white belly, and sides that may be plain, darkly spotted, or vertically striped. Under each side of the lower jaw is a row of at least six and occasionally up to nine noticeable sensory pores, whereas a northern pike has no more than five to a side. The scaleless lower halves of the cheeks and gill covers provide an additional

Musky, beached after slamming jointed plug.

means of identifying a purebred musky. A northern pike lacks scales on the lower parts of the gill covers but has fully scaled cheeks. In other respects the appearance of a musky is simply that of an oversized pike. It has the characteristic torpedo shape, the single rounded dorsal fin located over the anal fin, and the duckbill snout with deadly-sharp fangs jutting up from the lower jaw and smaller, rearward-pointing teeth on the roof of the mouth.

FISH HABITAT & FEEDING BEHAVIOR—ANGLING TACTICS: A musky's rate of growth is fastest during its first two or three years of life, and over the entire range of distribution most of those caught are probably between three and six years old. Biologists can estimate age by analyzing scale growth and vertebral rings; the oldest musky on record was a specimen that had lived thirty years and attained a weight of 69 pounds, 11 ounces. Size and weight increase most drastically during early summer and early fall, when water levels and temperatures are suitable and food is plentiful. The smaller individuals constitute a ready source of nourishment for faster-growing brood mates, as a young musky's feeding technique makes it extremely vulnerable to predation. Before attacking, the musky hovers motionless and gazes at a minnow or other potential food as if waiting for a closer approach

and using the time to make certain the victim is edible, alive, and easily killed. Sometimes an immature musky concentrates so intensely on prey that, in shallow water, it can be touched before it perceives an intruder and darts away. If this fish survives, it will become too wary for easy angling, but while a young one is absorbed in watching prey it may be struck by a larger sibling or adult musky. When forage fish are scarce, cannibalism is pronounced.

A minnow may escape when a musky hesitates too long or strikes too slowly, but with age this predator becomes more adept. Before charging, it coils itself slightly for extra power and speed, and it prefers to hit its target from above and behind. This may be why a musky sometimes rolls out of the water while lunging at a surface lure. The roll is likely to come from one side or at an angle rather than from straight behind, because prey is usually caught broadside and dragged downward before it is juggled around for head-first swallowing. A musky's mouth and throat look cavernous enough to make this maneuver unnecessary, but it is instinctive, and is advantageous when the fish attacks large prey, as it often does.

Although muskies spawn at night, there is some overlap with the diurnal spawning of northern pike, hence the occasional interbreeding. When the water temperature rises to about 42° the males begin their runs, and as it reaches about 46° the females follow them into shallow bays where breeding takes place near the shore in water often less than a foot deep and preferably over mud thatched with debris, brush, weeds, logs, or stumps. When the temperature rises another few degrees, a female will begin depositing her eggs at haphazard intervals along the shoreline, often scattering them over a distance of several hundred yards. She is escorted by one or more males ejecting milt. The eggs are about an eighth of an inch in diameter, and a big female—a fish weighing between 30 and 40 pounds—may spew more than 250,000 of them, enough to fill a 5-quart bucket. The nonadhesive eggs tumble about freely, without any nest or parental guardianship, and many perish as water levels fluctuate or through consumption by various fish and invertebrates.

In Wisconsin, spawning often begins in early April and can last until mid-May, but in many parts of the range the season is a month later; it may continue until the water temperature reaches 60° or so. The fry behave much like the hatchlings of northern pike after the yolk sacs are absorbed, staying in very shallow water at first and subsisting on waterfleas and other tiny crustaceans, insect larvae, and whatever else they may find among the habitat's zooplankton. Soon they are feeding on minnows, sucker fry, and one another, as well as on crawfish, tadpoles, frogs, and salamanders. When they grow large enough to be attracted by bigger prey, they will snap up a mouse or a muskrat, a duckling or a snake—anything that comes their way. In parts of Canada, studies revealed that yellow perch constitute more than half of their diet, but an adult musky will consume a wide variety of victims: smelt, walleyes, trout, bass, bluegills, suckers, minnows, and so on. Food preference is a synonym for food abundance, and a big minnow or sucker (up to a full foot long) always makes good bait.

Both in lakes and rivers, a musky favors submerged weed beds and little current. Usually it lurks in water less than twenty feet deep, but it will go as deep as fifty feet to escape heat, to find cover if weeds are sparse in the shallows, or to forage if prey is found at considerable depths. In most regions the musky populations are densest in clear waters, although West Virginia's finest musky streams are muddy.

A solitary and rather sedentary gleaner of unwary prey, the typical musky stays in a desirable lair unless forced away by a decreasing food supply, killed or driven out by a larger competitor, or taken by an angler. A good-sized river musky is inclined to remain in one pool all summer long. If it does move, it will probably swim a little way upstream, yet in the fall many big ones go downstream while the younger muskies stay behind, safely hidden in the shadows of submerged objects. These minor migrations amount to a search for food and for optimum water levels and temperatures.

Weed beds attract baitfish and the eaters of baitfish, and some beds are in particularly attractive locations—at drop-offs, near stream mouths, or where points of land dip into the water and must be skirted by schools of prey. Similarly attractive are banks with overhanging trees or other vegetation, where aquatic prey is supplemented by anything that might land in the water: a frog, lizard, bird, small rodent, anything. However, since feeding activity is greatest at a temperature of about 68° and stops altogether at 90°, an angler may read his water thermometer or electronic thermistor and decide to move on, fishing the thermocline as a bass angler would. The largest muskies will generally loaf down near the bottom of the thermocline, where the temperature approaches 60°.

It is not temperature alone that causes muskies to ignore baits and lures. They tend to gorge themselves on easily available food and then lie somnolent, digesting and resting like sated cougars, often for many days in succession before hunger returns. This is one reason why musky fishing sometimes becomes an exercise in frustration. But a dozing musky is awakened by any disturbance, including water turbulence, wind, or a barometric change. And once awakened, it is hungry. Fishing is therefore most promising just before, during, or after a squall, when the barometer is on the rise. It is also good with a light to medium chop on the water, especially in a wind from the northern quadrant.

The most venerable (or perhaps most gratifying or picturesque) way to catch muskies is casting—tireless, repeated casting until a watchful musky is teased into abandoning its lair and striking. But the most productive way is trolling where trolling for muskies is legal, and the most successful trollers (unless they are thoroughly familiar with the waters) generally go armed with hydrographic maps and electronic depth-finders whose intermediate blips reveal fish as well as submerged trees and the like. These men often use color-coded lead-core lines to keep baits or lures down, now and then bumping bottom. Some guides and experienced sportsmen have taken to using marine-type downriggers to troll lures or baits at two or more depths simultaneously. A large sucker is excellent trolling bait on a big treble hook, or with tandem hooks to handle short strikes.

Suckers and big minnows are also used for still-fishing with a heavy sinker and a large bobber. This is generally most successful in water ten to twenty feet deep off a point of land, and it is simply a heavyweight version of still-fishing for nothern pike (which see). There is a drawback, however. A musky may drag a bobber under and then go nowhere in particular for ten minutes while savoring, juggling, and playing with its meal. The angler waits, unable to interpret the bobbing and yanking and pauses, knowing that if he tries to set the hook too soon he will reel in

an empty hook. At last he feels a stronger surge and he sets the hook—two, three, four, five times to make certain. As often as not, he has done so too late. The bait is swallowed, and a gut-hooked musky cannot be returned to the water.

Typical trolling tackle is a stiff-action boat rod whose bait-casting reel is spooled with braided Dacron or lead-core line testing 50 pounds. At the end is a big, strong swivel snap holding a yard of steel or braided wire leader. For casting, however, an angler wants only half that length of leader and a lighter spinning or baitcasting outfit with monofilament line testing perhaps 12 or 15 pounds. Fly fishing is also practicable, using a 9-foot salmon rod, nylon shock tippet, and floating or sinking line with a weight-forward taper—the same assembly recommended for northern pike, but with all the backing the reel will hold. Like northerns, muskies will charge a big, bright bucktail streamer. And like

Angler boating muskellunge taken in weeds.

northerns, they will prey on ciscoes and other comparatively large species, which means that a sizable plug of the Cisco Kid type can be effective. For that matter, so can big bucktailed spinners like the Paul Bunyan 66, and a great many big plugs and wobbling spoons. The list of favorites includes the Rebels and Rapalas, Pikie Minnow, Lazy Ike, Pike Getum, Mepps Musky Killer, Musky Devle (or any big Dardevle), Red Eye Wobbler Spoon, and many more. For casting in the shallows, many experienced anglers prefer their plugs to be of the surface type and with churning propellers, flapping tails, or chugging cupped heads. But spoons, spinners, and spinner-flies also work in the shallows, and so do subsurface plugs if they have plenty of action and are retrieved with changes of speed and direction. Many anglers put all their faith in a fast retrieve, and their rule is never to stop a lure before it reaches the boat and is given a last figure-eight sweep. Others insist—with greater logic and at least equal success—that the key is in changing speeds frequently and making a great many short to medium casts, thereby goading hesitant or barely interested muskies into explosive attack.

For trolling, medium- to deep-running lures are preferred, often on lead-core lines where such lines are legal. Most anglers do their trolling at a low speed, and this can be a necessity when using a spoon, which will usually rise—plane through the water—when pulled quickly. Significantly, slow trolling harvests at least as many muskies as fast retrieving. Of course, the troller can cover large expanses of water.

A few fishermen daub their lures or even baits with commercial blood bait—the same reddish-brown dough containing animal blood that is used by many catfishermen. Some years ago an angling writer published a magazine article in which he described his homemade blood bait for muskies. He saturated cotton balls with fish and beef blood, then stored them in his freezer and brought them to the water on ice or in a cooler. He threaded a frozen blood ball ahead of his lure, and as he trolled or retrieved, it slowly exuded a blood trail. Whether or not this can be classified as chumming, it must whet the appetite of fish like muskies which, though they are primarily sight-feeders, have sensory pores and well-developed olfactory nerves.

Those who cast can copy nature closely by tossing lures outward from spots near shore and then drawing them toward the

shallows. Small prey seldom swims directly toward deep, open water but frequently panics upon realizing it has ventured too far out, and then it races for the shallows. The lure can mimic this race for shore and, if moved spasmodically, can look still more like a creature in trouble—injured or indecisive about the direction of safety. If a musky follows the lure but fails to take it, an angler can add to the trickery by speeding it up, either without a pause or after just an instant's hesitation, and he can sweep his rod from side to side when the lure comes close. The musky is an unpredictable animal that may strike at any point or may follow a lure or bait several times before rushing it. Even a plug or a big spinner or spoon is usually grabbed sideways. The fish clamps its jaws and plows downward, and for a brief interval the lure cannot be budged, so there is no possibility of setting a hook. Of course, a treble hook, even if it is not attached near the front or middle of a plug, may already have driven into the musky's jaw, but the fisherman cannot count on such luck. He waits until

Tired fisherman holding his catch; note musky's teeth.

the fish has gone down and begun to relax its hold, either in the realization that it has caught something inedible or in the effort to maneuver it for swallowing. Then the angler sets the hook hard, several times in fast succession. The reaction is furious, and the fish is still capable of mayhem when brought to the boat.

A small one can be managed with a deep, wide landing net or handled with the eye-socket hold described in connection with northern pike. But anything much over 10 pounds is a hazard when lifted with this head grip. Its teeth are murderous, and it is a very slippery species. Sometimes beaching a large one is easier than boating it. There is wisdom in holding a musky down with an old towel while using longnosed pliers to remove a hook. Since large specimens are almost always going to be eaten or mounted as trophies rather than released, a short gaff is a valuable tool for safely boating them. Once aboard, they can be clubbed.

In the summer, when few muskies seem to be available for gaffing, an angler can troll the depths of a lake, or he can investigate a river for pools, channel edges, and backwaters with good cover. He can also try fishing at night and early in the morning, although afternoon is best through most of the season. Or he can fish for other species until fall, satisfied in the anticipation of September and October—the best months for capturing a muskellunge.

Northern Pike *(Esox lucius)*

COMMON & REGIONAL NAMES: *pike, northern, great northern, great northern pike, jackpike, jack, jackfish, hammer handle, pickerel*. (The term *waterwolf*, seen occasionally in angling literature, has become a popular terse description if not a name for pike.)

GAME IDENTIFICATION & LOCATION OF FISHING REGIONS: In the summer of '42, a fisherman and his eleven-year-old son drifted away the morning on Big Pine Lake in Minnesota, casting toward the lily beds for bass and pike. Now the man was slowly winning a tug of war with an 8-pound pike that backed into the weeds and hung low, threshing and yanking. Thus absorbed, the father took no notice as his son, awkwardly wrapping both hands

Assortment of lures that take both musky and pike.

around the butt of a light baitcasting rod, heaved a perch-sized, cigar-shaped, two-piece jointed plug almost to the weeds and then leaned close over the reel to unsnarl a bird's nest. With the backlash cleared, the boy began a fairly slow, erratic retrieve, swishing the rod to make the big plug zigzag. Behind the plug, flecks of froth appeared, and a long swirl like a wake. Tensing, he gave the reel handle a quick couple of turns to make the lure dart faster. All the same, the abrupt jolt sent an unexpected thrill over his nerves, as it always did when the rod quivered and flexed.

He knew the fish was hooked, but he hauled back to make sure because he also knew that it was a big one, and there is never any real certainty in this game. He said nothing—simply concentrated and cranked the handle and wished he had been given a good stiff boat rod and a reel with a tighter drag. For a moment he wondered if he had a fish, after all, or had snagged an immovable log. And for a few more moments, leaning back with the rod, then lowering it as he gained line, he wondered alternately whether he had the strength to haul this fish to the boat and whether he was horsing it too much, straining the braided linen to the breaking point.

But then the resistance melted away, as if the fight had gone out of the fish. He did not know that a pike will occasionally swim toward the source of its difficulty, in curiosity perhaps, or in confidence that it can smash whatever challenges it.

Now the fish was at boatside, close to the surface, and even before it rolled and surged away he saw its gleaming torpedo shape, more than 3 feet long.

"Pop!" he shouted. "The net, Pop."

But his father had his hands full of his own thrashing fish and longnosed pliers, as he disgorged a big coppery spoon from the tooth-studded jaws of a pike. The man looked down into the water but did not see the boy's fish, which had come toward the boat again. He looked at the boy's rod, which was bending only slightly now. "Come on, Bob," he said, "you don't get any help with the little ones. Just reach—oh, my God!"

The fish had rolled out of the water again, shaking its massive head, half-coiling its body. "My God," the man said again. "My God, it's got to go at least twenty pounds." He dropped the pliers and reached for the landing net, but it was too late. His son's fish shook itself once more and the plug flew through the air and struck the gunnel. The monstrous pike was gone. For the next two weeks the man paid closer attention to his son's fishing than to his own, remaining instantly ready with the net, helping to boat every pike the boy caught. The excitement did not wane, for every pike, even a small one, is a fighter capable of doing the unexpected. And every pike has the toothy, baleful-eyed, stream-lined, and powerful look of a freshwater barracuda, a waterwolf.

On big northern and midwestern lakes it is not unusual to catch 20-pounders, and in the weedy shallows there are frequent strikes from pike weighing 3 or 4 pounds and occasionally several times that much. The world's record was a northern caught in 1940 on New York's Sacandaga Reservoir; it weighed 46 pounds, 2 ounces. It has been closely rivaled by several fish taken in Minnesota and Saskatchewan. The fly-rod record, a 27½-pound northern caught in 1971 on Lake Mistassini in upper Quebec, was equally impressive in its own way; it was taken by André La Chance, public relations director for that province's Parks Department, on a tippet testing only 6 pounds.

The northern is the second largest of the pike family, out-weighed only by the closely related muskellunge. It is a species

of ancient lineage, probably having evolved to its present form in southern Europe during the Cretaceous period, and it is found in many of the world's fresh northern waters. The European pike is indistinguishable from the American. Of two Asian varieties, one is an extremely similar subspecies and the other looks like an intergrade between the pike and the muskellunge. (In the United States, the pike and musky occasionally hybridize.) There is excellent pike fishing in some Scandinavian rivers and in the basin of the Danube, but reports of the largest specimens come from Ireland, where a 53-pounder was caught in 1920; only a lack of proper documentation prevented its acceptance as the world's record. Since then there have been reports of still larger pike in America as well as Ireland. It is possible that the present record weight may be nearly doubled by pike lurking in the deep waters of several wilderness lakes in Canada.

Young pike are among the fastest-growing of freshwater fish, gaining about half a pound for every pound of food eaten. Neither growth nor voracity ends with maturity. During the summer months in good habitat, a pike's daily food intake may equal

Head of northern pike.

a fifth of its own weight. The typical life span is ten years, but some pike live twenty. Longevity is greatest in the North, while growth is fastest in the southern part of the range. On the average, a year-old pike is 8 to 12 inches long and weighs less than a half-pound; a two-year-old measures 16 to 19 inches and weighs 1 to 1½ pounds; at four it measures 24 to 28 inches and weighs 4 to 6 pounds: Males seldom grow any larger, but by the time a female is seven years old she measures 33 to 38 inches and weighs 10 to 14 pounds; and at ten she measures 39 to 45 inches and probably weighs between 16 and 23 pounds. But despite the long, slim, compressed contours of all pike, the length-to-weight ratio is extremely variable. A 45-inch ten-year-old may weigh only 15 pounds or as much as 30.

During a pike's first summer, until it reaches a length of 6 inches or so, its sides are tiger-striped like the sides of grass and redfin pickerel and some muskies. However, its tail is rounded and lacks the pronounced fork that marks its relatives, and there are other ways to distinguish it. A pickerel has fully scaled cheeks and gill covers; a pike has fully scaled cheeks but the lower halves of its gill covers are scaleless; and a musky lacks scales on the lower halves of its cheeks as well as the lower halves of its gill covers. Another way to tell a pike from a musky is by the number of sensory, or mandibular, pores which form a row of little holes under each side of the lower jaw; the pike has no more than five to a side, while the musky has at least six.

Like its relatives, the pike is a long-bodied fish with a single dorsal fin located well back over the anal fin. It has a long head, flattened on top, and a duckbill snout. Its back is dark green, almost black, its sides a lighter green or greenish-gray, often with a yellowish or bronze flush on the lower parts, above the white belly. The fins are darkly mottled, and the sides of an adult have numerous yellowish or creamy oblong spots, like irregular rows of beans from head to tail. A mutant type, discovered in a Minnesota lake in 1930 and since then in several Canadian lakes, is called the silver pike. It is probably an ancient form that existed when pike first spread to this continent by way of the Bering Strait, for the same silver variant has been found in a Swedish lake. Dark silver or gray in color, it is a very hardy fish but rarely weighs more than 10 pounds.

The English name "pike" is a venerable metaphor, likening

the sharp-toothed, spear-headed, quick-thrusting, belligerent fish to the weapon of that name. According to an old fishing adage, the catch of pike decreases in midsummer because the fish then shed their canine teeth and must virtually fast until new ones grow. Actually, new teeth grow if old ones are broken from the jaw—a common occurrence during a pike's smashing attack on prey—but there is no shedding. Midsummer fishing is often poor in the southern part of the range, but only because the pike have a great abundance of natural, easily caught prey and because high water temperatures affect their metabolism. They lose their appetite, and the big ones retreat to deep, cooler water. Throughout a pike's life, it has an average of sixteen wickedly pointed teeth studding its lower jaw, and the roof of its mouth is lined with smaller, rearward-pointing teeth.

In America, the natural range of the pike extends through most of the northern lakes and rivers: in Canada, from Labrador and New Brunswick westward across the Prairie Provinces, into eastern British Columbia, and up through the western half of the Northwest Territories; in the United States, from New York down to western Pennsylvania and westward through the Great Lakes drainage to the Dakotas, northern Iowa, and eastern Nebraska. Pike are also indigenous to most of Alaska, except for the southeastern portion of the state. There were no fish of this species to help alleviate the colonists' hunger at Plymouth, but in the third decade of the nineteenth century pike were introduced into a pond of the Connecticut River drainage and they spread through New England. In more recent years they have been brought to the waters of Montana, Colorado, lower Pennsylvania, Maryland, and North Carolina, but they do not always reproduce naturally in habitat warmer than their accustomed environment.

A great many northerly waters have become famous for large and plentiful pike: New York's Sacandaga Reservoir and the backwaters of the St. Lawrence River; Michigan's Bond Falls Basin; Minnesota's Leech Lake, Basswood Lake, and Mille Lacs; Quebec's Lakes Mistassini, Camachigama, O'Sullivan, and Whiskey; Ontario's Trent Canal, Dog Lake, Kesagami Lake, Lac Seul, Lake of the Woods, Ogoki Reservoir, Savant Lake, Eagle Lake, and Lake Nipigon; Manitoba's McGavock, Reed, and Kississing; and Saskatchewan's Tazin, Tobin, Black, and Wallaston. Large northern pike flourish in many other waters, and the biggest may well inhabit some nameless wilderness lake whose mirror surface has rarely borne the reflection of a canoe.

FISH HABITAT & FEEDING BEHAVIOR—ANGLING TACTICS: Primarily a lake fish, the pike is also found in the backwaters and almost still, weedy stretches of northern rivers. It can, in fact, tolerate mildly brackish waters, though high salinity will kill it. In spring, when pike have recently been visiting streams and marshes to spawn, they will buck fairly heavy current to intercept the baitfish that tumble toward them below falls, dams, riffles, and around stream mouths. They are not school fish, these lone waterwolves, and they do not hunt in packs, but they can be caught in good numbers at these spots. And later in the summer, if the weed jungles become relatively barren, they return sporadically to these cool feeding troughs.

It is the lengthening of daylight rather than the warming of the water that accelerates hormonal production and awakens the breeding instinct in pike, for they gather in the shallows as soon as the ice goes out, when the water temperature is only about 40°. In Alaska they may not spawn before July, or before May in Saskatchewan, but in Minnesota and Pennsylvania they do so in April, and by then the pike in Iowa have finished spawning. In the southern part of their range, a few yearlings may reproduce, but most of them attain sexual maturity at two or three years of age. Some of them come to the shoreline swamps and marshes, often spawning in places that will be dry land when the water recedes in the summer. Others migrate into rivers, moving as far as 25 miles upstream in some areas. The largest pike seem to travel the greatest distances. They make their runs chiefly at night, but spawning activity is usually diurnal, peaking in the afternoon. The process is much like that of pickerel (which see) except that a good-sized female pike carries over 200,000 eggs.

The fry remain on the bottom for a few days after hatching, and then keep to very shallow water for several weeks, at first subsisting on small insect larvae, waterfleas, and the like, but soon preying on larger creatures and on one another. The adults subsist chiefly on fish—fingerlings of their own kind, shiners and other minnows, yellow perch, suckers, ciscoes, trout, sticklebacks, bluegills, crappies, bass, whitefish, young walleyes, and so on. A hungry pike is an opportunist, eager to snap its jaws shut

Top: Pike going up.
Bottom: Pike going down.

on whatever comes its way—a tadpole or frog, a mouse, duckling, muskrat, crawfish, shrimp, snail, leech, even a nymph. A night-crawler dangled for bass sometimes catches a pike instead, but large, very lively minnows or suckers—from 3 to 7 inches long or even larger in waters known to hold big pike—are by far the best live bait. (In the shallows, frogs nearly rival minnows in eliciting ferocious strikes.) Because large pike take baits and lures so eagerly, and also perhaps because they often forage deeper than fishermen suspect, not many big ones seem to be left in the most easily accessible waters. There are plenty in the 3- to 8-pound class, but most of the real trophies come from lakes that receive relatively light fishing pressure.

Angler getting grip on heavy northern taken with baitcasting rig.

In any lake or river, the pike's preferred food is whatever fish happens to be most abundant, most easily available. This is likely to be a minnow found in the weedy shallows, but it may also be a deep-diving species like the cisco. Studies in Wisconsin and Canada revealed that where ciscoes were plentiful, more big pike were being caught at depths of fifty feet than at ten or fifteen. Anglers were collecting trophies by trolling with lead-core lines, as if in search of lake trout or walleyes instead of northerns. Even where most of the bait species are denizens of the shallows, pike will go deep in midsummer, because they cannot tolerate warm water for very long. All the same, they prefer to take up feeding stations in or near weed patches where the depth is only about four feet, and most are taken in less than fifteen feet of water.

Unlike pickerel, they will sometimes cruise. In a small lake, most of the pike will find the prey-rich weed patches and stay there unless heat forces them out. But in a big lake with scattered expanses of vegetation, some of them will wander from patch to patch, occasionally visiting stream mouths or spills, going deep to escape the heat, gathering around submerged thickets and bars, hovering where points dip into the water, and in the fall lingering near steep banks, often on the windy side of a lake rather than in the lee. Neither moderate turbulence nor extreme cold will deter them from the quest for food and, like pickerel, they can be caught through the ice. In winter they return to summer habitat—the small ones to fairly shallow water, the big ones to deeper parts of a lake.

In the traditional weedy summer-fishing haunts, they often hang motionless, their tails characteristically drooping, their immovable eyes taking in a wide area to each side, their underslung jaws pointed toward open water. There is truly something lupine in the appearance of a big northern as seen from above by an angler.

While spawning, nothing distracts them from the reproductive process, and they seem to stop eating. Afterward, because their stomachs are empty and they are ravenously hungry, the fishing is at its best, and it remains excellent until June in the warmer pike waters. Even the trophy-sized pike are still in the weedy or brushy coves. Feeding activity is intense, and the fishing is therefore good, as long as the water temperature stays under about 65°. On many of the Canadian lakes, therefore, the action may be as frenetic in July or August as in June. Regardless of season, pike tend to be daytime foragers. On most waters, a majority of strikes can be induced between 8 and 11 in the morning and then, after a warm midday lull, again between 2 and 4 in the afternoon. In the North, where summer days are longer, the action may peak a little later in the afternoon.

Trolled lures or baits should be kept fairly far behind the boat, and casts must be long, because pike are more leery than pickerel of any alien presence. On the other hand, they are bolder in leaving their hiding places to capture prey. When trolling or retrieving a lure, a pike fisherman likes to run it about a foot above submerged weeds or brush, and he casts into the openings in weed and lily patches as well as along the edges, in the open water two or three feet out from the thickets.

One good tactic for such spots is to fish the surface with a popping bug, a popping plug, a hair-bodied frog or mouse, or a live frog hooked through the lips from the bottom up. Another is to attach a large bobber high enough on the line to let a minnow down to about two feet from the bottom. Either deep or shallow water can be worked this way. To keep the minnow down without unduly hobbling its swimming action, a sinker is attached a good two feet from the bait. When trolling deep water, many anglers use two rigs, one to pull an offering along just three or four feet below the surface, and the other down near the bottom. The deep-runner often seems to be most productive with a big pike plug or a very large spoon. The shallower runner might be a plug, a brightly flashing and wobbling spoon, a big streamer, a spinner, or a spinner ahead of a big minnow.

Around the weed beds, most anglers favor lively minnows or lures that dig only a little way beneath the surface. There are many traditional and perennially effective lures, such as the big jointed Pikie Minnow plug and the red-and-white Dardevle spoon (which often proves all the more productive when fluttering a pork-rind banner). There are also big, colorful surface disturbers like the bucktailed, cedar-bodied, 5-inch Skipping Bug on a 1/0 to 3/0 hook. Favorite color combinations are red and white, red and yellow, and black and yellow. And there are big streamers, both traditional minnow patterns and 5- to 7-inch concoctions like the McNally Magnum—another of the many lures that seem most tempting to a pike in a red-and-yellow or red-and-white combina-

Gill-squeezing grip and hook removal; pliers would add margin of safety.

tion. Bright feathering is needed, and it can be enhanced by some silver tinsel around the body. Pike come readily to big, tandem-hooked streamers trolled on the surface. On the basis of frequent if not particularly scientific observation, many anglers are convinced that bad temper rather than hunger triggers many pike attacks on lures. To a pike, perhaps anything that is colorful enough to attract its attention and that has a lively movement looks like it must be either food or competition.

There is no need for a fast retrieve, as with pickerel, but the lure must attract attention and must move along realistically. It can be allowed to rest for a moment after the cast and then brought back haltingly, with stops and starts and sideward swims. If this brings no strike, it can then be moved more quickly and steadily for a little distance. Often this draws a pike out to follow it, and the fish charges at the next change in speed, action, or direction, even if the lure is almost at the boat. Some anglers impart an extra, vibrating action by strumming the line. In pike fishing, a retrieve is not finished until the lure is lifted for the next cast. Sometimes a pike follows a plug or spoon all the way, but indecisively, attacking only when the angler has scant inches of line in the water and dips his rod tip in to give the lure a final figure-eight movement.

Most pike fishermen use medium- to heavy-action spinning or baitcasting rods with monofilament testing 8 to 15 pounds (depending on the size of the pike expected in the waters being fished). A short steel or braided wire leader is used because pike will often cut monofilament. For fly fishermen, a 9-foot salmon rod is a good choice, and the line—floating or sinking, depending on the flies and type of water—should terminate in about 9 feet of leader tapered from 30-pound test to 12 and ending with a foot of 30-pound shock tippet. This tippet need not be wire (which is difficult and even somewhat hazardous to cast with a fly rod) as nylon is tough enough for the purpose.

Prudence requires three other items of equipment where northerns run large. One is a deep, wide-mouthed landing net. The second is a longnosed pliers for disgorging hooks from a pike's tooth-crammed jaws. The third is a short club—anything from a length of pipe to a commercially manufactured "priest"—for administering the last rites to a big, unmanageable pike. Caution must be employed while holding a pike in order to extract a hook. There are fishermen foolhardy enough to hold one by the gill cover, as if it were a harmless species. A safer way is to place a hand over the rear part of the head and hold it tightly, with the thumb and fingers squeezing the gills shut. Another way to immobilize a pike is to place the hand a little farther forward over the head and press its eye sockets with the thumb and index finger. There are some old-time fishing guides who use no club to subdue a catch; they simply force the pike's jaws around a canoe thwart and press down behind the head to break the spine.

There are also old-time midwestern anglers who have been catching pike and pickerel all their lives and have yet to keep one. "Love to catch 'em," one of these anglers is fond of telling visitors, "but eat one of them bony snakes? Never." The firm white meat of a northern (or, for that matter, any of the pike family) is excellent table fare, but the thick upper section near the backbone, above the pike's lateral line, conceals a daunting row of thin, flexible, branched bones, the infamous "Y-bones" that turn the eating of pike from a delight to a nuisance. Few anglers seem to realize that these are easy to cut away during the filleting process.

To fillet a pike quickly and thoroughly, first remove the head, taking the pectoral fins with it, and eviscerate the body.

With a sharp filleting knife, cut around the dorsal fin and lift it out. Lengthen that first cut back to the tail, keeping the knife close to the spine so that no meat is wasted. Cut the flesh away from the tail, freeing the end of a fillet on one side of the fish, and work forward, removing the remaining fins and their attached bones. When the ribs are reached, sever them rather than trying to pare the thin cover of flesh from them at this point. Put the first fillet aside, turn the fish over, and slice off the second fillet in the same manner. Now shave away the ribs, leaving as much meat as possible. Run an index finger along the inner side of each fillet,

Pike fisherman proving value of wide-mouthed landing net.

above the rib cage, near the back, to locate the butt ends of the Y-bones. Ease the knife in, close along each side of this line of bones, tilting the blade to get down under and free a thin strip of flesh containing the bones. Run the knife along the entire line and lift out the thin strip. Only a little meat—the flesh clinging to the bones—is lost when the strip is pulled away.

What remains is a large, quite boneless fillet. Some camp chefs insist on skinning their pike, but if it is scaled before filleting, baked pike is reward enough for the small effort.

Pickerel (*Esox niger* and *Esox americanus*)

COMMON & REGIONAL NAMES: *jack, jackfish, pike, black pike, green pike, eastern pickerel, pond pickerel, snake.* (The chain pickerel is also called the *chainsides* or simply *chain.* The grass and redfin pickerels are known collectively as the *little pickerel.* The grass pickerel is also called *mud pickerel* or *grass pike* and the redfin is called *redfin pike, barred pickerel,* or *banded pickerel.*)

GAME IDENTIFICATION & LOCATION OF FISHING REGIONS: On a cypress slough or a weedy southeastern river, a cane-poler swings a short line holding a spoon or spinner, a chunk of pork or a frog. "Skittering" for pickerel, he skims his bait across the surface at the edges of weed beds, right over lily pads if need be. On an Appalachian beaver pond, a spin fisherman casts a tiny red-and-white blade with a trailing tuft of squirrel tail. On a shallow New England lake, a fly fisherman uses an 8½-foot rod with a weight-forward line. His Royal Coachman has taken a single 16-inch fish and now he ponders whether to try the same pattern tied as a streamer, or perhaps switch to some other streamer like the Maribou Matuka or Brass Hat Bucktail, or maybe a hair-bodied mouse or a cork-popping bug. Where a stream empties into an impoundment in the upper Midwest, a bass fisherman, skunked until now, decides to rig his light baitcasting outfit for a different kind of quarry. He attaches a small bobber about a yard from the end of his line and puts a 3-inch minnow on a long-shanked no. 2 hook.

They are all hoping for the slamming strike of a pickerel, a fish gratuitously maligned when caught by anglers wielding stiff, heavy rods in pursuit of bass and walleyes. After a savage attack, a slim, light pickerel puts up a disappointing struggle against overweight tackle. Moreover, this fish has a tough, toothy, hook-resistant mouth that can throw a lure if the angler horses it. But when played tactfully on "hairline" tackle, a sizable pickerel duplicates in miniature the flair of its larger relatives, the northern pike and the muskellunge. It whips about in lateral surges or breaks into the air in tail-fanning, head-shaking violence that can loosen a hook if the flustered angler permits his line to slacken.

The largest of the bellicose pickerel clan is the chain pickerel, a long, slim fish whose mature weight is usually between 1 and 3 pounds but quite often exceeds 4. The record was set by a mill-pond chain in Georgia in 1961; it was 31 inches long and weighed 9 pounds, 6 ounces. Recently, pickerel weighing up to 9 pounds have been coming from Connecticut waters, and there is no way to predict where the next record will be made. Wherever the trophy may be caught, it will probably be a female. As with bass, the female outgrows the male.

The chain pickerel is greenish or greenish-gray, sometimes with golden glints or a bronze wash. Its tail is forked and its rounded dorsal fin is set well back, above the anal fin. Its back is black, its belly cream, its sides blanketed with a network of broken black lines that form a chained pattern or, to those of us whose visual associations tend that way, a pattern like the mesh of a net. Its long, bony snout is often described as a duckbill. Its teeth constitute a mouthful of needles but they do not justify the notion of some anglers that a wire leader is essential to prevent terminal tackle from being snipped off. Wire may be helpful to a fisherman who habitually lets his bait be swallowed, as too many pickerel fishermen do. When hooked this way, a small specimen cannot be returned to the water uninjured and a large one cannot fight well. A premature attempt to set the hook will often lose a pickerel, but adept timing usually sinks the barb securely into the forward part of the mouth. As a rule, a monofilament leader will then slip down into one of the many gaps between the teeth, where it will not be cut.

The chance of leader breakage is even smaller with a "little pickerel"—the apt collective name for the redfin pickerel *(Esox americanus americanus)* and the grass pickerel *(E. a. vermiculatus)*. Both average only 10 inches or so in length and seldom go more than 14 or 15 inches or weigh more than a pound, yet on

ultralight tackle they, too, are sporting adversaries. All three of the pickerels look rather like immature northern pike or muskellunge, and the grass variety bears the strongest resemblance. However, pickerels have fully scaled cheeks and gill covers, whereas the northern pike and musky do not.

The little pickerels have vertical side bars rather than a chain pattern. The bands on a grass pickerel tend to be wider but less distinct than the long, wavy, sometimes branched markings on a redfin, and the latter can also be distinguished by its reddish fins. However, where the ranges of these subspecies overlap—particularly in the South—they hybridize, and some taxonomists classify them as regional strains of a single subspecies, subtle anatomical differences notwithstanding. The "barred pickerel" caught in Alabama often display intergraded characteristics.

The redfin occurs in small numbers in the Northeast but is chiefly distributed over the coastal plains of the Atlantic drainage from Maryland to northern Florida and westward across the Gulf states. The grass pickerel ranges from the lower St. Lawrence watershed through the Great Lakes into the Midwest, down the Mississippi drainage into eastern Texas, and along the Gulf into

Chain pickerel.

Alabama. In the early part of this century it was established in Colorado lakes and ponds near Colorado Springs, and at an unknown date it was also successfully introduced into northeastern Washington. The chain pickerel claims the widest distribution, having been transplanted to a number of states beyond its original range. It is indigenous to most of the East and part of the lower Midwest—from Maine to the Great Lakes, southward to Florida, across the Gulf region, and up into Oklahoma and Missouri. Chain pickerel are native to additional midwestern states, but the greatest abundance is found east of the Alleghenies, with the center of concentration running from New Jersey and Pennyslvania up into New England. All members of the pike

Spin fisherman reaching for chain pickerel.

family have roughly similar feeding habits (which include preying on one another). Since the small ones cannot compete with the large ones, it is a fairly reliable rule that pickerel are caught in waters where the larger pike species—the northern and the muskellunge—are scarce or absent.

FISH HABITAT & FEEDING BEHAVIOR—ANGLING TACTICS: A chain pickerel rarely lives the nine or ten years necessary to attain a weight of 9 pounds and a length of nearly 3 feet, but it grows faster as well as larger than its two closest relatives. A three-year-old chain may be 14 inches long, and a six-year-old may have a length of 20 inches or more. All three types can tolerate a slightly brackish habitat, and chain pickerel often grow large in coastal ponds and creeks. Whereas the chains are partial to lakes and ponds, the other two, especially the redfin, are a trifle more common in sluggish streams. Aside from these minor differences, the three are much alike. They seek soft-bottomed, weedy shallows with little or no current, and they prefer clean, cool "blackwater" ponds and rivers that are darkened by the tannic acid leached from vegetation. Their haunts are weedier and swampier than those of the northern pike. In fact, they shun open expanses unless driven there by a lack of prey in the shallows.

Among freshwater game species, the pikes are the earliest spawners. Like the northern pike, pickerel in Pennsylvania breed in April, and earlier in parts of the Midwest. Southern pickerel may do so as early as February. The presence of new fry indicates that grass pickerel sometimes spawn again in the fall, but most of a late hatch probably dies, owing to the autumnal meagerness of the zooplankton that provides much of a pickerel's first food.

Spawners gather in the more or less open patches of shallow, weedy backwaters and swamps, where one male or several will swim alongside a female and eject milt as she deposits a glutinous ribbon along the bottom. No nest is made, and there is no guarding of the young. A small pickerel may produce fewer than five hundred eggs, a big chain close to thirty thousand. They hatch in a week or two, depending on water temperature. Although most of the young linger in or near the spawning area for the first year of their lives, they quickly develop into efficient predators. Their first foods are algae, a great many small crustaceans, and the larvae of midges, mayflies, stoneflies, and the like.

Soon they begin to capture big, active insect larvae such as hellgrammites and dragonfly nymphs, as well as tadpoles and small fish.

They also eat annelid worms, yet that most universally seductive bait, the nightcrawler, is a poor attractor of adult pickerel. They will devour frogs, mice, crawfish, newts, lizards—anything they can waylay in the shallows and catch by a sudden lunge, without any real pursuit. Studies have shown that after pickerel have grown to more than 6 inches, over 60 percent of their diet consists of fish. Minnows are either their favorite prey or the most easily available, followed by perch, sunfish, darters, and bullheads. Hence, minnows are the most productive of all baits. They should be live minnows, because pickerel are primarily sight-feeders and they associate movement with prey.

Pickerel rarely cruise in search of food. A large pickerel is especially sedentary—like a patient, experienced deer hunter who finds a good stand and waits there, immobile, watching for his quarry to pass close, ready to intercept it. The pickerel is built for this kind of hunting. It hangs motionless inside the fringe of a weed bed, lily patch, brush, or tangle of snags, facing out, invisible to the passing schools of minnows that swim by unharmed and unaware of danger until the pickerel, feeling a twinge of hunger, snakes forward and smashes the next moving target.

If an opening exists between the bank and the pickerel's weedy lair, the fish will most often stay on the shallow side of the vegetation, facing the bank, sometimes in water barely a foot deep. But if the vegetation extends to the shore, the pickerel will be stationed on the outer side, facing open water. Thus an angler can easily read a promising site and decide where to cast. Most strikes come between the shoreline and a depth of seven or eight feet, or in slightly deeper water during midsummer. The fact that pickerel are lone hunters rather than school fish does not prevent them from lining up in a loose column along the edge of a good feeding lane.

Sometimes, it seems, experienced anglers need to be reminded of these and related details. Once, several of us marooned a young lady, a comparative novice, while we drifted past lush beds, casting fruitlessly into the lilies. She kept the bait bucket while we used small spinners, a fine choice for pickerel. She hung a minnow under a small bobber to probe a shoreline gap where beavers had been working. At first she hooked her minnow in accepted fashion behind the dorsal fin, taking care to avoid the spine and organs, but the bait soon lost its liveliness in the shallow water. Next she hooked one through the lips (a better method, many of us feel, even though a short strike may easily take the bait). The minnow came loose when it skirted a little snag, whereupon she improvised a modification—running the hook up through the lower lip and out through the snout between the upper jaw and the brain. A short cast placed the bait at the rim of a lily patch, where she left it for a few minutes. Then she reeled in several inches of line, and suddenly she was coaxing a recalcitrant 20-inch pickerel to the water's edge. After putting the fish on her stringer, she hooked a fresh bait in the new manner, cast it out past the site of the first strike, again waited, and then began reeling in. This time nothing happened, but she confirmed that the minnow was still lively and so she placed it still farther away along the inshore lily fringe. Five minutes later the stringer received a second pickerel, almost as large as the first.

She had made her first casts short not for lack of strength or skill but to avoid spooking any close-lying pickerel while taking one farther along the lily border and having to draw it right past their snouts. She was right about that. Evidently, she was right about the minnow, too. And she was right to cast parallel to the weeds rather than into them, for a pickerel often slices at a bait or lure moving by but is less inclined to follow one out, away from the weeds, as a retrieve is made.

Whether or not the pickerel happen to be engaged in one of their unpredictable feeding orgies, small weedless spoons and spinners do work rather consistently. So do hair-bodied frogs and mice, small popping bugs, and spinners with streamers or pork rinds in tow. For that matter, so do plain wet flies and streamers in colorful, minnowlike patterns.

The fly rod is an appropriate tool for these relatively small but spirited fish. A light, short spinning rod is equally appropriate, and there is no need to spool line testing more than 6 pounds even with live bait. As for lures, if they weigh a quarter-ounce or less they—and the pickerel—can be handled on line testing 2 or 3 pounds. Lightness of tackle can increase productivity as well as excitement, because pickerel occasionally must be a bit leader-shy in clear, shallow waters.

The attraction of a spoon or similar lure is intensified if, after the cast, it is allowed to sink and is then retrieved moderately fast and erratically. A carnivore perceives this action as an escape effort by a small fish. The tactic often induces a pickerel to leave the weeds and, at the next change in the lure's speed, smash it. This is likely to hook the fish. Setting a hook is not quite so easy with a live bait. A pickerel usually hits a minnow amidships, swims with it, then quickly juggles it around for head-first swallowing and moves off again. Most anglers wait for the second run before setting the hook, but by then the minnow may be in the pickerel's throat or stomach. Some of us would rather risk a few lost fish; it seems better to use a very sharp hook and set it after perhaps five or six seconds of the first run. More often than not, the barb is inside the jaws even then.

Pickerel are among those species that feed ravenously in defiance of cold, and minnows are the best bait not only during the warm months but when fished through the ice. In late fall or winter, pickerel are also taken from streams that have not frozen over. At such times and places they seem especially susceptible to streamers and spinners; it is a susceptibility cordially appreciated by the light-tackle devotee.

Salmon *(Salmo salar* and *Oncorhynchus)*

GENERAL DESCRIPTION & DISTRIBUTION: North America has a half-dozen species of salmon—gunmetal-backed, silver-sided, heavy-bodied but streamlined, capable of streaking, surging runs, adept at jolting switches of direction when defying the rod, and given to wild aerial pyrotechnics. At spawning time they leave the sea to converge in rivers and work their way to the gravelly upstream shallows, making the arduous journey without eating, yet exerting an incredible store of energy that empowers them to breast heavy rapids, to climb, swim, and leap over waterfalls. Though all six are classed as anadromous (an adjective taken from the Greek *anadromos,* literally "upward-running"), two species include landlocked races and two more have thrived astonishingly when stocked in suitable inland waters.

An angler who speaks of salmon may be referring to 5-pound grilse or their 10- and 20-pound elders, still carrying a few of the little isopod crustaceans called sea lice when they rise to gaudily feathered flies in the streams of Maine or the Maritimes. He may mean a grilse-sized Sebago or ouananiche, taken on a trolled streamer or smelt in a lake of that region, or a 50-pound sea-run trophy of the same species caught in the roaring waters above a Norwegian fjord. Perhaps his salmon is a 2-pound ko-kanee, attracted to a morsel of worm fluttering behind a beaded spoon at Lake Pend Oreille in Idaho. It may be a 7-pound coho that struck a spinner on a Lake Michigan tributary or gobbled a salmon fly on a British Columbian river or snapped at a tinsel-ribbed tuft of bear hair in Puget Sound. Perhaps it is a small but aggressive chinook—a "jack salmon"—taken with a rigged her-ring and a flashing Herring Dodger attractor in Vancouver's bay or with a streamer on Oregon's Rogue River or Vancouver's Campbell. Or perhaps it is a tyee chinook, a trophy weighing over 30 pounds but nonetheless susceptible to the presentation of a steelhead fly on British Columbia's Skeena River. The salmon has many forms, and is sought in diverse places by diverse strata-gems.

The single eastern species is the renowned Atlantic salmon *(Salmo salar)*. The five Pacific species endemic to this continent are similar in many respects but belong to another genus, *Onco-rhynchus*. They are the chinook *(O. tshawytscha)*, chum *(O. keta)*, coho *(O. kisutch)*, pink *(O. gorbuscha)*, and sockeye *(O. nerka)*. Of these, the chinook and coho are the largest and the most important to the angler but the others, too, enliven western fishing. A sixth member of the genus, the medium-sized cherry salmon *(O. masou)*, is found in Asian waters.

Both the eastern and western varieties have the soft-rayed single dorsal fin and the adipose fin typical of salmonids and, in the adult stage, a tail whose rear edge is only slightly forked or concave. The body is generally about five times as long as it is deep, and the head is small for the size of the body. The jaws and front of the palate are toothed. At spawning time the tip of the male's lower jaw or both the upper and lower develop a pronounced cartilaginous hook called a kype. Spawning females tend to change color somewhat, and the spawning raiment of the males becomes far more vivid in most species—red, yellow, or black.

Before they go to sea and again when they reach spawning

age, the Pacific salmons range through the rivers from California to Alaska and from Siberia to China. In the intervening time—while developing from smolts to spawners—they roam along vast, roughly elliptical routes through the Gulf of Alaska and the northern Pacific.

The North American rivers of the Atlantic salmon indent the coasts from Greenland and upper Canada down to Cape Cod and the Connecticut River. The species enters European rivers as far north as Russia and Scandinavia, down through the British Isles, and along the continent all the way to Spain and Portugal. On either side of the Atlantic, the salmon that are spawned in some rivers wander only a comparatively short way along the coasts, while those from other rivers travel enormous distances, many of them gathering at a common feeding ground off the west coast of Greenland. All have a seemingly miraculous navigational and homing sense that guides them back to the individual streams where they were hatched.

GENERAL LIFE CYCLE & ANGLING STRATEGIES: Salmon spawn in the fall and hatch in the spring, yet there is a winter coho run in Oregon, there are spring runs of Atlantic salmon in Maine and Quebec, and many of the rivers on both coasts have salmon in

Chum salmon pushing upstream through white water.

them at various times from early spring to late fall. One reason, of course, is that some species differ from others in the timing of their heaviest runs, and early arrivals simply require a longer stay in fresh water before spawning. Another is that some species (and some populations within a species) travel farther upstream than others and are therefore in the rivers for longer periods. Furthermore, spawners of several age classes within a single population in a single river may run at different times. Thus nature appears to have accomplished a complex staggering of migrations, without which the gravelly spawning shallows might well be too crowded for successful reproduction.

An angler planning a trip to an unfamiliar region should make advance inquiries as to the most promising weeks, and also the most promising waters during the period he allots himself. Runs of large Atlantic salmon typify the Quebec rivers in June, for example; in New Brunswick, where the fish tend to be more abundant, the big ones are more often caught from July to September. On the West Coast, there are several races of chinook, commonly called spring, summer, and fall salmon. On one part of the coast or another, they enter rivers from January to late fall. Some of the northern populations travel immense distances—up to 2,000 miles in the big Yukon rivers. On the Washington-Oregon border, the Columbia has a spring chinook run, most of which spawns in the side streams all along the waterway, and a fall run that spawns almost entirely in the main river. Not only should a nonresident angler make careful plans regarding time and place; he should also schedule as long a stay as he can afford, because salmon fishing is affected somewhat unpredictably by the weather. As the fish begin to gather in the estuaries, heavy spring rains and high water can spur a fast run upstream, soon leaving a river's lower "beats," or fishing stretches, barren. Conversely, drought can delay the upstream surge and keep the upper beats fishless until the water rises sufficiently to ease the passage of the salmon.

A specialized, traditional vocabulary is used by fishermen as well as biologists to denote the ages, or developmental stages of a salmon's life cycle. Newly hatched fry—larval salmon—are termed alevins. Once their huge red, orange, or yellow egg sacs have been absorbed and they are foraging in the streams, they are called parr. Their colors change as they grow. At the fingerling stage they are spotted or speckled—"parr-marked"—but gradually they become silvery as they head toward the sea. Still juveniles, they are now called smolts. Among some species, particularly the Atlantic salmon, the amount of time spent in the ocean varies considerably. The youngest, smallest spawners, those that return to the rivers after only one winter at sea, are called grilse. The specialized nomenclature in general usage ends there. Larger catches—the older individuals—are simply called salmon. In the Northwest, however, a trophy chinook is honored with the name tyee, the Siwash word for chief; specimens weighing 30 pounds or more qualify for recognition by the Tyee Club at Campbell River, British Columbia.

An account of spawning behavior will be given for the Atlantic salmon. With exceptions (noted, where applicable, in the descriptions of other species) the Pacific varieties spawn in roughly the same manner. The most important point for the angler to bear in mind is that, apart from the landlocked populations, salmon feed rarely if at all once they enter fresh water. They are intent only on reaching their birthplaces, there to reproduce. Why they will smash an attractive and well-presented lure is still a matter of conjecture. Some anglers and biologists speculate that the strike is a conditioned reflex, ingrained by constant, ravenous feeding at sea. Others believe the impulse is strengthened by a kind of reflexive memory of stream foraging when they were parr. It is also possible that they are simply irascible, as some animals are at breeding time, and inclined to attack any seemingly live and conquerable creature that approaches. Or perhaps they have an instinctive desire to rid the habitat of creatures that might prey on their eggs and alevins or compete for spawning room or the plankton that feeds the parr. In any case, they can be surprisingly selective, and more so regarding the presentation than the design of the lure. Recommendations will be given under the species headings.

Oceanic salmon migrations have been studied by scientists for half a century, but much remains to be learned. A large store of information has been acquired in recent years by tagging and releasing smolts, many of which are subsequently recaptured at sea by trawlers. A tagged Irish smolt, for example, was recaptured as a grilse one year later off Greenland, 2,025 nautical miles from its release site; it then weighed 6 pounds, having gained over 5½ while in the ocean. The longest recorded Atlantic salmon migration was from the northern arm of the Baltic to Greenland, 3,300 nautical miles (a nautical mile is over 6,000 feet, substantially longer than a statute mile). According to Anthony Netboy, an eminent authority on the world's salmon, most Atlantic salmon travel only 50 to 200 miles from the rivers of their birth, but they remain in the ocean from one to six years, and the longer they remain, the farther they are likely to wander. Recaptures off Greenland have included fish from Canada, the British Isles, France, Spain, Scandinavia, and Russia.

These fish begin their oceanic stage as zooplankton feeders, following the masses of plankton that drift with the currents. They grow quickly, and are soon devouring larval fish, crustaceans, squid, and mollusks. The rich pink of their flesh is derived from their intake of shrimp and other crustaceans. Their diet renders their meat delectable as well as colorful. The popular ways of preparing salmon are almost uncountable, though some of us are saddened by the notion of anything more complicated than poaching, baking, or broiling, as the pure, natural flavor is too good to excuse the slightest adulteration.

Pacific salmon have the same basic diet as Atlantics but they roam much farther during their growing stage (having a larger ocean in which to do it). Some of the cherry salmon of Asia stray into the Gulf of Alaska. Most of the pink salmon from southeastern Alaska and British Columbia linger in estuaries and bays for several months after coming downstream, reaching the ocean in July and then fanning out across a vague path, about 20 miles wide, to move counterclockwise past the Aleutians. The smallest and most numerous of the continent's anadromous salmon, pinks live only two years, more than half of that time in the ocean. When outward bound, they travel about 10 miles a day. In the spring and summer, turning north toward home, they sometimes hurry along at 45 miles a day to reach the spawning grounds in the fall. Their elliptical orbit stretches at least 2,000 miles. Chum and sockeye salmon generally remain at sea for two to four years, making an even wider circuit than that of the pinks, and some of them repeat the circuit a second and third time—a total distance of 6,000 to 10,000 miles. Coho spend only a single winter at sea, and most of them stay in coastal waters, but some cross 1,400 miles of the North Pacific. Some chinook also remain

relatively close to their ancestral rivers. Others travel 2,500 miles
to the central Aleutians, and some spend five years at sea,
covering as great a total distance as do chum and sockeye. Now
and then several species mix into loose, tenuous convoys a
hundred miles long.

Biologists and anglers alike have wondered what mysterious mechanisms lead salmon back unerringly to the streams
where they hatched. To some degree, of course, they follow major
currents, but they depart from these along the way. As salmon
are sensitive to light intensity, the beacon of the sun may help
to guide them on rare clear days in the North Pacific and again
when they reach coastal waters. Scientists investigating bird
migrations have found evidence for a theory of avian sensitivity
to magnetic fields, so perhaps this, too, guides migrating fish.
Researchers are reluctant to speak of anything more definite than
a "searching recognition mechanism"—a kind of physiological
compass—and a genetically inherited knowledge of routes that
might be described as racial memory. One aspect of their homing
ability is better understood and proved by laboratory experiments:
when they reach the final maze of estuaries and river mouths,

Bay fishermen with good catch of kings—chinook salmon.

they recognize their home streams by scent. The nostrils in the snout of a fish connect to very sensitive olfactory organs somewhat different from those of mammals, and they respond to very faint, long-remembered chemical combinations and intensities. The ability seems all the more impressive in view of man's interference—the pollution that constantly alters the chemistry of coastal waters.

Man's interference has affected migrating salmon in other ways. Fish ladders are built at dams to facilitate upstream migration, but no way has been found to enable the smolts to pass the dams without high casualties as they head downstream to mature at sea. Then there are races of Pacific salmon, such as the Columbia's fall-spawning chinook, that use the main river for breeding; the slack water created by dams has ruined much of their spawning ground. On the East Coast, logging and other riverside industry has done comparable damage. On both coasts, some waters are so badly polluted that salmon would die off even if no migration barriers existed.

The results of commercial fishing have been equally disastrous. In coastal waters, salmon are harvested by drift nets and trap nets, and at sea they are taken by trawlers. Japanese and Danish vessels have made the most severe incursions. The Japanese began their high-seas operations in 1952 with fifty-seven "catcher" boats and three "mother" ships for canning and freezing. Three years later they had fourteen mother ships and 407 catchers on the Pacific, accounting for 162,000 tons of salmon annually, about 40 percent of the world catch. Most of those salmon came from Siberia, but many came from Alaska, British Columbia, Washington, and Oregon. The United States has now extended its maritime jurisdiction to a 200-mile distance from the coasts; Japan, for its part, has signed a treaty with the United States ending operations closer than the mid-Pacific, and another with Russia setting catch quotas, but the toll of Siberian and American fish remains too high. Japanese boats still take 23 percent of Alaska's sockeye.

Denmark, too, began its intensive operations in the 1950's, when the great salmon shoals were discovered off the west coast of Greenland. The Greenland tonnage rose from 60 in 1960 to 2,615 in 1971—20 percent of the world's Atlantic salmon catch. An American organization, the Committee for the Atlantic Salmon

Emergency, launched a publicity campaign advocating a boycott of Danish imports, and in 1971 Congress passed the Pelley Act, authorizing the President to ban imported fish from any nation failing to conduct an "acceptable fishery conservation program." Within five years, Denmark phased out its operations in international waters and now, even in Greenland's territorial waters, the harvest is limited. Controversy persists, however, for both the Japanese and the Danes have been accused of continuing to overharvest salmon.

Regulated sport fishing has no impact on the salmon population because anglers catch only a small percentage of the fish preparing to spawn. Evidently the commercial devastation has been alleviated in time—barely in time—and intensive efforts are under way to correct the decline by a combination of stream improvement and experimentation in hatchery rearing and transplantation. At one time, Atlantic salmon ranged as far south as Long Island Sound and they thronged the Connecticut River; they have long been gone, but efforts are being made to restore them to the Connecticut.

Atlantic Salmon *(Salmo salar)*
COMMON & REGIONAL NAMES: *salmon, eastern salmon*

GAME IDENTIFICATION & LOCATION OF FISHING REGIONS: An adult sea-run Atlantic salmon has an almost square tail, a long body, and a metallic gleam that is lost on the way upstream. Its fins and tail are dark, almost black, and the top of its head and back are dark blue, shading to silver on the sides and white on the belly. On its head and upper body, glimmering with traces of pink, lilac, and blue, are numerous black spots and X-shaped markings. As it moves along the river, it gradually turns dull yellowish or brown. A female may become dark gray, almost black, while a male usually acquires black patches or dusky red on the flanks, and his jaws eventually become so hooked that they meet only at the tips. The fins thicken, the skin grows slimy, and the body is emaciated by the time spawning is over.

A fish newly arrived from the ocean, with sea lice still clinging, is a "bright salmon," the fish coveted by anglers. One that has finished spawning is called a "black salmon." Whereas all Pacific species die after spawning, a few Atlantic salmon—

usually less than 10 percent—survive, wintering beneath the ice of the rivers. In the spring these fish move slowly back to sea, where they revive and grow fat enough to spawn again. In New Brunswick, spring fishing for black salmon is legal, since the catch represents only a minuscule percentage of the next year's spawners, but these fish cannot put up the dramatic fight of a bright salmon.

Apart from insignificant numbers around Cape Cod and those released in the Connecticut River, North America's Atlantic salmon range from Greenland (which has only a single salmon river) to Maine. Since they take a fly more readily than chinook salmon and grow to comparable size, numerous quixotic attempts have been made to establish them along the Pacific coast. These efforts have failed, but sea-run Atlantic salmon have been successfully stocked in Oregon lakes, giving that state a small landlocked-salmon fishery. One can only wonder why the introduction was not accomplished with naturally landlocked Atlantic salmon (which will be described separately) rather than with anadromous fish.

Most rivers have runs of grilse or mixed runs of grilse and older fish, and in some regions—Newfoundland's eastern coast, for instance—grilse predominate. These fish usually are three to five years old and have spent only one year at sea. They are mostly males (females do not attain sexual maturity as soon) and most of them weigh between 2 and 5 pounds. A typical grilse is a salmon that entered the ocean as a 6-inch smolt and returned a year later as a 4-pound premature spawner. A salmon that has spent two years at sea is likely to weigh between 9 and 12 pounds, the average size caught on North American streams. Those that remain at sea for three years (as many do) usually weigh from 18 to 30 pounds, and the few that linger in the ocean for another year or two may attain a weight of 45 pounds. In parts of Europe, particularly in Norwegian rivers, fish of this age sometimes attain a weight of 70 pounds. Perhaps this is explained by a rich feeding ground, comparable to the Greenland shoals, recently discovered off the coast of Norway. The world-record Atlantic salmon was caught in 1928 on Norway's Tana River. It weighed 79 pounds, 2 ounces. (This, of course, was a sporting record; a few even heavier fish have been taken by trawlers.)

Maine's formerly great salmon rivers are now, slowly, being

revived. The best of them are the Sheepscot, Narraguagus, Pleasant, Machias, and Dennys. The fishing in Maine is commonly done from the banks or by wading, yet there are stretches along these rivers where the best holding waters can be fished more thoroughly from a canoe. Although the heaviest fishing pressure occurs in May and June, a majority of Maine's salmon enter the rivers in early fall. The banks are not lined with anglers then and the fishing is better.

Canadian salmon fishing is better yet. There are good salmon rivers in Nova Scotia, better ones in Newfoundland, and truly fine ones in New Brunswick and Quebec. They include such famous waters as Nova Scotia's Margaree, Newfoundland's Gander and Humber and the streams of the Labrador peninsula, New Brunswick's Miramichi and Restigouche, and Quebec's Matane and Matapedia. The finest fishing of all may well be on the Miramichi and along the Quebec-New Brunswick border, in the region where the Restigouche and Matapedia join.

Salmon tend to be slightly larger in Quebec than in New

"Bright" Atlantic salmon—still ocean-fresh.

Brunswick, but not quite as abundant. Unfortunately, Quebec has little public water other than the Matane. Most of the productive beats are privately owned or leased, and the right to fish them is by invitation or fee—often a high fee. In Canada, as a rule, a nonresident salmon fisherman must employ a guide. The guide may work with as many as three clients simultaneously, and may charge each of them as much as $30 a day. But a guide who is familiar with the local waters is worth his fee. There is also the expense of a nonresident license—$35 or $40 a week—and lodging, food, travel, and so on. A Canadian salmon-fishing trip is not an excursion to be undertaken casually. Only the splendor of Canadian salmon (and trout) justify it. A stranger to the region ought to make arrangements long in advance, beginning with a letter to one of the provincial departments of tourism to request addresses of local guides and fishing-camp operators.

In Quebec, the waters tend to be larger and deeper than in New Brunswick, and the little fly rod used by a typical New England trout fisherman is not really adequate. An 8½- or 9-foot salmon rod is recommended. A somewhat shorter rod will serve well enough on most New Brunswick streams, but in either province the reel should be big enough—at least 3½ inches in diameter—to accommodate the line and 200 yards of backing. A big salmon can take most of that out in an early run. In the low water of summer or fall, light tackle (and small flies) can be rewarding. There are quiet, easily waded American salmon waters where a fisherman can use a very light 7½-foot rod that would astonish a Norwegian accustomed to roaring rivers, gigantic fish, 14-foot rods, and tippets testing 60 pounds. Generally, however, a good rod for Canadian salmon is a conventional salmoner that handles no. 8 or 9 floating line. For use with dry flies in the summer, a leader can be tapered to a 3X tippet (testing about 5 pounds). But what is needed more often is a long leader with a 9- to 12-foot tippet section testing 6 to 12 pounds.

Fishing in New Brunswick is somewhat more homespun than in Quebec. A guide is likely to do as much fishing as the client. The usual New Brunswick style is to cast from shore or wade out. When a salmon is hooked, an angler in the stream does his best to reach shore without tripping and filling his waders. Then, as he plays the fish he jogs along, following its run. trying to get below it so that the fish will turn upstream against the tiring

current. If the salmon does not escape, it can be beached after a sufficiently fatiguing fight. In Quebec, canoe fishing is often a necessity. The guide paddles to a favorite pool and works it from head to tail, anchoring at one or several spots while the angler casts across-stream and slightly downstream, first to one side and then to the other, letting the fly drift down. Strikes come most often near the end of a drift, when the fly is about ten yards beyond the bow of the canoe. If a fish is hooked, the angler does not fight its initial run. The best he can do is to keep his rod high and his line reasonably taut while the guide paddles for shore. Then, perhaps, he can start to take in some backing—a process that will have to be repeated more than once before the fish tires enough for the guide to use his long-handled, oversized net.

In Quebec this kind of action most frequently erupts early

Angler tailing Atlantic salmon.

in the season and early in the day—from mid-morning to noon. In New Brunswick it comes later, an ideal session being a summer or early-autumn evening from about teatime until dusk. Whatever may motivate them to take a fly, salmon do not strike with the hit-and-spit impulsiveness of trout, demanding instant hook-setting. Sometimes they come up under a fly very deliberately, swelling the surface before reaching the lure, and causing an overeager fisherman to snap his rod up and then mutter about a short strike. Sometimes they slap at a fly, or take it with a splashy jump, or roll out and snatch it on the way back in, or turn in the water to grab it in a flipping lunge. Any of these maneuvers can fluster the angler, and the reflexive, rod-snapping reaction must be overcome. The surest technique (none is absolutely sure) is to let the salmon mouth the fly and start back toward the bottom, and then, when the fish is felt, lift the rod to tighten the line. With dry flies, false rises—salmonid changes of mind—are common enough to make an angler tense. With dries, moreover, the line may be slack enough to require a more forceful setting of the hook, but it should still be timed to let the salmon close its mouth. Then, for insurance, a couple of additional tugs can drive the barb deeper.

A salmon almost invariably jumps, and usually the first leap comes when the pull of the line is felt. The long initial run may be punctuated by another leap, and another—arcs and flips and high, wrenching cartwheels that somehow accentuate the salmon's strength rather than its agility, making an angler question whether with his frail tackle he can hope to rein in this bucking runaway.

•

FISH HABITAT & FEEDING BEHAVIOR—ANGLING TACTICS:
Since a migrating salmon is no longer actively feeding, the realistic mimicry of food has less importance than in most angling situations. Of course, some salmon are caught in salt water, and some countries condone the use of spoons, plugs, and even natural baits for Atlantic salmon. These enticements are appropriate to the fishing tactics demanded by several other salmon species but they are neither necessary nor desirable—nor legal, as a rule—for Atlantic salmon in North American rivers. If a fly is hard to cast far enough on some big waters or hard to present to a distant lie in a turbulent stretch, the difficulty is an accepted

part of the eastern salmon-fishing mystique. Furthermore, an attractive and attractively presented whisk of feathers or hair induces strikes at least as well as anything else concocted by man for deceiving Atlantic salmon.

Since no importance is attached to the imitation of specific salmon foods, flies tend to be impressionistic or fanciful. When an angler's assortment of famous, exquisitely tied salmon flies is disdained by the fish, a guide may try to hide his own disdain or he may be kind enough to offer something from his personal armamentarium. A "guide's pattern" may be based on a standard design or on nothing in particular. Either way, it is liable to prove efficacious since it has worked for the guide himself. Sometimes, on a given beat, river, or day, only one or two out of many patterns will provoke fish into striking, or one pattern will take mostly grilse while another takes salmon. An angler's dilapidated lamb's-wool fly book may therefore bulge with standard wet salmon flies— Black Dose, Cosseboom, Jock Scott, Night Hawk, Black Bomber, Brown Bomber, Butterfly, Green Butt, Squirreltail, Oriole, Lady Amherst, Red Abbey, Silver Abbey, Rusty Rat, Silver Rat, Nepisquit Gray, Silver Gray, Silver Blue, Blue Charm, Blue Doctor, Silver Doctor, Squirrel Doctor, March Brown, Silver Wilkinson, Green Highlander, Dusty Miller, Durham Ranger, Black Silvertip, and so on.

Many of the favorite patterns are tied in the hair-wing style, which has gained favor both in Maine and Canada. In fact, hair wings have nearly replaced feather wings on this side of the Atlantic. Sizes should range from no. 6/0 all the way down to 8 or even 10 in order to suit stream conditions as well as the whims of the salmon. Early in the season, when the water is high, roiled, perhaps muddied, the need is for big, easily visible flies, and an angler might prefer his dressings on 1/0 to 6/0 hooks. Later, when the water is low and clear, he wants short, sparse flies on smaller hooks—usually from size 6 to 10. A "low-water" dressing is a fly on a hook that seems a trifle big for it, a fly whose dressing looks as if it ought to be a no. 10 but is on a no. 6 instead. The larger size is a surer hooker and holder of large fish, while the scant dressing gives a more natural impression of an aquatic creature.

Dry flies would be impractical on many turbulent European rivers, and have never achieved great popularity on the murkier Irish and Scottish rivers, yet they work well in Canada and Maine whenever a small fly can be fished on a floating line—especially during late summer and early fall. Popular patterns include the Salmon Skater, White Wulff, Gray Wulff, Irresistible, Bomber, Badger Bivisible, Brown Bivisible, Dr. Park, Hair-winged Rat-faced McDougal, Pink Lady Palmer, Hunt's Wasp, and Bird's Stonefly.

In many rivers the salmon migrations have two peaks—an early summer run and an autumn run. One may be dominated by large or small fish, or may be more plentiful than the other. On some streams, the late run tends to be much denser than the early one. A large percentage of a river's salmon may simply be late runners, or the fishing may be improved by the fact that the commercial season has ended. As spawning time approaches, the quality of salmon meat deteriorates slightly and the market fishermen quit for the year.

Sometime in the fall, the salmon reach the shallow, gravelly upper reaches of the streams. In Maine, for example, spawning peaks in late October. A female searches about, selects a site, and turns on her side to dig her redd. Her flapping tail raises and sweeps away the gravel. The nest is usually spacious, a yard or so wide and perhaps 10 feet long. A big female may dig 18 inches down into the stream bed. She generally carries about eight hundred eggs per pound of her own weight, and as she begins to deposit them a male lies at her side emitting a cloud of milt. Smaller males—even parr—sometimes lie near and release additional milt, thus helping to assure fertilization. She then covers the eggs, and in doing so she may cut a second redd in which she will also deposit eggs. When the second clutch is fertilized and covered she may rest, but she is likely to spawn several times.

The young hatch in the spring. Parr look very much like young brown trout, but with a more deeply forked tail, a duller adipose and dorsal fin, and usually no more than two black spots on each gill cover rather than several. Because size and growth rates vary, some parr remain in fresh water for two years, some for four; the average is three. Until then, like trout, they feed on aquatic insects and zooplankton. By the time they reach the sea, they are 5 or 6 inches long and have turned silver—the smolt stage. It is life at sea that gives them adult size and coloration.

When they return to the streams as adults, they stop feeding or feed very little, a fact the angler must take into account because the lie of a salmon is only a resting place, not a feeding station as a trout's lie is. It may be in a slight depression near shore, in a slick, in a pool, or at the tail of the pool. There is no sure key, but the most common lies are in shallow places, perhaps 3 or 4 feet deep, and they tend to be used over and over by successive fish and in successive years. A guide who seems to have a miraculous ability to recognize holding spots is generally a guide who knows his locale and remembers past successes.

On a bright summer day, with the water low and still, salmon are often seen in their lies, or are betrayed by a ripple, a stir of the surface. This is the ideal time for casting a dry fly, quartering it downstream to them. It may be necessary to present it repeatedly, coaxing a strike. Repeated presentations will not alarm a salmon as they will a trout.

Wet flies are presented in either of two ways. One, developed by A. H. E. Wood on an Irish river in the summer of 1903, is called the greased-line method, though very few anglers still use greased silk since they can rely on modern floating lines. Basically, the method is to cast a slack line and fish it downriver, close to the surface, constantly mending line to assure as little drag as possible. The other method is to cast a straight line across-stream and down, at an angle depending on the speed of the current, mending line if it bows, not letting the fly race too fast but making a salmon lunge after it. This, too, is done with the fly high in the water. There is no certainty as to which method works more often. Probably a more important consideration is the need to cast across and slightly downstream—not upstream— bringing the fly around to let the fish view it broadside, and mending line in upstream curves to slow down the fly and keep it ahead of leader and line. Strikes sometimes come near the end of the drift, when the fly is allowed to hang in the current a few moments and then is drawn out gently to avoid frightening the fish before making another cast.

Landlocked Atlantic Salmon *(Salmo salar)*
COMMON & REGIONAL NAMES: *landlocked salmon, landlock, Sebago salmon, ouananiche, lake salmon*

GAME IDENTIFICATION & LOCATION OF FISHING REGIONS:
The Ice Age sealed off many rivers, preventing Atlantic salmon

from reaching the ocean. The survivors adapted to a life cycle spent entirely in fresh water, and their descendants populate lakes in Maine, New Brunswick, Quebec, Newfoundland, and Labrador. They have also been introduced into New Hampshire, Massachusetts, New York, and the big, trout-rich lakes of Argentina. The landlock record was set by a 22-pound, 8-ounce fish caught on Maine's Sebago Lake. The record has stood since 1907; sooner or later it may be broken by one of the trophy-sized Argentine fish whose ancestors also came from Sebago, a lake that remains very productive.

There are two regional types of landlocked salmon, the Sebago form that evolved in Maine and New Brunswick, and the ouananiche of Quebec, Labrador, and Newfoundland. Both are simply freshwater strains of the sea-run *Salmo salar*. The ouananiche tends to be smaller and more heavily speckled than the Sebago, and its tail and fins are slightly larger. In some waters it takes a fly more readily and is caught by conventional trouting tactics. However, most taxonomists regard the ouananiche and Sebago landlocks as too similar to be called separate subspecies. They have slightly bigger eyes, scales, fins, and tails than the anadromous type; their bodies are more streamlined, darker, often with a deeper wash of pink, and more heavily spotted.

The original landlock range was diminished by shoreline deforestation, which raised water temperatures. Maine began a restocking program in 1875 and lake salmon are now the state's most important gamefish. A 14-inch Sebago is a legal keeper there and most of the fish weigh 2 to 3 pounds, but 10-pounders are still caught now and then on Long Lake, the East Grand, and the West Branch of the Penobscot. Moosehead, Sebago, and Rangeley are also very good, and over the New Brunswick line are the famous Palfrey and Spednick. Because ouananiche aver-

Landlocked salmon from Maine's Sebago Lake.

age 2 pounds or less, and a 6-pound catch is rare, the Sebago strain of Maine and New Brunswick is commonly used in transplantations. It is now found in more than 250 New England lakes and streams.

FISH HABITAT & FEEDING BEHAVIOR—ANGLING TACTICS:
Early in September, landlocked salmon leave the deep lake waters for the inlets, outlets, and feeder streams where there are swift, gravel-bottomed riffles for spawning. The peak of reproductive activity comes between mid-October and the end of November. At other times the chief habitat requirement is deep, cold water with plenty of oxygen and plenty of baitfish—preferably smelt.

The parr remain in the spawning streams for a year or two, feeding on aquatic insects and other invertebrates. The lakes are to them as the sea is to anadromous smolts, and when they move into bigger waters (though they continue to eat nymphs and flies) their diet changes dramatically. They feed on smelt, minnows, perch, and alewives.

They can be taken on spoons, spinners, or nightcrawlers, and in the evening on a lake cove or a river slick they will rise to dry flies as small as no. 16 or 18, but there are two methods that eclipse all of these. One is to troll with a long, smeltlike wobbling spoon or a real smelt, putting it only a few inches below the surface in the spring but down about twenty feet when summer temperatures have discouraged the salmon from feeding near the surface. A good way to rig a smelt is to run a size 6 hook through its mouth and out the gill, push the bait up onto the leader, then loop the hook through the same way again, draw it tight, and insert the barb about an inch from the tail. This makes it move naturally in the water and cuts down the number of short strikes. Some anglers attach a spinner ahead of the smelt.

The second method, streamer fishing, is more worthy of the quarry and just as productive from ice-out through June and often into July. The streamer, like the smelt, should be trolled a little under the surface, but faster—about 6 miles an hour—and with action imparted to it by sweeping or nodding the rod. A number of smeltlike bucktails and feathered streamers were originated in Maine for precisely this purpose. Today's popular patterns include the Ghosts (Black, Gray, and Green), Nine Three,

Supervisor, Barnes Special, Mickey Finn, Jane Craig, Parmachene Bell, Dark Edson Tiger, and the numerous guides' patterns. Sometimes they are tied on no. 4 or 6 hooks, sometimes as big tandems. The tandems, like the smelt rig, reduce the chance of short strikes.

A still lake and a sunny day will drive the fish deep, but they chase smelt at the surface on rainy, blustery days shortly after ice-out. The smelt are moving from deep water to spawn in the streams, and an angler can troll rocky shorelines, ledges, bars, islands, and drop-offs. Cold, deep spring holes in the lake will be good later, but now a windy shore is best. The wind stirs up the little organisms on which smelt feed and thereby attracts concentrations of baitfish which, in turn, draw landlocked salmon. Later the angler will use sinking line and in midsummer he may resign himself to heavier tackle—wire line, perhaps, or a downrigger that will let the sinker snap free at a strike so that it will not impede the fight. But in spring and again in fall, he wants

a floating line with plenty of backing and a 30-foot leader tapered to 8-pound test.

With sweeps of the rod and changes of trolling direction, he enhances the smelt mimicry. If streamer trolling becomes boring or unproductive, he can cast wets such as the Mar Lodge, Black Dose, or Jock Scot, and he may have luck with bushy dries of the Wulff persuasion.

Success is felt as a very sudden, very heavy pull. Landlocks sometimes hook themselves, but the barb should be set with a smooth, line-tightening sweep followed—when the fish is definitely on—by a couple of sharper tugs. The salmon's reaction is immediate, often in the form of a vertical leap that evokes images of rockets or catapults.

In the event of a short strike, the only hope lies in stripping off line to encourage a second attack; it sometimes happens. But a proper strike is followed by the leap and a run and more leaps and runs. Coils of line in the bottom of a boat can become unmanageable, and the fish should be played from the reel whenever possible. However, a salmon may double back after a run, forcing the angler to strip in line wildly. After that it may depart again. It may strain one's skill, credulity, and tackle with quivering tailwalks, and when it is close enough to notice the boat, it may dive straight for the bottom and renew the fight.

Chinook Salmon *(Oncorhynchus tshawytscha)*

COMMON & REGIONAL NAMES: *king salmon.* (The name *tyee* is correctly applied only to trophy chinook, generally those weighing 30 pounds or more. The name *jack salmon* is sometimes applied to young chinook. The names *spring, summer,* and *fall salmon* merely denote seasonal runs.)

GAME IDENTIFICATION & LOCATION OF FISHING REGIONS: A 30-pound chinook can wage a half-hour battle against heavy spinning tackle. Such a fish has a combative resilience manifested in aerial headstands and whip-cracking switches of direction; and it has the muscular power to tow a dory backward. King salmon. Tyee. It is worthy of such titles. Though the average catch is a 10- or 12-pound fish, the chinook generally weighs twice that at maturity. It is the largest of the salmons. In 1959 on the Skeena River in British Columbia, a new sporting record was set by a tyee

Spin fisherman with landlock that struck near surface.

weighing 92 pounds and measuring 4 feet, 10½ inches long and 3 feet around. A 126½-pound chinook was once hauled up in a commercial net.

The broad back of this salmon is bluish-green, darkening to black on top, and its sides are silvery. It has irregularly scattered black spots on its body above the lateral line and on its dorsal fin and both lobes of its tail. The canine teeth of spawning Pacific salmon grow long and ferocious-looking. Those of the chinook are set in blackish gums. Coho can be caught in the same waters with chinook, and there is a similarity of appearance. A coho can be identified by its whitish gums and the lack of spots on the lower lobe of its tail. Like all salmon, spawning chinook change color and soon their fins begin to fray. The female takes on a brassy hue. The male becomes hook-jawed and turns blackish.

Chinook salmon enter rivers on both sides of the Pacific: from central California to Alaska and from China to Siberia. They come into North American streams beginning in March or sometimes a little earlier, and there is a heavy spring run consisting of younger, more brightly colored fish than those arriving later. The run subsides until most of the summer has passed; then it begins again, developing into a heavy autumn run. Some chinook travel no farther than Atlantic salmon. Others make extremely long spawning journeys, threading their way through the Columbia River, for example, into the Snake and finally into Idaho's Salmon River, where they spawn. Their longest known odyssey winds 2,400 miles from the Bering Sea up Alaska's Yukon River to Lake Teslin on the Yukon-British Columbia border. In some rivers, the late-fall and early-spring runs nearly merge, or spring migration may begin so early that it is called a winter run.

Before the fish move upriver, while they are actively feeding in the coastal bays and sounds, they are caught in great quantity along the coast of California, Oregon, Washington, and British Columbia. Party boats and charter boats as well as private craft work the waters from San Francisco northward, slowly trolling herring or big spoons and plugs. Plugs, spoons, and spinners are used in some of the rivers, but fly fishing is a more rewarding method. Standard salmon flies, steelhead flies, and gaudy streamers and bucktails are used. British Columbia has a number of famous salmon rivers such as the Campbell, Fraser, Skeena, and

Stikine; Washington has the Skagit and Chehalis, and the Columbia on the Oregon line; two of the best fly-fishing rivers are the Chetco in Oregon and the Smith in California.

In 1967, shortly after coho salmon were introduced into the Great Lakes, a similar stocking program was initiated with chinook. Smolts from Washington and Oregon were released in the Little Manistee and Big Huron, streams feeding Lake Michigan. Subsequent plantings were made in other Lake Michigan tributaries and then in rivers feeding Lakes Huron, Superior, Erie, and Ontario. Now, in addition to the parr growing in the region's streams, millions of hatchery-reared smolts are released in the lakes annually. The Erie stockings have brought excellent late-summer and fall salmon fishing to Pennsylvania's Elk Creek, Walnut Creek, and Presque Isle Bay, and to Ohio's Sandusky, Huron, Vermillion, and other river outlets. At Lake Ontario, New York's Salmon River (off the St. Lawrence) is getting 30-pound catches in August—earlier in the salmon season than the tributaries of the other Great Lakes. Superior has excellent chinook fishing at Marquette Bay and at L'Anse on Keweenaw Bay, though the fish are seldom quite as big. Lake Michigan is best, and Huron is almost as good. The entire Wisconsin shoreline of Lake Michigan can be recommended, though Sturgeon Bay is probably the finest spot on that side; on the Michigan side, some of the best spots are at Petoskey, Manistee, Ludington, Muskegon, Grand Haven, South Haven, and Benton Harbor. The areas to troll are the drowned river mouths. On Lake Huron some of the best are Thunder Bay, Harrisville Harbor, Oscoda, the Au Sable, Au Gres, and down around the Detroit and Huron rivers.

Pacific salmon were brought east to supplement the dwindling lake trout (victimized by pollution and the spread of sea lampreys into the Great Lakes) and to help control the population of alewives. Today the salmon are flourishing as splendidly in the Great Lakes as in the salty bays of the West Coast. King salmon can be established only in very large lakes that support teeming populations of baitfish, because an average chinook consumes more than 200 pounds of small fish during its lifetime. But the Great Lakes are not the only inland bodies of water suitable for kings. A stocking program has begun at North Dakota's Lake Sakakawea, and similar experiments are certain to follow elsewhere. The king's realm is going to be enlarged.

FISH HABITAT & FEEDING BEHAVIOR—ANGLING TACTICS:
Pacific salmon spawn in much the same manner as Atlantic
salmon, and the young have more or less troutlike parr markings.
The eggs hatch in about two months. The smolts of chinook that
enter the rivers in the fall generally go out to sea when they are
only a few months old, while the smolts of some of the spring
chinook remain in fresh water for almost a year and a half. (The
landlocked chinook of the Great Lakes are fall salmon, requiring
only six months from spawning time to the arrival of smolts at
the stream outlets.) Their time at sea varies even more drastically
—from two to eight years. The huge trophies are those that matured
slowly and stayed at sea longest.

River-running chinook, especially the females, become
less emaciated than other salmon. All the same, they have
stopped feeding actively, for they return only to spawn and die.
They seem to strike lures merely out of irritation, and they take
colorful streamers and steelhead flies as well as the patterns used
for Atlantic salmon. However, a chinook rarely rises to a fly near
the surface, as an Atlantic does. It notices only the creatures near
the stream bed, so weighted flies are used. For rapid sinking and
the long casts needed on many western rivers, a lead-core
shooting-head is spliced between the monofilament backing and
the leader; tippets testing about 10 pounds are usual.

Chinook are still feeding when they gather around the river
outlets. Big, red-beaded silver or brass spoons used to be popular
for salmon fishing on the coast, but recently bottom-raking silver
or fluorescent orange plugs have gained ascendancy. Out on the
ocean—in the bays, straits, sounds, and estuaries—anglers
watch for gulls dropping to grab herring, just as East Coast anglers
do when trying to locate bluefish; the birds show where the baitfish
are, and that is where the salmon should be—sometimes. Tide-
rips also mark good trolling spots since they collect baitfish; they
are indicated by long lines of debris, foam, and floating weeds.
The most common bait is a frozen herring, though a sardine or
anchovy will do just as well. Small hooks such as no. 2/0 can be
used in tandem, one behind the head and one near the tail, rigged
to bend the bait slightly and make it wobble. A variation is a single
long-shanked hook with a plastic clip near its eye to hold the
herring's head, and a rubber band to hold the body just forward
of the tail against the hook's bend. Sometimes a brass spinner

Netted chinook, almost in tyee class.

is attached ahead of the bait, and sometimes a silver or chartreuse Herring Dodger is used. This is a shiny metal flasher that has gained favor on the Great Lakes as well as the West Coast. It is used not only with bait but with a spinner-fly or a big trolling fly, and it seems to work best when attached to the leader about a foot ahead of the lure or bait. A sinker is needed, and it should go about 1½ to 2 feet ahead of the Dodger.

Sometimes chinook are seen at the surface, rolling like porpoises and relieving the angler of any need to look for gulls or rips. However, the salmon are not actually feeding on top; they dive down again to capture their prey. Very early in the morning, at night, or beneath an overcast sky, they may be close enough to the surface for an angler to fish his bait and Herring Dodger with a 2-ounce sinker while trolling very slowly—only a couple of miles an hour at most. But chinook are extremely light-sensitive, and they may go deep enough to require a snap-off downrigger with a 3- to 12-pound sinker that looks like a miniature cannon-

ball. In some waters, even heavier downriggers are needed. Aboard the private runabouts as well as charter and party boats, the usual tool for this kind of endeavor is a long trolling rod with a star-drag reel and line testing at least 20 pounds. Fairly heavy saltwater spinning rods are also used.

The sportsmen of the Great Lakes fishery have adopted or modified the western methods. In October, when the fly fishing is good on the California rivers, it is also good on the Great Lakes streams and is done in much the same manner. And beginning in late August, trolling is excellent on the lakes, particularly in rain or when a chop is on the water to stir up plankton and arouse the hunger of baitfish. It is most rewarding at the edges of deep drop-offs, steep banks, points, and river outlets. Depth-sounders are often used to locate likely spots or feeding schools. Water thermometers are used, too, because chinook prefer to cruise at depths where the temperature is in the mid-50's.

In September the chinook begin to crowd the areas around the river mouths but they are still feeding, and heavily. Bait-fishermen on the lakes sometimes use smelt or bagged roe, but nightcrawlers are most common and they are used on no. 1 or 1/0 single or treble hooks. They work well in the shallows, especially on a rainy evening. After dark the fish bite even in calm water. The technique is to set the hook when a light tapping is felt. A chinook does not strike bait hard, the way it strikes a lure. With a lure, if the fish fails to hook itself, it can be hooked in the same manner used for other salmon. Sometimes, though, it will merely slap at an offering and take it only if it appears to be injured. The trick then is to let the lure drop back, as with landlocked Atlantic salmon.

Surfcasting has become popular at the lakes with big, long-handled spinning and baitcasting rods that can toss a lure or bait far from a shore, pier, or jetty. More fish are taken by this method on the Wisconsin side of Lake Michigan than elsewhere.

Boat equipment includes hefty spinning rods, trolling rods, and—for a few midsummer anglers—large-frame reels with wire line. The fish are boated with long-handled nets, but now and then an angler is seen slipping a tailer-loop onto a chinook. Trying to tail a big one from a boat seems like an unnecessary gamble.

In fresh water these salmon are much like lake trout; they need cool, deep, well-oxygenated water. Sometimes they can be caught by trolling eighty feet down in two hundred feet or more of water. For success with wire line, the throbbing of a Herring Dodger is recommended. More common than wire-lining is trolling with a pair of downriggers and a pair of flat lines. Effective lures include Rapalas, Thin Fins, and silver U-20 Flatfish plugs, as well as spoons—Dardevles, Flutter Spoons, Sagamores, Sugar Spoons, Manistee Wobblers. Often the fish will be fifteen to twenty feet down, and the flat-line lures will work at that depth with a sinker of appropriate weight—generally a half-ounce to 2 ounces. The lures on the flat lines should be at least fifty feet behind the boat, preferably more, because chinook are easily spooked. The downrigger lines trail their lures only thirty or forty feet back, and sometimes right under the prop wash. Evidently, the fish that are deep enough are attracted rather than repelled by the bubbling commotion. When a line snaps away from a downrigger, or a screeching drag signals a first run, all lines but that one are brought in fast. A chinook may race in any direction, tangling lines as well as tempers.

The fish are not always lake-trout deep. They may be only knee-deep when they herd and harass the alewives around river mouths. Occasionally it is possible to cast to the edges of the schools, but chinook are so easily alarmed that even in these waters a more common procedure is long-line trolling. And here, as in deeper waters, a chinook that has fought long and acts spent may end the contest with a barrel roll, wrapping line around its body, whipping off in a new direction, cutting under the boat, inspiring anglers' laments about last-moment break-offs.

Chum Salmon (Oncorhynchus keta)

COMMON & REGIONAL NAMES: dog salmon. (The terms summer salmon and fall salmon are sometimes used to denote seasonal runs.)

GAME IDENTIFICATION & LOCATION OF FISHING REGIONS:
The chum salmon looks like a small chinook but with only a very faint sprinkling of dark spots on its back. As a male travels upstream to spawn, its back darkens until it is black, and its upper sides turn green. A rusty or bluish-red mottling appears along the sides, the vertical splotches merging to form a ragged longitudinal band and sometimes spreading down to the belly. Most

spawners are four-year-olds, weighing between 5 and 10 pounds, although anglers occasionally catch 12- and 15-pounders.

In North America, chum range from San Francisco Bay to Alaska. On the far side of the Pacific they are found from Siberia to Korea and Japan. Commercially, they are almost as important as pink and sockeye salmon. In 1956 Russia introduced them into the Barents Sea, near Scandinavia, and they have now become established in Russian and northern Scandinavian streams. Chum enter North American rivers from July to December, forming a summer run and a bigger fall run, but spawning does not occur until November and December. The fall fish travel farther, mature more slowly, and grow larger than summer chum. They enter the rivers used by the larger salmons. Most of them spawn in the lower reaches but some travel as far as the chinook—to Teslin Lake, for example, near the head of the Yukon River.

FISH HABITAT: The parr of the smaller Pacific salmons, the chum and pink, begin to work their way toward the sea when they

are hardly more than alevins—almost as soon as their yolk sacs are absorbed. Thus they spend almost their entire lives in the ocean. On this continent, anglers have paid little attention to chum salmon in the tidewaters and almost none at all in the rivers. In part, this is due to the fact that most chum enter fresh water late in the season, when only the most fanatic anglers want to be on the streams. Another reason for neglect is the availability of larger, more glamorous species in the same region.

In Norway, chum are sometimes caught on flies or spinners, and there is no reason why they should not be taken on the same lures in American streams. Even in Alaska, where they are most abundant, relatively few "rod-hours" are spent in quest of chum, but these salmon do have a following among light-tackle saltwater anglers off British Columbia's Queen Charlotte Islands. The fish assemble there in large numbers from September through mid-October, before moving up the Skeena, the Nass, and other nearby rivers. While lingering in the island waters they are still hungry, and they display a decided preference for spinners and small wobbling spoons. Blades with bright red or fluorescent red spots or stripes bring the greatest number of strikes. A hooked chum fights very well but is small enough to be handled with a fairly light spinning rod.

Coho Salmon *(Oncorhynchus kisutch)*
COMMON & REGIONAL NAMES: *silver salmon, hooknose*

GAME IDENTIFICATION & LOCATION OF FISHING REGIONS: At sea or in tidewaters, the coho is a dark-backed, silver-sided fish that looks very much like a chinook except that it has white rather than black gums and has no spots on the lower part of its tail. The male's spawning colors are green on the upper sides and rose or rust on the fins and from the area of the lateral line to the belly. Coho salmon generally spend only one or two years in the ocean. A few weighing more than 30 pounds have been taken, but most are in the 5-to-10-pound class when they return to the rivers to spawn. They are abundant, and they rival the usually bigger chinook in popularity because they often feed at the surface, fight near the surface—very hard—and shoot into the air even more often, more spectacularly than chinook of comparable size. They also outperform chinook in their readiness to attack a fly.

Big male chum, taken on spinning gear.

Coho range from California to Alaska and from Siberia to Japan. They have enhanced the reputation of many American rivers—the Navarro, Klamath, Rogue, Columbia, Chehalis, Skagit, and dozens of more northerly streams along British Columbia's coast. In the spring of 1966 coho smolts were planted in the Platte River, in Michigan, and soon the species was well established in the Great Lakes. The best coho-fishing spots on the lakes coincide with the best spots for chinook (which see), but coho are more migratory in their seasonal quest for comfortable waters. Observations and catch statistics at Lake Michigan furnish a key to their movements. During the winter they travel to the lower end of the lake; shortly after ice-out they begin to move north again, reaching the outlets of their parent streams in late summer and fall. Very early in spring, the fishing is excellent at Michigan City, Indiana, and within sight of the Chicago skyline. A few weeks later they are gone. In April and May they are at Benton Harbor, South Haven, Saugatuck, and Milwaukee. From June through August they are at Grand Haven, Muskegon, Ludington, and Manistee. In late August and September they gather near river mouths at Ludington, Manistee, Frankfort, Platte Bay, and

Hooked coho, or silver, salmon.

Traverse City. For reasons still mysterious to ichthyologists as well as anglers, most of the biggest ones are caught in the area of Grand Traverse Bay.

There is a definite possibility that coho and other Pacific salmons, until recently limited in distribution and severely threatened by power dams and industry on the western rivers, will assume an importance rivaling that of all other gamefish in the Midwest and East. The success of the stocking endeavor in the Great Lakes has encouraged analogous experiments elsewhere. As a result of New Hampshire's coho-stocking program, begun in 1969 in the tributaries of Great Bay, 7- to 9-pound Pacific salmon are being caught in the coastal and estuarine waters of the Atlantic. In early September, New Hampshire anglers troll and cast spoons for them in the coves of Great Bay and at the mouths of the Lamprey and Piscataqua rivers. A few weeks later these anglers put aside their spinning tackle for fly rods and move upstream to cast bright streamers, mostly tied on no. 4 and 6 hooks and used with a tippet testing 6 pounds at the end of a sinking line.

FISH HABITAT & FEEDING BEHAVIOR—ANGLING TACTICS:
Most coho spawn in November and December, the time varying with locale, climate, and the length of the spawning journey. There are streams near the sea where coho dig their redds in October, but Oregon's coho are chiefly February spawners. The eggs hatch in spring and early summer. Some of the young swim to sea almost immediately, while most remain in fresh water until the following spring. The coho stocked in the Great Lakes are planted in streams as one-and-a-half-year-old smolts, 4 to 6 inches long. A few mature quickly and spawn the next fall, by which time they weigh about 6 pounds. More of them remain in the lakes until they are three years old and weigh about 15 pounds. These and the few that feed in the lakes for yet another year before spawning provide trophy fishing in the streams. Their growth rate is credited to dense schools of alewives that may render a salmon's life more voluptuous in fresh water than in the Pacific.

On the West Coast, good coho fishing comes at different times to different locales, depending on when the fish run in the nearest rivers. Coho begin to show up in the Puget Sound catches in late August. A little farther north, in the Strait of Georgia off Vancouver Island, they congregate chiefly in mid-September. (It may be worth noting, however, that the author and his father once caught 10- and 11-pounders on anchovies trolled beneath an August-morning fog on the bay outside the mainland city of Vancouver, near the mouth of the Fraser River.) Trolling is done with anchovy and herring baits, spoons, spinners, spinner-flies, and colorful streamers. Candlefish—the slender surf smelts known as hooligans in Alaska—are also trolled in some areas. Popular streamers, generally tied on no. 1 to no. 3/0 hooks, include the Coho Special, Howells' Coho Fly, Candlefish, Silver Killer, Coronation, Blue and White, and Alaska Mary Ann. Most of the good ones utilize bear hair and tinsel. Howells' Coho, for instance, has a wing of peacock herl over green and white polar-bear hair and a body wrapped in oval silver tinsel.

An angler can find good trolling water in the same general way he looks for chinook (which see), but with a couple of important differences. First, as a rule, when coho are rolling and breaking on top, they are actually feeding there—chasing herring and candlefish at the surface—so there is no need to troll deep. Second, the greatest activity usually occurs from an hour before to an hour after a high or low tide. When a school is sighted at such a time, a boat crisscrossing ahead of the fish will get strikes. As with chinook, plenty of line should be let out, but trolling speed should be considerably higher than for the bigger salmon; about 4 to 6 miles an hour will do nicely. If flies or other lures are cast rather than trolled, the retrieve should be jerky and fairly fast.

The fish are still feeding when they reach the mouths of rivers, and bait there includes spawn bags. Farther upstream, many anglers use spinning rods to troll or cast spinners, spinner-flies, and small wobbling spoons. A spinner seems to provoke strikes most regularly when cast upstream and brought back along the bottom. Migrating coho prefer to rest in slow or almost still water near the protection of a bank, sunken tree, log, or brush tangle. Deep holes and confluences with other streams are also customary lies. Some of the streams, both east and west, are well suited to fly casting with a 9-foot rod. Western fly-rodders, using the aforementioned streamers as well as steelhead flies, standard salmon flies, and various other colorful streamers, employ the same methods as for steelhead (which see).

The eastern fishery is developing methods that merit a trial in the West. David Richey, a Great Lakes guide and angling writer, has described his fishing on the Platte (southwest of Traverse City) and the Big Manistee in September and October. Both rivers are governed by regulations to maintain quality fishing; anglers may use only single, unweighted hooks no larger than no. 4, and the landing nets may be no longer than 36 inches, including handle and hoop. As these streams are clear and shallow, Richey walks the banks until he sees a coho in its lie, and then wades in downstream and casts his fly so that it touches a couple of yards upstream of the salmon. As soon as it has passed the coho's snout, he lifts it out and casts again. Several casts may be needed to annoy a salmon into a response, which generally takes the form of a hard strike. Richey varies this approach with a technique more like the classic Atlantic salmon presentation, casting across and down. He gives the fly a few twitches as it passes the fish. Among the streamers he has recommended are the Green Maribou, Mickey Finn, Golden Girl, and Royal Coachman.

Pier and jetty fishermen on the Great Lakes bait their hooks with nightcrawlers or spawn bags, as they do for chinook, and some of them wade the shallows to cast spinners. In the spring, when the water is still cold, the trollers work the top ten feet, using no sinker, keeping lures eighty feet or more behind the boat unless crowded by other fishermen, and moving relatively fast. The most productive waters are almost invariably within a mile of a creek or river.

In the summer, many trollers use electronic thermometers and depth-finders to locate drop-offs or the fish themselves, and to gauge the water stratum that provides the 53° to 56° temperatures preferred by coho. Some use downriggers, some content themselves with wire line, and some use a Pink Lady—a red planing device that pushes a lure down without adding excessive weight. Supplied by Luhr Jensen, the company that makes Herring Dodger attractors and Fireplug lures, it has been described as a "poor man's downrigger." Lure-enhancing attractors include Lake Trollers and Cowbells as well as Herring Dodgers.

On Lake Ontario, fishermen have been reporting outstanding success with fluorescent red plugs. Some, like the Tadpolly and the Fireplug, can be bought in that color; many anglers paint their own. A rule of thumb on Lake Michigan seems to be springtime use of drab-colored plugs that realistically mimic alewives or minnows, and a summertime switch to fluorescent red, orange, and yellow plugs, spoons, and spinners. Rapala, Rebel, and Thin Fin plugs are popular, and the size 4 and 5 Mepps spinners trailing plastic minnows or squirreltail also produce strikes.

Pink Salmon *(Oncorhynchus gorbuscha)*
COMMON & REGIONAL NAMES: *humpback salmon*

GAME IDENTIFICATION & LOCATION OF FISHING REGIONS:
Smallest of its group, the pink salmon usually weighs 3 or 4 pounds when it comes to the rivers to spawn, but on rare occasions 10-pounders have been caught. Commercially, pinks and sockeye are the most important Pacific salmons. On the far side of the Pacific, the range of the pink stretches from Siberia to Japan and Korea; on the near side it extends from Alaska to California, as do the ranges of other Pacific species, but the pink is abundant farther south than its relatives. In the 1920's, pink salmon were introduced into Maine's Dennys River but failed to establish a fishable population. They have, however, been established in northern Norway, where chum salmon have also been introduced.

Before spawning time the only pink about a pink salmon is an occasional very faint blush on the sides. It looks so much like an undersized king salmon that anglers often call it a "young chinook." However, it has considerably smaller scales and its tail is covered with oval black splotches, much larger than the speckles on a chinook's tail. At spawning time, the male develops not only the hooked jaws typical of ripe salmon but a pronounced— in fact, rather grotesque—hump behind its head. The name humpback salmon refers to this, of course, and the name pink salmon refers to its color at this time, a deep rosy pink.

FISH HABITAT: The fry of pink salmon lack the dark parr marks of their relatives, and they remain in fresh water for only a very short time, moving into the ocean soon after their yolk sacs are absorbed. Invariably they live only two years, most of that time at sea. Late in the spring of their second year they come back into the coastal waters near their home streams. Although they

enter some of the rivers in July and do not spawn until fall, only a few of the runs extend inland. Most pinks use suitably gravelly spawning shallows very close to the sea, only a little above the reach of high tide in the rivers. The timing of the runs varies more widely from year to year than among other salmons. Abundance varies, too, but as a rule the fish provide good sport around Puget Sound and, like chum salmon, in the waters of the Queen Charlotte Islands. Later in the season they are numbered among the popular game species in the many rivers of British Columbia.

In the ocean and in brackish tidewaters they can be caught on the same baits and lures that take chinook and coho. Like chum salmon, they greedily attack spinners and small wobbling spoons. And like chum and coho, they are suitable quarry for fairly light tackle. But like chinook, they go deep to forage, and they are most often caught on or near the bottom in tidewaters. Once they are in the rivers, they can be caught on wobbling spoons, spinners, and streamers. As in the case of chinook and steelhead, flies must sink readily and be drifted or twitched over the bottom, and a shooting-head line is sometimes needed.

Sockeye Salmon *(Oncorhynchus nerka)*
COMMON & REGIONAL NAMES: *blueback salmon, red salmon*

GAME IDENTIFICATION & LOCATION OF FISHING REGIONS:
The sockeye has silver sides and a gray-blue back marked by very

Pink, or humpback, salmon in spawning shape.

small black spots. A ripe female turns pale red or darkens to a dingy olive shade. The male undergoes a more pronounced metamorphosis; its head becomes greenish, its body bright red, its jaws kyped, and its back humped almost as high as that of a pink salmon. Most of those caught are four years old and weigh 4 to 7 pounds, but there is a record of a five-year-old, 15-pound sockeye, and a few live as long as eight years.

They range from Japan to Siberia and from Alaska to California, but few sockeye enter rivers south of the Columbia. Although they contribute a high percentage to the commercial catch and are prized for their excellent meat, they are the least important of salmons in the sport fishery. Once hooked, they fight very well, but when they enter coastal waters they seem to lose their appetites faster than other salmons, and in many tidewaters where other salmons are taken the sockeye sometimes ignore baits and lures. In recent years, however, anglers on the Washington coast have been plug-fishing for sockeye with fairly consistent success, and river fishermen have been taking them on bright wobbling spoons and spinners.

FISH HABITAT: Though a few sockeye spawn in rivers, most seek their gravel beds in the shallows of lakes or in adjacent inlet and outlet streams. The best sockeye rivers, therefore, are those fed by lakes. Spawners crowd together in relatively small areas, forming dense concentrations. A sockeye is content with only a couple of square yards for its redd, and in the lake shallows a colony can have the appearance of shimmering scarlet cobblestones spaced for a man to step across without waders.

The fish come from the sea in spring and early summer and arrive on the spawning grounds from August to December. The young stay in the lakes and streams for a year or more—sometimes three years—migrating to the sea in springtime. Most spend from two to four years at sea and some stay longer before returning to spawn and die.

Since they subsist chiefly on crustaceans, one might think that shrimp would be a tempting bait. Yet in the tidewaters they are more readily caught on plugs. In Washington's bays and estuaries, anglers use depth-sounders and deep-running plugs. When a school is located, the fishermen flutter their plugs just off the bottom, where the salmon are accustomed to foraging for soft-shelled crustaceans. This type of fishing situation would seem to call for experimentation with jigs of various forms and colors. Farther upstream, anglers with spinning rods and, less often, fly rods use bright or flashing lures to elicit annoyed strikes, pretty much in the same manner as with other Pacific species.

Kokanee (Oncorhynchus nerka)
COMMON & REGIONAL NAMES: *landlocked sockeye, redfish, Kennerly's salmon, blueback, kickaninny, silver trout, silversides*

GAME IDENTIFICATION & LOCATION OF FISHING REGIONS:
The kokanee is merely a landlocked and dwarfed form of the sockeye salmon—a form to be expected since the sockeye spawns in northern lakes. Like the sea-run sockeye, kokanee are silvery until spawning time. Males then turn red, while females tend to become slaty rather than the pale red or olive of ripe females from the sea. Mature kokanee generally weigh only about a pound, but they grow larger in some lakes. The record specimen, taken in 1975 from Priest Lake in Idaho, weighed 6 pounds, 9¾ ounces.

Kokanee occur on both sides of the Pacific; in Japan they are known as *benimasa*. Their indigenous North American range is from Alaska southward through British Columbia, Washington, and Oregon, and eastward into Idaho. They have been introduced into lakes in California, Nevada, Utah, Colorado, Wyoming, Montana, North Dakota, New York, Connecticut, Vermont, and Maine. Unlike the anadromous form, they are fairly easy to entice. Kokanee and big rainbows have made Idaho's Lake Pend Oreille famous among sportsmen.

FISH HABITAT & FEEDING BEHAVIOR—ANGLING TACTICS:
Kokanee generally mature in three or four years, though longevity varies with locale. They die after spawning in streams like those used by trout. The time of spawning also varies regionally, from August to February; generally speaking, it peaks in late fall. A male and female pair off, and the male drives off intruders while the female clears a small, shallow redd mounded on the downstream side with sand or gravel. The young soon begin feeding on plankton, and their diet changes little as they mature. More than half of what they eat consists of waterfleas and other small

crustaceans. They also feed occasionally on craneflies, midges, and other diptera, plus almost microscopic planktonic life.

In the West, a popular way of taking kokanee is with maggots or corn on a handline, hardly a just way of treating vigorous fighters that can be caught on spinning tackle or a fly rod. Some anglers use spinning rods to still-fish with the same baits or with salmon eggs or worms. They also troll with red-beaded wobbling spoons trailing a gob of worm on a small hook.

Shortly before spawning, as the weather cools, kokanee can be seen rolling and jumping repeatedly. It is a time for fly fishermen to cast midges and whatever small dries roughly match the local stoneflies or mayflies. Fish will rise to these often enough to hold an angler's interest, though strikes will be fewer than the spoon-and-worm trolling rig. The lightest possible rod assures the best sport, of course. By comparison with larger salmon, kokanee have very fragile mouths; they must be played delicately on a rod with accommodating "give."

Sauger *(Stizostedion canadense)*
COMMON & REGIONAL NAMES: *sand pike, gray pike, river pike, spotfin pike, jack salmon, jackfish, horsefish, pickering.* (See **WALLEYE** for additional names, associated interchangeably with both species.)

GAME IDENTIFICATION & LOCATION OF FISHING REGIONS:
The sauger is a true perch, a close relative of the walleye and very much like a small walleye in appearance and behavior. Tradition-

Kokanee in stream, about to die after spawning.

▲ Fly fisherman laying out line. ▼ Chain pickerel.

Coho on spawning run. ▲ Angler with coho. ▼ Atlantic salmon. ▶

▲ Sockeye near end of run. ▼ Chum salmon with bright streamer that took it.

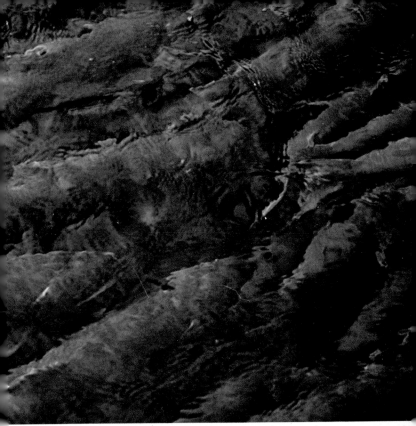

▼ Female (left) and male sockeye on spawning ground.

Pink salmon on run. ▲ Salmon angler removing hook. ▼ Angler gaffing chinook. ▶

▲ Seven-pound sauger, brought to net. ▼ Sturgeon.

ally, sauger fishing has been regarded as a kind of footnote to wall-eye fishing, but this smaller species has risen in popularity and numbers, owing to the construction of big hydroelectric dams in the central and southern states.

For biological reasons not yet understood, sauger fare poorly when stocked in smaller waters, so the species has not been as widely transplanted as the walleye. But in deep, sprawling reservoirs, 6- and 7-pounders are occasionally taken. Heretofore, such catches were very rare except on the Missouri River and its tributaries. Biologists, unable to find any conditions on the Missouri to account for increased size, have speculated that the sauger there may be a distinct subspecies. Mature specimens of this strain have an average weight of 1 to 3 pounds and a maximum (attained in the Missouri's reservoirs) of about 8. Elsewhere, the maximum is about 5 and the average little more than a pound. As a rule, a 14-inch sauger weighs nearly a pound, an 18-incher weighs about 2 pounds, and a 20-incher weighs 3.

The sauger has the big glassy eyes for which its larger relative is named, and the same long, rounded body, forked tail, sharp teeth on the jaws and roof of the mouth, and stiff spines on the anal fin and forward dorsal fin. It has an olivaceous back and three or four dark, amorphous saddles spilling onto the olive-gray, sometimes brassy sides. The white of the belly reaches to the end of the tail but does not spread to form a white lower tip as it does on the walleye. An angler can identify a sauger by its tail and fin markings. The tail has vertical rows of dark spots like the walleye's, but without the white patch, and both of its dorsal fins have longitudinal bands of dark spots, whereas the walleye's forward dorsal has streaks or vague blotches.

Sauger are caught in large lakes and impoundments from Labrador to the Prairie Provinces, through the eastern and central states, and down the Mississippi, Ohio, Missouri, and Tennessee rivers and their tributaries. The Great Lakes have always had an abundance, as have Minnesota's Rainy Lake, St. Croix, Kabetogama, and Lake of the Woods. The big dams on the Missouri, the Tennessee, and the Tennessee's tributaries have now accumulated concentrations, not only by supplying excellent habitat but by blocking upstream migrations. Occasionally sauger will abandon food-rich havens and will travel great distances—another mystery that has resisted biological investigation.

FISH HABITAT & FEEDING BEHAVIOR—ANGLING TACTICS:
Night fishing is excellent, and the waters near shore may be remunerative by twilight. Like walleyes, sauger schools often hunt
in fairly shallow water at night, but during the day they seek even
dimmer light and deeper water than the walleye haunts. The
temperature zones are similar, however. Where the water is between 55° and 70° both species feed well, and their activity peaks
at about 60°. This and other factors contribute to the superiority
of fall and spring fishing.

There are late-fall runs to the tailwaters below dams, where
the sauger become gluttonous for the prey that spills about. They
seem to be fattening themselves for winter, when food supplies
diminish, but they keep biting during cold weather. A great many
are caught through the ice on shiners and jigs. And in spring, their
spawning runs again make them both hungry and easy to locate.

Breeding begins just a trifle later than that of walleyes—as
late as May in icy northern waters, as early as February in the
South. The males run first, when the water temperature reaches
45° or so, and the females join them in the shoals of lakes and
rivers. The beds are in one to five feet of water, over a gravelly
or rubble-strewn bottom, where there is some current or wave action. The eggs are dropped at night—some 25,000 or more per
pound of the female's weight. She and several escorting males
thrash about, ejecting eggs and milt, after which they depart.

The fry generally hatch in less than three weeks, or less

Sauger taken on spinner-bait at dusk in shallows.

than two if the water warms up. They are about a half-inch long and so thin as to be almost invisible, an advantage in a predator-infested environment. They drift about for several days while absorbing their yolk sacs, and then feed on progressively larger morsels of zooplankton as they head for deeper water. By late summer they are several inches long and feeding mostly on fish—as they will all their lives.

In spite of a preference for small live fish, sauger take baits other than a minnow, darter, sculpin, or eel. Additional choices include a frog, newt, crawfish, hellgrammite, or nightcrawler. Nor must the bait always be live. Sauger will often grab cut bait such as a strip of perch belly. But they will grab gently, no matter what bait or lure is offered.

Some fishermen rig their baits (or long, soft-bodied lures such as plastic worms and eels) with tandem hooks to counter short strikes and tentative nibbles with a tail hook. Experienced anglers also tend to acknowledge the slightest tug with a hooksetting yank or sweep of the rod. It is usually a light spinning rod carrying monofilament that tests no more than 4 to 6 pounds. The fish are mostly too small and their behavior too delicate for lead-core line, even though deep, slow trolling is a primary method of locating wandering schools. Trolling is done with bait, plugs, soft-bodied lures, and weighted spoons and spinners. A fine trolling combination is a June Bug spinner ahead of a minnow, eel, or worm. Another is a Flatfish plug with flanking angleworms trailing

Angler with typical sauger.

from the treble hooks on its midsection.

It pays to go on trolling the area where a first fish is caught. This is most likely to be over a sand, gravel, or rock bottom, particularly at the site of a drop-off, deep hole, bar, or a deep river channel or pool. Unlike walleyes, sauger will tolerate somewhat silted or murky water, and although they prefer the deepest abysses of a lake, in some localities they are more partial to rivers.

As a change from trolling, a nightcrawler or 2- to 3-inch minnow can be drift-fished, or a crawfish or two on a dropper rig can be crawled over the bottom. Or a deep-running plug, wobbling spoon, or weighted spinner can be cast. Popular plug colors are red, minnow-silver, and green with a light belly. A spinner will often attract more sauger if a worm or pork rind is added. The wobbling spoons are especially good at spawning time and in tailwaters and eddies.

The species is also susceptible to a yellow jig scraped and bumped along the bottom. An effective tactic is to cast the jig to the upper part of a drop-off or submerged ridge and twitch the rod to make it skip and tumble down the slope.

Fly fishing is less productive, but minnow-patterned streamers on sinking lines can take sauger in the evening or at night. A streamer should be drawn or drifted slowly over a shallow bottom. Sand or gravel patches can be prospected right up to the edges of weed thickets but not into the vegetation. Sauger cruise the edges but seldom hound their prey into a thicket. About the only time a hooked sauger ever jumps is during an evening or night session, when the fight takes place in these shallows. But in windy, rainy weather, sauger become so active that strikes may come frequently, regardless of the hour.

Shad *(Alosa)*

COMMON & REGIONAL NAMES: *poor man's salmon*. (The American shad is equally well known as the *white shad*. A northerly race of Alabama shad is sometimes called *Ohio shad*. The golden shad is more commonly known as the *skipjack, skipjack herring,* or *river herring,* and is also called *river shad* or *blue shad*.)

GAME IDENTIFICATION & LOCATION OF FISHING REGIONS: In late April, when stream fishermen traditionally celebrate the opening weeks of trouting, many on the Connecticut River watch

instead for the first runs of American, or white, shad *(Alosa sapidissima)*. Down near the mouth of the Susquehanna, others await friendly telephone calls announcing that the aggressive hickory shad *(A. mediocris)* are appearing in Chesapeake Bay, soon to be followed upriver by the bigger whites. Farther south, on Florida's St. Johns River, the white-shad fishing now dwindles fast, the run having begun in November or December and peaked between January and March; while on California's Russian River the white shad will probably be most abundant in May, and to the north, where the Columbia cleaves Oregon from Washington, they will crowd the waters in July.

Some few anglers still abide by the belief that shad arrive with the white flowering of the various serviceberries, appropriately called shadbush (genus *Amelanchier*), and the dingy brown hatch-clouds of sedges, or caddisflies, of the species *Brachycentrus fuliginosus,* known to some as the grannom and to others as the shadfly. A more accurate herald is the rising of a river's temperature to 50° or so. That is when the hickory schools run in from the bays, and the more widespread American shad follow as the temperature climbs another few degrees (or, on rivers in the deep South, when it drops to the 60's).

American shad taken on flies.

An angler may be casting a white or yellow streamer, or perhaps he is trolling or casting a red-and-white shad dart—a little leadheaded jig—when the first strike bows his rod so solidly that he fears he has snagged a log. He is relieved of that pessimistic notion as a 3-pound shad breaks out like a silver rocket and then plunges for the bottom. He lifts his rod tip high, but the fish sounds nevertheless and holds for a few seconds before plowing downstream. Knowing how fragile a shad's mouth is, the angler gives it the head it demands as it runs with the current. He plays it carefully, trying to outmaneuver rather than outpull it, and he thinks he is winning the contest until the fish rips off more line, then turns and hangs broadside to the current so that the rush of high spring water is added to its own resistance. The shad has a fairly deep-bellied, laterally compressed shape, and a swift current against the slab of its side is like a stiff wind against a sail. Too much strain and the fish will break off. The angler decides to compensate, moving toward the fish when he is afraid to move the fish to him. Its strength is disproportionate to its size.

Several minutes pass before the shad is within reach. Still concerned lest the hook tear out, the angler slips his net into the water and gingerly scoops up the glimmering coin-silver catch.

Shad are anadromous species of herring, members of the family Clupeidae, wanderers of the sea for most of their lives, sparkling river runners and gamefish only at spawning time. The earliest spring catches are mostly "buck shad"—males—but as the season progresses, more and more females, or roe shad, appear. Many fishermen, eager to play as many as possible before limiting out, release all or most of the males once the females arrive. Male or female, both hickories and whites—the important game species—are delicious. But females grow larger than males and hold a treasure: roe to be crisply fried. An angling gourmet confirms a shad's sex by the look of its vent; if it is reddish and slightly protruding, he has caught a ripe female.

The American shad is not exclusively American. An Atlantic native, it enters coastal rivers on both sides of the ocean. On the American side, it probes the eastern seaboard all the way from the Gulf of St. Lawrence to Florida, but the best fishing is from lower New England southward, in rivers like the Connecticut, the Scantic, and the Salmon in Connecticut; the Hudson and Delaware in New York; the Delaware for the remainder of its course down

Pennsylvania and New Jersey; the Susquehanna in Pennsylvania and Maryland; the Gunpowder, Patuxent, Pamunkey, Rappahannock, York, Appomattox, Chickahominy, James, and others emptying into or near Chesapeake Bay; additional Virginia streams and many in the Carolinas such as the Cape Fear, Neuse, Pee Dee, Roanoke, Cooper, and Edisto; Georgia's Ogeechee, Satilla, and Altamaha; and the St. Mary's on the Florida line and the St. Johns just below it.

White shad have also become well established on the Pacific coast, from Alaska's southern seaboard to southern California. There, as on the East Coast, dams have impeded spawning runs, and such devices as fish ladders have not entirely alleviated the problem. Pollution and commercial fishing have also lowered the populations. All the same, California's American, Russian, and Feather rivers have become meccas for shad fishermen. Other fine California streams are the Yuba, the Trinity, the Klamath, and the lower Sacramento and San Joaquin. North of that state, shad are caught in good numbers on Oregon's Umpqua and Coos rivers, on the Columbia, around Puget Sound, and on British Columbia's Fraser River.

The American shad rather resembles its little baitfish relative the alewife. It has the same deeply forked tail and silvery, vertically broad, compressed body. Its back is a dark, metallic green, gray-green, or blue-green that spills a little way down onto the sides. Along the "shoulder," behind the top of the gill cover, is a row of several round black spots, each smaller and fainter than the one in front of it. The species has a slight overbite, the upper jaw enclosing the lower jaw when the mouth is closed. Specimens caught on sporting tackle are invariably adults—ready to spawn— and most are about 19 to 21 inches long, with a weight of 2 to 3 pounds. (Because the combination of upriver migration and spawning activity exhausts them, they ignore lures as they turn back toward the sea.) The American shad is the largest of herrings, occasionally growing much heavier than 3 pounds; a new rod-and-reel record was set in 1973 by a Connecticut catch weighing 9 pounds, 2 ounces.

The hickory shad, though smaller, tends to be more acrobatic in battle and, because it spawns in shallower water than the American, it is an even more attractive fly-fishing species. Its distribution is rather limited, however. It enters streams from New

Brunswick to Florida but is abundant only in the mid-coastal states, from the Susquehanna, Potomac, and other rivers around Chesapehanna Bay down into the North Carolina creeks. The hickory is not quite as tasty as the American, but its roe is equally good. The average weight is between 1 and 2 pounds or so; anything over 3 is a rare trophy. Dark markings on the upper rows of scales tend to form dim lines, but to anyone who is not an accomplished ichthyologist the hickory looks like the white. An angler tells them apart by the mouth, as the hickory has a projecting lower jaw.

Two other species, of still more limited distribution, smaller size, and minimal culinary distinction, are sometimes sought by fishermen in the mid-South and Gulf region. They are the Alabama shad *(A. alabamae)* and the skipjack, or golden shad *(A. chrysochloris)*. The Alabama is slightly smaller than the hickory, chunkier, and with a relatively slim, pointed upper jaw. It is found in streams as far north as the Ohio, but its chief distribution is in the Alabama, Apalachicola, and Suwannee river systems. It is most often caught in the tailwaters of reservoirs. Tandem jigs sometimes catch two of these shad at a time.

Once in a while someone nets a hickory-sized skipjack, but usually this species is smaller than the Alabama shad, averaging less than a pound. It looks like the Alabama variety but has a more compressed body, a very protrusive lower jaw, and a thick lid covering part of the eye. Adults of these small species usually retain weak teeth in the lower jaw, unlike the hickory or white, and they lack the black shoulder spots of the larger varieties. Fishermen often mistake a big skipjack for an Alabama shad, as it inhabits many of the same waterways—the Ohio, the Tennessee, and streams emptying into the Gulf from Texas to Florida. In coastal streams these species share the anadromous characteristics of the American and hickory, but some spend their lives in the big inland rivers.

FISH HABITAT & FEEDING BEHAVIOR—ANGLING TACTICS:
Until late summer, shad fry remain in streams, subsisting chiefly on plankton; then they head out to sea. Trawlers have netted them in sixty fathoms, more than a hundred miles from shore. White shad remain plankton eaters; hickories and the smaller species prey on baitfish and assorted invertebrates. The shad caught by

sportsmen are usually five to seven years old; they mature in salt water, most of the males returning to the rivers to spawn in their fifth year, the females in their sixth or seventh. In rivers south of Cape Hatteras, they almost invariably die after spawning. They stop feeding as soon as they enter fresh water, and if river temperatures are too high to slow their metabolism significantly, they soon burn up the fat reserves that would give them strength for a journey back to sea. But in some of the cooler northern rivers, at least a quarter of them may survive the downstream migration, regain their strength in the ocean, grow larger, and spawn again the next year. A few spawn a third and even a fourth time. The biggest trophies—white shad weighing 8 pounds or more—are these older fish, invariably caught in waters from Massachusetts to Maryland.

Most shad spawn in the streams where they hatched, locating home waters as salmon do, evidently by light intensity and the scent and taste of familiar chemical combinations. But a small number will enter any suitable river on their part of the coast. The hickories begin their runs a trifle earlier in the spring than the whites, and they spawn in shallower water. Both species travel up the Delaware and Susquehanna, for instance, but only the hickories turn off into the smaller feeder streams where fly casting assumes the classic style of brook fishing.

A roe shad typically carries about thirty thousand eggs, and

Hickory shad.

a big white may hold four times as many. One or more males will swim along with her to fertilize the eggs as they are broadcast. They sink quickly, adhere to almost anything they touch, and hatch in about six days. The process is fast, but shad fishing does not end quickly, for the early spawners are followed by larger and larger waves as the water temperature reaches about 60° to 67°.

Strangely, shad in the South bite well in bright sunlight, yet those in the North, especially the hickories, strike most actively on overcast days, in a light rain, early in the morning, or just before sunset. North or South, very clear or muddy water will curtail strikes; slightly turbid water is ideal. Promising spots include the waters below dams, falls, and other impediments to upstream progress. Lacking these, an angler can work the swift runs and the tails of deep pools with heavy current. In the evening he can go up to the heads of such pools.

Probably the most common fishing method is to troll with light spinning or baitcasting tackle, keeping close to the bottom with a small silver spinner or spoon such as a no. 00 Drone and tweaking the rod to snap the blade flashily. When casting to known or suspected gathering spots instead of trolling, an angler can impart more varied movement to the lure, but in swift streams many fishermen take shad simply by hanging a spinner or streamer in the current and occasionally twitching it. A West Coast meat-fishing method called "shad bumping" consists in moving a boat slowly downstream while holding a long-handled, rigid hoop-net in the water to intercept shad swimming upstream. A more respectable California technique is to drift a weighted fly on a dropper eighteen inches above a sinker that just clears bottom.

In some locales the shad may savage a particular type of lure most avidly, while in other locales a different offering is more productive. On the Delaware, small silver spoons are very popular, and a quarter-ounce wobbling spoon should work well anywhere. On stretches of the Susquehanna and other waters, a favorite is the shad dart, or "quill minnow"—a leadheaded descendant of the old Quilby Minnow. It is a small, weighted bucktail jig, often with a white body and red head. On many streams the shad, being unaware of the long tradition associated with that color combination, seem to strike impartially at white or yellow jigs of the same type. In Connecticut and parts of Pennsylvania, casting bicolored shad darts has attained the status of a traditional art. After casting into the current, an angler usually lets the jig swim around and hang there—"on the dangle"—before making his retrieve.

An efficient tool for this fishing is a 6- or 7-foot medium-action spinning rod or a shorter baitcasting rod with 6-pound mono-filament. (Some baitcasters switch to braided line testing as much as 12 pounds for working big, deep, swift rivers.) A wide landing net is recommended, because a weak-mouthed shad can break off if it bumps a gunnel or when a wading angler fumbles to get a grip on it.

Fly fishing can make the sport more difficult as well as more rewarding. Some southern rivers are too deep, and many streams, though negotiable with a fly rod, require long casts and a retrieve or a battle with a strong fish in strong current. A good rod for this work would be a bass-bugging stick with a fairly hefty action and a length of 8½ or 9 feet. On the upper Delaware, when flying ants are abundant or aquatic insects are hatching at dusk, dry flies sometimes bring shad to the surface to strike. Elsewhere, as a rule, wet flies and especially streamers are the flies of choice. Whether or not an angler is fortunate enough to fish a shallow stream with big, concentrated shad schools, he is well advised to cast up and across and let the fly swing down and around, bouncing along the gravel. For weight, copper wire is wrapped under the fly's body material, and a fast-sinking line is used with a fairly short, tapered leader.

Years of experimentation by shad-obsessed anglers have produced an array of bright, wet, weighted shad flies in red, white, silver, yellow, gold, even bright blue. They work, as do various bright salmon flies and steelhead flies that are used for shad. Probably more reliable in more locales, however, is a plain yellow-winged streamer, descendant of the old Enfield Shad Fly, or any deep-swimming, sparsely tied, dominantly yellow, white, or orange streamer with a tinsel-wrapped body, on a no. 2, 4, or 6 long-shanked hook for whites; 6, 8, or 10 for hickories. The veteran fisherman may not bother to invent flies just for shad since he can adapt such standard patterns as the White Miller, Royal Coachman, Parmachene Belle, White Maribou, Dark Edson Tiger, or the lesser-known Silver Yank, but he will take the trouble to thread several glass beads onto the tippet ahead of the fly. Red, orange, and yellow are the favorite bead colors, though some anglers also use blue and green, and others insist that the chief value of beads lies in their weight, not their color. Perhaps. But in clear water shad have been known to attack a hook adorned with bright beads alone.

Flashy visibility may well be the crucial quality of anything intended to trigger the strike reflex of migrating shad. In the usual high, roiled flow of spring, a white wing, a white jig, or a silver flash may be the only thing an angler can count on to distract a migrating shad as it struggles against the river's thrust.

Sturgeon *(Acipenseridae)*

COMMON & REGIONAL NAMES: Names in common usage identify each species—Atlantic, or common, sturgeon *(Acipenser oxyrhynchus);* green sturgeon *(A. medirostris);* lake sturgeon *(A. fulvescens);* pallid sturgeon *(Scaphirhyncus albus);* shortnose sturgeon *(A. brevirostrum);* shovelnose, or hackleback, sturgeon *(S. platorynchus);* white sturgeon *(A. transmontanus).*

GAME IDENTIFICATION & LOCATION OF FISHING REGIONS:
Big, grotesque, slow-moving except in battle, sturgeon look and act like relics of an early geologic age. Their family has changed little in the eons since its emergence. Found in oceans, rivers, and lakes throughout the Northern Hemisphere, there are four genera comprising sixteen species. The largest species is the European beluga, whose weight has been known to exceed a ton and whose jet-black roe is the world's finest caviar. North America has seven species, listed above. Their bizarre appearance is unappetizing to some people but they all furnish excellent caviar, and all but the green sturgeon are delicious either cooked or smoked. To an angler, their strength and stamina are equally interesting. Sometimes they leap in fierce resistance.

Unfortunately, they have been depleted by overfishing for the market and for private consumption. Their meat was in great demand for generations, and on rivers like the Snake a single catch could assure a family of protein-rich food for many months. Still more detrimental was the construction of dams that blocked the spawing runs. The sturgeon is a slow-growing fish with a life span comparable to man's, and it seldom attains sexual maturity before it is at least twelve years old. When the big ones have been

removed from a river or lake, decades pass before the population can replenish itself. Sturgeon fishing has therefore declined, and is governed by stringent local laws regarding sizes and seasons.

Like some other primitive fishes, all species have cartilaginous skeletons, and there are several other distinguishing features. They have a long, somewhat flattened snout with the mouth and four short barbels on the underside. All teeth are lost long before maturity. The thick-lipped, almost tubular, protractile mouth is built for sucking morsels off the bottom of the habitat.

The upper lobe on the large tail is longer than the lower lobe, as on paddlefish and sharks, and the single dorsal fin is set back over the anal fin. The body is long and rounded. There are no scales in the usual sense, but the head is covered with bony plates, and the body has five longitudinal ridges of scutes—raised, horny plates. Most species tend to be a dull, somewhat blotched brownish or grayish color.

The green sturgeon ranges from the Gulf of Alaska to northern California. River mouths, estuaries, and shallow coastal waters are its primary habitat. Though it will go a little way upstream to spawn, it is not strongly anadromous and is rarely found in fresh water. Its color is olive-green, with an olive stripe along its side above the row of lateral-line scutes, and a similar stripe along the pale belly. It can attain a length of 7 feet and a weight of more than 300 pounds, but most specimens are much smaller. Alone among the American sturgeons, it has dark, distasteful flesh.

Lake sturgeon.

The Atlantic sturgeon, which ranges from Maine to Florida and the Gulf of Mexico, is another anadromous but chiefly marine species, of more interest to commercial fishermen than to sportsmen. Other species of minor importance are the anadromous shortnose sturgeon of the East Coast; the pallid sturgeon, a freshwater species of the upper Mississippi drainage; and the shovelnose sturgeon of the Mississippi valley. At one time the shovelnose was avidly sought, despite the fact that it is the smallest American sturgeon, but diminished numbers have reduced its significance. Most worthy of notice are the lake sturgeon, a freshwater creature found chiefly in the Great Lakes region, and the anadromous white sturgeon of the Northwest.

The lake sturgeon has the tastiest meat. It is a typically grayish-brown species but easily identified. On its head, forward of the gills, it has a pair of spiracles—breathing vents containing a rudimentary gill. Its barbels are farther back, nearer the mouth, than those of its relatives; its rather pointed snout is almost conical, much less flattened than that of any other American species; and the narrow stem of its body, near the tail, is not completely covered by scutes as on other sturgeons. It has become rather scarce but is still encountered from Hudson Bay and the St. Lawrence through central Canada, Michigan, Wisconsin, Minnesota, Nebraska, and Missouri, and thence southeast to Alabama. It has all but vanished from the Mississippi River.

A lake sturgeon can attain a length of about 8 feet and a weight of about 300 pounds, but with most of the big ones either caught or dead of old age and the normal spawning runs blocked in some locales by dams, today's catches are likely to weigh between a couple of pounds and 60. In some areas it is illegal to keep a sturgeon over, rather than under, a stipulated size because the big ones are valuable spawners.

Much the same remarks apply to the white sturgeon, another excellent food fish whose harvest is now governed by stringent regulations. It is the largest fish of inland waters in North America. An 800-pounder would be a female—the female lives longer and grows larger than the male—and she might be carrying 50 pounds of roe, potential offspring or caviar. The record white caught by rod and reel weighed 360 pounds, measured 9 feet, 3 inches long, and was taken on the Snake River in 1956. The largest authenticated white, taken by gill net in the Columbia

River near Vancouver, weighed 1,285 pounds. She must have been very old, as a sturgeon more than 14 feet long has probably lived more than sixty years. A two-year-old may be 19 or 20 inches long, and a seven-year-old can measure 40 inches.

This species dwells along the Pacific Coast, from Alaska to Monterey Bay in California. Adult white sturgeon travel great distances up such rivers as Oregon's Columbia and California's Klamath, and on into Idaho's Snake and Payette rivers. In a few headwaters—on the upper Columbia, for example—they have become permanently landlocked. Locale and size would serve to identify these big, relatively pale sturgeon. Their species is also distinguished by a short, broad snout on which the barbels are located far forward.

FISH HABITAT & FEEDING BEHAVIOR—ANGLING TACTICS:
Some of the Pacific's white sturgeon begin their eastward spawning migration in winter, and reach the confluence of the Snake and Columbia before spring. Since they return downstream during the summer, they remain present along inland waterways in the upper West for a large portion of the fishing season. Most lake sturgeon head upstream to spawn from April to June, while some remain behind to spawn in lakes. Both varieties breed in the shallows over gravel. Too little has been learned of the life cycle, but it is known that there is no care of eggs or young. The adults disperse, leaving the fertilized eggs adhering to gravel and detritus. The young feed on minuscule plankton. As they grow to more than half a foot long, they begin to suck up much larger bottom-dwelling organisms—insect larvae, mollusks, shrimp, crawfish, and vegetable matter. Of all plant foods, the most heavily browsed is the algae known as river moss, a good bait when scraped from a stream's rocks, kneaded into a ball, dried, draped over a large, sharp hook, and rolled slowly along the bottom with a heavy sinker to keep it down. (This bait is also used for eastern sturgeon on such rivers as Florida's Apalachicola.)

Other recommended baits are meat scraps, lampreys, doughballs, and nightcrawlers. In both lakes and streams, sturgeon prefer fairly shallow waters, and a big gob of worms fished on a shallow bottom is a good choice. On rivers like the Snake and Columbia, cut bait is commonly stripped from suckers and other easily available small fish. Where set lines are legal, meat fishermen rig them with big, heavy hooks, but warm-weather sport fishing for sturgeon is done with hefty spinning or surf tackle. It is a popular diversion in the upper western rivers and on lakes in Ontario, Michigan, and Wisconsin. In the mid-1950's Ted Trueblood, a knowledgeable angling writer, experimented with tackle for Klamath River sturgeon. He found that he needed line testing at least 45 pounds. Fighting a big sturgeon is not a matter of hauling dead weight, as with trash fish. The tactics, however, are simple in the extreme: the bait is cast out and left on the bottom or moved along very slowly.

Lures are useless except in winter, and then they are of a novel kind, employed for spear-fishing through an ice hole in a darkened shanty. The lures are hookless fish decoys. Most are painted blocks of wood resembling plugs, but ears of corn are also lowered. The spearman sits for hours, hoping to see a big shadow ooze into view. Then he thrusts hard and fast with a large, roped harpoon whose weighted head helps to drive it home. Some spearmen are convinced that sturgeon have habitual feeding runways on each lake, and they locate their shanties accordingly. Harpooning is something of a tradition in Wisconsin's Lake Winnebago region and on Michigan's Lower Peninsula.

Conventional ice fishing, with baited line, can also harvest a sturgeon now and then. During the brief February season when Wisconsin permits sturgeon to be caught through the ice, an angler who has been bringing up pike, walleyes, and panfish may have a chance to manhandle something much weightier.

Sunfish *(Centrarchidae)*

COMMON & REGIONAL NAMES: *sunny, sun perch, panfish, bream.* (The name *bream,* or *brim,* a popular term for the bluegill, is used in parts of the South to denote other sunfish species or as a collective name for all sunfish. Some species are known by several additional names, which will be included in their descriptions.)

GAME IDENTIFICATION & LOCATION OF FISHING REGIONS: An inch-long Everglades pygmy, a 2-pound shellcracker, and a 20-pound largemouth bass are all true sunfish, members of a North American freshwater family comprising eleven genera and thirty species. Some are too small to be of direct interest to anglers, but

▲ Redbreast sunfish. ▼ Cane-poling the shallows for panfish.

▲ Casting fly for brown trout on Madison River. ▼ Arctic char.

▲ Fanwing Coachman floating on hackle.

◀ Brown trout. ▲ Netting Dolly Varden. ▼ Mouth of large brook trout.

Brace of fine rainbows. ▲ Brown trout rising to fly. ▼ Lake trout taken in shallows. ▶

▲ Head of walleye. ▼ Angler boating inconnu, or sheefish.

even the dwarf varieties are important either as desirable forage fish for larger game species or, where natural balances have been knocked askew by man, as undesirable competitors that can stunt or crowd out larger fish. Only a few varieties are sizable enough to have much sporting glamour, yet more sunfish are caught than any other freshwater group. Each of the three major sporting varieties—black bass, bluegill, and crappie—is treated separately in this book. Of the remaining species, those that have angling significance will be described here.

These Centrarchidae share several family characteristics. They are rather deep-bodied fish whose forward spiny and rear soft dorsal fins are joined as a single long fin. (The largemouth bass, with its deep notch between the forward and aft segments, is almost an exception.) Aside from one species, the Sacramento perch, all sunfish are native to regions east of the Rockies, but sunnies of one kind or another have been established in every state, for they are easy to stock and manage, and even among the smaller ones several are admired for their scrappiness in the water and delicately savory quality on the table. All of them spawn in spring or summer, generally when the water temperature is between 60° and 70° or so. All but the Sacramento perch and one pygmy species are nest-builders. Two of the pygmy sunnies build nests from bits of vegetation. Among all the remaining species, the males sweep saucerlike depressions in sand or gravel near shore. After fertilizing the eggs, they drive the females away and stand guard until the fry have hatched, have begun to absorb their yolk sacs, and can swim freely. Among the larger species such as bass, nests are spaced at fairly wide intervals and the males exhibit territorial behavior; some of the smaller species nest in dense colonies, an adaptation that probably offers collective defense. In either case, the high survival rate can cause crowding and stunting where predation of fingerlings is light.

Because of close physiological relationships and similar spawning habits, crossbreeding occurs, especially among species of a single genus. A bluegill, for example, may breed with a green sunfish, a pumpkinseed, or a longear. Yet each species maintains its identity because nearly all the hybrid progeny die without reproducing. Fisheries biologists have been able to use hybridization to control overpopulations of some species.

Some sunnies are particularly colorful and handsome, and

some exhibit foraging peculiarities that influence fishing tactics. To an angler, all the same, the primary differences among species are the differences in size. Almost any sunfish may delight a child with a willow pole, a length of string, a hook, and a can of worms. But an adult who wields a fly rod or a short, whippy spinning rod and gossamer-light monofilament is inclined to be more selective. On such tackle, most of the larger species have enough fight to pique an angler's interest. They hit baits and lures greedily.

Half a dozen marginal species are sometimes sought but more often added to a mixed bag while an angler is taking whatever comes his way or prospecting for more exciting quarry. One such is the longear *(Lepomis megalotis),* which is caught in clear, weedy ponds and streams throughout most of the East and Midwest, from the St. Lawrence watershed to Florida and from North Dakota to Texas. Northeastern longears are quite small, but once in a while in the lower Midwest or the South a 9-incher is caught and it may weigh over a half-pound.

It can be identified by its bright hues and the very long, flexible, reddish-edged black gill flap for which it is named. It has orange or yellowish fins, often with some green at the base of the dorsal. The upper part of the almost discoid body is greenish, speckled with yellow or blue. The lower part and belly are orange or yellow-orange. Some anglers would describe the head and cheeks as bluish-green with streaks of yellow-orange, while others would insist the base color is yellow-orange, the streaks bluish-green. It subsists principally on aquatic insects, crustaceans, and small fish, and since it does much of its feeding on the surface it provides quick diversion for the caster of dry flies and small popping bugs. A close southern relative, formerly thought to be a longear subspecies, is the dollar sunfish *(L. marginatus),* which rarely exceeds a length of 6 inches. It is olive with orange spots and blue-green streaks, and it has a shorter, light-edged gill flap.

Sometimes comparable in size but usually smaller is the mud sunfish *(Acantharchus pomotis)* of sluggish streams and ponds from lower New York to Florida. A relatively slim variety, it is dark green with five to eight dark, vague longitudinal bands. Another half-foot member of the clan is the spotted sunfish *(L. punctatus),* which ranges from South Carolina to Florida and along the Mississippi valley from lower Illinois to the Gulf. Like the warmouth—a sunfish caught in some of the same waters—it is regionally known as the stumpknocker, a reference to its habit of taking cover around shallow-water obstacles such as stumps and logs. Olive or olive-bronze with a brassy or orange belly, it is heavily stippled with black or brown. The subspecies of the Mississippi valley has longitudinal lines of red spots. Like the other small species, it takes small natural baits or artificials.

The rock bass *(Ambloplites rupestris)* is slightly more popular because it reaches a 9-inch, half-pound size with fair frequency, and once in a while a portly, foot-long specimen weighs a full pound. Its indigenous range blankets the East from Vermont to Manitoba and down to the Gulf, and it has been widely introduced elsewhere. Its name is indicative of habitat. Loose schools congregate amid boulders and jumbles of stones in the same lakes and streams where smallmouth bass and redbreast sunfish are often caught. A predator of crustaceans, insects and fish—as are most sunnies—it will take such baits as worms, grubs, crawfish, small minnows, and crickets. An angler on a big northern bass river or a southern trout stream will find that rock bass also hit flies, spinners, spoons, and small plugs. In some locales the species is called a rock sunfish, and in some its appearance has inspired the name redeye, goggle-eye, and black perch. Its color is dark olive, sometimes with a bronze tone and splashed with amorphous blotches of brown or brass. Dark basal spots on the scales form interrupted longitudinal streaks.

Quite similar but very limited in distribution is the Roanoke

Pumpkinseed sunny.

bass *(A. cavifrons),* which is found chiefly in Virginia's Roanoke River but also in North Carolina. It can be distinguished from a rock bass by the slightly concave profile of its head, its scaleless or almost scaleless cheeks, and the three spines of its anal fin—half as many as the rock bass has. It tends to grow a bit larger than the latter; 1-pounders are not uncommon, and there have been reports of fish weighing 4.

Another fish of the same size and general appearance as the rock bass is the warmouth *(L. gulosus).* It can tolerate muddy water and it prefers soft bottoms, weed beds, stumps, and snags. It, too, is sometimes called a stumpknocker, goggle-eye, or goggle-eye perch. Its color is mottled olive, brownish, or gray, and it has a big mouth and big eyes. It can be distinguished from the rock bass by small, pronounced spots on its dorsal fin, a patch of teeth on its tongue, and three rather than six spines in its anal fin. Its range is chiefly west and south of the Alleghenies, from Minnesota through the Great Lakes region into western Pennsylvania, and southward to Florida and the Gulf. It seeks the same prey that rock bass hunt, and takes the same baits and lures, but it fights no better, is not very tasty, feeds most actively in the early morning, and stops biting by afternoon.

Half a dozen other sunnies offer better sport and food or occupy an ecological niche that might otherwise be usurped by less desirable coarse fish. For example, the flier *(Centrarchus macropterus)* thrives in waters too acid for some of its relatives. It inhabits bayous, swamps, and lowland streams in the Mississippi valley from lower Illinois to Louisiana, and in the East from

Rock bass.

Virginia to Florida. Short-bodied, almost round, it seldom grows beyond 6 inches or so but is fairly scrappy on ultralight tackle. It can be identified by its anal fin, which is nearly as long as the dorsal fin, and by its coloration: greenish, with small dark spots on most of the scales, the lower ones forming longitudinal lines. A larger dark spot is located under the eye, and another marks the rear of the dorsal fin. An eater of assorted small organisms, it has a particular fondness for mosquito larvae. This fact alone might win the esteem of many sportsmen who ordinarily scorn sunnies. It will take worms, but there is more challenge in luring it with popping bugs and flies.

The green sunfish *(L. cyanellus)* grows a little larger—up to 8 or 9 inches. Also known as the green perch, sand bass, rubbertail, and blue-spotted sunfish, it is a stocky species, olive-green with a brass wash over the belly, blue-green spots on the cheeks, and blue glints on the sides. It has a dusky blotch on the rear of its anal and dorsal fins, and a black gill flap with pale, sometimes rosy edging. Originally its range extended from the Great Lakes region and the Mississippi valley westward to Colorado and New Mexico, but it has been widely transplanted. It can tolerate siltation that would prevent the establishment of many species, and it thrives in lakes, ponds, streams, rivers, and reservoirs. An angler can offer it worms, grubs, crickets, grasshoppers, spinners, or flies—both wet and dry.

An even more abundant, widespread, and popular species of the same size is the pumpkinseed *(L. gibbosus),* or "common sunfish." A denizen of lakes and ponds with soft, weedy bottoms, it is one of the colorful little opportunists that swarm about a small gob of worm dangled around weed patches, brush, fallen trees, docks, and floats. It has a rigid black gill flap with a red or orange tip and a light olive dorsal fin with dark spots. The pumpkinseed's name describes the shape of its light olive or green body, speckled with blue or darker green on the upper parts and with orange below. The forward part of the belly is generally a solid yellow or orange. The cheeks and gill covers are also orange but with bluish streaks radiating from the snout. It is found from North Dakota eastward into the Maritime Provinces, southward along the coast to Georgia, and through the upper Mississippi valley and tributary systems from western Pennsylvania to Iowa. Its principal foods are mollusks, insects, and fishes. It is caught through the ice on

worms, and it will also take grubs, but warm-weather angling for this species is more fun with lures—popping bugs, wet and dry flies, small spinners, or even small plugs. During the spring spawning season, yellow flies seem to be especially productive.

The redbreast *(L. auritus)* grows a little larger—sometimes nearly a foot long and weighing almost a pound. Regional names for it are yellowbelly, longear, sun perch, and redbreast bream. It can be caught in lakes, ponds, and reservoirs, but is most plentiful in the smallmouth rivers where rock bass also flourish. Its primary range is east of the Alleghenies, through the Atlantic drainage from New Brunswick to Florida. The redbreast is one of the more flamboyant species, with the dark olive of its back shading to yellowish on the lower sides and red-orange on the forward part of the belly. The red turns an even brighter crimson during the spring spawning season. The tail, too, is reddish or orange and often quite bright. On most specimens, faint, dark vertical bands run down the olive parts. The cheeks and gill covers have light bluish streaks mixed with orange, and there is a long, black, narrow gill flap. An adult redbreast will take a worm, grub, cricket, grasshopper, or small minnow. It will also take a variety of small spoons, spinners, spinner-flies, midget plugs, wet flies, and streamers. When feeding on the surface, as it often does, it will snatch a dry fly or a popping bug. Unlike most sunnies, it can be caught at night because it continues to forage after dark.

In many parts of the country the redear *(L. microlophus)* is better known as the shellcracker and is the most esteemed of

Warmouth, or goggle-eye.

sunfish. It is especially admired in states like Virginia, North Carolina, and Florida, where 1-pounders are common, 2-pounders are caught with fair regularity, and shellcrackers weighing more than 3 pounds are taken now and then—which may startle anglers who scoff at sunfish. The record redear, caught in Virginia in 1970, was over 16 inches long and weighed 4 pounds, 8 ounces.

This is one of the species also known as the stumpknocker; although it inhabits fairly large, still lakes and is bolder than the pumpkinseed in leaving the weeds to venture into open waters, it prefers the security of stumps, roots, and similar cover. It is also called the yellow bream. Its body varies from silvery bronze to bluish-green, with dark spots that sometimes form vague vertical bands. It looks rather like the pumpkinseed but with a dark, unspotted dorsal fin and without the bluish streaks about the head. Its red-tipped black gill flap is somewhat flexible, whereas the pumpkinseed's is rigid. Originally the redear was distributed from lower Illinois southward in a sprawling fan of territory to Florida and across the Gulf region into the Rio Grande drainage. It fares well in farm ponds without quickly overcrowding them, and is now stocked in a number of northern and western states. For sustenance it relies heavily on mollusks (snails are its favorite), which it crushes with a pair of rough-surfaced bones located in its throat —hence the name shellcracker. Although this fish sometimes takes a wet fly, plug, or spinner, it is not easily fooled by artificials. The best baits are angleworms, small minnows, freshwater shrimp, and catalpa worms or other grubs. The best fishing is at

Green sunfish.

the weedy spawning beds from April to June.

The Sacramento perch *(Archoplites interruptus)* is the largest of the group (excluding black bass) but it is also the only one that has declined in size and numbers. Weights approaching 10 pounds were reported in years gone by; today a catch weighing 3 pounds is rare. Unlike other sunfish, the Sacramento perch evolved where competition was light and there was no pressure to develop defensive behavior with regard to eggs and fry. A female emits her eggs in a gelatinous ribbon that clings to rocks, algae patches, and weeds. The adults then depart. Man has altered the ecosystem by introducing such eastern species as catfish and crappies, which prey on the abandoned eggs and emerging young. However, there is a basis for optimism concerning a resurgence of the Sacramento perch, the only far-western sunfish. Attempts are being made to study and manage the species in its native waters—the drainages of the Sacramento, San Joaquin, and Pajaro rivers—and stocks have been successfully transplanted from California to Nevada and Utah.

The species has a blackish back and somewhat mottled sides that blend a dominant blackish-brown color with a paler, almost white shade. Usually seven wide, irregular, soft-edged blackish bands run down the sides. This large sunny eats insects, fish, and crustaceans, as do most of its family, yet it ignores many baits. It rarely takes worms but responds well to live minnows. It also hits small spinners with satisfying regularity. For that matter, it will attack almost any lure retrieved slowly across its spawning

Redear sunfish, or shellcracker.

bed. When spawning, the Sacramento perch seems to grab lures not as it captures food but in an effort to clear the bed of alien creatures. Probably this is a vestige of the guarding instinct common to other sunfish. The result is excellent fishing in May and June, after which it deteriorates.

FISH HABITAT & FEEDING BEHAVIOR—ANGLING TACTICS: The Sacramento perch spawns around algae-covered rocks in water a foot or two deep. The shellcracker will nest on a sandy bottom as deep as four to six feet among weeds or in shoreline fringes of such grasses as maiden-cane, but in lakes supporting lush growths of spatterdock—common yellow water lilies—fishing the beds means fishing the pads. Spawning shellcrackers exude a musky odor, and some veteran anglers have a keen enough olfactory sense to detect it. Others look for air bubbles, floating debris, trembling weeds and pads, or the pale saucers of the nests. Another indication of spawning may be schools of minnows darting about in a hazardous effort to feast on eggs.

The spawning sites and habits of redbreasts and pumpkinseeds are much like those of the bluegill (which see). In fact, most sunnies spawn more or less like bluegills and can be caught in large numbers in the same kind of habitat at the same season. Sunnies are so prolific that fishing the beds amounts to a beneficial harvesting of the surplus. In parts of the South they breed several times a year.

After spawning ceases, the best sunfishing generally continues to be in waters no more than six feet deep, but some of the larger species often cruise about at more than twice that depth. The redbreast and others that inhabit streams are likely to be caught in pools, runs, and beneath undercut banks. Almost all sunnies like the shade of overhanging vegetation. Those known as stumpknockers hide around obstacles and brush; similarly, the primary haunts of the rock bass are indicated by its name. The remaining species tend to school in weeds or brush; around floats, docks, and shallow drop-offs; in coves and near shoreline points. Since shellcrackers root about for snails and usually ignore lures, the best redear tactic is to fish the bottom with bait. Redbreasts, on the other hand, frequently hit sizable bass plugs.

Generally speaking, the best sunfish baits are worms, small minnows, and freshwater shrimp on short-shank no. 6 or

8 hooks. Still-fishing, drifting, or wading is productive, and in shallow water a bait can simply be dangled under a bobber. However, it is usually best to reach at least midway down or nearer the bottom with a slip sinker or a couple of split shot. For sunnies feeding on top, fishing with lures is more effective as well as more satisfying than bait-fishing. Early in the evening, particularly when the water is mirror-flat and insects are abundant, small dry flies are sipped in with a little flurry by various sunnies.

Both spin fishermen and fly-rodders are understandably partial to small, long-shanked popping bugs, particularly those with "rubber-band" legs that flex tantalizingly with each twitch of the rod tip. Though yellow is a favorite color, all the bright hues work well and are easily visible for efficient handling when flicked into little openings or deep shade. Artificial grasshoppers and crickets are also tempting to sunnies, as are sponge-bodied, rubber-legged spiders. A spider lure is usually allowed to sink and then moved slowly—an effective method—but it can be transformed into a twitchable floater by searing the sponge to seal the outer cells. Among flies, an equally versatile lure is a fur-bodied nymph. It usually has the shank wrapped with lead wire for bottom-fishing, but some anglers tie a few as floaters and let the actions of the sunnies dictate their tactics. Wet flies take some sunfish, but more are caught with gaudy little streamers on size 8 or 10 hooks. Very small minnow-shaped plugs get frequent strikes, too. Subsurface models are worth trying, but in the shallows the surface types work best. They should be twitched gently, with the line kept taut for instant setting.

In deeper water, very small marabou-tailed or plastic twister-tailed jigs nicely mimic prey but, deep or shallow, nothing outperforms small spinners such as the Abu Reflex, Mepps, and Rooster-Tail. Silver blades draw fish in murky water or on overcast days, but as a rule gold is best. Some anglers prefer metal alone while others rely on spinners with buck or squirrel hair or a miniature strip of pork rind. A spinner blade should turn and flash at low speed because fast movement looks to sunfish more like a predator than prey.

A traditional southern sunfishing rig is a long cane "bream pole" with a short line tied to its tip. It can dap a bait or lure along bushy shorelines as an angler moves slowly past in a johnboat. But such equipment provides more satisfaction in reaching into

tight spots and presenting an offering gently than in the subsequent playing of the fish. Delicate spinning gear, on the other hand, magnifies the wrenching tremors. A casting bubble can aid in tossing very light, small lures, but it is seldom needed because casts can be short. The line has to test no more than 4 pounds, and the rod should be short, very light, and springy.

Probably most sporting of all is a light, fast-tipped fly rod, preferably no longer than 7½ feet, with a weight-forward line. With a short tippet, it can penetrate all the tight pockets. A 7X tippet will do nicely, since it need not test much over a pound. Bait-fishermen may claim that sunnies are too stupid or gluttonous to be frightened off by coarse tackle, but anglers who depend on lures often find these fish to be engagingly cautious.

Trout *(Salmo)* **& Char** *(Salvelinus)*

GENERAL DESCRIPTION & DISTRIBUTION: If an ichthyologist were bound by a vow never to wet another line until he had defined the trout and char genera in simple terms, he could stipulate (as he donned his waders) that these fishes are closely related, globally distributed, handsomely colored, sleek, swift, powerful, cold-water salmonids, some of them anadromous, some of them land-locked and nonmigratory. But he would be shamefully aware that such a generalization fails to convey the essential reality of the trouts and chars. It is a fisherman's reality, felt in the cold, clean, heavy thrust of current against the legs; smelled in the damp musk of hemlock and willow, moss and watercress; heard in the crunch of wet gravel, the gurgle of a small eddy, the hiss of white

Longear sunfish.

water; seen in the little bow wave created as an artic char swerves to overtake a Warden's Worry streamer, the sip and roll of a squaretail or a brown trout risen to the first buoyant Quill Gordon of the spring, the taut line thrumming into depths where a laker wallows, rolling tangled leader around its massive body, or the rose-and-silver pinwheel blur of a jumping rainbow trout.

The various trout and char species are much like their close relatives, the salmons, except that they do not grow quite as large, and they can spawn and live to spawn again. All have soft-rayed fins, a single dorsal fin, and a soft, fatty adipose fin located more or less above the anal fin. The lake trout has a deeply bifurcated tail but the caudal fins of most species are only slightly forked, and two species—the brown trout and the brookie, or squaretail—have virtually straight-edged tails. All of them are trim, elongate, powerful swimmers even when they are bulged with roe or fattened and paunched with a rich food supply. They average about four and a half to five and a half times as long as they are deep of body. As the males grow older and larger, they develop kyped jaws, and the coloration of both sexes generally intensifies at spawning time. Those that go to sea pale to the color of silver and pearl in the marine habitat but regain their reds and blacks and other markings soon after returning to fresh water.

Hatchery fish tend to be slightly less rich in hue than the wild ones but all display brilliant tints or streaks or speckling either throughout the life cycle or during some phase of it. The color of the flesh varies, too. That of hatchery-reared brook trout, for instance, is rendered considerably paler by artificial food than it is in the wild. And even among wild populations, the flesh of most species ranges from white to pink or brownish or even orange, depending on the primary foods and chemistry of the locale. Regardless of shade (and regardless of parochial preferences among epicures) it is always a delicacy.

Much has been written about "selective trout," because feeding preferences among some species are the crux of angling success. Such relevant preferences will be mentioned in connection with those species. Generally speaking, however, it is valid to state that the larger, older trouts and chars become predominantly piscivorous, even cannibalistic, yet retain a sufficient appetite for insects so that at certain times they will rise to a well-presented fly. All of them can be taken on baits at one time or

▲ Trout taken on wet flies, bucktails, and streamers. ▼ Fly-rodder on trout stream.

another, and on lures that mimic baitfish or insects. It is also a valid generalization that most of them leap when fighting the rod —some considerably more than others—and all are battlers.

Among the native species of sufficient abundance, size, and widespread distribution to claim angling importance, North America has three "true" trouts, as the taxonomists rank them: the cutthroat, the golden, and the rainbow. (Steelhead are automatically included, since they are anadromous rainbows.) All three were originally western—primarily either northwestern or alpine. However, the rainbow trout has been successfully established in the Great Lakes and other midwestern and northeastern waters, as well as in cold lakes, impoundments, and rivers surprisingly far south. A fourth true trout, the brown, was imported to the Northeast from Europe late in the nineteenth century and has since been established across most of the United States and Canada. Like the rainbow, it is a bit more adaptable to alien habitat than are most trouts and chars.

America's four other major species are not really trouts but chars—the arctic char, brook trout, Dolly Varden, and lake trout. Originally the brook trout and lake trout were eastern species (although the laker occurred in diminishing numbers across northern parts of the continent.) Both of these species have been successfully introduced to cold, clean waters from coast to coast. The Dolly Varden is a far-western species, known in some regions as the western char. The arctic char is circumpolar in distribution and can be caught in waters throughout the arctic and subarctic regions of North America. Thus, one or more species of trout or char can be found in every part of the continent.

Chars have smaller scales and rounder, less compressed bodies than true trouts, but the genera can be more readily distinguished by mouth structure. A trout's vomerine bone, centered in the roof of the mouth, has teeth all along it. A char's vomerine bone has only a few teeth at the front end. Both trouts and chars have maxillary teeth, better developed in some species than in others, and in all but subtle anatomical respects they are much alike. They are closely enough related so that species with similar spawning habits and times can interbreed, although the progeny of trout-char crosses are infertile whereas fertile hybrids may be produced by crossing species of the same genus. To an angler, the differences are largely academic. He cares little that a brook trout is, scientifically speaking, a brook char. There are steelhead cultists for whom neither the brookie nor any other char is worthy of the title trout. On the other hand, the eminent fly-fishing authority and writer Vince Marinaro has remarked that a typical square-tail aficionado would shrug off scientific distinctions and call it a true trout's misfortune not be be a char.

GENERAL LIFE CYCLE & ANGLING STRATEGIES: Human beings associate warmth with the production of foods, both animal and vegetable organisms. Warmth, however, is a relative concept. Some of the planet's most biologically productive ecosystems exist in the colder parts of the oceans and in northern and alpine lakes and streams. Given a hospitable chemistry, such waters support a rich growth of algae which, in turn, supports a varied population of planktonic and larger organisms. And this life, in turn, supports still larger creatures, including fish. Since trouts and chars require high oxygenation, they seek cool water, which holds more oxygen than warm water. They live in lakes as well as streams, but ideal habitat is in or near moving water—current, eddies, riffles, falls, obstructions, gradients, breeze-driven ripples, springs and seeps, tributary infusions, and so on—because moving water absorbs oxygen through interaction with the air. Even browns and rainbows, though less demanding than their relatives and able to thrive in slower, warmer water, need relatively cool, clear, unpolluted habitat. Brook trout cannot survive for long periods in water much warmer than 65°, and most of the other species cannot tolerate temperatures consistently much higher than 70°.

In addition to aerated water and adequate nutrients, a number of physical attributes mark a good trout stream. Because constant strong sunlight can raise the temperature, reduce the oxygen content, and even lower the water level, there should be at least intermittent shade. Deforestation and the erosion caused by poor farming practices and human habitation have ruined many fine streams. Occasional stretches of fast water are needed not only for aeration but to carry away silt. Clean, shallow gravel beds are needed for redds at spawning time. (Spawning habits of the brook trout will be described in detail under the species heading; those of most trouts and chars are roughly similar, with exceptions that will be noted in describing other species.) Deep pools and springs are needed for coolness, yet the likeliest trout lie is not situated in just any pool. The best are often those separated by riffles. In the riffles themselves are rocks and ledges that provide resting spots or feeding stations for trout as well as hiding and growing places for such creatures as caddisfly, mayfly, stonefly, and fishfly nymphs, and for crawfish, shrimp, scuds, other crustaceans, and small mollusks. Thus, some of a trout's food is carried to it by the current and some grows on the spot, where the trout spends much of its time. Aquatic vegetation also holds prey for trout; in watercress, for example, there are the flat, wide-bodied, segmented little crustaceans known as cress bugs.

Just outside of the strong current there are frequent logs, snags, and exposed roots that provide lairs, just as boulders do. And at stream bends there are gouged channels, toppled vegetation, stones, and undercut banks along the outside curve to provide concealment for trout and collecting pockets for their waterborne food. Yet a trout stream need not be a raging mountain torrent. The same features may be present—in miniature, yet large enough—along some quiet meadow streams and in lakes or ponds fed by springs or cool streams.

It was on relatively gentle streams—England's stately chalk streams—that modern fly-fishing techniques were first developed. Many American waters are very different, and there are American anglers who still handicap themselves by adhering too dutifully to the tenets of English trout fishing, which work admirably on some waters but not on others. A successful angler recognizes the kinds of holding water just described, and he also recognizes two fundamental stream types: the limestone, or chalk streams, and the freestone streams. Each makes its own rules.

On this continent, limestone streams are not necessarily gentle flows but they are generally less violent and at lower elevations than the freestone type, and they are the finest waters for brookies and most of the trouts. Limestone streams exist in parts of Canada and everywhere in the United States except large portions of New York and New England (where, nonetheless, trout fishing is very rewarding). Pennsylvania's Letort may well be the nation's most renowned limestone river, but the Au Sable on Michigan's Lower Peninsula is an equally typical example. The cutthroat and rainbow streams of Yellowstone Park are chalk-based. Such waters are numerous in many parts of the West. They are the "spring creeks" that feed or branch from or comprise portions of some of the best-known western rivers. A typical Idaho, Montana, or Wyoming stream may originate as a freestone creek high in the Rockies and become transformed into the limestone type as it meanders through lower elevations, just as Pennsylvania's famous Yellow Breeches Creek begins as a freestone stream and becomes a limestone stream as it cuts through the Cumberland Valley.

Some of the world's limestone is formed by chemical precipitation. For millions of years, much more has been provided by a constant rain of tiny calcareous shells to the floors of the seas. These shells are the exoskeletons of organisms chiefly belonging to the order Foraminifera (such as globigerina, biloculina, and related protozoans), so small that fifty thousand of them may be compacted into a cubic inch of limestone. The shells have formed a large part of the oceanic sediment, accumulating in vast layers, a process that still continues in all oceans (enhanced by coral deposition in the warmer ones) to provide the calcium carbonate of ordinary limestone as well as its crystalline form, marble. Most of the limestone-enriched inland waters originated some six hundred million years ago as the seas receded, land masses were elevated, and the sediments buried and compacted. Rain and spring water percolated down through the earth, eroding the lime, cutting fissures and channels in it, and eventually forming subterranean caverns and watercourses. These underground reservoirs and rivers are the sources of the limestone streams, most of which do not issue from true springs but from limestone faults or cracks at relatively low elevations.

The lime-rich water is insulated in the underground reservoirs, and its large volume further helps to negate heat fluctuations; it issues from the ground at consistent temperatures of about 47° to 56°. Below the headwaters, additional feeder cracks or springs also help to stabilize the stream's temperature. A limestone stream is cool enough to hold the oxygen trout need, yet warm enough near its source so that it may remain ice-free in winter. Now that habitations and lumbering operations have removed the shady forest canopy from the banks of many streams, such stabilization has become all the more important.

The stream's chemistry is as vital as its temperature. In water, the calcium carbonate of lime forms soluble carbonates and bicarbonates that work with other nutrients to stimulate plant growth, making the stream fertile. The resultant plants furnish cover and food for aquatic creatures. Through photosynthesis, the plants also release additional oxygen into the water—a process especially important in the quiet streams that are not aerated by violent movement. Some of the additional oxygen is used directly by fish and other animals. Some is used by bacteria in the decomposition of dead plants and animals—organic matter that adds further nutrients. Since sunlight is necessary for photosynthesis, deforestation actually benefits some limestone streams, although pollution can turn an advantage to calamity by adding or altering nutrients, quickening the natural processes, choking portions of the stream with excessive weed growth, and thus encouraging eutrophication. There are exceptions to the rule that limestone streams support the most trout or the most good-sized trout. (As a matter of fact, the biggest trophies are more likely to come from lakes that nurture hordes of preyfish.)

Limestone water is relatively alkaline, of course. It may have stretches whose steep topography resembles that of freestone streams, but it can be recognized by a comparative wealth of alkaline-loving plant life: watercress, muskgrasses, pondweed, waterweed, duckweed, and the like. A stream that supports those plants is likely to be fine trout water. But it is also water where the fish are so well fed that they are harder to entice with artificial flies than are the hungrier denizens of freestone streams.

A freestone stream generally has its headwaters at a high elevation, where water is provided by melting snow, ice fields, and springs. It is more dependent on rainfall than is a limestone stream, and its volume, flow, and temperatures are less stable. In its course down steep gradients it is more susceptible to flooding, erosion, the choking effect of debris, the scouring away of life, suffocating bottom ice, suffocating heat, drought, and pockets of stagnation. Deforestation has been much more damaging to such streams than to the limestone type since the maintenance of fairly stable temperatures and volume depends more heavily on a spongy forest floor and a shady canopy.

Such water is also rendered less fertile because it is acid rather than alkaline. It consists primarily of surface water flowing over granite, sandstone, quartz, and other volcanic rocks—a source and bed having no enriching cargo of lime but carrying

the burden of humic or tannic acid leached out of surrounding land by rain. There are freestone streams that cannot yield ten pounds of fish food per acre, whereas some limestone streams contain five thousand pounds per acre. A trout in an impoverished freestone stream may never reach a length of more than 6 inches or so, yet it might gain that much length per year in a rich limestone stream. Some authorities (Vince Marinaro, for one) are convinced that many sterile waters can be made viable by adding crushed limestone and organic fertilizers at appropriate places and by retarding the flow over steep gradients in order to form plant-holding silt beds. Anglers and fishery experts have long practiced stream improvement—building Hewitt ramp-dams (where damming will not warm the water intolerably), installing rock and log cribbing on the strong side of a current flow to make the water scour deep undercuts and pools, riprapping sandy banks and planting willows to halt erosion and excessive siltation.

It would be wrong to imply that an unimproved freestone stream is not worth fishing. Many small ones are nearly barren,

Early-season fishing for squaretails.

but a large freestone river accumulates nutrients from fallen leaves and trees and other organic debris, thereby providing the algae and plankton to establish a healthy food chain along stretches that are not scoured barren by flooding. Brook trout prosper in the acid water of some New England streams that are stable and well oxygenated. They grow slowly but eventually become fairly large. Where there are fewer of them (apart from newly stocked brookies which, being unwary, are removed by anglers in large numbers soon after the hatchery truck deposits them) competition is relatively light. Fishing for small and medium trout in a peaty northern stream can be exciting; insect life there may be meager enough to keep the fish hungry and unselective.

This kind of water often calls for a slight change from classic angling strategy. On a limestone stream, a fly-rodder usually selects his flies on the basis of matching the color and size of a current hatch or the currently most plentiful insects. Because the water is usually clear (not roiled by upstream torrents) he favors small flies whenever possible and a very fine leader. Often he casts to an individual fish, watching it rise to sip insects from the surface, working to achieve a skill in timing and placement that will drift his presentation before the trout as it rises to find another insect. In roiled water, an ultrafine leader is less important and a fly need not be so precise an imitation of natural prey; it can be both larger and more impressionistic. But a freestone river can render its presentation harder rather than easier, because a degree of realism is still needed and an angler must learn to cope with fast, changeable currents.

PREFERRED FOODS & IMITATIVE LURES: Clear, low, relatively smooth water occurs even on portions of torrential freestone streams. Such stretches often provide hatches of insects—and trout to eat them. Many fly-rodders therefore become avid and accomplished entomologists who know which hatches to expect at a given time of year on their home waters, who observe or catch samplings to confirm or correct their expectations, and who tie or buy close imitations of whatever the trout are eating. Aquatic insects—a staple of most trout in most regions—appear in a rough, slightly variable, overlapping succession of genera and species. Some have lived underwater as nymphs—larvae—for several months, some for a year, some for several years. Certain types, such as midges and caddisflies, then pupate. (Most types of caddis larvae build a protective casing of cemented sticks, pebbles, or sand, and pupate within this odd cocoon.) Some aquatic insects, such as stoneflies and mayflies, metamorphose into adults without undergoing the pupal, or resting, stage. Most of them have truly ephemeral life spans in the adult stage. Their digestive organs have atrophied or disappeared, for they will not survive long enough to require food. They emerge from the water and take wing only to reproduce. Most shed their nymphal cases at the surface, though the Quill Gordon mayfly *(Epeorus pleuralis)* leaves its case underwater and rises as a winged adult, while the majority of stoneflies and at least one early-season caddis creep onto exposed rocks or logs to hatch. As a rule, the adults bob and drift on the surface for a few moments before they can open their wings fully and fly off. It is an opportunity for trout to gobble countless numbers, but countless more escape to reproduce.

Alone among these insects, mayflies undergo a sub-imago, or dun, stage during which they fly awkwardly. For about a day they rest and hide like most other aquatic insects beneath the leaves of trees. Then they shed a very thin outer membrane to reveal brighter coloring and more crystalline wings. Their shape is also changed slightly at this imago, or spinner, stage; they are slimmer, more graceful, with longer tails and legs. Now they fly very well, as do the imagoes of the other orders of aquatic insects, and they return to the stream to execute the aerial dance of their mating flight. Afterward they drop to the water, dying, their wings spread limply. This final stage is known to fly-tiers and anglers as the spentwing. Most females drop their eggs into the water and then fall to the surface, dead or dying, as the males have done. The females of a few mayfly species dive beneath the surface to deposit their eggs; some are devoured by trout even before they bob to the surface again. Various artificial-fly patterns imitate each stage of insect life: nymph, dun, spinner, and spentwing.

When no hatches are in progress and few flying insects are seen near or over the water, an angler may choose to use nymph patterns—or wets, bucktails, or streamers. Generally speaking, the wets mimic dead, current-carried insects while the bucktails and streamers are longer, fuller wets that mimic small fish. Bucktails and streamers are particularly attractive to trophy-sized trout, whose appetites are more piscivorous than insectivorous, and to the various kinds of sea-run trout that have returned to the streams to spawn. There are other wet flies such as the Fresh Water Shrimp—a popular choice on some western streams—tied to mimic small crustaceans. In midsummer, small flies tied to mimic mosquitolike craneflies and related midges also lure trout, as do Bivisibles and other flies imitating terrestrial insects that have fallen to the water. Leonard M. Wright, an erudite and sometimes iconoclastic angling writer, has remarked that an examination of a trout's stomach contents on a midsummer afternoon will usually reveal the bulk to be composed of ants, wasps, bees, craneflies, beetles, and houseflies. Only a few caddisflies, stoneflies, or mayflies are likely to be mixed in—sometimes none at all. But when a hatch is in progress, an angler will choose dun or spinner patterns, depending on what is hatching. And during a spinner fall, though he might begin with raised-wing patterns, he will probably rely on spentwings.

Generally speaking, in April and May most hatches occur after the day has warmed up—between two and five P.M.—and spinner falls take place slightly later in the afternoon. There are a few morning hatches, as well. Beginning in June, more hatches and spinner falls occur at dusk or later, and spinners assume their greatest importance at dusk. Hatches are less common during summer, but they do continue. In September both hatches and spinner falls occur most often in late afternoon.

Where streams do not freeze over, a few insect species, apparently impervious to cold, hatch in late winter. However, the heavy succession of emergence begins in April, or later in northern regions and at high elevations. Among the earliest mayfly hatches are those of the Hendrickson *(Ephemerella subvaria),* which emerges before the opening day of trout season on some Appalachian streams, or later in April in parts of Michigan and Wisconsin and on the Catskill streams made famous by Theodore Gordon. In the Catskills, it is preceded by the Quill Gordon *(Epeorus pleuralis),* earliest of the larger mayflies. Various shadflies of the genus *Brachycentrus* also appear in abundance then, but in June on the lower Beaverkill and many other streams the blue sedges—caddisflies of the genus *Psilotreta*—overshadow the brown Quill Gordon as well as the shadflies and any other mayfly. In the Midwest, around the Great Lakes, and on streams like the Ausable in the northern Adirondacks, mayflies such as the Light

Angler casting for rainbow trout.

Cahill *(Stenonema ithaca* and *S. canadense)* are among the last to emerge. A rainbow trout might be caught on a Light Cahill artificial in August or September.

Many books have been devoted to an enumeration of hatches and imitations. Standard references include, among others, J. Edson Leonard's *Flies,* Preston Jennings' *A Book of Trout Flies,* Art Flick's *New Streamside Guide,* and Ernest Schwiebert's *Matching the Hatch.* It is impossible (and needless) to duplicate these enumerations here, and not even the best manuals cover all the species on this continent—probably about a thousand mayflies, almost as many varieties of caddis, and a sizable number of stoneflies.

Most books have emphasized the mayflies, partly because large populations of some species are sprinkled over the continent, partly because some have a distinctive appearance that

lends itself to fly-tying, partly because trout eat them as avidly as any other aquatic insect, and partly because America's pioneering fly-tiers and angling writers were strongly influenced by their predecessors in England, where mayflies have always been an abundant trout food on the chalk streams. Mayflies are important here, too, particularly on limestone streams, but there are times when stonefly or caddis hatches predominate. Moreover, mayflies are less tolerant of pollution or environmental alteration than other orders, particularly the hardy caddis. Eutrophication or other damage will often cause a preponderance of caddisflies.

For these reasons, an angler cannot simply rely on a few of the best-known floating imitations of mayflies (or any other aquatic insects) for all waters. He can do fairly well by carrying an assortment of famous patterns—mentioned frequently in this book and in most fishing publications. He can do better by studying the waters where he fishes and matching the insect life he finds there. Wherever he goes, he can tie his own or buy locally tied patterns, and he can also have with him a basic selection that will serve in most locales. His rule of thumb in collecting them is that more than 90 percent of American stream insects can be imitated by patterns in three color categories: dun, or salty bluegray; cream; and the brown-and-grizzly mixture exemplified by the Adams. As to sizes, he ought to have all of these color categories on hooks ranging at least from no. 10 to no. 18. And as to shape, he needs only two varieties—the raised-wing mayfly profile and the low-winged caddis silhouette. In nature, the mayfly has upright wings, while the caddis folds its wings down, like a tent, and the stonefly keeps its wings flat—horizontal. The profiles of the caddis and the stonefly are so similar that a tie simulating one can simulate the other.

Traditional, delicately tied dry flies, though excellent at appropriate times on appropriate waters, probably receive disproportionate publicity in angling literature. Significantly, they fared poorly in a symposium conducted by *Outdoor Life* magazine, whose editors asked each of ten outstanding trout anglers to name his favorite fly—the pattern he would choose if he were limited to just one. There were five easterners and five westerners among the respondents, and they included nationally known guides, angling writers, and fly-tiers. The western choices included the Troth Bullhead, a long, bulky streamer imitating a sculpin; the Royal Wulff, a big, fluffy, high-floating dry, tied full in imitation of nothing in particular except perhaps the more traditional if less durable Fanwing Coachman; the basic deerhair Muddler, another sculpin type; the Coachman Trude, or Western Coachman; and the Bitch Creek Nymph, a variation on the stonefly-larva theme of the Montana Nymph, modified by tying on a rubber-band tail and antennae. The eastern choices were the Brown Stonefly Nymph; the Letort Cricket (with its overwing intact or trimmed to mimic a black caddis instead of a terrestrial); the Slate-Tan No-Hackle, which roughly resembles about half of all the hatching mayflies of importance on eastern and midwestern streams; the Olive Matuka, a stickleback-minnow pattern; and the Cress Bug, which imitates the natural cress bug, or water sow bug (*Asellus communis*), a small, flat-bodied isopod crustacean that is very fond of the watercress and elodea, or common waterweed (*Philotria canadensis*), in limestone streams—an excellent choice where trout have withdrawn, under angling pressure, to feed on the bottom or under cover. Since seventeen related isopods are scattered about the continent, the Cress Bug should take western as well as eastern trout.

Western flies tend to be vaguer in their mimicry and larger than eastern patterns, especially on big, roiled waters. In addition to those previously mentioned, popular ones include the Bird's Stonefly, Elk-Hair Caddis, Little Brown Caddis, Fluttering Caddis, a number of other sepia sedge patterns, and the Bucktail Caddis. Its name notwithstanding, the Bucktail Caddis does not imitate a caddis as closely as it does the big stoneflies on rivers like the Yellowstone and Madison. Reasonable impressions of assorted low-winged naturals are also rendered by hair-winged patterns like the Mormon Girl and Rio Grande King, and by a number of "all-purpose" flies like the Irresistible, Goofus Bug, Humpie, and several Wulffs. Variations on some of these can also pass for mayflies, which are represented by most of the traditional eastern and midwestern patterns.

The no-hackle patterns float best if simply drifted. Some caddis imitations can be given twitches during the drift to mimic the tiny upstream lurch of a caddis preparing to take off or expiring after reproduction. Most other dry flies are cast across and slightly upstream and simply allowed to drift down. This, obviously, is a realistic method with a spentwing pattern or a terrestrial as well as with mayflies. When a fish is seen, a very effective alternative is to cast quickly to the rise. Another alternative (and a relief to those who are not adept at casting flies) is to stalk from the bank and lightly drop a fly to a known or suspected lie; this is the venerable technique of dapping.

Wet flies and streamers can be drifted, or they can be given swimming retrieves. Nymphs, too, can be drifted; generally they are cast slightly upstream, but when trout are gorging near the surface a nymph sometimes can be presented more effectively by casting across and down. Often a strike is triggered by making a nymph rise like an emerging insect as it passes a trout.

There are streams, and sections of streams, where only fly fishing is permitted, and there are waters where barbless hooks are common because all trout must be released. When skillfully chosen and presented, flies can be as deadly as any other lure, and sometimes more deadly than bait. But because many casual anglers do not acquire the requisite skill, fly-fishing rules can be used as a conservation measure to perpetuate quality fishing on some streams where anything but a fly rod somehow strikes the addict as a sacrilege. However, spinning gear and even trolling rods are more common for certain types of trout and char fishing, and recommended methods will be covered under individual species headings. More relevant at this point are some generalizations regarding various methods at various times.

Early in April, when the season is new, the water is usually high and in some regions still icy. The trout are sluggish—almost winter-torpid—and are generally caught by fishing deep. Yet those in ponds (especially brook trout) stay surprisingly near the surface during the first week or so, and an angler may have his choice of fishing tactics. Nightcrawlers always tempt trouts and chars. Appropriate lures include small spinners, spoons, spinners enhanced by a dab of worm or a feather or hair tail, bright jigs, and weighted wets and streamers. In some waters insects are scarce and the trout seem too sluggish to take much interest in realistic minnow imitations, but they may take traditional attractor patterns—bright flies like the Parmachene Belle, Reuben Wood, and Scarlet Ibis. Dark Spruce Flies also seem to work well at this time, as do Spuddler and yellow Maribou Muddler streamers. An angler who does not use a fly rod can cast a streamer or wet fly with a spinning rod. This works best if a small transparent bobber—a "casting bubble"—is attached to the end of the line, with the fly 2 feet behind on a 6-inch dropper.

Small sinking plugs such as the Countdown Rapalas and Rebels take early season trout, and among the spinners and spoons some effective choices are the Mepps Comets and Aglias, the C. P. Swings, Rooster Tails, and gold-finished Fighting Fish. They take many trout in the riffles at midday. Where worms are used, they should be fished near bottom and near the banks. A single salmon egg on a small egg-holder hook also takes some trout, especially rainbow (which will also attack a morsel of orange cheese). In regions where the law permits the use of live nymphs, they seem to be most effective on rising rivers. Small minnows can be cast, drifted, or trolled. Sometimes they seem to be most effective if hooked near the tail to permit free swimming, or threaded on with the hook protruding from the vent and the leader going through the mouth.

Regardless of region, stream fishing seems to be improved by a west wind. In lakes, good spots to prospect are sloping shorelines and points where trees or rocks have fallen into the water. When the season is a few weeks old, artificials such as Woolly Worms and Stonefly Nymphs are productive, especially with a dropper and split shot, in eddies, gentle whirlpools, the edges of slackwater, riffles, shoals, heads and tails of pools, and the depths of pools below falls. If these and similar artificials fail to bring strikes, brighter lures can be be flicked or drifted over the bottom. Strikes will not be violent; the rod tip should be raised at the mere suggestion of a hit. Once a fish is on, an angler may want to lower his rod and give a little slack to a jumper that seems likely to pull the hook out or break off.

Toward the end of April, sombèr wet flies sometimes enthrall trout. A size 12 March Brown, Quill Gordon, or Gold-Ribbed Hare's Ear—or a dropper combination of such patterns—may catch fish. It is a good time to cast a point fly and two droppers across and down, jiggling them gently as they swing around in the current. Baits, spinners, and spoons continue to take fish now, as they do throughout the season.

In May and June the dry flies gain ascendancy, beginning with drab ones because the early-hatching mayflies and many other aquatics are drab. The brownish-gray Adams, tannish-buff Light Cahill, and blue-gray Quill Gordon are prime examples, generally in sizes ranging from 10 to 18, depending on the water and the trout it holds. As the season progresses, an angler should begin experimenting with paler buff and cream dry flies, and switch to smaller sizes and a finer tippet if fortune eludes him. Summertime selections depend on the hatches and spinner falls, of course, but summer also calls for large wet flies. A no. 6 is not at all too large to be snapped up by a brown trout.

Arctic Char *(Salvelinus alpinus)*

COMMON & REGIONAL NAMES: *charr, arctic charr.* (The name *silver char* is used to describe the sea-run fish, fresh from the ocean; the name *red char* applies only to landlocked populations or those that have been in fresh water long enough to darken. In a few far-northern regions, char are sometimes called *ilkalupik,* the Eskimo name for the species.)

GAME IDENTIFICATION & LOCATION OF FISHING REGIONS:
Near Goose Bay, in Labrador, an angler detaches the treble hook from a small red-centered spinner and replaces it with a no. 6 single hook. He casts into a deep, slick glide a little distance below a waterfall and begins a slow, deep retrieve, nodding and wagging the rod and stripping line to make the spinner weave and swim. Suddenly a strike yanks his rod tip forward and down. Before he can yank back to make sure the hook is set, line is whirring from his reel. The fish runs less than 35 yards, but so fast that it seems more of a dart than a run. It leaps, runs again, leaps, and plummets to the bottom. After a few more leaps and dives, it seems to be subdued, but the angler knows better than to hand-tail it from the water; the fish struggles with renewed vigor as the net is slipped under it. The catch is a 4-pound silver-bright arctic char with a few pale, indistinct spots on its sides, a light green wash along its back, and a slight coppery cast on its fins.

On a river where Alaska and the Yukon meet, a fly fisherman casts a streamer of his own devising—a silver-ribbed orange chenille body wrapped on a long-shanked no. 4 hook, winged with a crest of pink-and-red bucktail over gray squirrel hair. He has pinched a lead shot onto the tippet right ahead of the fly, so that he can work it over the gravel three feet beneath the surface of a riffle, upstream from a white, foamy chute. A 2-pound char sights the fly and stalks it, swerving methodically after the streamer the way a Dolly Varden will, raising a curved swell in the rumpled surface. The fish follows for almost ten yards without taking. The angler hesitates, wondering if he might as well lift the streamer, when he is saved from decision by a snatch and run. Despite the shallow water, this fish jumps less than the silvery 4-pounder, yet it seems to fight at least as hard. It fights as a grilse does, with sudden thrusts, swift dashes, the power and stamina of the hardy salmonids. Finally the angler beaches it, wets his hands to prevent abrading the char's delicate skin, gently removes the hook, holds the fish in the water, and moves it from side to side or back and forth to encourage gill action. With a satisfied grunt he watches as his catch flicks its tail and swims away. It is a pink-spotted scarlet fish with an almost blackish head and tail and a lateral darkening like a shadow. The only traces of silver are glints on the cheek, yet it, too, is an arctic char.

In conformation the species looks like a big, well-fed brook trout, trim and elongate but moderately deep-bodied when it has been feasting in prey-rich waters. The tail has a very slight fork or inward curve, almost but not quite as straight as a brookie's. As with most chars and trouts, coloration varies considerably, and there are a few waters where the arctic char and brook trout live together and look much alike. Neither the slightly concave tail nor the slightly rounder body of the arctic char will readily differentiate it from the brookie, but the markings will. Unlike the brook trout, an arctic char has no streaks or dots on its tail or dorsal fin, no blue-rimmed red spots, no wormwood pattern of vermiculations on its back. Like the lake trout, this char has well-developed teeth on its tongue; and like the brook trout, it often has carmine anal, pelvic, and pectoral fins with pale leading edges. As with other salmonids, old males develop hooked jaws.

A landlocked specimen or one that is simply nonmigratory usually has an olive-green back, sometimes bluish, sometimes brownish, and its sides vary from orange to rose or brilliant carmine. Its spots—usually pink, sometimes orange or creamy—are fairly large but less distinct and numerous than those of its relatives. An occasional char, especially an anadromous one fresh from the sea, may be unspotted. A sea-run fish is almost entirely silver when it first enters fresh water, and it is then commonly called a silver char. As it makes its way upstream toward spawning areas, it gradually darkens and turns as red as the nonmigratory variety. Anglers call such fish red char.

Some of the nonmigratory forms are dwarfed, but a typical adult weighs from 1 to 3 pounds. Those that mature in salt water grow large on a diet of fish and crustaceans. It would be difficult and probably misleading to speak of an average size; an angler can generally expect catches running from 2 to 10 pounds. A char weighing more than 30 pounds was taken at Quebec's Finger Lakes, but the official record is 29 pounds, 11 ounces, and it has stood since 1968. It was set by Jeanne P. Branson on the Arctic River in the Northwest Territories in the month of August—a very good time for catching large sea-run char in the rivers.

The species has a circumpolar distribution through the arctic and subarctic latitudes. Both sea-run and landlocked populations occur in Alaska, northern Canada, Baffin Island, Greenland, Iceland, northern Europe, and Siberia. Landlocked char are also caught in the British Isles, central Europe, and Russia. In Alaska, the range overlaps that of the closely related Dolly Varden (which see) and in cohabited waters the two species can be hard to tell apart. However, the arctic char's spots are larger than the iris of its eye; the Dolly Varden's are smaller. Probably the two chars were evolved from ancestral stock split by the formation of the Bering Land Bridge. Those in the Arctic Ocean became arctic char while the Pacific population developed into Dolly Vardens.

The char fishing is good in Alaska and across upper Canada from the Yukon to Labrador. Anyone planning a trip for silver char should first ask the fishing-camp operator or fish and game department about the local timing of the run, because big fish may be plentiful near the river mouths for only a couple of weeks. Farther upriver, the run becomes more leisurely, and the fishing for red char may be good from summer to early fall in and near lakes, below falls that impede migration, and at the mouths of tributary streams where the char tend to assemble. Quebec, like parts of western Canada, has excellent August runs; among the best waters are the George River and the Finger River and Finger Lakes in the Ungava region. Nonmigratory char, like the sea-run populations, can be found in lakes and in lakelike widenings of rivers, but they generally stay deep and they seldom measure more than 15 inches long or weigh more than a pound or two.

There are several additional, isolated forms of arctic char. The blueback trout, formerly classified as *S. oquassa,* is now con-

sidered to be a landlocked strain of arctic char. Once abundant in Maine's Rangeley Lakes, it has been extinct there since the early years of this century and is now found in only a few Maine ponds. Whereas most arctic char are natural associates of brook trout, the blueback seldom strays into water shallower than the upper part of the hypolimnion—the cold bottom layer of thermally stratified water—and it feeds chiefly on plankton. Its back and the upper parts of its sides are bluish-lilac, marked with a few vague white spots. It has a white belly, forked tail, and scarlet lower fins. It can be caught on small spoons or natural baits jigged deeply with light spinning tackle, but it seldom exceeds 12 inches. Moreover, it is scarce and efforts are being made to preserve it.

Another isolated strain of similar size is the Quebec red trout formerly classified as *S. marstoni* and sometimes called the Marston trout. It is a slender fish with a more deeply forked tail than that of typical char. The male's belly turns crimson at spawning time. It inhabits a few Quebec lakes and the streams feeding

Spin-fisherman playing arctic char.

them, can be caught in shallower water than the haunts of the blueback, and sometimes jumps like a rainbow trout.

The Sunapee, or Sunapee golden, trout is classified by some taxonomists as *S. aureolis* and by others as just another race of *S. alpinus*, arctic char. Named for New Hampshire's Sunapee Lake, it is found only in a few deep, cold lakes in that state, Vermont, and Maine. It has a grayish back, white spots, and a yellowish tinge along the underparts. As with the Quebec race, spawning males acquire a reddish stain on the belly. This race or species spawns in the shallows during October and November, evidently winters in shallow water, and remains near shore for a brief springtime period. It prefers a water temperature of 50° or less, however, and as the weather warms it goes to depths of sixty to one hundred feet. It readily hybridizes with lake trout or brook trout (though brook trout usually spawn in the feeder streams). Floods Pond in Maine has the only remaining population that is definitely pure. There are just two ways to catch a Sunapee: either by deep trolling as for lake trout or by handlining with cut bait or live smelt in deep water. Foot-long Sunapees are legal keepers in New Hampshire, but few of them grow even that big. One additional closely related char, the aurora trout *(S. timagamiensis),* is found in a few lakes in northeastern Ontario. It looks like a brook trout but without red spots or vermiculations, and its habits evidently resemble those of the Sunapee.

Good-sized male char.

FISH HABITAT & FEEDING BEHAVIOR—ANGLING TACTICS:
The arctic char worthy of a fishing trip are the migratory populations. After the ice breaks up they begin to head downstream, going to sea in late spring and coming back in summer or early fall. A char lives in fresh water and remains small until it is five to seven years old. Good char rivers are almost invariably characterized by deep, wide sections—living space for the young fish and for those returned from the sea. Some live for more than two decades, but they attain most of their growth during the first few seasons in the ocean. In midsummer they can be found in bays, feeding heavily, yet once they have started upriver their stomachs are usually as empty as those of salmon in spawning streams. Most trouts and chars continue to eat until almost ready to spawn, and it may be that the arctic char does, too—altering its diet and temporarily subsisting on tiny, quickly digested organisms. The schools winter inland, more than a hundred miles from the coast in some rivers, and fatten themselves again after spawning.

Little is known of their breeding habits, and some observations are puzzling or contradictory. For example, Eskimos have reported finding full quantities of roe and milt in silver char—fish that are thought to be unripe. They spawn in cold streams over gravel, or over lake shoals and reefs, from late September or early October into December. Often they do so under a covering of ice.

By spawning time the good fishing is over. The time to be on hand is in the summer, when they are seen jumping and rolling with the incoming tide, or a little later, when big schools may be found far upriver. Because the fish travel and rest in groups, a mile of water may be full of char while the stretches immediately above and below are empty. Sometimes a bit of prospecting is needed to locate a large school of large fish. Often such a group is comprised of one age class, one size. This kind of angling is for hardy souls who shrug away the hikes over rocky, muddy terrain, in cold, wind, and rain, to fish swift, heavily bouldered water. On some of the big rivers, guides run freight canoes for trolling, but wading is sometimes a necessity.

Seagoing char feed on sand eels, sculpin, young cod, crustaceans, and capelin (a northern variety of smelt). Nonmigratory char feed on small fish, crustaceans, and insects. In the tidewaters and for a little distance upstream, the anadromous schools also take a few insects. There are Icelandic rivers where they rise to dry flies that match local hatches of grayish caddisflies, but neither dries nor conventional wets account for many Canadian char. Though sometimes they will snatch one that mimics a small shrimp, more often they succumb to spoons, spinners, and bright streamers that either resemble minnows or are nonobjective works of fantasy. Among the standard streamers are the Pink Lady, Warden's Worry, Red-and-White Bucktail, Supervisor, Nine Three, Light Edson Tiger, and Gray Ghost. Some anglers prefer the bright European wet patterns developed for sea-run browns and embellished with gold or silver tinsel—flies like the Teal-and-Yellow, Bloody Butcher, Teal-and-Green, Demon, Railbird, and Carson. And still others concoct original designs, emphasizing pink, orange, or red. (For unknown reasons, yellow arouses few char.) Most of these flies are tied on no. 4 or 6 hooks, weighted, and fished on a 7-foot leader with a sinking line or shooting head.

Whether or not char continue to feed as they go upstream, they behave like famished carnivores in the tidewaters and lower reaches of a stream, where they are surprisingly easy to catch with spawn bags (though they seem only mildly interested in other baits) and on spinners, wobbling spoons, bright plastic or bucktail jigs, and small sinking plugs. They seem to prefer red, red and white, or red and gold on the metallic lures. Hardware presents a problem, for a char hits a spoon or spinner almost too eagerly—gulping it deep into the mouth, where a treble hook impedes the fight and can do serious enough injury to dissuade an angler from releasing a small catch. Most char fishermen therefore favor single or double hooks rather than trebles.

The fish often cruise near the surface and along deep banks. Silvers like to rest in pools, especially below falls or other barriers, and in deep glides within a main current or in slower water just outside such a current. The reds lie in shallower water as a rule, often in pools or riffles just above or below white water, or near boulders in a heavy flow. They seem to be resting before or after the exertion of fighting the rapids. They commonly school in riffles up to about four feet deep, especially riffles next to bars or near the mouths of tributary streams. Sometimes they can be seen. When they are not visible, an angler ought nevertheless to probe the fast shallows, casting his fly upstream, letting it sink and swing downstream, then sweeping it in quickly and erratically. Hard lures should be retrieved or trolled in a similar manner, always within a few feet of bottom. In tidewaters, casts can often be made into passing schools. The char is not a timid fish and will not be dismayed by a bit of disturbance.

Brook Trout *(Salvelinus fontinalis)*
COMMON & REGIONAL NAMES: *brookie, squaretail, speckled trout, native trout.* (The name *salter* denotes sea-run brook trout.)

GAME IDENTIFICATION & LOCATION OF FISHING REGIONS:
There are larger and more colorful fish, but none more beautiful than a brook trout. Its back and upper sides—usually olive but occasionally brown, green, or blue-green—are marbled with dark and light vermiculations. Its flanks are paler but sometimes orange or rosy, its body speckled with yellowish spots among which there is a sparkling of pink or red spots with soft blue halos. Dark vermiculations, streaks, or occasionally spots mark the dorsal fin. The tail has a straight or very slightly forked rear edge, and it may bear similar markings or it may be solid in hue—the color of the back or sides. The lower fins are sometimes dusky, more often amber, orange, rose, or carmine; their leading edges are creamy white, usually with a vague black line separating the pale trim from the brighter rear portion. The flanks of a spawning male often darken to a sooty shade, and the creamy or orange tinge of the belly often turns bright orange. Wild squaretails are more colorful (externally and internally) than newly released hatchery kin, and some races are more brilliant than others.

As with other chars, the jaws and the head of the vomer are toothed, the fins soft-rayed, and an adipose fin is located over the anal fin. The conformation, too, is typical of chars; trim, tapered, about five times as long as its depth. None of these details can evoke the sparkling, spray-throwing élan of a rolling or jumping brookie. Leaps are not only occasioned by the alarming jab of a hook or pull of a line; sometimes brookies, especially those of small or medium size, leap clear of the water in their zeal to snatch an insect from the surface, though at other times they feed with a delicacy and caution that can tax an angler's artful dodges. Typically, a fighting brookie alternates surface thrashing with deep, long pulls and tugs.

In the vestibule of the Presbyterian church at Brookhaven, Long Island, hangs an effigy of a 14½-pound sea-run brook trout

—a salter, as the anadromous form is called. According to tradition, it represents a trout caught nearby, on the Carmans River, in 1827. The angler was Senator Daniel Webster. If Senator Webster were plying those lower New York waters today, he would find the neighborhood's fishable streams and the trout themselves to be as drastically abbreviated as a modern sermon, despite intensive stocking. This is not to say that big squaretails no longer exist, but only that they cannot exist where they once did. The current official record is an inland duplicate of the great orator's brook trout: a fish weighing 14 pounds, 8 ounces. It was caught in 1916 by Dr. W. J. Cook on the Nipigon River in Ontario.

A typical trout stream today is easily accessible, heavily fished, degraded along some of its stretches, and likely to yield a majority of brook trout weighing half a pound and measuring 10 inches or so—barely above legal keeping size in most regions. Yet brookies 16 inches long and weighing over 2 pounds are not uncommon in well-managed rivers; 4- and 5-pounders are not uncommon in lightly fished, unspoiled Canadian lakes and rivers.

Originally, brook trout ranged from Georgia's cool highland streams to lower Canada and westward over a roughly fan-shaped zone to the tributaries of the upper Mississippi. They may have been most populous in Labrador and Quebec, where squaretail fishing is still outstanding. Brookies were preeminent in the development of American fly fishing, and in spite of shrinking habitat they remain one of the primary game species in the Northeast, the region where that development took place. They benefit from intensive management in the form of hatchery propagation, genetic experimentation, and stream improvement. Moreover, they have become the most widespread of chars, having been successfully transplanted to cold streams, lakes, and ponds throughout the United States and Canada and in many parts of Europe and South America. The biggest brookies have always occurred in the northern part of their range, where water conditions are most suitable and human settlement is light.

Maine's wild rivers still furnish plenty of big brookies. The Allagash, Kennebago, and Kennebec are among the finest such streams. But even bigger brook trout—the biggest today outside of Argentina—are caught in the lakes and streams of Labrador, the Ungava, Hudson, and James Bay drainages of Quebec, and northern Manitoba. About 4 pounds is the average size caught on

Gods River and Gods Lake in Manitoba. Bigger ones come from Quebec's Broadback, Nemiscau, and Rupert rivers, near James Bay. Significantly, all of these streams are long and wide; only big, food-rich waters produce really big squaretails.

Sea-run brookies seem to be on the increase from the New Jersey coast northward, probably because many of the Atlantic seaboard streams are heavily stocked. An average New Jersey or New England salter outweighs its landlocked brethren of the same region, but salters cannot rival the inland trophies of the North. They seldom weigh 4 pounds. They acquire oceanic coloring—dark greenish-blue on the back and silvery on the sides—but they revert to type after about two weeks in fresh water.

Seth Green established the first brook-trout hatchery in 1864, near Mumford, New York. Hatcheries now operate throughout the country. They produce chiefly domestic strains, developed over many generations to assure ease of husbandry and high birth and survival rates under hatchery conditions. Experiments have been conducted to achieve fast growth and the hardiness of wild populations, and some continuing experiments hold promise. Stocked trout have become a necessity, though they do not survive as well in the wild as the native fish.

Crossbreeding has also been conducted for many years. A brookie-lake trout hybrid is called a splake—a name coined by Canadian biologists who crossed the terms speckled trout and lake trout. Smaller than lakers but larger than brookies, splake lack the red spotting of brook trout. They have the lake trout's yel-

Brookie, displaying typically vermiculated back and dorsal fin.

low spotting, but after some time in the wild they acquire the red-dened flanks of a brook trout. Unlike most hybrids, they are fertile. They are also hardy, and so fast-maturing that they may be able to withstand lamprey predation better than lake trout. They have been introduced to the Great Lakes and to many Canadian waters. Another interesting hatchery hybrid is the brookie-brown cross, called a tiger trout. It has some of the orange-gold color of a tiger, as well as a tiger's determined ferocity in attacking prey, but its markings are marbled rather than striped. Though infertile, it has value for stocking club or private waters. Brook trout are much less cautious than brown trout, and tigers are still less cautious.

FISH HABITAT & FEEDING BEHAVIOR—ANGLING TACTICS: In the northeastern brooks most familiar to the author, squaretails spawn in late October and November. The time varies from September in the northernmost part of the range to December in the southernmost. Any angler living near a shallow, gravelly trout stream probably watches with reverence, fascination, and optimism regarding future seasons as a female brookie hovers over

Brook-trout waters in Labrador.

her chosen bed, attended by at least one male and often two. If there are two, one may drive the other off, or the two may wait on each side and slightly to the rear of the female. The site is clear, gravelly, cleaned by current, and sometimes so shallow that dorsal fins cut the surface.

If trapped in a lake without suitable feeder streams, brook trout will seek gravel, twigs, or other debris near the shore, and this adaptability has caused crowding and stunting in some stocked lakes. But an ideal spot has cold, flowing brook or spring water, with cleansing current pouring down through the gravel. The female clears a small, shallow redd and deposits her eggs, turning on her side with spasmodic movements as if flapping must promote the extrusion of roe. Milt is immediately ejected by the male or males. In a little freestone brook, an adult female may be 6 inches long and carrying about a hundred eggs; a 14-inch hen in fertile water may deposit twelve times as many.

Since incubation requires more than a month even if the stream temperature is above 50° and more than four months if it is very cold, most wild fry probably hatch in late winter or early spring. Those in a single clutch do not emerge all at once but over a period of about a week, and more than another month may elapse before all the yolk sacs are absorbed.

Salter fingerlings spend their first winter in fresh water, then go to sea in March and April and begin to return in September. After spawning, they head out to sea again. Unlike some salmonids, they continue to feed as they move upstream in fall, suspending their foraging only during four days or so of actual breeding activity. Both salters and sea trout (anadromous browns) are most often caught on standard bucktails and streamers. They are less susceptible than landlocked trout to insect imitations. They can also be taken on small spoons and spinners—brass and black ones, especially. Among baits, sandworms and bloodworms tempt them in the estuaries, nightcrawlers and small minnows in the streams.

Brookie fingerlings can withstand ice and a reduction of oxygen better than the young of browns or rainbows, but they are less tolerant of warm water. The best brookie fishing is therefore in headwaters, cold spring streams, or rivers and lakes with sufficient volume to maintain optimum temperatures—from the mid-50's to about 61°. The fish are never abundant in water warmer than the upper 60's. Some Canadian brook trout have a longevity of about ten years, but three is the average in most waters. They continue to grow after maturity if they suffer no crowding, no severe competition.

Brookie fry soon progress from a diet of the smallest planktonic morsels to larger prey, and the adults seldom limit themselves to insects. They eat crustaceans, mollusks, small fish, worms, an occasional leech, any edible windfalls. Among insects, the preferred foods generally are abundantly available ones—mosquito larvae, the larval and adult forms of mayflies, stoneflies, caddisflies, and midges, and a chance array of beetles, flies, bees, wasps, crickets, grasshoppers, and other fallen terrestrials. When aquatic insects are active, squaretails rise to dry flies perhaps more readily than any other chars or trouts; some choice pattern types are enumerated above, with standard methods of presentation, in the section on preferred trout and char foods and imitative lures. Dry flies will often take brook trout even in the absence of natural hatches or spinner falls, and of course hatches have no effect on the use of terrestrial patterns such as the Black Gnat, Bumble Bee, Ant, Woolly Worm, Hunt's Teagle Bee, Hopper Fly, the Bivisibles, Green Caterpillar, Wet Spider, and McGinty.

When terrestrials and dry aquatics are of no avail, an angler can work the bottom with nymphs such as the Leadwinged Coachman, Stonefly Creeper, Long-Tail March Brown, Flick's March Brown, Fish Fly Larva, Little Marryat, Quill Gordon, Breadcrust, the Athertons, Trueblood's Caddis Nymph, Hellgrammite, Light Cahill, Iron Blue, Greenwell's Glory, Green Drake, Montana, Michigan Nymph, and others—when possible, choosing patterns that resemble locally prevalent stream life. In addition, there are the standard (and some outrageous but effective) wets, bucktails, and streamers. Patterns that come to mind include the Coachman in all its guises, the Iron Dun, Silver Doctor, Mallard Quill, Blue Dun, Blue Quill, Parmachene Belle, Grizzly King, Butcher, Cowdung, Alder, Grannom, the Cahills and Hendricksons, Montreal, Hare's Ear, Spruce, Ginger Quill, Burlap, Nine Three, Supervisor, Light and Dark Tigers, Gray and Black Ghosts, Black-Nose Dace, and Mickey Finn. For the big northern trophies, streamers should be appropriately big, from about no. 6 to no. 2, but generally speaking, small flies should be used for average fish and clear water. The angler who does not use a fly rod can present the same concoctions with spinning tackle and a casting bubble, or he can use spinners and spinner-flies. For that matter, a gob of worm on a no. 8 hook will inveigle brook trout. But there is an excitement in the classic use of flies, and no fish is more compatible with the art of fly casting.

Brown Trout *(Salmo trutta)*
COMMON & REGIONAL NAMES: *German trout, German brown trout, Loch Leven trout.* (The name *sea trout* denotes sea-run brown trout.)

GAME IDENTIFICATION & LOCATION OF FISHING REGIONS: It is the wariest member of its tribe and one of the strongest for its size. A merely average brown trout is a special joy to an angler, whether he keeps it or returns it to the water and watches its darkly lustrous back vanish into the shadows of its lair. If it is a juvenile its tail is slightly forked, but a mature brown is as square-tailed as a brook trout and sometimes deeper-bodied. A big one—say, 28 inches long—probably weighs 8 to 10 pounds. The brown of its back lightens to tan, bronze, ocher, or gold on the sides, liberally sprinkled with black spots and usually a few red ones. Some of these spots have faint blue or creamy aureoles. A similarly faint blue wash often glimmers on the cheeks or gill covers or along the lateral line. Additional black spots may appear on the tail or dorsal fin, and red or orange spotting or edging frequently adorns the dorsal or adipose fin. The lower fins are brown or dusky yellow, the belly almost white on a young specimen, yellow or ocher on an older one.

A brown trout caught in a big lake may be pale enough to look like a landlocked salmon, but some of a landlock's black spots are generally X-shaped and the roof of its mouth shows only a single row of poorly developed vomerine teeth (or none at all, as they are easily broken off). A brown trout has an irregular double row of teeth on the vomer. Anadromous browns, called sea trout, look like small Atlantic salmon—grilse—until they return to fresh water and darken again. There are small runs of sea trout along the East Coast of the United States and Canada as well as the coasts of Chile, Argentina, New Zealand, Iceland, and northern Europe. They generally weigh from 2 to 10 pounds when they return to the rivers, though the sea trout of Scandinavia and the Argentine range from 10 to 30 pounds. The migratory instinct depends more on genetics than locale, and until 1958 very few of the browns in the coastal waters of the United States ever ventured into the ocean. Then Connecticut imported a European strain of sea trout and enlarged the runs somewhat.

The brown trout of the interior average a pound or less—or that weight is the average of those fooled by anglers. But some grow much larger, not only because they prey on smaller trout and other fish, but because they are harder to catch than such relatives as rainbow trout and chars. Being wary, they often live longer. For more than a century, the accepted world record was 39 pounds, 8 ounces—a fish caught in 1866 on Scotland's Loch Awe. As this fish was discovered to have been snag-hooked—and may have been a salmon rather than a brown trout—it has been disqualified. The new record is a 33-pound, 10-ounce brown caught in 1977 at Utah's Flaming Gorge Reservoir, where even bigger ones may be taken in the next few years. Second place is held by a 31-pound, 12-ounce fish taken in 1975, third place by a 31½-pounder taken in 1972 from the White River in Arkansas, another home of exceptional browns.

Originally, brown trout ranged through Europe from the Mediterranean to Scandinavia and across Russia into Siberia. There are four subspecies and numerous strains within those races. One strain of the Caspian brown trout is the largest of the genus *Salmo*—larger than the Atlantic salmon.

Brown trout were introduced to America in 1883, and the earliest arrivals came from Scotland and Germany—hence the names Loch Leven and German trout. Since then, several strains have been intermixed and the subtle characteristics of the original stocks are no longer discernible in American brown trout. They are now distributed from coast to coast in the United States and Canada, and they have been established in South America, New Zealand, Africa, and Asia. Among the American rivers famous for brown trout are the aforementioned White, Pennsylvania's Letort, Wisconsin's Brule, Michigan's upper Manistee, and Montana's Big Hole, Yellowstone, Gallatin, Madison, and the upper Missouri. Brown trout also prosper in large lakes and impoundments, as do other trouts and chars. Flaming Gorge, on the Utah-Wyoming border, vies with the White River as the continent's best water for trophy-sized brown trout.

Brown trout lying just off bottom.

FISH HABITAT & FEEDING BEHAVIOR—ANGLING TACTICS:
Like several other trouts and chars, browns provide good fishing
in waters ranging from brooks to big rivers and lakes. Suitable
temperatures and adequate oxygen are needed, yet brown trout
are more adaptable than most of the group. If they are not quite
as resistant to warm water as rainbows, they are more so than
brook trout. Their preferred temperature range is about 54° to 64°
but they can survive in heat up to about 84°. And although they
grow best in very alkaline water, they resemble brook trout in their
tolerance of mild acidity. It is because they are so adaptable that
they have become naturalized American quarry.

Those that reside in lakes or big rivers move to the mouths
of feeder streams in mid-September, providing prime fishing
there. If suitable tributaries are lacking, they will breed in rubble
near shore, but they prefer to make their redds on shallow, gravelly stream bottoms, typical sites for all species of the group. They
spawn from October to February, depending on region and climate, and they cover the redds with fine gravel as most other
trouts and chars do. A small female may develop only a couple
of hundred eggs, while a large one can produce six thousand.

The young generally hatch in early spring. If they are sea trout, they may spend from two to six years in fresh water, though most head for the ocean when they are three years old, the age at which nonmigratory browns reach maturity and begin spawning. Browns have an average life span of seven or eight years, and a few live as long as twelve. They are not fast-growing fish; a two-year-old is likely to be only 6 or 8 inches long.

The anadromous populations go to salt water in early spring, beginning in February or March. Their first oceanic sojourn usually lasts a year and a half, ending in summer or fall. As with landlocked browns, September is the month when concentrations of sea trout can be intercepted at stream mouths or a little distance up the spawning streams. Little is known of their marine existence, except that most linger near the estuaries and a few travel along the coasts as far as a hundred miles. On their first return to fresh water, their life stage is comparable to that of salmon in the grilse stage. Called whitling at this time, they generally measure 15 to 19 inches and weigh 1½ to 3 pounds. After three summers at sea, most of them are six years old; they are now 17 to 22 inches long and weigh 3½ to 4½ pounds. They are comparable to landlocked browns of the same age in prime habitat. Older browns—repeat spawners—are generally just a trifle under 2 feet long and weigh 4 to 9 pounds.

A big trout of any kind may gobble a frog, lizard, newt, mouse, or small bird, but browns subsist on a primary diet of aquatic and terrestrial insects, fish, shrimp, crawfish, and mollusks. Browns weighing over 2 pounds feed chiefly on minnows. They are so predaceous and such efficient competitors for available food that stocking them can be unwise in a limited habitat where native fish are to be maintained.

Night fishing accounts for some of the biggest browns, as these fish acquire a pronounced habit of nocturnal activity. Sea trout are even more nocturnal than nonmigratory browns. They are worth the tangles and snarls, fumbling and stumbling, and insect attacks of a night-fishing session because they are even better fighters—given to sudden rushes, twists, turns, and jumps. Like salters, they can be taken on streamers, spinners, spoons, jigs, and occasionally on minnows, sandworms, and bloodworms. Upstream, browns will take nightcrawlers, minnows, grasshoppers, hellgrammites, softshell crawfish, tailed spinners and

spoons, and small plugs, any of which can be cast or trolled.

A good springtime bait is a strip of sucker, and lunker browns will hit big streamers, tied on hooks of no. 2 size or larger, as well as big, flashy spinners trailing worms. However, since these fish are leader-shy, spinning or baitcasting tackle should be light; monofilament testing 6 to 8 pounds is sufficient.

In spacious waters, brown trout will strike spoons and plugs as big as those used for largemouths. Sculpin minnows are a favorite prey in some waters. The Flaming Gorge browns feed mostly on chubs, gaining 5 or 6 pounds a year on that diet, and some of the biggest have been taken on assorted Rebels, no. 9 and 11 Countdown Rapalas, and similar minnowlike sinking plugs finished in gold, red, blue, green, or black. Color matters less than fishing method. The most productive tactic is to troll very slowly, fifteen or twenty feet down and close to the steep bluffs that form much of the shoreline. This is where the Flaming Gorge browns

Angler versus brown trout on Montana's Big Hole River.

find chubs, and the same tactic should work in similar water else-where. It is most effective in spring and fall, evening and early morning, and on calm water.

In deep water, big browns fight a twisting, running battle without jumping much, and they seldom hit a plug hard. The an-gler may feel little more than a nudge or tap. To make a barb pene-trate the trout's tough jaw he must set the hook with a long, smooth, forceful pull.

Stream fishing provides a better opportunity for traditional dry-fly techniques. Browns favor clear water, often seeking calmer lies than those of brook trout—quiet pools and runs. When a fly is presented to a rising brown the fish may take it or, being a consummately suspicious feeder, may dart back down to cover. A brown may also inspect a fly that drifts past—may even move as if to follow it—but there is no certainty whether the fish will ac-cept or refuse it. In the latter case, a brown frequently goes to the bottom and stops feeding. The species is easily put down by a sus-pect pattern, inept presentation, or missed strike. But if the fish does not actually retreat from a refused offering, a change of fly size is indicated and, if that fails, a change of pattern as well. A no. 10 is easy to track on clear water but is larger than natural prey. A no. 14 is often much better. If that meets refusal, a 16 or 18 may be accepted.

Sparsely winged patterns, spider types, and variants are good because they can be dropped to the surface with little com-motion, and are buoyant on calm water. Among the flies famous for tempting brown trout are the Cream Variant, Light and Dark Cahill, Hendrickson, Adams, Royal Coachman, March Brown, Blue Dun Spider, and Quill Gordon—all excellent choices in wa-ters that also hold brook trout and rainbows. This is not to say that all the previously listed patterns will not work; a consistently suc-cessful quest for brown trout demands experiments.

In early spring and fall, nymphs and wets are more repre-sentative of available foods than are dries. These times also call for streamer and bucktail simulacra, the big minnow patterns such as the various Muddlers, the Missoulian Spook (essentially a white Muddler), the Perch and Dace streamers. Another type that often works is exemplified by the Spruce Fly, a shorter streamer that can be fished as a standard wet. Big tandem flies also catch browns, and so do saltwater designs like the Honey

Blond. The success of the big streamers overshadows the difficulty of casting them, and on big western or northern rivers they perform marvelously when trolled very slowly.

Where winter trout fishing is permitted, some anglers work the big rivers with two-handed, 8½-foot spinning rods from which they can cast weighted jigs with yellow, brown, or black marabou dressings, or big streamers with a sinker attached two feet up. With a three-way swivel, the sinker can be put on a dropper to reduce hang-ups on rocky or snag-strewn bottoms. This kind of fishing has become popular on the upper Missouri.

Night fishing is best from midsummer through fall. The trout are most susceptible to trickery at the darkest times of night, before the moon rises or after it sets. However, they stop feeding in mist or fog, when the air is cooler than the water. Lights should be kept to a minimum and not shined into the water. It is the better part of valor to scout the water during daylight, and to use a 1X to 3X tippet (testing about 5 to 9 pounds) rather than a light daytime leader, and to have plenty of backing on the reel since there may be no possibility of following a running fish. The nocturnal foraging areas are shallow bars, mud flats, and gravel shoals where the browns capture minnows and crawfish. Also try the heads and tails of pools, bends where the current sweeps a bank, springs, and the cool mouths of tributary streams.

During a nighttime hatch or spinner fall, standard dry flies can be used. Heavy nocturnal hatches include those of the brown drake *(Ephemera simulans),* several green drakes, and the pale evening dun *(Ephemerella dorothea).* On many midwestern streams, one that cannot be ignored from late June to mid-July is the giant known as the Michigan Caddis *(Hexagenia limbata),* which is really a mayfly and is also called a sandfly or fishfly. Nymph and dry patterns for this species are included in the Compara series of flies, described by Al Caucci and Bob Nastasi in *Comparahatch* and *Hatches.* When most of the nighttime naturals are stoneflies, caddisflies, and terrestrial insects, a hatch or a common terrestrial can be matched, or the angler can try a big attention-getting floater such as a moth concocted of deerhair—the same kind of fluffy dry that takes smallmouths.

In the absence of aquatic and terrestrial naturals, the aforementioned baits and hard lures can be used at night, but many of us prefer to continue fly fishing with meaty-looking wets

and streamers—a wet caddis or green drake pattern, a Royal Coachman, a Sculpin Spuddler, or a Matuka Muddler, to name a few. The Muddler types lend themselves nicely to coating with floatant so that they bob up if fished slowly. One way to encourage a take by a cautious brown is to retrieve slowly, alternating drifts and darts. Whether done by manipulating a fly line or whipping a spinning rod, it elicits strikes from habitually skeptical lunkers.

Cutthroat Trout *(Salmo clarki)*
COMMON & REGIONAL NAMES: *cut, black-spotted trout, mountain trout, Rocky Mountain trout, native trout.* (The name *harvest*

Angler netting cutthroat in high country of Wyoming.

trout is applied to those sea-run cutthroats that are taken in autumn. Regional subspecies are denoted by many other names—
*Paiute trout, Utah cutthroat, Yellowstone trout, Colorado cut-
throat, Rio Grande cutthroat, Lake Tahoe trout,* etc.)

GAME IDENTIFICATION & LOCATION OF FISHING REGIONS:
Named for the blood-red, crimson, or orange slash mark under
the dentary bone on each side of its jaw, the cutthroat has a handsomely unique appearance when in its most brilliant freshwater
raiment. Color varies considerably, however. Its tail has the same
black spotting and slight fork as that of the closely related rainbow, and the two can look very much alike when the cutthroat's
dentary slashes are faint. The cutthroat is slightly heavier-shoul-
dered and longer-jawed. Field identification can be confirmed by
the prominent hyoid teeth on the back of its tongue, which the
rainbow lacks.

The typical inland forms usually have a yellowish-green or
bronze back, blending to rose, amber, or orange on the sides. The
belly is pale, sometimes white. Some races are silver-sided while
others have a mere wash of silver here and there. Black spots are
scattered over the body, small ones on some races, larger and
more numerous on others, and usually most plentiful near the
spotted tail. Where their ranges overlap, races intergrade, and the
cutthroat and rainbow species hybridize in a number of Wyoming
and Montana streams. The result is a fish with the rainbow's pink
lateral band and the cutthroat's red slash marks. In a few high-
country lakes, the cutthroat also crossbreeds with the golden
trout, thereby bestowing slash marks on the offspring and somewhat muting their golden hue.

Sea-run cutthroats are silver-sided, with bluish-green
backs. When ocean-bright, they are meagerly spotted and sometimes their slashes are faint. After they have been in fresh water
for a short while, their spotting and slash marks intensify, but
their sides usually remain silvery—a description that also fits the
sedentary coastal races of cutthroat.

The sea-run forms average between 1 and 4 pounds, while
those of the interior mostly run from 1 to 5 but with an occasional
giant scaling 15 pounds or more. The record was set by a 39-inch,
41-pound fish—very nearly as big as the record rainbow—taken
at Nevada's Pyramid Lake in 1925. The record will probably stand

forever, as the fish was a Lahontan cutthroat *(S. c. henshawi);* as a result of stream diversion, reckless commercial harvesting, and other human meddling, that subspecies is now extinct. The cutthroat races that still prosper are smaller.

They range from the Gulf of Alaska down to northern California and inland to the Rockies. Attempts to establish the species in the East have failed, and in a few western areas intensive stocking has failed to reverse serious depletion due to the cutthroat's tendency to hybridize, its inability to compete well with other species (both native and introduced), and its vulnerability to fishing pressure. Probably the best cutthroat waters now are along the upper Snake, Yellowstone Lake and River, the Wind, Green, Shoshone, and several other Wyoming rivers; Montana's smaller Yellowstone tributaries; Idaho waters such as Pend Oreille and Priest lakes; and the streams along the coast of British Columbia as well as on the Vancouver and Queen Charlotte Islands.

Two other closely related and rather similar-looking trouts merit description, if only to assure their release when caught. They are the Apache, or Arizona, trout *(S. apache),* which resides chiefly in the waters of the Fort Apache Indian Reservation in the White Mountains; and the Gila trout *(S. gilae),* which is found in New Mexico and Arizona, primarily in the Gila River drainage. They are small, chunky, deep-bodied trouts with much amber or brown or pink on their bodies, or with an olive-green dorsal surface paling to gold on the lower parts. Both have a very long adipose fin, and a purebred Gila always has a golden belly. The Gila, which interbreeds with the rainbow, sometimes has a few large black spots but usually can be distinguished from the Apache by the smaller size and greater profusion of its spots. Either species may resemble the cutthroat but without its red slashes, and both lack hyoid teeth. The Gila is currently a protected species. The slightly larger Apache seldom exceeds 12 inches.

FISH HABITAT & FEEDING BEHAVIOR—ANGLING TACTICS:

Cutthroats, goldens, and rainbows are all spring spawners; hence the frequency of interbreeding. The breeding instinct draws some ocean cutthroats back to the estuaries in early spring, others in fall, when they are aptly called harvest trout. They dally long enough to provide good fishing, for most of the coastal races spawn from February to March. The inland forms spawn primarily

in April and May. Some of them do not attain sexual maturity until their fourth year and thereafter breed only in alternate years. Since the longevity of inland cutthroats is only about six to eight years, many reproduce no more than twice. Their spawning activity is like that of other trouts, but over a long period it obviously produces fewer fish—another factor in their decline, another reason to release most of those caught.

Some of the anadromous races are more prolific. They go to sea when two or three years old, stay there for another year or two, then spawn annually and live as long as ten years. The young of all the races are insect-eaters. In the ocean, cutthroats feed on sand lances (small, slender fish resembling eels) and other small fish and shrimp. Inland cutthroats feed chiefly on freshwater shrimp and insect larvae (mostly midge and damselfly nymphs). Less dependent on minnows and mollusks than most trouts, they also eat fewer terrestrials and ephemera.

Tidewater cutthroat fishermen troll or cast small silver spoons, wet flies, streamers, and natural baits matching the customary foods. In the bays, cutthroats snatch at streamers simulating local baitfish and sometimes at nymph-ties imitating shrimp. The fishing is best near rocky shores, especially those with drop-offs. From April through July, migrant cutthroats school off gravel beaches flanking river mouths. The trolling is most productive at ten- to fifteen-foot depths from ebb through slack tide.

Cutthroat in shallow riffle.

From late August through October the trout move up into the rivers, taking all kinds of bait, still-fished or drifted, cast or trolled spinners, spinner-flies, baited spinners, wet flies, and streamers.

Whereas steelhead feed only meagerly until after they spawn, cutthroats feed avidly until they are ready to make their redds. Both steelhead and nonmigratory rainbows provide a more sensational aerial show, but cutthroats fight very well, indeed. They do not hold in current as steelhead will. They prefer to rest and watch for food in dead or slow water—around brush, stumps, roots, logs, and boulders. Strikes can be induced with no. 6 attractor-type wets such as steelhead flies carrying crests of yellow, orange, or red and white. The fly should be moved near bottom with short spasms to make the hackle pulsate.

Inland cutthroats choose lies comparable to those of brookies, in quiet pools, behind boulders, near logs or snags, and in holes under cut banks. They take live baits—worms, crawfish, or minnows—and the same spinners, spoons, and bright wet flies and streamers used for anadromous fish. They are attracted to flashing spoons finished in gold, brass, silver, and red and white. Because big hatches of aquatic insects prompt cutthroats to vary their customary diet, they rise to dry flies in spring and early summer. However, they seem to be more cautious than sea-run cutthroats, so the rule is to use a fine leader and small flies.

Dolly Varden *(Salvelinus malma)*
COMMON & REGIONAL NAMES: *Dolly, bull trout, western char, salmon-trout, red-spotted trout*

GAME IDENTIFICATION & LOCATION OF FISHING REGIONS:
Though not always cherry-spotted, America's far-western char was named for a Dickensian character in the historical novel *Barnaby Rudge*—Miss Dolly Varden, who wore cherry-colored ribbons and other adornments. Often her namesake does, too, but the spots liberally sprinkled over its greenish back and paler sides are just as often orange, pink, or yellowish-white. In salt water it turns silvery and the spots grow dim or disappear. In the northern part of its range it bears faint vermiculations on its back, and sometimes its lower fins have a pale border. Its belly is white, its tail moderately forked. In mountain streams where forage is meager, it is slim; in lakes rich with kokanee and other preyfish,

Fisherman with good-sized Dolly Varden.

it grows big and very fat. In Alaska, where its range overlaps that of the arctic char, the two species look very much alike. Some taxonomists would prefer to classify the Dolly Varden as a subspecies of the arctic char. For field identification, look to the spots: if they are smaller than the iris of the eye, the fish is a Dolly Varden; if they are larger, it is an arctic char.

In average size, the stream-grown Dolly Varden is comparable to a brook trout—a pound or two. Only in lakes does it normally acquire trophy proportions. The record fish was a 32-pounder caught in 1949 on Idaho's Lake Pend Oreille.

The distribution of this western char extends from Alaska to northern California and eastward to Idaho, Montana, Utah, and Nevada. It also occurs along the far side of the Pacific. The anadromous form occurs only in the northern part of the range.

FISH HABITAT & FEEDING BEHAVIOR—ANGLING TACTICS:
Many fishermen deride the Dolly Varden's game qualities, though it fights well, and some would like to see it extirpated from lakes and streams where coho, chinook, steelhead, or kokanee are caught. The Dolly Varden is a voracious predator with a reputation for consuming salmonid eggs and fingerlings. But other trouts and chars also prey on salmonid eggs and young. The Dolly Varden is not a serious enough predator to deserve condemnation. In northern estuaries and in headwater streams where other salmonids provide no important fishery, it is esteemed.

Runs of anadromous Dolly Varden enter the rivers from

September into November and go back to the sea in the spring. Some of the nonmigratory populations leave the lakes for their spawning streams in June or July even though they will not spawn until fall. A stream fisherman can therefore catch good numbers of them through the summer. Those that run up the spawning streams in summer are usually feeding half-heartedly, but repeated casts or trolling passes can tease them into striking. They are not alarmed by repeated presentations. A small, slim female may deposit eight hundred eggs in her redd; a big, lake-fattened fish may deposit three thousand. Incubation requires from one to three months, depending on water temperature, and the emerging fry burrow deeper into the gravel, as if they were insect nymphs, remaining there for about two to four more months. Those that enter the ocean do so in the spring of their fourth year. Until then, both migratory and nonmigratory types are small and much less active than most chars.

The young are largely insectivorous, but the adults eat more fish than insects. In streams, small and medium Dolly Varden sometimes rise to dry flies. The larger ones tend to be bottom feeders. They are most often caught on minnows or other baits, streamers, spinners, bright plugs, and big wobbling spoons. Red and white is a preferred color combination for spoons. In streams, the places to probe are the bottoms of holes and pools, swift runs above pools, and the kinds of lies where one might expect to find a brook trout. In lakes, the good holding waters are usually along the edges of reefs and drop-offs. Any streamer that attracts cutthroats or rainbows (which see) will take these fish, too.

Golden Trout *(Salmo aguabonita)*
COMMON & REGIONAL NAMES: *mountain trout, Volcano Creek trout, Kern River trout, Sierra trout*

GAME IDENTIFICATION & LOCATION OF FISHING REGIONS:
The statement has been made in this book that no fish is more beautiful than a brook trout. It is a subjective appraisal, and one that western fly fishermen might dispute. Among the many paeans to other species was one written at about the turn of the century by the zoologist David Starr Jordan. "The most beautiful of all our beautiful western trout," he declared, "is the famous golden trout of Mount Whitney."

The subject of Dr. Jordan's praise attains its most brilliant coloration as a stream resident, though it also flourishes in lakes. Its sides are sometimes brassy, sometimes truly golden. Its back is olive, grayish, or bronze, paling on the upper sides above the lateral line, which is marked by a red band extending from the gill cover almost to the black-spotted, slightly forked tail. The band cuts through a series of about ten round or oval darkenings —smoky shadows like the parr marks on young salmon. A red flush also runs over the gill covers and lower fins and along the belly. Black spots are scattered over the dorsal fin and upper part of the body. The tip of the dorsal is gold or white, and the tips of the anal and pelvic fins are white, often with a black line of demarcation. Coloration varies from one region to another. The hue of the belly ranges from cadmium to white, and fish bred at low altitudes tend to become steel-blue instead of gold and red.

Golden trout average less than a pound in weight, but 3-pounders are occasionally caught in the lakes of Wyoming's Jim

Goldens—some taken on spoons, some on flies.

Bridger Wilderness and in Idaho's Golden Trout Lake. The fishing is good, though the trout are smaller, along parts of the Kern River and nearby waters in the Sierra Mountains of California—the original home of golden trout. The largest ever caught was an 11-pounder landed at Cook's Lake, Wyoming, in 1948.

Biologists believe the golden may be descended from an isolated race of rainbow trout—with which it interbreeds—or from rainbow-cutthroat hybrids. It was first discovered late in the nineteenth century, in the high, cold mountain streams and lakes of California's upper Kern River drainage. Since then it has been established in Washington, Idaho, Wyoming, Colorado, and Montana. Though widely stocked, it thrives only in cold lakes and streams, mainly at or above timberline. Unable to endure high temperatures, it fares best in water ranging between 40° and 60°. Its indigenous waters in the high Sierras are fairly acid and not very fertile but they are cool and well oxygenated. They flow—violently in some places and gently in others—over dull red gravel, granitic sand, and algae-yellowed tufa that may have caused the evolution of the golden trout's colors.

Unfortunately, brown and rainbow trout have been introduced to those waters, and goldens have been transplanted to lakes and rivers already inhabited by those two species as well as brook trout. Brown trout reduce golden populations through competition and predation. Brookies also reduce them through competition. And rainbows reduce them through crossbreeding. Because rainbow-golden hybrids are fertile, few purebred goldens remain in most waters. Western anglers catch an illusory abundance of fish that look like purebred goldens, yet some biologists consider the golden trout a threatened species.

FISH HABITAT & FEEDING BEHAVIOR—ANGLING TACTICS:
Snow still blankets some of the slopes of the Kern River drainage in April and May, when goldens make their redds in the gravel of cold, swift streams. They first spawn at three years of age, and a breeding male can be recognized by an intensification of color and an enlargement of his upper jaw. He extrudes milt as a female deposits her three hundred to seven hundred eggs, which hatch in about twenty days. After another eighteen days the yolk sacs are absorbed and the fry, almost an inch long, emerge from the gravel to begin browsing on plankton. As they mature, their diet

changes to small crustaceans and insects—mostly caddis and midge larvae in winter and early spring, supplemented by fallen terrestrials in summer.

When aroused by a hatch, the fish will take small dry flies of appropriate size and color. A typical choice would be a dark midge pattern on a no. 18 hook. Since goldens are timid and the water is usually very clear, a 4X to 6X tippet is recommended. These fish will come to worms, salmon eggs, grubs, small spoons, and spinners, but somehow it seems shameful to use anything other than flies to beguile the delicate, aristocratic trout of the high country. If dries are rejected, a no. 14 or 16 caddis nymph is a suitable ploy. Small bucktails and streamers also whet the appetites of goldens. The range of fly size is said to be from 12 to 20, but Ted Trueblood, a notable western angling writer, has caught goldens on a no. 10 Bucktail Coachman.

A lake is easily fished by casting or trolling, and many anglers simply drag spinners or streamers over the edges of dropoffs. The pools of small, clear streams can be much harder to cover without alarming the quarry. Sometimes the only recourse is to stalk, crawling along the banks and dapping a fly over the edge. A trout in shallow water can see movement on a nearby bank or a profile against the sky, and that—or a shadow falling across the water—is enough to send it darting away.

Lake Trout *(Salvelinus namaycush)*

COMMON & REGIONAL NAMES: *togue, mackinaw, laker, gray trout, forktail trout*

GAME IDENTIFICATION & LOCATION OF FISHING REGIONS:

The lake trout is the largest of chars, a ponderous, deep-dwelling, fork-tailed relative of the squaretail. Its body is generally bronze-green or blue-gray, sometimes almost black, with a great many pale yellowish or pinkish spots on the back, sides, dorsal fin, and tail. It has more prominent vomerine teeth on the roof of its mouth than the brook trout. The splake (a hatchery cross between the brookie, or speckled trout, and the laker) retains the markings and teeth of the lake trout but has a squarer tail and the reddish ventral color of the brook trout; in size and shape it is intermediate between the parents. This hybrid is fertile, and because it matures quickly it is thought to be more resistant than purebred lake

trout to the ravages of lampreys; it has therefore been released in the Great Lakes and a number of Canadian waters.

The lake trout has several subspecies which differ slightly in color and shape. One of these, the siscowet, is sometimes caught in the Great Lakes and especially Lake Superior. Some biologists grant it separate status as a species *(S. siscowet).* It is deeper-bodied than most lake trout and its flesh is much oilier.

Called togue in parts of the Northeast, mackinaw in parts of the Northwest, the lake trout is a species peculiar to America, with no very close Asian or European relatives. It is the only far-northern freshwater fish that is not also found in Siberia; unlike most chars, it never migrates to the ocean. Its original distribution was densest in the Northeast, particularly in the region of New York's Finger Lakes and the Great Lakes, with diminishing numbers scattered across Canada and Alaska. Transplantations have made it fairly plentiful in deep, clear lakes throughout most of Canada and the northern United States and in some of the high lakes of Colorado, Nevada, and California.

The construction of the St. Lawrence Seaway, linking the Great Lakes to the Atlantic, permitted incursions of sea lampreys and alewives into the lakes. The alewives have become a primary food for lake trout, salmon, and other gamefish in the Great

Lake trout, about to be boated.

Lakes. The parasitic lampreys, on the other hand, were so devastating that lake-trout fishing—sport fishing as well as commercial—was ruined in those waters for a number of years. However, some authorities believe it would have been ruined in any event by pollution and overharvesting. Through a combination of corrective measures, including a curtailment of the harvest, an effort to alleviate pollution, and selective poisoning to curb the lamprey population, the fishery is slowly being revived. Because Superior is the coldest and cleanest of the big lakes, more and larger togue come from it than from the others.

Some of the upper New England lakes have an abundance of togue, but those fish are usually of small to medium size. Waters closer to the Great Lakes—Big Green Lake in Wisconsin, and a great many others in Minnesota, Wisconsin, and Michigan—may well offer the nation's best fishing for this species. Some of the finest Canadian waters are Ontario's Rainy Lake (on the Minnesota border) and Lake Simcoe; Manitoba's Gods Lake; Reindeer Lake (on the Manitoba-Saskatchewan line); Saskatchewan's Black, Wollaston, and Cree lakes and Lac La Ronge; and Lake Athabasca (on the Saskatchewan-Alberta line). The finest of all may be Great Bear Lake, in the Northwest Territories. That was where, in 1970, a new record was set by a mackinaw weighing 65 pounds and measuring 52 inches long. The average lake trout is between 3 and 10 pounds, but in clean, cold lakes there is nothing very unusual about catching one that weighs well over 20. It is therefore not surprising that the Alaskan lakes vie with Great Bear as havens for lakers and laker fishermen.

FISH HABITAT & FEEDING BEHAVIOR—ANGLING TACTICS: Although this species is sometimes caught in rivers connected to lakes, it prefers the lakes themselves, chiefly because it seeks spacious habitat with a temperature of 50° or less. A big lake in the far North may be sufficiently cold in its upper and middle strata; elsewhere, the best lakes are thermally stratified and oligotrophic—oxygen-rich in the lower depths during summer.

In the northernmost waters, lake trout up to about 8 pounds may be caught wherever baitfish are found, even at the surface in summer, and bigger ones follow the ciscoes that come up to spawn in autumn. To the south, lake trout frequent the shallows from late fall until early spring, and they furnish good sport and good eating when taken through the ice with live smelt or minnows jigged over the bottom. But in the summer they move to the deepest water, often several hundred feet down.

They come closer to shore again as early as September in some waters. Depending on region, spawning occurs from that month until December, but chiefly in October and November. Preferred sites are over rocks or gravel, preferably in deep spots near shore but in shoals if they find no suitable deep spots. This species of char makes no redd. Instead, a sizable area is swept clean by a small group of spawners—one female or several, together with several males. Then the females merely scatter their roe and the males spread their milt. Many of the eggs are picked from the gravel by small lake trout that are not spawning and by suckers, eels, perch, bullheads, and other predators. The survivors generally hatch in the spring and remain in deep water.

The fingerlings eat insects and crustaceans. When they grow big enough to be efficient predators, they progress to the adult diet of sculpins, ciscoes, alewives, ling, chubs, kokanee, whitefish, and the like. Many of these preyfish can be captured in deep water during summer but school in the shallows during spring and fall. Before and after the heat of summer or in the far North an angler can work areas that look like bass water, fishing the reefs, rocky shorelines, drop-offs, and edges where steep bluffs rise from a lake. Here he can troll or cast streamers, spinners, spoons, plugs, jigs, or live minnows. Where the trout run fairly small—say, 2 to 5 pounds—he can make the most of his sport by using a fly rod or light spinning tackle. Later, he will have to switch to a medium spinning or baitcasting rig or something even stouter. Many fishermen prefer big saltwater spinning or trolling rods. They want at least 250 yards of line, testing 15 or 20 pounds. A popular terminal rig is a 6-foot monofilament leader on a three-way swivel, with a bell, dipsey, keel, or drail sinker on a dropper of somewhat lighter monofilament. To reduce weight and enjoy an unimpeded contest, some anglers troll with a metal or plastic planer tied to the line; the planer digs down without the need of a heavy sinker. But the fish may be cruising hundreds of feet beneath the surface and, as with lake fishing for chinook salmon (which see), depth-sounders and electric water-temperature gauges are often used, together with lead-core lines, wire lines, or downriggers with sinker releases.

Trolled baits include strips, as well as whole fish, alive or dead. Tandem hooks with a wire minnow harness are excellent for trolling live bait. Though the best is probably a 6- to 8-inch smelt, the choice may depend on what is locally plentiful—sucker, cisco, chub, lake shiner, alewife, or whatever. Lakers sometimes take foot-long suckers and ciscoes. As a change of pace from trolling, bait can be still-fished or drifted in the shadow of a bluff or over deep reefs, spring holes, and points.

The most popular lures are silver, brass, and copper spoons, ranging from 2 to 9 inches in size, depending on the local fish. Other good colors are green, yellow, orange, red and white, and black and white. Big, minnow-shaped or jointed plugs are also favored.

For deep trolling, attractors are often used as for lake-dwelling chinook. Some anglers drag them as teasers on a separate line. Some mount thin chrome or fluorescent flashers on the

Laker caught on Alaskan stream during spawning season.

line being fished. Perhaps the most traditional attractor is the Cowbell rig, a series of big spinners mounted several inches apart on a heavy wire that is attached several feet ahead of the bait or lure.

Unless a lake has a reputation for productivity at a particular depth, a troller might begin only fifteen or twenty feet down and go progressively deeper until he connects with fish. By then, however, his lure might be three hundred feet below. It is not typical trout fishing but it is fishing. Trolling is best done at moderate speed and in long, lazy-S curves or by motoring upwind and drifting down. This method is very good with leadheaded jigs. If tedium sets in, the jig can be cast and given a pumping retrieve.

But if the lake trout are within fifteen feet of the surface, as they often are in spring or fall, a great deal more fun can be had by using a light spinning rod or a fly rod to cast jigs, spinners, wet flies, nymphs, and streamers. A good choice for casting flies is a salmon rod or an 8½- to 9½-foot bass-bugging or bonefishing rod. Bright, weighted streamers on 1/0 to 3/0 hooks are especially inviting to lakers. Most fishermen are partial to streamers 3 or 4 inches long. However, where the fish are known to be big there is no reason not to try something as massive as a 5-inch McNally Magnum. A red-and-yellow streamer of that size must appear as a banquet to a hungry laker. It is unwieldy to cast but can be worth the effort. Whatever lure is used, the retrieve should be slow and erratic. By stripping in line a foot at a time, a darting and halting action can be imparted.

When the fish are near the surface, trolling surface streamers may not be quite as deadly as trolling weighted ones, but it can be more fun. The angler sees a wall of water rise behind a fly as a laker comes to it. A wild surface roll and the fish is on! If a laker drops back instead of striking, temptation can be intensified by stripping line out and then pumping the streamer again like a darting minnow. Many fishermen troll at the surface with the biggest streamers they can obtain—the tandem-hooked kind supplied by Bean, for example, which are at least 5 inches long.

Every angler has pet streamer patterns, but two that should not be overlooked in favor of others are the Gray Ghost and the Supervisor. In a reasonably controlled angling experiment conducted over a period of three summers, the Gray Ghost was the top harvester, closely followed by the Supervisor.

Rainbow Trout *(Salmo gairdneri)*

COMMON & REGIONAL NAMES: Alternate names in common usage denote races such as the Kamloops, Shasta, and Kern River trout. (The name *steelhead* denotes sea-run rainbows.)

GAME IDENTIFICATION & LOCATION OF FISHING REGIONS: At the height of a spray-misted leap, an arching rainbow trout—cobalt-backed, silver-sided, pink-banded—may, indeed, look for an instant like a rainbow hanging above the water. The fry of rainbow trout have pronounced parr marks like those on the fry of brown trout and salmon. The adults display extreme variation in markings. Those in streams tend to be heavily spotted with black on the upper body, dorsal fin, and tail; those in clear lakes often have few spots or none. Some have a bluish cast over the silvery sides. Some have golden overtones. Some have a bronze rather than blue-green back. Some resemble cutthroats, though without the red cutthroat slashes. And on some the lower fins match the pink lateral band while on others they match the back.

The migratory form, better known as the steelhead, has a steely appearance—silvery, without the long pink stripe and usually with no spots or very faint ones until it eventually regains bright colors in the spawning stream. (Technically, a steelhead is any migratory rainbow, whether it dwells in the sea or a large lake between spawning periods, but by popular definition it is a sea-run rainbow.)

Size varies with locale as much as color does, and at one time the rainbow was classified as a dozen separate species. As a rule, steelhead and Kamloops rainbows grow larger than the others. Apart from those two types, most of the rainbows caught range from 1 to 4 pounds—from the size of an average brookie to about 18 inches. Steelhead, though a trifle less deep-bodied, are much larger. Many 5-pounders are caught but the average is heavier, probably about 8; nothing less than 15 or so will impress an old steelhead hand.

Not surprisingly, the current rainbow record was set by a steelhead. It was a 42-pound, 2-ounce fish caught at Bell Island, Alaska, in 1970 by David Robert White. Surprisingly indeed, in 1970 White was nine years of age—not much older than his trophy.

Kamloops rainbows often grow larger than steelhead,

though none has yet rivaled that Alaskan giant. The Kamloops race inhabits some of the mountain lakes and streams of lower British Columbia and the northwestern United States. The average size varies with locale and diet. In some insect-rich British Columbian lakes such as Babine, 8-pounders may boil the surface during an evening hatch of caddis, and those fish stage a spectacular aerial fight in the manner of landlocked salmon. They also abound on British Columbia's Kootenay River and the streams around Kamloops—north and northwest, respectively, of Idaho's Priest Lake, where the same form of rainbow provides outstanding sport. On Kootenay Lake, where the Kamloops rainbows have more fish than insects in their diet, anglers troll for 20-pounders. Additional good waters are situated in northeastern Washington, and one additional famous one—Pend Oreille—is in Idaho. The Kamloops in Pend Oreille have a surfeit of kokanee to eat, and they rival those of Kootenay. In either of those lakes, a 30-pounder would not be considered a rarity.

The far West has many famous steelhead streams: California's Eel, Klamath, Trinity, and Smith; Oregon's Rogue, Umpqua, Kalama, Lewis, Willamette, and Cowlitz; Washington's Klickitat, Skagit, Skykomish, and Wind; British Columbia's Kispiox, Thompson, Campbell, and Skeena; and a great many more along the Canadian and Alaskan coasts. A steelhead even larger than the sporting record has been authenticated at Jewel Lake in British Columbia. It was a 52½-pound fish, netted during a spawn-collecting operation by fishery biologists. At the Great Lakes, the largest steelhead are generally caught in the rivers that empty into

Rainbow seen from below as it cuts surface during fight.

Lake Michigan, but there are good runs on the rivers that feed into the others, too. Among the excellent streams are the Au Sable, Platte, Big and Little Manistee, Père Marquette, Muskegon, Black, Elk, Grand, St. Joseph, Au Gres, Chagrin, Conneaut Creek, Bois Brule, Cranberry, and the Two Hearted River (a trout stream made famous by Hemingway).

For ordinary rainbows (if the term "ordinary" applies at all in connection with these fish) waters such as the Snake and its tributaries in Idaho and the Dean in British Columbia are often recommended. But one offers recommendations hesitantly these days, because rainbow fishing has become extremely good in the Midwest—particularly the Great Lakes region—and in countless eastern lakes, rivers, and impoundments.

Originally the species ranged principally from the Rockies to upper California and northward through western Canada to Alaska. A few additional populations were also sprinkled through the upper Midwest. And on the Siberian side of the Pacific, the Kamchatka trout *(S. mykiss)* is suspected by many taxonomists of being just another rainbow subspecies. Rainbows can adapt to alien habitat if the water is clean and fairly cool; they have been established through most of Canada, the Great Lakes, the East, and as far south as Georgia, Tennessee, Arkansas, Oklahoma, and Texas. They have also been transplanted to New Zealand, Chile, Argentina, and other distant lands.

FISH HABITAT & FEEDING BEHAVIOR—ANGLING TACTICS: Rainbows prefer a water temperature between 50° and the low 60's, but sometimes they continue feeding near the surface of a lake even when it has heated up almost to 70°. Some of them can survive water temperatures in the mid-80's—higher than the tolerance level of the other most adaptable trout, the brown.

Sometimes, of course, water that is barely livable for them is changed by man into habitat that suits them better than the natives. The cold tailwaters produced by the dams on the White and Little Red rivers in Arkansas have turned Ozark smallmouth habitat into rainbow habitat. There is reason to mourn the passing of good bass pockets. However, excellent trout fishing can now be had by casting into those tailwaters with minnows, crawfish, plugs, spinners, and flies ranging from Cress Bugs to shrimp imitations to mayfly patterns.

Human activity on many other rivers has harmed rather than helped the rainbow fishing. The migratory trout, in particular, have been hurt by the construction of power dams that block spawning waters on steelhead rivers. They have also been hurt by excessive nitrogen and other pollutants poured into streams.

Most rainbows spawn in spring, but a few do so in fall, and a few spawn twice a year. Most inland forms spawn from January to June, and may still be spawning in early summer in some high, cold waters. There are hatchery strains that breed in every month of the year. Spawning takes place in streams or lake inlets and outlets and is fairly typical of trout reproduction. A female resorbs her roe if she finds no suitable site. Most redds are dug in riffles and near the tails of pools. A female and one or two males arch their bodies and simultaneously eject roe and milt. Then the female loosely covers the eggs with gravel while already clearing a second redd upstream of the first. Some females deposit eggs in only a few redds, while others continue to spawn for a week. Then, somewhat drooping and spent, they move downstream to revive. The eggs hatch in about two months. Some fry move into a lake; others remain in the spawning stream up to three years.

Among the steelhead races, some of the young go to sea quickly and others remain in fresh water for three years. Then they stay in the ocean for several years before returning to spawn. Along the Pacific coast they can be seen entering rivers in one locale or another during every month. Some, known as spring or summer fish, have returned as immatures and will linger in fresh water for half a year to a year before reproducing for the first time. Winter fish are more widespread; they come into the streams in fall and early winter. Though a few may spawn as early as December, most do so from March to May. Not much is known about their lives at sea, but captures of tagged steelhead prove that some of them, like salmon, travel as far as 2,200 miles in the Pacific. Many that come back to the stream mouths in July make their way upriver for several hundred miles and hold there, waiting to spawn the following spring before going back to the ocean. A prime summer run of this sort provides good steelhead fishing as far inland as Idaho's Clearwater River.

Apart from steelheading techniques (which will be treated separately), rainbow fishing can be divided into two general, flexible, and somewhat overlapping categories: fly fishing where in-

sects and shrimp are the dominant foods; trolling or casting baits and hard lures where the major prey is the cisco, kokanee, alewife, or some other fish. Either way, the period from April through June is excellent in the East and at the Great Lakes; mid-June through mid-July is excellent in the West; September through November may well be best in all regions; and the majority of strikes come in early morning and late afternoon. Those strikes are a problem to describe because they vary considerably. Sometimes a nonmigratory rainbow hits as hard as a summer-run steelhead—which is occasionally hard, indeed—and sometimes it takes a lure or bait gently, tentatively, as if to test an angler's nerves, timing, and hook-setting skill. There is less diversity in the actual fight; it almost always involves sensational leaps, headlong runs, sudden switches, speed, and power. And it is safe to say that native rainbows are more determined battlers than the stocked variety. Wild fish fight wildly.

In rivers, the rainbow is a denizen of fast water, which means that a fly fisherman must try the swift runs and riffles of large streams, the tailraces below dams, and the fastest portions of streams that also hold browns and cutthroats. This picture may be daunting to an angler accustomed to dropping dry flies on pools and placid runs, but the shallows above pools can be

Angler removing fly from hefty rainbow.

worked during an actual hatch, and 2- and 3-pounders rise well to dries on many waters; the Dean River in British Columbia comes to mind, and in Idaho parts of the Snake and its tributaries are equally good. As might be expected, rises come fastest in the evening, but most of the catches are of small to medium size when an evening hatch triggers repeated rises. The dry patterns of choice are, generally speaking, those already listed for other trouts; they are governed by locale—a matter of matching a hatch or the region's most common insects. Wherever a strong current is likely to be carrying nymphs, duns, or spentwings, a nymph, wet, or dry pattern ought to work at the appropriate times.

Assorted wet flies, nymphs, bucktails, and streamers are effective in all regions. A deeply fished shrimp-pattern nymph is usually worth trying, and so is a Muddler (most often tied on a no. 6) fluttered right over the bottom. Where the fish are known to be large, streamers must also be large, and some anglers troll or put aside their fly rods, using spinning tackle to cast flies or bait, often with spinners or other attractors.

Crawfish, worms, spawn bags, minnows, even kokanee— all kinds of baits are used. Salmon eggs on egg-holder hooks will take rainbows (and most trouts and chars, for that matter); as a handy substitute for eggs, kernels of canned corn will also inveigle rainbows. The same spinners that take other trout species will take big rainbows, and deeply fished spinners may well account for the majority of the largest fish. Streamers take some big ones, too, but on the lunker water like Kootenay Lake (to cite one example among many) the experienced fishermen tend to favor trolling with spinners, spoons, jigs, deep-running plugs, or bait. They troll the reefs, bars, and shoals, and the river mouths where the current is strong. The technique is the same as for coho (which see) but in shallow water.

STEELHEADING TECHNIQUES: Steelhead fishing is an exceptionally rewarding (though often difficult) sport from the western slope of the Rocky Mountains to the Pacific, and north from the Russian River to Alaska. It has also become a major form of recreation around the Great Lakes, particularly in Ontario, Michigan, Wisconsin, and Minnesota. The runs are best on some rivers from April through June and on others from October to December.

As often as not, a summer-run steelhead will crash into a

lure the way a well-bred bull is supposed to charge a red cape. Most of the time, however, the strike is light. A steelhead will, for instance, often mouth a salmon egg or spawn bag, then take it gently or spit it out and ignore it, or spit it out and take it again. The process can be trickier with a lure. The bite may be so gentle that it feels as if something—a slight snag, perhaps—has merely stopped the lure's swing across the current. The safe procedure is to set the hook. Thus the steelheader loses many flies, spoons, and other lures, hooks a great many "fish" that turn out to be rocks or twigs, and once in a while hooks a fine steelhead.

Another problem (the first problem, really) is the recognition of good holding water in unfamiliar streams. Steelhead move into rivers in groups, a succession of fish using the same holding waters repeatedly, so the good spots are known by local anglers. A visitor without a local friend or guide must do some exploring. One rule of thumb is to ignore both dead water and water too fast for comfortable wading. Try the tails of pools, the slicks that form below them or above rapids, the long, uniform runs—right in the channel or the deeper parts—boulder-strewn bottoms, edges of heavy flows, deep pockets, and the heads of runs or riffles. Likely waters should be covered thoroughly. This necessitates wading in at the head of a run or riffle and casting across repeatedly, first making short casts, then longer ones, and then moving down

Angler handling jumping steelhead on Alaskan river.

eight or ten steps and casting again, moving and casting until the whole run has been probed. A fly can be drifted or twitched. Either way, the rod ought to be kept fairly low, with its tip directed toward the fly's position as the fly moves down and swings in, because a majority of strikes will occur during the last quarter of the drift.

Many fishermen use spoons, spinners, yarn flies, or salmon eggs for steelhead because these fish continue to eat at least sporadically during the spawning run and they will grab offerings that represent food. In one locale or another, spawn bags, single salmon eggs on egg-holder hooks, and even nightcrawlers are drifted on the bottom or bounced downstream with the current. On Lake Superior, fishermen cast bait into the stream mouths, using sinkers as heavy as an ounce to stay on bottom. Around the river outlets they also cast small copper, silver, and silver-and-blue spinners, as well as silver-and-blue minnow-shaped plugs. In the fall, they troll very slowly off the river mouths, often using 2½- to 3-inch wobbling plugs. They tow the lures a hundred feet or more behind the stern because steelhead are leery of boats, and they set the hook hard at any suggestion of a strike. With drifted bait, a very light nibble is a signal to let out more line for encouragement and then set the hook. In the West, bait is used the same way, and wobbling spoons or spinners are often trolled or fished across- and downstream, retrieved with a downstream swing as in fly fishing. In both regions, spinning equipment is common; the line generally tests 8 to 15 pounds.

Fly fishing at the Great Lakes is rather different from the western variety, however, because the streams are smaller and more placid. The fish hold longer in deep pools and runs, and sometimes they can be stalked from the banks of clear, shallow rivers. A man can cast to a lie then, whether with a fly or a small spinner. Repeated casts sometimes trigger a response. This technique works well in October and November, April and May.

In the West, some of the best waters are wide and deep enough to require skill in double-haul casting. For 60- to 80-foot casts, many anglers dispense with short, light fly rods, preferring a 9½-footer with a reel holding 100 to 150 yards of 15-pound backing, then another 75 feet of monofilament, 28 to 32 feet of single-tapered shooting-head line, and finally a 9- to 12-foot leader (or 15-foot for clear rivers like the Rogue) with a tippet testing 6 or 8 pounds. For use with a heavy steelhead rod, an angler wants a heavy shooting head—320 grains or more.

All the same, a summer run in clear, low water may call for big dry flies—about size 8. The best are the standard trout and salmon patterns, but tied bushily. In the tidewaters, streamers and many weighted wets take fish, but the standard river patterns are those that have proved valuable for years, some of them designed in the West specifically as steelhead flies. They may be tied on hooks ranging from no. 2 to 10. Since they will have to take punishment on rocky bottoms, Limerick bend and Mustad round-bend hooks are favorite types. Double hooks are popular on some streams. Patterns, tied sparsely to sink well, range from somber to gaudy: the Boss, Sky Komish Sunrise, Silver Hilton, Umpqua Special, Umpqua Red Brat, Thor, Burlap, Lady Godiva, Jock Scott, Thunder and Lightning, Black Prince, Golden Demon, Gray Hackle, Badger Hackle Peacock, and so on.

When an angler sets the hook as one of these creations pauses in its swing, his steelheading problems are not at an end. Since clear water demands a long, fine leader, he has to be skillful and cool-nerved while playing a heavy battler that has no intention of leaving the water except to hurtle through the air.

Walleye (Stizostedion vitreum)
COMMON & REGIONAL NAMES: *walleyed pike, pike-perch, pike, jack, jackfish, dore, pickerel*

GAME IDENTIFICATION & LOCATION OF FISHING REGIONS: A walleye by any other name (including such misleading aliases as walleyed pike and pickerel) remains an oversized species of perch. That description should not be construed as disparaging. Like yellow perch, walleye makes estimable table fare, and its high angling value prevents overharvesting for the market.

It is not as spectacular a fighter as bass, pike, trout, or salmon. Though a big walleye can wage a ten- or fifteen-minute battle, it rarely leaps or makes sudden dashes, stunning switches, or powerful runs. Its teeth may fray a repeatedly used leader (or an angler's fingers if he neglects to use a hemostat or pliers to disgorge a hook), but it will rarely break a light line if the rod is kept arched and the line taut. Its style is a matter of short runs, dives, and straightforward resistance—dogged if the fish is large, brief if it is small. The species should not be too casually damned

with faint praise, however. Now and then, in the spring or fall, merely passable ferocity is counterbalanced by sheer numbers of strikes. In the dead of winter the walleye can be caught through the ice, and in the dead of summer, when other game species become almost somnolent, it provides rejuvenating sessions of night fishing. Furthermore, since it is relatively easy to rear in hatcheries and takes well to stocking in large bodies of water, it enriches many fisheries outside of its original northerly domain.

In some areas a 14-inch walleye is no keeper, but most catches range from that size (the average length of a 1-pound specimen) to a length of nearly 2 feet and a weight of 4 or 5 pounds. Each year anglers boat a good number of 7- and 8-pound walleyes, as well. In the better walleye states, the annual records are often set by yard-long fish weighing 14 or 15 pounds. The record is held by a 25-pound Tennessee walleye caught in 1960.

The walleye has an elongate, rather evenly tapered body, a moderately forked tail, spines on the forward dorsal fin and the anal fin, and sharp canine teeth along the jaws and on the roof of the mouth. Its name refers to its big, glassy, milkily opaque, light-sensitive eyes, which easily spot prey or a dark lure at night. Experienced night fishermen take care with running lights and flashlights; a glare on the water near the boat will alarm walleyes.

The walleye's dominant color is olive-green, usually with a yellowish cast, dark on the back and paling to white on the belly. It generally has six or seven dark, irregular, dimly edged saddles over its back and sides. The white of the belly reaches to the tail and spreads onto the end of the lower lobe. This white tip is the marking most often used to distinguish a walleye from its closest relative, the sauger (which see). It also differs from the sauger in having dark streaks or blotches on the forward dorsal fin, but no clear rows of spots.

Typical walleye; this one was caught in Montana.

Originally, its range extended through the states around the Great Lakes and across most of Canada, as far north as the lower reaches of Hudson Bay. Widespread, intensive stocking has now established the species throughout the East and most of the South and West. It is abundant—and grows to its largest size—in the deep TVA impoundments of Tennessee and Kentucky and the drainages of the Alabama and Tennessee rivers. Lake Erie has always had excellent walleye fishing. Walleyes are plentiful in a number of New York and Pennsylvania lakes, the best known probably being New York's Oneida and Pennsylvania's Pymatuning. The species ranks first among all the gamefish in the Minnesota lakes (where, incidentally, ice fishing produces some of the heaviest catches), and Wisconsin has an equal abundance. Every Canadian province has walleyes, except in the most northerly portions. The lakes of Saskatchewan can produce nothing to rival the Tennessee trophies, but in terms of numbers caught, they probably have the continent's best walleye fishing.

FISH HABITAT & FEEDING BEHAVIOR—ANGLING TACTICS:
Walleyes are not often caught in lakes covering much less than 80 or 90 acres. They need large, shallow spawning areas over gravel or rubble, plus extensive living and foraging quarters more than ten feet deep—and preferably much deeper. They inhabit rivers with suitable spawning sites and deep pools and channels, but the ideal habitat is a sizable lake or impoundment. Good fishing waters are usually fairly clear and have hard bottoms or big patches of sand or gravel. There must be plenty of minnows or comparable baitfish, the primary food, and plenty of water that remains cooler than 85° in summer. During the warm months, strikes come most frequently at depths where a water thermometer shows a reading of about 60°, the temperature at which the walleye's metabolic rate induces a hearty appetite.

Fishing the spawning sites in spring is prohibited on many waters, but it is frequently permissible to fish the approaches then, or to fish the beds themselves very soon after spawning. Reproduction generally takes place in clear water, between one and five feet deep, over gravel, rubble, or cluttered rocks. Walleyes in rivers seek gravel bars, ledges, deltas, and other such sites. Those in lakes migrate up tributary streams or, if suitable streams are lacking, they congregate in shoals where springs or wave action can substitute for the flow of river water. The males head into such areas soon after the ice breaks up, and the larger females move in as the water temperature reaches 45° to 50°. Spawning occurs in April over a large part of the range; it starts earlier in the South, slightly later in the northernmost waters.

The average number of eggs dropped is about fifty thousand, but a small female may deposit only half as many and a large one may produce half a million. Several males escort her across the bed, zigzagging and thrashing as eggs and milt are ejected. The eggs lodge amid protective gravel and debris where moving water keeps them clean and oxygenated during the twelve to eighteen days of incubation. The unguarded hatchlings drift for several days, absorbing their yolk sacs, protected only by near-invisibility; they are about a half-inch long and almost as thin as paper. Perhaps one in ten thousand will survive the first year, but thereafter the odds improve enormously—to one out of two or three. They grow fast in the South but live only six or seven years, while in the North they live about twice as long. Depending on latitude and the water's food supply, a walleye may measure 4 inches or a foot long by the end of its first summer. Fry subsist on tiny zooplankton, progressing to larger prey as they move into deeper water. As fingerlings, they are already feeding on baitfish.

In the spring, walleye fishing is usually best near the spawning areas—around the mouths of a lake's feeder streams, for example. The males, especially, linger in the shallows. Then they begin to go deeper, temporarily scattering and thus giving some anglers the erroneous notion that they "go off their feed" for a few weeks in late spring. Actually, they have not yet gathered in their summer haunts; this is a time to probe the six- to twenty-foot depths and then, a little later, the twenty- to forty-foot depths. Both spring and fall offer excellent fishing in comparatively shallow water, but even then walleyes do their hunting far below the surface where the light begins to dim; baits and lures should be kept down at least eight feet in rivers, a couple of feet deeper in lakes, and experienced trollers let out 60 feet or more of line because walleyes hardly ever venture near the vibrations of an outboard—even a quiet little electric trolling motor. Such a motor (or a gasoline motor running in reverse) is recommended, for trolling or retrieving must be slow. The walleye is a plodding hunter and must be given time to eye its prey—whether real or simulated—for

a few moments before striking.

Particularly in spring and fall, walleyes often share the habitat of smallmouth bass, yet their reputation for lying deep prompts many anglers to troll more or less blindly across the deepest valleys of lake bottom. What the walleyes seek is a rich minnow-hunting ground adjacent to deeper water—bars, rubble, boulders, drop-offs, delta ridges, reefs, ledges, points, and break-waters around dams and bridges. Such spots are most promising if oxygenated by current or wave action. Even in the heat of a mid-summer night, repeated action is associated with the old midwestern technique of "bar hopping"—casting for about fifteen minutes over each sand or gravel bar, then moving on to another.

As spring warms into summer, the fish school again and cruise the deeper waters—generally thirty to sixty feet—over hard bottoms. Some anglers now switch from 6-pound monofilament or light braided line to high-density, wire, or lead-core line. Others simply double (or nearly double) the test weight since the heavier, larger-diameter monofilament sinks well enough and permits a walleye to fulfill its fighting potential. Many anglers also use

Fisherman hoisting walleye caught on spoon.

piano-wire leaders to withstand walleye teeth but, since this fish does not often break off, some of us prefer the low visibility and high flexibility of ordinary monofilament leaders. With a no. 6 hook snelled to a 16-inch monofilament leader and a slip sinker affixed above the snap swivel, a minnow can be effectively trolled, drifted, or retrieved. Hung from a 7-foot spinning rod or a shorter baitcasting rod, this is a very practical, versatile walleye rig.

In walleye-smallmouth habitat, crawfish make good bait. Nightcrawlers (as well as plastic worms or eels) work well in summer, perhaps representing a tantalizing change of diet to deep-cruising walleye schools. For ice fishing, minnows are the finest bait. Regardless of season, the favorites are live minnows and comparable fish, including madtoms and those otherwise undesirable parasites, lampreys. A very different kind of parasite, the leech, is unsurpassed in the spring. A leech should be hooked just once, through its sucker, so that it writhes naturally when drifted or slowly trolled with a slip sinker.

Often a walleye mouths its prey tentatively or else cripples it, backs off for a better view, and hits it again. When a knowledgeable walleye fisherman uses bait, he feeds out line as soon as he feels a bite, awaiting the real strike before lowering the rod tip to set the hook with a snap of his wrist. A lure is generally hit harder, sometimes hooking the fish without any assistance from the angler. The strike is not a smash but a sudden stop, almost as if the lure had snagged. Occasionally it is only a bump—the crippling-and-backing-off maneuver. The lure-fisherman does not feed out line then; instead, he accelerates the lure's speed to trigger a strike by simulating an escape attempt.

In Canada and around the Great Lakes, an old standard lure-and-bait combination is a June Bug spinner with a minnow or worm trailing behind it. This is a superlative walleye rig, but probably the most popular lures today are leadheaded jigs with marabou, plastic, or bucktail dressing and size 4 or 6 treble hooks. Models like the Upperman Bucktails and the Dollflies are perennially effective. Wobbling spoons and deep-running plugs are equally deadly walleye deceivers. Minnowlike plugs are the obvious rule, the exception being the extremely productive flatfish style with outrigger hook attachments.

Streamers can be trolled, but they are at their best for fly-rodding the shallows in the spring and fall. They should be weighted, of course, and used with a sinking line and a leader testing about 10 pounds. Though size is not critical, they are usually tied on no. 4 or no. 6 hooks. Most of the favored patterns are dominantly white or yellow, with or without a dash of red—patterns like the Nite Owl, Ambrose Bucktail, White Maribou, Royal Coachman, Brass Hat, Golden Darter, Doctor Oatman, Colonel Bates, Mickey Finn, Dark or Light Edson Tiger, Sky Komish Sunrise, White Muddler, Yellow Butcher, and so on. Some anglers also catch walleyes on various salmon flies or Mylar-bodied saltwater flies.

Regardless of which baits or lures are used, walleye fishing improves when the sun goes down. The species is primarily a nocturnal forager, the star of freshwater night fishing. On bright nights and in clear water, light-colored lures receive the most strikes, while dark nights demand a switch to dark lures, even black ones. Writers have speculated about the effects of the moon on tides and water levels, not only on the sea but on large inland bodies of water. The moon's pull may well influence the activity of aquatic life, but the influence of the moon's light must be stronger. Even a night prowler like the walleye is aided in its foraging by a slight penetration of light beneath the surface—not the frightening glare of a bumbling angler's flashlight but the gentle moonglow; walleye fishing is best under a full moon.

White Bass *(Morone chrysops)*
COMMON & REGIONAL NAMES: *barfish, sand bass, streak, striper*

GAME IDENTIFICATION & LOCATION OF FISHING REGIONS: On Fall River Reservoir, a sprawling Kansas impoundment, an angler inches his boat along with an electric trolling motor as he peers through binoculars, scanning thousands of acres of water. He has a small, deep-running, white-and-silver plug in the water, but he pays little attention to it. After a few minutes he spots a ruffled patch of surface perhaps a hundred yards off. Heading for it, he reels in and switches to a cup-headed yellow surface plug from which a white jig trails on a 16-inch strand of monofilament. It will be awkward to cast, but no matter. He cuts the motor and drifts toward the ruffled patch—a furious boiling of the surface now that he is within range. He casts along the fringe of the boil,

taking care not to charge in and scatter either the prey or the predators that churn the water. As he begins the first retrieve, his light spinning rod bows deeply, and he is playing the first white bass of the day, a 3-pound, black-lined, pugnacious slab of silver.

After a few minutes, when he has caught two more, the churning subsides, but he knows that the school of half-grown gizzard shad, forced to the surface by the ripping attacks of a pack of white bass, may soon come up again elsewhere in the vicinity. Before long he is sneaking the skiff toward another boil, jumpfishing for white bass as a hunter jump-shoots ducks on prairie sloughs. Because the species is cyclic in numbers and occasionally capricious in its choice of foraging areas, white-bass angling can degenerate into boredom, but when it is good the action can reach wild crescendos. And since there is no danger of overharvesting, neither seasons nor limits are imposed in many areas. Whether an angler releases his fish or saves them all for the freezer, he may hook a score in half an hour. At Lake Pleasant, a big Arizona reservoir that may be America's best white-bass water, a zealot once confessed to catching ninety in an afternoon.

Lake Pleasant is one of many reservoirs stocked with white bass in recent years. The world's record was set in 1972 on Ferguson Lake, California, by a 19½-inch, 5-pound, 5-ounce lunker believed to be one of a group transplanted a couple of years earlier

White bass.

from the Arizona reservoir. It outweighed the previous record-holder, a Kansas specimen, by an ounce.

There was a time when many anglers snubbed the white bass, but since the 1950's it has been widely stocked and enthusiastically received. Fishermen have come to appreciate its schooling habits, its eagerness to hit lures, its fine meat, and the adequacy of its fight—a jumpless tussle but quite vigorous for a fish averaging between a half-pound and 2 or 3. Moreover, it is easily bred in hatcheries, and because it is very prolific but also short-lived, the populations renew themselves with little need of management and no hazard of fishing a lake out. Finally, its voracity significantly helps to control soaring reservoir populations of small panfish and such baitfish as gizzard shad and threadfin shad, which crowd the game species.

Originally, the white bass was found from the Great Lakes to Missouri, Arkansas, and Kansas, along the Mississippi River drainage, and eastward to the western side of the Alleghenies. Wisconsin's Wolf River, Kentucky's Dix River, and Missouri's Lake of the Ozarks have a reputation for white bass, but now these waters are rivaled by many throughout the Missouri River system and in most of the South and Southwest.

The species is a freshwater member of the Percichthyidae, the "temperate bass family" that includes white perch, yellow bass, and striped bass. Above its faintly yellow-tinged belly, it is a silvery fish with an average of ten thin, blackish longitudinal stripes (five of them above the lateral line), a spiny forward dorsal fin, and a soft hind one. Thus, it looks much like a small striped bass, but it has a more deeply forked tail and a deeper, more compressed body, a shape midway between that of the true striper and that of a sunfish. In waters where the catch might be either a white bass or a landlocked striper, an angler can make positive identification by examining the tongue; the white bass has a single patch of glossohyal teeth, whereas the striped bass has two. In some regions the similarity of yellow bass may also cause confusion, but the stripes of the yellow bass are fewer and usually broken, the forward and hind dorsal fins joined at the base, and the lower jaw almost even with the upper rather than jutting distinctly forward, as on the white bass. The yellow variety is usually smaller and darker, often with golden sides.

In 1965 a team of South Carolina and Tennessee fishery

biologists crossbred a 2-pound male white bass with a 20-pound female striped bass and produced extremely hardy hybrids that exhibited faster growth and a higher survival rate than either parent species. The experimental project is being continued at lakes and reservoirs in Texas and Florida as well as in the two states where it originated. On some of these waters, 6- to 8-pound hybrids are becoming common, and one 18-pounder has been caught. In size the hybrids are more like stripers than white bass, but they bite as eagerly as the smaller species.

Where water temperature drops below 55° or so in the fall, the metabolism of white bass slows down and they eat very little from then until spring. Yet the fishing for hybrids seems to be best from November to April. They strike leadhead plastic jigs that imitate grubs, deep-running plugs that imitate shad, and the fly fisherman's popping bugs and light-colored streamers. A typical hybrid has the striper's double patch of teeth on its tongue, but is deeper-bodied. It usually displays broken stripes.

FISH HABITAT & FEEDING BEHAVIOR—ANGLING TACTICS:
The construction of giant reservoirs in the South and Southwest has been a boon to white-bass anglers, as this fish almost never maintains a healthy population in lakes covering less than several hundred acres. The species fares best in large, relatively clear lakes and impoundments, but also frequents some rivers and fairly big streams. It requires water with considerable expanses deeper than 10 feet, because its daytime feeding strategy is chiefly to cruise the depths where prey can be pursued in the open, without much escape cover such as brush, weeds, or drowned woods. A school of white bass stays low, hunting groups of shad or other small fish flitting about a little higher. When victims are sighted they are attacked from below, crowded toward the surface and into a tight mass that can be ripped and gobbled as it flails the water in a panicked effort to escape.

However, these fish need gravel, rocks, or rubble for spawning, and in spring they often concentrate at the mouths of feeder streams. The run begins in April or as early as March in some southern waters but is delayed until May or June in parts of the North. Fishing is best during the run, as the bass are hungry and aggressive and assembled in very large mobs in easily recognized stretches of water. There will be more action in the streams and near stream mouths than out in the lakes where most of the summer action will occur.

A female is likely to carry 250,000 eggs or more, frequently several times that number. She seeks a rumpled bed under about six or seven feet of water. Males hover about, fertilizing the roe as it is ejected. Millions of eggs settle amid the gravel and, theoretically, can hatch two or three days later. However, they require near-perfect conditions: moving water and a steady temperature of 58° to 64°. Since large percentages fail to hatch, a really successful brood is generally spawned only once in three or four years. Of those that hatch, perhaps one in 25,000 will survive the first year, after which the annual survival rate soars, probably fluctuating between 20 and 40 percent. These factors account for the peaks and dips in fishing success every two or three years as abundant broods of large fish begin to die off.

The tiny fry form great schools, and after a few weeks of feeding on minute zooplankton they begin to devour larger crustaceans and insects. By summer's end, a northern white bass is about 5 inches long, a southern one more than 7 inches, and it has started feeding heavily on small fish. The species does not show a pronounced cannibalistic appetite; it prefers assorted minnows and sunfish, perch, crappies, bluegills, and especially shad—the gizzard shad of eastern waters and the smaller threadfin shad of the West. White bass become rather torpid at fall temperatures, and growth stops until spring. A half-pound 10-incher is probably in its second year; a white bass measuring over a foot long and weighing a full pound is two or three years old, and a 16-inch, 2-pound fish is four or five years old—nearing the end of its natural life span. Since white bass do not mature until their third year in the South or sometimes their fourth in northern states, a large percentage must reproduce only once or twice.

The adults continue to travel with companions of their own size in big, dense schools, and they continue to hunt the same prey. Unfortunately for the angler, gizzard shad die on the hook too quickly to provide good bait. Threadfin shad are occasionally used, but a trolled or cast minnow is the general favorite, by dint of its hardiness and strong appeal to white bass and other game. Whether an angler uses light spinning equipment or a fly rod, he can elicit action by casting small minnows into the current at places where the white bass normally feast on vulnerable prey—

below dams, for example.

White bass become so agitated as they whip into prey that they seldom distinguish between the real thing and a counterfeit. Being so easily fooled, they are more often caught on lures than on bait. They hit hard, and generally hook themselves without any tricky setting by the angler. Perhaps the deadliest of white-bass lures is a half-ounce white, marabou-dressed, leadhead jig. Yellow may rival it when the fish are located in deep water. Another favorite is any small "crankbait" plug, big-lipped for deep running and white with silver stippling to simulate a shad. Sometimes a half-ounce sinker is attached above a short leader to get the plug down still deeper. A heavy silver spoon can also be wobbled over the bottom to mimic an injured shad. Plugs with trailing jigs work well, too, and so do fairly big spinners, especially if enhanced with small pork rinds. White or yellow bass bugs and subsurface or surface plugs also take many white bass.

Fly fishermen may prefer medium-sized light or dominantly white streamers to simulate small shad and minnows—a Doctor Oatman, for example, or a Silver Darter, White Maribou, Black Ghost, Blacknose Dace, or Royal Coachman. For that matter, nothing prevents experimentation with wets like the White Miller or, when the fish are on top, dries like the White Wulff.

In early morning, late afternoon, or evening, the fishing may be good in the shallows, and even during the day it can be excellent around stream outlets that have deposited clean sand deltas. White bass like to hunt over sand flats and bars or other bare-bottom patches. An angler can drift across an outlet, casting a spoon toward open water and jigging it in. Some night-fishing specialists employ a more arcane method—hanging a light on a pole to attract minnows and dipping a jig through the gathering school. The minnows come like moths to a lantern and the white bass sometimes come to the minnows in like fashion.

Many anglers stay too shallow in the daytime and put few white bass on the stringer until they happen to see a boil of bait where they can jump-fish. The bass cruise widely, and some sophisticated aficionados locate them with depth-finders that signal audibly when passing over a school. Usually they locate two schools—shad or other bait above white bass. A shrewd bit of duplicity consists in lowering a jig through the shad, perhaps five feet under them, twitching it, and bracing for a hard strike.

Winter fishing for mountain whitefish.

Whitefish & Inconnu *(Coregonus, Prosopium,* and *Stenodus)*

COMMON & REGIONAL NAMES: Names in common usage denote each species. The lake whitefish *(Coregonus clupeaformis)* is also called *common whitefish, high-back whitefish, Otsego bass, Great Lakes whitefish,* and *Labrador whitefish.* The mountain, or Rocky Mountain, whitefish *(Prosopium williamsoni)* is also called *Montana whitefish.* The round whitefish *(P. cylindraceum)* is also called *Menominee whitefish, grayback,* and *pilotfish.* The inconnu *(Stenodus leucichthys)* is also called *sheefish.*

GAME IDENTIFICATION & LOCATION OF FISHING REGIONS:

Fork-tailed, small-headed salmonids common to America, Europe, and Asia, whitefish have the fleshy adipose fins of their relatives, the trouts, but no healthy trout has the big, loosely attached scales of a whitefish. The whitefish family includes eight graybacked, pearly-sided, herringlike species of ciscoes, all sharing the genus of the lake whitefish. Ciscoes inhabit lake waters from New England through the Great Lakes and across much of Canada. Ice fishermen jig for them with spinners, small spoons, and leadheads; and fly fishermen take them in June or July, depending on region, when cisco schools rise to big hatches of mayflies. A few varieties reach the size of an average lake whitefish—2 to 3 pounds—and occasional lunkers are twice as heavy. Generally,

however, they are smaller and less game than other members of the family. Some cisco species rarely grow much longer than 6 inches. Usually when an angler talks of whitefish, he means one of the medium-sized, relatively widespread types, but, technically, American whitefishes range from midget ciscoes to the far-northwestern inconnu—the "unknown one"—which has been reported to reach more than 50 pounds.

The major species are the lake, mountain, and round whitefish and the inconnu, or sheefish. ("Shee" is derived from the Eskimo word for the species.) The most popular is the lake whitefish. It is also the tastiest and the most heavily harvested by commercial means. Its populations have declined somewhat in easily accessible waters where gill netting is permitted, but it remains abundant in many northern lakes. A whitefish, especially this kind, is excellent fried, sautéed, broiled, or poached. However, those of us who are not barbarians question why anyone should want to do any of those things to what might otherwise be alchemized into smoked whitefish, the third or fourth highest achievement of western civilization.

Its name notwithstanding, the lake whitefish is found in many northern rivers such as the Kanuchian and Gods in Manitoba and the streams that feed Lake La Ronge, Reindeer Lake, and Cree Lake in Saskatchewan. It is plentiful in the Great Lakes and in Great Slave Lake and Great Bear Lake. It provides fine sport in a number of Maine lakes—Moosehead, Sebago, Chamberlain, and so on. It ranges from New York and New England through the upper Midwest and across Canada and Alaska. Although it is most common in deep lakes, it can be found in other cold habitats—not only inland rivers but brackish and even salt water.

Regional races exhibit subtle physiological differences, and in some locales the species seldom grows much bigger than a cisco. Generally, the lake whitefish has appropriately white sides, with a soft, silky sheen and silver glints. The color darkens on the back to bronze or olive-green, and the fins and tail tend to be dusky or a bronzy gray. The deeply forked tail is dark-edged. The head is small, the snout blunt, the mouth small, fragile, and toothless. Sometimes the species is confused with the closely related cisco, but the cisco is more cylindrical while the lake whitefish is ovate in cross section, and the cisco's back is more bluish or greenish-gray. An adult lake whitefish is quickly recognized by

an angler because its back arches high behind the head, forming a bulge almost amounting to a hump. If there is any doubt, the mouth will tell; the upper lip of a lake whitefish overhangs the lower lip. Most sporting catches weigh less than 4 pounds, but commercial fishermen have dredged 20-pounders out of deep waters. The record on rod and reel was set in 1974 on Great Bear Lake in the Northwest Territories; it weighed an even 13 pounds.

The round whitefish has the rather cylindrical, uniformly tapered body implied by its name. Its sides are silvery with a brownish wash, and the head and back are greenish-bronze. Some mature specimens are more colorful—reddish or orange on the belly. A few 4-pound catches have come from the Great Lakes, but this species rarely exceeds half that weight or a length of 15 inches. It is primarily a lake inhabitant, ranging from Maine and New Brunswick north to Ungava Bay and west through the Great Lakes, across Canada and Alaska and into the Arctic Ocean.

The mountain whitefish belongs to the same genus and looks somewhat like the round variety. It, too, is fairly cylindrical. Its back is olive-brown, shading to pearly silver on the lower sides and white on the belly. It can grow to 5 pounds, but the average catch weighs a pound or so. It inhabits clear, deep lakes and high, swift streams from the Rockies to the Pacific Northwest as far up as lower British Columbia. It is plentiful in Washington, Idaho, and on the eastern slopes of the Sierras in California. Good mountain-whitefish waters include stretches of such rivers as the Snake, Payette, Wind, Madison, Gallatin, Bitterroot, Flathead, and Deschutes. This species is not as hardy a fighter as the lake

Inconnu, also known as sheefish.

whitefish, and many anglers consider it a pest in streams where it competes with trout for space and food—and sometimes for dry flies. It is, however, an acceptable summer gamefish, and an appreciated winter quarry where steelhead are absent—in Colorado, Utah, Montana, and Wyoming.

The inconnu, largest of the group and most limited in distribution, is a long, silvery, cylindrical fish averaging 5 or 6 pounds but often weighing 25 or 30. Unlike other members of its family, it has bristlelike teeth. Its habits are also unlike those of its relatives, for it resides in brackish estuaries of the far Northwest and, just once in every three or four years, migrates upriver to spawn. That is, each individual spawns only that often, but considerable numbers of sheefish are ready to breed in any given year. Every June and July, they invade the rivers of Alaska and northwestern Canada. Some travel nearly a thousand miles. There are also landlocked populations in big lakes such as Great Slave and Great Bear.

FISH HABITAT & FEEDING BEHAVIOR—ANGLING TACTICS:
They are cold-water fish and autumn spawners, all of them, but the inconnu's life cycle is not typical of the group. It probably has the greatest longevity, as sheefish over twenty years old are not uncommon. Being the largest of the clan, it deposits the greatest number of eggs—about 125,000 to 325,000. Because evolution has programed it to travel great distances on its spawning run, it begins migrating in the spring in order to spew its eggs over gravel bottoms in the fall.

In relatively warm waters, the eggs of many fall-spawning salmonids hatch during the winter, but winter food may be too meager for the survival of fry in cold habitats. Incubation periods are lengthened by low temperatures, and the eggs of the inconnu and other whitefish species lie dormant until conditions favor hatching. (Those of the round whitefish, for example, are fertilized in November and December but generally do not hatch until April.) Though whitefish cluster at entrances to spawning streams, at resting and feeding spots along the way, and around suitable gravel beds, they are not colonial spawners. They pair off, or a female is escorted by a couple of males.

The smaller species migrate in the fall, and their reproductive processes are roughly similar. Mountain and lake whitefish go to the shallows of lakes or ascend streams. Round whitefish seek shoals and usually deposit their eggs on gravel three to twenty feet deep. Mountain and round whitefish lay about 2,500 to 10,000 eggs per female, and a lake whitefish releases up to about 12,000. The eggs are heavily gleaned by winter-feeding predators. In the fall, mountain whitefish in particular feast on their own eggs.

Of all the American varieties only the inconnu becomes a true predator. Its young eat plankton at first and then gobble larger bottom-dwelling organisms; in their second year they begin devouring whatever small fish they can capture. Northern anglers sometimes take them while seeking trout; indeed, the way to catch inconnu is to fish the pools and promising lies in the same manner as for trout. They can be fooled by streamers, but the best lures are half-ounce to 1-ounce wobbling spoons, spinners, and spinner-flies. A small or medium sheefish is often a very agile, troutlike fighter, while those weighing more than about 10 pounds are inclined to make deep runs.

The primary foods of mountain whitefish are the larvae of stoneflies, caddisflies, and midges. Some anglers harvest such foods from stream riffles, turning over stones to gather stonefly nymphs, the best natural baits. Salmon eggs, maggots, and fruit-flies also bring bites. Spinners work well, and a fly-tier can use artificial nymphs, but during the warm months the best lures are dry flies resembling local hatches. Mountain whitefish rise greedily to evening presentations of small dries, tied on size 12 to 16 hooks. A fly must be offered and worked daintily because this species can be as wary as a brown trout even when hundreds of whitefish are rising to a big hatch.

Winter fishing for mountain whites is a novel sport where main river channels remain open. An angler can reach past the ice with a spinning or fly rod to drift bait along the bottom, but some specialists prefer a long cane pole with a line of about equal length. A bobber, a sinker, and a hook as small as a no. 12 are used to offer a stonefly nymph or other natural bait.

Where lake whitefish are plentiful, round whitefish receive scant attention because of their small size. However, they frequent the shallows more regularly than lake whites and can be taken near shore. In May and again in early fall, they congregate near and around the mouths of streams flowing into Lake Superior, and anglers on Michigan's Upper Peninsula catch them by casting a small gob of worm on a size 8 hook, weighted with a small sinker. These fish feed chiefly on insect larvae and small crustaceans, and can be caught by the same tactics used for lake whitefish, whose diet is similar but supplemented by baitfish.

All of these species are slow-growing. A typical lake whitefish in Lake Erie is three years old when it reaches a length of 16 inches. The big ones are hard to find. In far-northern lakes, whitefish schools often accompany grayling as they hunt near shore, but in the thermally stratified lakes near the Canadian border the whitefish, especially the big ones, prefer deep water in the summer. They may be several hundred feet down in Lake Superior. This creates two problems for the angler. First, unless he has learned some choice locations from experience or a local informant, there is no telling where most of the whitefish may be cruising or resting. Second, whitefish cannot be hauled up from the depths as easily as lake trout. All whitefish are slow, tentative nibblers with fragile mouths. The hook cannot be set hard; nor can heavy pressure hoist a fighting whitefish, because that, too, will yank the hook out. Playing one requires coaxing.

Where chumming is legal, some anglers lower a bucket or metal "baiting cone" with a trip-catch lid to spill chopped minnows, boiled rice or pasta, doughballs, even canned corn over the bottom in waters up to about sixty feet deep. The spot is marked with a buoy, and the fishermen wait until the next day or night (night fishing is good) for whitefish to gather there. Cut bait can then be lowered with a sinker. Some anglers dispense with bait, snagging the feeding whitefish almost as paddlefish are snagged, by a method called "snatching." The rig is an ordinary lead sinker with bare hooks soldered on. Some anglers also use a handline with a dipsey sinker and a pair of no. 8 hooks baited with chunks of sucker flesh. The baits are jigged gently until a whitefish nibbles one, expels it, nibbles and spits again, and finally takes it with a slow, strong pull. The hook is set by tightening, not jerking, and the fish is brought up slowly. Ice fishermen, too, drop chum through spud-holes and then jig minnows, cut bait, or corn on a broad-bend hook for these nibblers.

But although whitefish are deep-water associates of lake trout, they can be caught more often than lakers in the shallows, and therein lies the best sport. River fishing is good in the spring and fall. During the day a river angler can use small spinners and leadheaded jigs. In the evening the fish rise as trout do, and they can be taken on dry flies resembling local hatches.

If a lake is calm and a good hatch of mayflies or caddisflies is under way, a fly caster probes the bays in search of swirls. Unlike a trout, a rising whitefish moves continually and in a predictable direction. The angler notes a rise and watches for another, several seconds later and some yards from the first. Now the line of movement is known. The fly is cast along that line, perhaps ten yards beyond the second rise, to intercept the quarry. The whitefish may take it from below, turning and sucking it in, or may roll almost clear of the water to come down on it. Either way, if the hook is set too fast the fish will have no time to inhale the fly, and if it is set too hard it will tear loose. There can be no horsing as the fish makes short, strong runs, seldom jumping but rolling out like a seal or porpoise until it is netted or goes free.

White Perch *(Morone americana)*
COMMON & REGIONAL NAMES: *silver perch, sea perch*

GAME IDENTIFICATION & LOCATION OF FISHING REGIONS:
The derivation of the word "perch" follows a meandering path back through Middle English, Old French, and Latin to a couple of Greek terms (of equally roiled background) meaning "spotted" or "dark." Taxonomically, a true perch—the yellow perch, for example—is a member of the Percidae, but many unrelated species have been named perch because they were thought to resemble other fish that had been so named for a fancied resemblance to still other fish. The white perch neither looks nor acts very much like the true perches. It belongs to the family Percichthyidae, genus *Morone.* It has two freshwater clansmen of comparable size, the white bass and yellow bass, but in its easy tolerance of fresh, brackish, or sea water it is more like its larger relative, the striped bass.

A young white perch sometimes has a faint suggestion of the horizontal stripes that mark all three relatives, but they fade completely with maturity. It also has the same squarish, almost unforked tail and high, triangular dorsal fins. It looks rather like a very small striper but with a deep, more laterally compressed body. Its back and tail are generally olive or greenish-gray or al-

most black, its sides silvery green, often slightly bronzed, grading to white on the belly. Its pectoral fins are also more or less bronzed, and its head is almost as dark as its back but with light cheeks and gill covers. Only when living in salty or brackish water is it pale enough to make its name reasonably descriptive.

It is an eastern fish, fairly common from the Atlantic coast to the Great Lakes and from Nova Scotia down to the Carolinas. Brackish waters seem to produce the largest specimens. In terms of size and numbers caught, the fertile tidal ponds of lower New England may be the country's best white-perch waters. Fish measuring 15 inches and weighing 2 pounds inhabit these ponds. In most bays, estuaries, rivers, and ponds where white perch are abundant, the average size is no more than 10 inches, the average weight a pound or less. Where the species is present at all, it tends to be plentiful, as it is hardy, prolific, and long-lived. But it is cyclic in population density, and during peak periods it may be sufficiently stunted by crowding to resemble a sunfish.

FISH HABITAT & FEEDING BEHAVIOR—ANGLING TACTICS:
Near the coast, saltwater fishermen occasionally catch white perch at depths of more than a hundred feet, but the pursuit of the species is generally confined to brackish bays, estuaries, rivers, and headwater ponds and lakes. Some white perch are landlocked, but most are anadromous, and anglers watch for the April and May spawning runs. As the fish move up the rivers, they are taken on worms, grubs, and small minnows drifted into deep

White perch.

pools. They migrate in schools, spilling into streams where they spawn colonially, without pairing. The females release their roe—perhaps 150,000 eggs spewed from a 1-pound fish—and this stimulates an immediate release of milt by the males. Enormous numbers of eggs are thus fertilized. They adhere to gravel, sand, and plant stalks, and within a few days they hatch.

The adults quickly move off to deeper waters. During the winter they have lain dormant in the deep holes of bays, ponds, and tidal creeks, so they must now feed heavily. Those in salt water prey chiefly on small fish, shrimp, crabs, and squid. Those in fresh or brackish water feed on what is seasonally plentiful. They dredge the bottoms for midges, mayfly nymphs, and other larvae in the spring; in the summer they hunt waterfleas and similar scuds and shrimp as well as small fish; in autumn, when many of the baitfish have grown too large, they capture whatever insects and crustaceans they can find. As a rule (a rather flexible rule) they consume relatively few minnows because they prefer water too deep for such prey. But at dusk a school of white perch frequently cruises fairly close to shore if prey abounds there.

In the spring, when landlocked salmon have begun to hit on the surface, eastern anglers sometimes gather a mixed bag, taking white perch on the streamers they are trolling for the salmon. At that time, too, a diverting change of pace can be arranged by drifting the boat over a perch school while fishing a small minnow or smelt on a free line or with a light sinker.

A hungry white perch will make a grab for any standard panfish bait such as a worm, grub, or small minnow. The schools seem to indulge in feeding sprees. It may be that when a few members of a school capture food, their action functions as a behavioral stimulus to the others. Extremely active foraging continues until the food source in the immediate area is depleted and then the school, abruptly losing interest, may drift away. Locating a feeding school is therefore a key to good white-perch fishing. Generally, the most promising spots are those where a more or less firm mud bottom underlies about fifteen to thirty feet of water —good habitat for burrowing mayflies and bloodworms (both true bloodworms and midge larvae, which go by the same name). A school may also be over sand or gravel, feeding on crustaceans and small fish, but white perch show little enthusiasm for chasing minnows through weed patches.

If an angler is unfamiliar with the local feeding grounds, a logical way to find them is to still-fish one promising area after another. A more enjoyable way is to deep-troll a worm or little minnow behind a small spinner. As soon as this produces a white perch, the angler drops anchor and, if he intends to continue using bait, he can bottom-fish with a worm or minnow for a few minutes. If this proves unrewarding, he should not leave before trying the middle depths and then the upper stratum. If frenzied action is followed by a sudden lull, the school has probably departed and the angler might as well follow suit.

Both for trolling and casting, small spinners often work superlatively without the added attraction of bait, and so do spinner-fly combinations. Usually the best way to fish a spinner for white perch is to let it sink all the way, then crank it just a short distance and let it begin to sink again before cranking a bit more. The spinner must have built-in liveliness since the retrieve is slow. Trolling a wet fly or a streamer can also induce strikes.

At about sundown a school may concentrate on the surface, rippling large patches of water even when there is no big evening hatch of insects to incite foraging. Surface feeding sometimes continues until dark, and the white perch become sufficiently excited to snap up a bass bug or small popping plug. However, these fish are quick to take alarm, so the retrieve of a surface-disturber must be gentle or it will send them down instead of attracting them. A selection of dry flies may therefore serve better. Moreover, a light, limber fly rod and long, delicate, tapered leader will magnify the excitement of playing the fish, transmitting every quiver as a white perch sounds and circles.

As to the dry flies most likely to succeed, white perch are especially attracted to dull blond, brown, or black patterns representing either aquatic insects or terrestrials. The bee-mimicking McGinty is productive, as are the black-ant and black-gnat patterns. Appropriately subdued imitations of ephemera include, among others, the Leadwinged Coachman, Light or Dark Cahill, March Brown, and Black or Brown Bivisible. A size 10 or even 12 hook is not too small. And when the mosquitolike diptera swarm, an angler can salve his annoyance by reflecting, first, that midges do not bite and, second, that a small, sparsely dressed representation—a Harger's Black Midge on a no. 16 hook, perhaps—may be just the temptation for white perch.

Yellow Bass *(Morone mississippiensis)*
COMMON & REGIONAL NAMES: *barfish, stripe, streak, streaker, brassy bass*

GAME IDENTIFICATION & LOCATION OF FISHING REGIONS: By late spring, yellow bass have begun feeding avidly after a winter of near-dormancy, and their spawning activity has made them all the hungrier. It is a time when light-tackle enthusiasts cluster almost as thickly as their quarry—schools of "streakers" and other panfish—on lakes in the Midwest and South. On delicate spinning gear or a fly rod, a yellow bass is a spunky welterweight.

With its forked tail, its moderately deep, compressed body, and its longitudinal striping, it closely resembles its relative the white bass, which inhabits some of the same waters. Since the dominant color of a yellow bass is not always a quickly identifiable yellow, it can be mistaken for the other species. It has an olive-green back, white belly, and sides that vary in color from brassy or gold to the silver of a white bass. But a yellow bass has fewer dark longitudinal stripes than a white bass—only six or seven, as a rule, with three lying above the lateral line. Moreover, those below the lateral line are not solid, as on the white, but broken into irregular segments toward the rear. The yellow species has no teeth on the base of its tongue, as the white has, nor does its lower jaw protrude beyond the upper. Another distinguishing characteristic is the membranous joining of the spiny forward and soft rear dorsal fin at the base of the notch between them. Finally, there is the matter of size. Every yellow bass on a stringer is likely to measure about 8 to 11 inches and weigh 12 ounces or less. A 2-

Yellow bass.

pound white is merely a nice catch; a 2-pound yellow bass is a rarity, just 2 ounces shy of the record.

This little panfish is nonetheless popular in its native waters, and probably would gain favor elsewhere if it were easier to stock. It occurs in scattered midwestern lakes and large rivers from Minnesota, Wisconsin, and Michigan southward into the drainage of the Tennessee and by way of that system across a portion of the deep South—Alabama, Mississippi, Louisiana, and eastern Texas. Like the white bass, it is a freshwater member of the Percichthyidae, but unlike the white, it resists transplanting. Even within its natural range, efforts to establish it in new waters or propagate it have been disappointing. Evidently, the primary impediment is a habitat requirement—extensive spawning shallows over gravel beds, stony rises, or rocky reefs.

FISH HABITAT & FEEDING BEHAVIOR—ANGLING TACTICS:

When the water temperature rises to the high 60's in May or early June, mature yellow bass—those at least three years old—seek gravel or jumbled rock expanses in depths of just a few feet. A ripe female may carry a quarter of a million very tiny eggs or, occasionally, almost a full million. Since the normal life span is about three to five years and very few individuals live much longer, she may spawn only once or twice before she dies. Even so, severe crowding would occur if the immense reproductive potential were not countered (as with most very prolific species) by a high mortality rate among eggs and fry. Within a few days, if conditions are favorable, a relatively small percentage of the nestless, unguarded eggs will hatch.

The schools of fry remind one of swarming no-see-ums as they flit about the shallows feeding on minuscule zooplankton. In late summer they are fingerlings, capable of swallowing larger components of the plankton—chiefly crustaceans, insects, and insect larvae. By September or October they have acquired their full year's growth—2½ to perhaps 5 inches—and their metabolism slows as the water cools. Fingerlings may be very plentiful, but because sufficiently favorable conditions prevail no more often than about one year out of three, the population fluctuates.

In their third year, when they attain maturity, their food intake changes abruptly to an almost exclusive diet of small fish, with only occasional insects or crustaceans. Now, at last, they begin to be worth catching. They fight well, and many anglers prefer their meat to white bass. Bait-fishermen catch plenty of them on both worms and minnows.

By the end of the third summer, many of these bass are a good 9 inches long, and they grow another inch or so in their fourth year and again in their fifth. Schools of these adults generally cruise deep during the daytime but hunt the shallows very early in the morning and again near dusk. Throughout most of the day, the usual angling method is to locate a feeding school by trolling, then stop to fish the area hard until the action dwindles and trolling is resumed. During the hours of dim light an angler can also fill a stringer by casting in the shallows near shore.

Sometimes the schools feed on top, but since they are usually pursuing fish, dry flies are only sporadically effective. More often, yellow bass are located near the bottom or in the middle strata and are caught on all manner of spinners, spinner-fly combinations, spoons, small plugs, and streamers.

Yellow Perch *(Perca flavescens)*
COMMON & REGIONAL NAMES: *perch, striped perch, ringed perch, raccoon perch, coon perch, jack perch, red perch*

GAME IDENTIFICATION & LOCATION OF FISHING REGIONS:
Hardly anyone will disagree that the sweet white meat of a freshly caught, pan-fried yellow perch is among the more savory of an angler's rewards. Yet most of us assume a defensive tone when we talk to other sportsmen about our perch fishing. For one thing, despite a particular fondness for small minnows, the species is not a selective enough feeder to challenge our knowledge of baits. For another, it is justly known as a lazy man's fish because it feeds more actively in the daytime—especially at noon and sundown— than at night or early in the morning. It is not the most wary of panfish and, finally, it puts up a brief if spirited struggle.

All the same, if numbers caught are a criterion of popularity, the yellow perch ranks among the several best-loved species. The lack of caution, power, and size is offset by abundance, widespread availability, generous legal limits, long seasons (or no closed season at all in most regions), and lively action wherever a hungry school is encountered. Moreover, when artificial lures are substituted for natural baits, the species is not taken in quite so easily. And if it is readily enticed by baits, it is not always readily hooked. Its instinctive feeding behavior is to nibble delicately at a dead bait or to run a short distance with a live minnow and then maneuver the prey into its gullet. Since either of these actions will strip an offering away from a hook, the yellow perch presents interesting if minor angling challenges.

The yellow perch has a trim, elongate shape but with a slightly humped back that becomes most noticeable on a large, relatively deep-bodied specimen. Its tail is moderately forked and its two dorsal fins are completely separated. It is a golden-sided fish with an olive back and six to eight wide, greenish-black or olive vertical bands running down the sides almost to the white belly. The anal, pelvic, and pectoral fins are yellowish or orange. The fins are said to be most colorful on spawning males, but sometimes even in midsummer, long after spawning has ceased, an angler may marvel at the fiery orange of the pectoral fins.

More widely distributed than its larger relatives, the sauger and the walleye, it is the most common of the Percidae. The American race is barely distinguishable from the European perch (*P. fluviatilis*), which is common throughout Asia as well as most of Europe. Originally, America's yellow perch ranged from the eastern seaboard to the Midwest, as far north as lower Canada and as far south as the Carolinas, Tennessee, Missouri, and Kansas. The Great Lakes, particularly Erie, Huron, and Michigan, have always been known for large and plentiful yellow perch. But equally large specimens are now added to the stringers of Montana fishermen. The species has been successfully stocked in impoundments and lakes west to the Pacific.

Being a prolific, hardy, and fairly long-lived species, it can overpopulate a pond or small lake. One result is stunting. In crowded waters, a five-year-old perch may be hardly more than 6 inches long. Such crowding brings about competition with larger game species whose predations (together with diseases and parasites) normally control the numbers of perch. Larger lakes with moderate weed growth provide sufficient food, space, and proper habitat to maintain a diversity of species and a balance of numbers. The biggest perch generally come from such waters. They grow slowly, attaining a length of about 3 inches in their first year, another 3 in the second. In the South, where yellow perch seldom live longer than five or six years, a ¾-pound catch

▲ Mate gaffing big amberjack. ▼ Bonito.

▲ School of young Pacific barracuda. ▼ Lingcod.

▲ Angler with boated bluefish. ▼ Snapper blue and larger specimen.

▲ Netting big bonefish. ▼ White sea bass. Female dolphin. ▶

▲ Black drum. ▼ Flounder, camouflaged to match bottom. Red grouper. ▶

▲ Crevalle jack. ▼ Horse-eye jacks.

is exceptionally large. In the North, where yellow perch have a life span of ten or eleven years, a specimen weighing a pound and measuring over a foot long is not very unusual. Sometimes a lake will produce a few 2-pounders. A yellow perch weighing 4 pounds, 3½ ounces was caught during the last year of the Civil War; that fish, taken by Dr. C. C. Abbot at Bordentown, New Jersey, set a record that has stood for more than a century.

FISH HABITAT & FEEDING BEHAVIOR—ANGLING TACTICS: Although yellow perch are occasionally caught in creeks and rivers —especially during the spawning period—they are primarily denizens of lakes and ponds. They can thrive in a small, shallow farm pond or a deep, sprawling reservoir, and they can tolerate mud and thick vegetation, but their ideal habitat is cool, clean water with big patches of sandy or rocky bottom.

Spawning, which peaks in April throughout much of the perch range, begins almost as early as that of the walleye, when the water temperature reaches 45° or 50° soon after the ice goes out. The perch then congregate in shallow coves, about the mouths of streams, and in the feeder streams themselves. Breeding takes place in several feet of water. A mature female, at least three or four years old, may release ten thousand to more than seventy thousand eggs in a gelatinous ribbon festooned over weeds or brush. As she does so, she may be flanked by one or two males or a swarm of them. Neither the female nor her escorts will take any further interest in their offspring until the fry grow large enough to be appetizing.

Yellow perch do very little feeding at night, and it is chiefly at night that spawning occurs. However, the fish linger at the spawning beds during the day, and there they furnish excellent sport. They bite weakly but repeatedly, with a persevering hunger. Later in the season, live minnows seem to be more tempting than dead ones, but while the perch are spawning their hunger appears to overwhelm any selectivity. All an angler needs is a conveniently pocketed jar of preserved minnows, procured at the nearest tackle shop. Angleworms or grubs will also keep the perch biting.

Perch hunt crawfish, snails, nymphs, worms, and any small fish they can catch and kill. Much of their food consists of minnows and equally small darters—members of the perch fam-

ily that are often mistaken for minnows in spite of their bright colors, big fins, and slender bodies. Darters, especially the spawning males, flash pinks, reds, and yellows in contrast with their darker colors. Perch are drawn to these bright hues, and yellow is probably the most tantalizing of the lot. This explains the effectiveness of many colorful streamer patterns such as the Mickey Finn, Supervisor (and Supervisor Special), Light Edson Tiger, Colonel Bates, Golden Darter, Silver Darter, Yellow Perch, Green Ghost, Red-and-White Bucktail, Male Dace, Black-Nosed Dace, and so on. Such streamers may be meant for nobler game, but on no. 10 hooks they serve as well for perch. (It is worth noting parenthetically that yellow perch are frequently, if surprisingly, taken with streamers tied on hooks as large as size 4.)

These fish school at all times and seasons and throughout their lives. For safety's sake, they school with other perch of the same approximate age and size; hence, an angler can decide on the basis of the first one caught whether to move on or continue fishing the same spot. Though schools may wander all over a lake, those consisting of large perch tend to stay in relatively deep water almost until sundown; then, for a brief period, they may patrol the shallows. This does not mean they cannot be caught close to shore at any time. Perch like to forage in coves, over bars, and around docks, floats, and breakwaters. In the heat of summer, however, good catches are most frequent over deep, weedy ledges.

Yellow perch feed voraciously even in winter, and they are

Typical yellow perch.

caught through the ice on grubs, small minnows, and weighted ice-jigging spoons that can be fluttered up and down to attract a school. However, these fish are most active in water temperatures ranging between 60° and 75°—just under 70° is about perfect—which means that their temperature preference is close to that of crappies, smallmouths, pickerel, and pike. If other factors are favorable, a perch fisherman may catch more than perch. And he may also catch perch when nothing else is biting.

One of the two most traditional ways of catching them is to lower a bell sinker to the bottom with a couple of droppers above it so that a 2-inch minnow or an angleworm hovers a foot or so above the lake bed and a second one hovers a foot higher. Size 6 or 8 hooks will do nicely. The other most venerable technique is to use a bobber over a minnow or worm, with a split shot or two about six inches above the hook to keep the bait down. Where weeds are sparse, the rig can be fished close to the bottom, but it works best just above the swaying tips of vegetation.

There are less traditional but more interesting techniques. One is slow trolling with a minnow, worm, beetle, grub, crawfish tail, or shrimp. Any of these baits can be enhanced by a small bright, willow-leaf spinner. Trolling can also be effective with a baitless spinner, a spinner-fly combination, or a streamer. With or without the spinner, a wet fly should be as bright as a streamer for yellow perch. Patterns that come to mind are the Silver Doctor, Red Ibis, Montreal, Oriole, Yellow Sally, and Parmachene Belle. Jigs work, too, and so do nymphs and small, deep-running plugs.

If a lure is used, the hook should be set quickly but not hard, and with the hope that the fish has done the hooking itself. When bait-fishing with a bobber, most anglers wait out any little dancing of the float, but they strike the instant it goes under. Unfortunately, there are some of us for whom this invariably results in lost bait. Even after the bobber has gone under, the perch may not be gulping the bait; instead, it may be using its rows of sharp little teeth to pull bits away from the hook. We therefore prefer to wait yet another moment, until the perch begins a definite run. Timing is more critical when a live minnow is used. The yellow perch is a relatively small-mouthed predator that uses its many teeth to position food for swallowing. The angler feels a little yank and a short run and then a quivering stop—the signal to set the hook and plan a lunch of sizzling fillets.

Saltwater and Brackish-water Game

▲ Fishing inshore Pacific waters. ▼ White marlin jumping.

▼ Tarpon fisherman.

Amberjack *(Seriola)* **& Rainbow Runner**
(Elagatis bipinnulata)
COMMON & REGIONAL NAMES: *amberfish, jack, runner*. (Names denoting various species will be included in the descriptions of those species.)

GAME IDENTIFICATION & LOCATION OF FISHING REGIONS:
Party boats, their rails bristling with rods, anchor at the California kelp beds; charter boats slowly troll and drift the inshore waters of the Gulf, as well as the Atlantic and Pacific seaboards from a latitude of about 38° southward; and trim little private runabouts patrol the reefs and coves along all the coasts. Chum slicks of chopped fish and weak live bait trail from the vessels as fishermen watch for swooping gulls and the quicksilver surface flurries that mark schools of baitfish being savaged by carnivores. The prey is under attack by toothless but crusher-jawed marauders—amberjacks of one species or another, blue or black and silver, often brilliantly streaked with yellow. Even when the anglers expect a mixed bag, as they often must in this kind of fishing, they hope that one of its chief constituents will be amberjack.

At least a dozen species occur along the American coasts, sometimes out at sea, more often cruising inshore areas or the reef habitat that swarms with food. Additional species are distributed around the world. Primarily denizens of tropical and subtropical waters, they roam northward into temperate zones during spring and summer. They belong to a large marine family, the Carangidae, numbering over two hundred species globally and nearly seventy in American waters. Some carangids—the scads, lookdowns, threadfins, and leatherjackets—are unimportant to anglers though they are caught occasionally and the small scads make good bait. Others—the pompano, permit, roosterfish, and such popular jacks as the crevalle—are included elsewhere in this book. The amberjacks have somewhat thicker, more elongate bodies than most of their relatives. They also differ in having an anal fin appreciably shorter than the dorsal fin, no scutes in the lateral line, and in a number of more subtle anatomical features as well as in some behavioral characteristics. In the adult stage, most of them have a yellow or amber streak along the lateral line which is lacking in many carangids. They also have a dark or black nuchal band—an inverted-V marking known as

Greater amberjack taken near wreck in North Carolina waters.

"fighter stripes"—running from the upper jaw through the eyes and obliquely back to the first dorsal fin. This is absent or less distinct in other species. It darkens or becomes more pronounced when a fish is excited (hence the term "fighter stripes").

Amberjacks and many other carangids have two detached spines in front of the anal fin, small scales, and a long, lunate tail with slender, deeply forked lobes. Some carangids have almost discoid bodies while others are thin as lances; most of the amberjacks resemble the common mackerels and tunas—fairly deep amidships, tapering to a slim "wrist" of caudal peduncle ahead of the tail. They have two dorsal fins, a very short, roughly triangular one immediately followed by another that sweeps back almost to the tail. The hind fin is narrow for most of its length but rises abruptly to a front peak. The anal fin is a shorter, inverted reflection of the hind dorsal fin. The meat of some species is very good, that of others barely palatable. Among American species, the California yellowtail and the rainbow runner are tastiest. Amberjacks caught in the West Indies may be unsafe to eat, as the flesh of some contains a toxin that produces ciguatera, a rarely lethal but often very painful poisoning. (A number of other West Indian gamefish produce ciguatera with equal frequency; the toxin is believed to accumulate from the eating of toxic prey.)

All amberjacks are strong, fast, swimmers, excellent game on light tackle. Juveniles and the younger adults travel in schools, but the oldest, largest specimens tend to be solitary or associated in small, loosely scattered groups. Surprisingly little is known of their other habits. The carangids are a confusing group, not yet thoroughly studied by ichthyologists. Many change shape and color as they mature, and there are slightly divergent forms with more than one common name.

Half a dozen of the true amberjacks—the genus *Seriola*—merit description. Principal player among the dramatis personae of the West Coast is the California yellowtail *(S. dorsalis)*. Unfortunately, it is also known simply as the yellowtail, a name used for several very different species, and as the Pacific amberjack, a name more properly associated with another species *(S. colburni)*. Immature California yellowtails, like the young of many amberjacks, are marked by vertical bars that disappear with maturity. Adults have greenish-yellow fins, a tail varying from greenish-yellow to bright yellow, and a yellow or brassy streak from eye to tail. Above the streak, the body is metallic blue or greenish; below it, the color is silvery. This is a fairly slender species, averaging perhaps 2 feet long and weighing 10 pounds or so, but the length-to-weight ratio varies considerably. Of two outstanding fish having equal lengths—both just under 4 feet, 10 inches—one weighed 63 pounds and one weighed 80. The record was set not in American waters but at Bay of Islands, New Zealand, in 1961 by a 111-pounder with a length of 5 feet, 2 inches and a girth of 3 feet, 2 inches. (Some biologists classify the giant yellowtails of Australia and New Zealand as *S. grandis,* a species distinct from the smaller though very similar California variety.) Yellowtails occur in the coastal waters of the Americas from lower Washington to Chile, and they are seasonally abundant from Los Angeles and the Channel Islands to the tip of Baja.

The Pacific amberjack *(S. colburni)* ranges from the lower Santa Barbara Channel, off California, to Ecuadorian waters. Its fins and upper body are dark, and it has a blunter head and slightly deeper body than the yellowtail. It, too, probably averages about 2 feet long, though occasional catches measure twice that.

The major species of the Atlantic, the Gulf of Mexico, and the Caribbean is the greater amberjack *(S. dumerili),* also called the horse-eye bonito. After it has matured and lost its bars, it has a yellow or coppery band from jaw to tail and a blue or blue-violet back. The yellow, which disappears after death, has an indistinct lower edge, blending into the silver of flank and belly. Often the lower body glows with gold, green, and lavender highlights. A young specimen may be only three times as long as it is deep of body, but a larger, older one is more elongate—about four and a half times as long as its body depth. The average size caught is 10 to 15 pounds, or up to about 2 feet in length, but 50-pound catches are occasionally reported. The record fish, caught in 1964 off Bermuda, weighed 149 pounds and measured 5 feet, 11 inches. The range of this species extends from Africa to the Mediterranean and from Brazil to Cape Cod. In American waters, it is most often caught from the Carolinas southward.

The lesser amberjack *(S. fasciata)* is a smaller, deeper-bodied fish ranging primarily from Massachusetts to the Bahamas, Cuba, and the Gulf of Mexico. Its body is olive-brown above, silver-gray below, and throughout its life it retains seven or eight split, wavy brown bars. Rarely exceeding 10 pounds, and averaging less than half that, it is nonetheless a very game fighter. Some biologists have speculated that the Almaco jack *(S. rivoliana),* or falcate amberjack, may be a subspecies of lesser amberjack, though it has fewer bars and loses them at maturity. Above its lateral ocher stripe it is gray, steel-blue, or olive, and its underparts are silvery. Often its sides have a lavender glow. Though it is usually small, fishermen have occasionally brought in 14-pounders measuring over 30 inches long. It, too, ranges along both sides of the Atlantic. It is found from Argentina to New Jersey, but is not abundant north of Cape Hatteras.

One additional species should be mentioned. The rainbow runner *(Elagatis bipinnulata),* also known as rainbow yellowtail, runner, or skipjack, is a resident of both the Atlantic and Pacific, from Massachusetts and lower California to South America. Physiologically it is similar to the *Seriola,* yet it belongs to a separate genus and its long, streamlined, almost spindly body and pointed snout are not characteristic of amberjacks. As a rule it is about 2 feet long and weighs less than 4 pounds. Off Kauai, Hawaii, in 1963 a new rod-and-reel record was set by a runner 47 inches long and just an ounce shy of 31 pounds. This species has a small detached finlet behind the second dorsal fin and another behind the anal fin. Its body is greenish-blue above the lateral line, yellowish below. Two light but brilliant, iridescent, blue lines run the length of the body, with a broad yellow band separating them.

FISH HABITAT & FEEDING BEHAVIOR—ANGLING TACTICS: For North American anglers seeking amberjacks, spawning time and good fishing coincide, but only because the fish move into temperate waters as the weather grows warm. Little is known about reproduction except what can be deduced from the capture of larvae and very small juveniles. Spawning evidently occurs in offshore waters from June or July to September or October.

Big yellowtails retain the schooling habit more consistently than most amberjacks and they can usually be found with companions of the same age and size. They are caught in greatest numbers in April, May, or June, depending on locale. They swarm off San Diego in April or sometimes in March. As spring progresses, the party boats become crowded progressively farther north. On both sides of the continent, amberjack fishing often remains good throughout the summer in the upper part of the

range. California anglers buy their party-boat tickets and come aboard the evening before they expect to fish. Usually they must sleep on board, because the boat will leave during the night for the coastal islands, reefs, kelp beds, or other known feeding grounds. The trip may take several hours, and fishing will be best for the first couple of hours after dawn—although amberjacks are diurnal feeders, more or less oblivious to light or tide.

Fishermen who dislike the crowding on party boats and cannot afford the usually high charter-boat fees often fish the surf with live bait, plugs, spoons, bucktails, plastic squid, and the big feathered jigs sometimes called Japanese feathers. Boat-owning anglers troll, drift, or still-fish the bays, coves, and reefs. The fish can move close inshore during high tide, but they are likely to feed over reefs and around the kelp beds at any time.

Some anglers favor strip bait or squid—whole or cut. Others prefer live baits such as anchovies, sardines, or herring on hooks as large as 10/0. Live mullet is among the best amberjack baits. Whatever is used, it is generally drifted or slowly trolled with very little weight, none at all, or a sinker on a dropper or far up, above a long leader, because the bait must move naturally. Trolling should be at low speed: it is most productive over rocks or kelp. Most of the fish will be cruising at about fifteen to thirty feet, but often they feed on or near the surface, or they can be attracted with chum.

Because a hooked amberjack sooner or later seeks escape amid sharp rocks, around coral edges, or in kelp thickets, the an-

Angler with enormous rainbow runner.

gler's most frequent defeat is a cut or broken line. Six-foot steel leaders are common, as are lines testing 60 pounds. However, the stiff, heavy, roller-guide trolling rods once regarded as standard boat equipment are giving way to medium saltwater spinning gear. Fly rods are also becoming popular, as well they should because blue-water fly-casting for game of this kind is easy and exciting. The rod's length is not particularly important, but it should be fairly stiff because it will have to stop a hard run short of coral or rocks, and it may have to be pumped strenuously. Some anglers use 250 yards of Dacron backing, testing 25 to 30 pounds, in case something bigger than an average amberjack is hooked. As a rule, the leader is at least 6 feet long, with a butt section of stiff, 30-pound nylon and a tippet testing perhaps half that or else a light wire or heavy nylon shock tippet.

The fly-rodder searches for surface-feeding activity or attracts the game by chumming. Then he motors upwind or upcurrent of the frenzy and drifts closer. Most casts are only about twenty-five to forty feet, but the retrieve requires a little more skill. It should be darting and erratic—a matter of stripping line in foot-long jerks the moment the fly touches the water, alternating these darts with longer sweeps and erratic stops to emulate prey.

The fly patterns are as simple as the fishing itself. White streamers (or combination popper-streamers) on 5/0 hooks are very effective. So is the Fry Fly, probably originated by Joe Brooks. Tied on a short-shanked hook (sometimes no. 1/0 or even smaller), it has a small white chenille body and a sparse white bucktail rear. It can be deadly when moved through a chum line.

The strike is usually hard, and sometimes it blends into an immediate dive. Amberjacks seldom jump, but they run hard and dive deep. With spinning gear, the safest tactic may be to stop the fish quickly—if possible—and wage a more or less unyielding tug of war to keep off bottom. With a fly rod, an angler may have to wait out the initial run, setting the hook soon after it begins but using no drag or very little.

Often, the first amberjack caught is trailed in the water to decoy others—a trick also used in fishing for dolphin. When one of their kind is in trouble they gather about. They continue feeding, evidently having no intention of helping a comrade; on the contrary, they are probably determining whether the unfortunate one is sufficiently weak to become easy prey.

Great barracuda.

Barracuda *(Sphyraena)*

COMMON & REGIONAL NAMES: *'cuda, snake, tiger.* (Names denoting various species will be included in the descriptions of those species.)

GAME IDENTIFICATION & LOCATION OF FISHING REGIONS: To those who are unfamiliar with the ways of the barracuda, it may look like a dark, thin log hanging motionless in the blue water. To a great many skippers of billfishing boats it is a pest, a snake, a purloiner of rigged trolling baits intended for bigger game. In deep water it dives and wages a head-shaking fight, a mild diversion at best for an angler winching it in with a stout boat rod and line of heavy enough test weight for marlin or sailfish. But to those of us who have used light tackle to stalk the barracuda on the shallow flats as if it were a bonefish, it is a handsomely sleek sea tiger awaiting victims. It overtakes a surface lure with incredible speed, strikes with a ferocity that froths the water or shoots it up in a geyser, then twists and jackknifes through the air in a manner befitting an outraged tarpon.

Many of the world's warm seas hold barracuda, and four species are found along North American coasts. The important variety on the Atlantic side is the great, or common, barracuda *(Sphyraena barracuda).* It has the long, slim shape of a northern pike or a self-propelled missile and, like the pike, it frequently lies still for long periods, its big eyes watching for prey. Large barracuda often hover alone or in scattered groups. Small ones lie in schools, frequently in attack formation, all facing in one direction. They are aggressive and peculiarly inquisitive. A lone barracuda

or one that has detached itself from a school will often charge a flashing object, or a disturbance in the water. It will investigate a swimmer or wader, following closely. Though attacks on human beings are very rare, the species must be considered dangerous. The big, pointed teeth that stud its jaws can slice a sizable fish in half very cleanly.

The back of a great barracuda varies from grayish-blue to black. This color spills down in short stripes or saddles onto the upper sides, which are silver above a whitish belly. The fish has a big, moderately forked tail and two small, widely separated dorsal fins. Scattered over the body, particularly near the tail, are a few irregular black spots or blotches. The average size caught is about a yard long, with a weight of less than 10 pounds, but there is nothing unusual about a 20-pound, 4½-foot catch. Now and then a 50-pounder is taken. The rod-and-reel record was set in Nigerian waters in 1952 by an 83-pound fish, 72¼ inches long. The primary American range is from Florida to Brazil.

It shares that range with a smaller variety known as the guaguanche, or guaguacho *(S. guachancho)*, which has a more deeply forked tail, no spots, an olive-gray back, and a length seldom exceeding 20 inches. This is also the range of the southern sennet *(S. picudilla)*, a still smaller barracuda that intergrades with a northern sennet *(S. borealis)* ranging as far north as New England. Some taxonomists consider the two sennets to be races of a single species. They resemble the guaguanche, but the saddles on their backs are longer and darker. Since they grow only to 12 or 15 inches, they are seldom sought.

Several more species are found along the western coasts of Mexico and South America but only one commonly ventures as far north as California. It is the Pacific barracuda *(S. argentea)*, also called the California barracuda, barrie, scoots, or scooter. It looks rather like the great barracuda but with a more deeply forked tail, a yellowish tinge there and on the dorsal fins, no spots, and often a brownish tone in the blue of its back. It reaches a weight of 12 pounds or so and a length of over 40 inches, but the average catch is smaller. Though it sometimes strays to Alaska, it is found chiefly from California's Santa Barbara Channel to the lower coves of Baja California. Barracuda move northward with warm spring weather. Along the Pacific coast of the United States the fishing for them is best in late spring and summer.

FISH HABITAT & FEEDING BEHAVIOR—ANGLING TACTICS:

The Pacific barracuda and probably most others spawn far off-shore from April to September, with a peak in June. The young soon drift to the coasts, where they school in bays, lagoons, coves, and quiet shoals. They are equipped with teeth and look surpris-ingly like thin miniatures of the adults. Those hatched in the spring are about 4 inches long by midsummer, and 16 inches long by the following summer. The large adults—those weighing over 8 or 10 pounds—are mostly females. Males spawn at two years of age but the majority of spawning females are at least three years old. They live for ten or eleven years, perhaps longer. Sight-feeders, able to overtake and kill almost any small fish that swims past them, they eat whatever is abundant. In Florida, for example, mullet is a mainstay but they will also capture small tuna, and in the more southerly waters balao is important.

Small barracuda of various species are often taken on live or cut baits fished from banks, bridges, jetties, and boats. They are also caught on flashing spoons, spinners, and surface plugs—wooden plugs, as a rule, because the first fish hooked might crack the plastic kind. Most of those caught in the shallows are 3- and 4-pounders, but 10- and 20-pound barracuda can also be taken in knee-deep water at certain times and places. Many of the big

Floridian anglers boating large barracuda.

ones head toward shore on the rising tide to hunt in coves, bays, harbors, and lagoons, over tidal flats, and along mangrove banks. If the water temperature drops below about 70° they usually head back into open water or the deeper channels; otherwise, the shallows provide exciting fishing during high water.

On the West Coast, most barracuda anglers troll near the surface or cast feathers ranging from a quarter-ounce to a full ounce, or they drift and still-fish with strip baits and live fish such as sardines or anchovies. Although these methods are also used in the waters of the Atlantic, the Gulf of Mexico, and the Caribbean, eastern anglers seeking the great barracuda put more faith in big flashing spoons and 4- to 5-inch silvery top-water plugs that simulate baitfish. The murderous teeth of a barracuda make a wire leader essential, but it can be as short as 6 inches and the line above it can be 8-pound-test mono, cast or trolled from a light spinning rod. Trolling is done at a good clip—7 or 8 knots. One must bear in mind that barracuda are speedy enough to overtake trolled marlin baits, and they are most strongly attracted to prey that is racing away, frantically attempting escape.

Good fishing spots include not only the flats and mangrove banks but channel edges, reefs, and coral heads. In parts of the Florida Keys and the Bahamas, a common tactic is to wade the flats or pole along the mangrove edges in a shallow-draft boat. High visibility in this habitat turns barracuda boat- and lure-shy despite their famous aggressiveness. Because they lie still, mere shadows over the bottom, they are harder to see than bonefish or the small sharks that undulate through these waters, but it is best to spot them at a distance and make long casts—seventy or eighty feet when possible. Since barracuda stalk a lure before taking it, a short cast allows insufficient distance for the retrieve before the fish sees the boat. The lure should touch down no closer to the fish than four or five yards or the startled barracuda may streak for deeper water. The lure is then drawn past the fish very fast and erratically. If it is followed but not taken, it should be reeled in even faster.

The shallows are not the exclusive domain of plugs and spoons, spinning and baitcasting tackle. Barracuda can be caught on the same fly-casting outfit used for amberjack (which see) but with a reasonably toothproof 12-inch tippet of nylon-coated no. 5 wire. A loop knot or a loop-and-barrel twist will let

▲ King mackerel. ▼ Sierra mackerel.

▲ Hooked white marlin, jumping. ▼ Boating white marlin.

▼ Black sea bass.

▲ Pacific rockfish. ▼ Opaleye.

▲ Roosterfish. ▼ Sculpin.

◀ Atlantic sailfish.　▲ Pacific sailfish.　▼ Boating Pacific sail.

▲ Blue shark. ▼ Hammerhead.

the fly move freely. Popping bugs draw barracuda, but the surest flies are usually bucktails or white bear-hair streamers with strippings of Mylar for flash. The same sizes used for amberjacks will do nicely, the only sensible rule being to use flies large enough to attract attention and resemble local prey species.

A subdued barracuda presents the question of what to do with it. Pacific barracuda and guaguanche (the tastiest of the Atlantic species) are both savory and safe. But barracuda taken from tropical Atlantic waters may contain the same ciguatera toxin described in connection with amberjacks. Too many big-game fishermen kill any barracuda caught and drop it back in the water, yet there is no evidence that these fish destroy game populations. On the contrary, they are part of the natural balance in their habitat. A barracuda can be lifted, without harming it, by slipping a gaff through the gill slit under the narrow jaw. Then— very carefully—the hook can be removed with longnosed pliers.

Bluefish *(Pomatomus saltatrix)*

COMMON & REGIONAL NAMES: *blue, chopper.* (The name *snapper* is applied to yearlings—blues up to 9 or 10 inches and weighing a pound or less. Slightly larger ones—about a foot long—are often called *harbor blues* or *tailors.*)

GAME IDENTIFICATION & LOCATION OF FISHING REGIONS: "The blues are running!" That signal crackles up the Atlantic coast from Florida in midwinter to New England in late spring or summer. Word of the first migratory wave, transmitted by telephone, newspapers, radio and television reports, sends anglers hurrying for beaches and boats, eager to meet the onslaught of a strange pelagic species. The first blues to arrive are spawners, heavy with milt or roe and feeding perfunctorily, difficult to entice. A couple of weeks or a month later, depending on region, they revert to their normal characteristics, becoming savage predators.

Though they are small by comparison with sharks and other well-publicized killers, they are perhaps the most ferocious, cannibalistic, bloodthirsty predators in the sea. At Florida beaches and elsewhere in recent years, bathers have been severely bitten by rampaging blues; the fish intend no attack on anything as large as a human being, but when bait schools excite them they slash almost blindly.

The lone representative of its taxonomic family, the bluefish is a long but moderately deep-bodied, flat-sided species with a blunt head and a downward-slanting mouth that looks harmless when closed but conceals an upper and lower row of conical, almost translucent canine teeth. It has a broad, forked tail; a short, spiny front dorsal fin; a hind dorsal more than twice as long, high at the forward edge and narrowing toward the tail; and an anal fin almost as large and of similar shape. The gray-tinged greenish-blue of the back pales to blue-powdered silver flanks.

Most of the blues caught by sportsmen measure only 1½ to 2 feet long and weigh hardly more than 3 pounds. But a good many 10-, 15-, and 20-pound choppers are boated or beached every year. The record is currently held by a 31-pound, 12-ounce fish with a length of 47 inches and a girth of 23. It struck a plastic eel at Hatteras Inlet, North Carolina, in 1972.

Except for the waters off the west coast of the Americas and most of the European coast, bluefish move through nearly all of the world's warm and temperate seas. They appear seasonally along the eastern seaboard of the Americas, from Argentina to Canada, but vanish from some sections for years at a time. Fluctuations in their coastal numbers evidently result from shifting migration patterns rather than from true population cycles. Seaside folklore notwithstanding, good or bad years cannot be predicted; in fact, oceanic researchers have not solved the mystery of the shifts. For many decades, the upper limit of distribution was Cape Cod. Bluefish are still most abundant from Massachu-

Bluefishing off New Jersey coast.

setts to Florida, but a recent northward expansion continues at the time of this writing; the upper limit is now Nova Scotia.

As a general rule, the heaviest fish are taken along the seaboard from Cape Cod to North Carolina's Outer Banks. Since they grow fast while lingering in coastal waters after spawning, the biggest blues are caught late in the season. In the North the fishing is usually best from July through September. Off New York and New Jersey, a last surge sometimes comes in October. Off Virginia and North Carolina it remains good through November or sometimes December. Fair numbers of blues are caught in midwinter near the southern tip of the United States, and a great many, including some big ones, are caught in March and April from Florida's Sebastian Inlet down to Miami or the Keys. "Summer blues," bigger than snappers or harbor blues but generally weighing only 2 to 5 pounds, remain plentiful during all the warm months from Maryland to the Caribbean and the Gulf.

The migration is more complex than most anglers realize. Although there is some northward movement as the coastal waters warm up, most of the eagerly awaited schools are approaching not from the South but from the East—from the depths of the Atlantic. Blues are essentially deep-water fish. They move into waters nearer shore only to spawn, and then linger to fatten themselves up on the prey swarming in those inshore and offshore regions before returning to the high seas.

Some of them come into tidal estuaries, and dense packs of snappers—yearlings—venture quite far up brackish rivers (though never into purely fresh water). Snappers provide remarkable sport on ultralight tackle, but they cannot match the aggressiveness, the occasional writhing jumps, or the invariably powerful runs and dives of their elders. They do, however, match the gastronomic elegance of the adults. The rich meat of the bluefish, slightly darker than that of many marine species, is among the finest viands of the sea. Most of the bigger ones are caught in open waters, and the very big ones are taken by surfcasters only occasionally because they rarely cruise the shallows. They move through the offshore waters in small schools like packs of hungry wolves, traveling with companions of their own size.

Bluefish are almost always present in Florida's waters. Their numbers grow even before spring comes, and the entire peninsula often has good catches before the end of March. In that month and in April the fish appear off Georgia and the Carolinas; late in April they gather off Virginia, Delaware, and Maryland; in May they come to New Jersey and New York, though they may remain well offshore for a little longer; some of them arrive off New England in June or July, and by August the fishing is good in Massachusetts waters and often as far north as Maine. They assemble in greatest numbers where the water temperature reaches about 68°. The northernmost grounds are generally abandoned sometime between September and mid-October, as the fish are driven away by the first squally northeasters. A couple of weeks later they leave lower New England; in another fortnight they are gone from New York and New Jersey. Even that late, mild, calm weather may delay them just as storms may hurry them, but fishing can be excellent through much of November in the middle and lower states, and it remains so in Floridian waters until early in January. Paradoxically, bluefish seem to like rough water, probably because it eases the capture of prey, and the action can become most exciting just before the schools depart.

FISH HABITAT & FEEDING BEHAVIOR—ANGLING TACTICS: Studies in the northern part of the range show that bluefish spawn in an area from about two miles offshore to the outer reaches of the continental shelf. Spawning there occurs in July and August, but obviously earlier to the south. Until breeding is finished, blues feed rather half-heartedly and mostly on or near the bottom. Anglers in several regions catch them, nevertheless, using chum pots of ground mackerel, butterfish, or menhaden (bunker, as it is known in the North) and drifting in the chum line. This is effective throughout the season, but at first it requires deep fishing, either with a heavy sinker or with wire or lead-core line. Strips of squid are good bait. Small live crabs are even better. The large claw, removed to prevent its clutching underwater objects, is added to the chum.

A little later in the season, any locally abundant preyfish makes good bait. Eels, which teem in the waters off coastal rivers, are particularly effective. Slippery but manageable with forceps or pliers and a rag, they can be rigged with a harness or simply hooked through both lips. They are used in sizes from a foot to a foot and a half long, generally on hooks from 3/0 to 7/0. Choppers smash lures as if consciously trying to break them, but they

take bottom baits rather gently. Particularly with a bait as long as an eel, a bluefish should be allowed to run at will for twenty seconds or so before the hook is set; otherwise, half a bait and nothing else is liable to be reeled in.

Anglers without boats can catch small to medium blues on baits fished from bridges, piers, jetties, and breakwaters. Still-fishing accounts for a good many blues, but a bait or lure is always most enticing to a bluefish if it is kept moving—the faster, the better. Surfcasters, using long two-handed rods with fixed- or revolving-spool reels, can heave baits far enough out to catch somewhat bigger blues, particularly if they fish breakwaters or wade out from the beach. A short wire or steel leader can withstand the wicked chopping teeth, but a tough nylon leader may have to be chanced on early-season occasions when the blues are still feeding cautiously. (It is then wise to use a thick bait or big lure to obstruct the teeth.) To keep a bait on bottom or prevent a surfcast bait from sweeping back to the beach with the current, a fairly heavy sinker (either the pyramid or egg type) can be attached on a dropper or slipped onto the line above the leader. When drifting or still-fishing for small blues, very light monofilament line is suffi-

Blues taken in one day by two anglers.

cient; for bigger blues and for trolling or casting, an angler might select line testing up to 15 pounds. Light, limber spinning rods enhance the sport, but on the crowded party boats, shorter, heavier baitcasting rods are more practical.

By midsummer, spawning is about over. The eggs, drifting in plankton, hatch after just two days of incubation. By summer's end the young are fingerlings, already equipped with wicked teeth. Two years later they measure 15 or 20 inches long and weigh up to 2 pounds. They usually double that weight in the third year and grow to a length of about 2 feet. The adults, as soon as they finish spawning, begin to feed ravenously, traveling in schools to hunt sculpin, menhaden, mullet, herring, mackerel, and other such prey. They move constantly, swiftly, driving bait schools to the surface and charging into them so violently as to churn the water, then moving off and returning for another attack as the scattered escapees begin to regroup. Upon returning, they also pick up mangled scraps sinking to the bottom, but a good number of choppers remain at or near the surface. Now and for the remainder of the season, lures are deadlier than baits. They should have some resemblance to bait species but need not match what is being eaten.

Rampaging schools are often spotted at a distance as they whip the surface, send up spray, and force baitfish to leap far out of the water. Even when the attack is fairly well submerged, an oily slick like that of chum often forms on the surface. Gulls and terns circle above, dropping to snatch morsels but not diving under; a dive would be extremely hazardous near these marauders. Some experienced fishermen can tell when they approach a concentration of feeding blues even if they see no sign; they can detect an odor somewhat like that of cucumbers or melons.

If no slicks of carnage are in evidence, it pays to cast or troll along a few yards from a tide-rip, or near reefs, breakwaters, river mouths, submerged boulders, channel edges, or turbulence where small fish are tumbled helplessly by clashing currents. Repeated passes should be made to arrest the attention of preoccupied blues, and various depths should be probed until a first fish hits. Trolling speeds are generally about 5 to 8 knots, and cast lures should be retrieved fast but at varying speeds.

Casting or trolling right through a tide-rip or feeding school will only send the fish racing away. A lure should touch on the near side of the surface disturbance or just ahead of moving blues to intercept them. When trolling, the lure should be let back perhaps a hundred feet to avoid spooking the fish.

Effective lures include big plugs (especially the popping type), trolling spoons, feathers, bucktails, and various nylon and other soft-bodied models, including plastic eels and squid and surgical-tubing eels. Metal squid and trolling spoons can be enhanced by a little pork-rind strip or bit of squid. In some regions the umbrella rig is popular for trolling. It consists of four to six rubber or plastic eels on spreader arms; this produces enough water resistance to call for fairly hefty tackle, but occasionally it draws two choppers at a time. Hard-bodied plugs should be wood rather than plastic, as a fighting bluefish continues to chew on a lure just as it continues to mangle bait. Since this chewing tends to rip treble hooks free, it is also wise to remove the factory-supplied trebles and arm a plug with two single hooks.

In some areas, night fishing is excellent, while in others (for reasons unknown) it is not particularly productive. Surf fishing, however, is almost always best early in the morning or at dusk because the heat of the day drives prey out into deeper water. Among the favored surf-fishing lures are metal and plastic squid, popping plugs, jigs, and plastic or rubber eels.

Fly fishermen can elicit strikes with popping bugs or big streamers—preferably double-winged streamers that throb through the water. Yellow, red, white, and combinations of those colors are recommended. A wire or tough nylon leader is needed, of course. The rod should be heavy enough to handle powerful fish in choppy water, and long enough for casting a good distance. But even then, it is usually impossible to cast a fly far enough to reach the edge of a feeding school without bringing the boat so close that it causes alarm. The same specialized two-man technique used for larger saltwater game can solve the problem. One angler wields a spinning or baitcasting rod to hurl a hookless teaser plug. His retrieve coaxes one or more fish out of the school toward the bait. The fly caster drops his offering in the wake of the teaser and hopes for the best. The best is a rushing strike.

Once a blue is boated, the hook should be removed with pliers and the utmost care. This is one of the few aquatic species that see very well out of water and direct their savage bites with nicely aimed belligerence.

Bonefish (Albula vulpes)

COMMON & REGIONAL NAMES: bone, ladyfish, alby, banana, macabi, raton. (In foreign locales, many other names are in use.)

GAME IDENTIFICATION & LOCATION OF FISHING REGIONS: Albula vulpes—in literal translation, the white fox. Angling writers have described it as the sea fox, fox of the flats, ghost of the flats. The bonefish is probably the wariest, or most nervous, of all marine species. Evolution, having equipped it to feed in the shallows, has also forced it to feed there, in a zone of perpetual danger. Every minute it forages is a minute of vulnerability to surprise attack by lurking barracuda and the small sharks that patrol the warm tidal flats. Constant alertness and instant escape are its only defenses. Although its keen sense of smell frequently helps it to find food, it relies more on vision. In the clear water rimming tropical islands it undoubtedly spots prey or an enemy at considerable distances, since it can see a pink no. 4 fly eight or nine yards away. It is also exquisitely sensitive to vibrations—including sounds—transmitted through the water. An outboard motor starting a hundred yards away can send a school of bonefish for cover or deep water as if released by a hidden spring. At closer range, a pole bumped against a skiff has the same effect.

A sizable bonefish fights with astonishing spurts of power, speed, and something akin to desperation. A 10-pounder can take half an hour to net when played on light tackle. (And lightness is a requisite, since anything coarse is too easily detectable.) Yet it is the stalking rather than the battle that furnishes the greatest excitement. Bonefishermen refer to their sport as a hunt.

The bonefish is a torpedo-shaped creature with a single high dorsal fin amidships and a slender-lobed tail that is widely and deeply forked. Its back, fins, and tail are gray or bluish-gray, its sides bright, pale silver with occasional faint gleams of pink or blue, its flanks and belly silvery white. The dorsal surface of a very young adult has dark spots that merge to form short saddles extending onto the upper sides; these fade on older fish, replaced by shadowy longitudinal streaks along the sides. The tip of the conical snout extends beyond the mouth, as if the fish had a slight overbite. The mouth itself is fairly small, with thick, rubbery lips. In open position for grubbing food off the bottom, it projects slightly, and it has been compared to a hog's snout or that of a carp. Most bonefishermen would take umbrage at the latter comparison if not the former.

The mouth is a marvel of adaptation. The tongue and palate are almost entirely blanketed with molars that look like seeds or tiny pearls, and behind the tongue are powerful grinding bones—pharyngeal teeth. This odd dental equipment can crush the toughest crab, the hardest clam. A hook is unlikey to pierce the molar armor completely, but quite often it snags there firmly enough to hold until a fish is netted or lifted by hand, and the angler's odds are improved by the fact that a bonefish usually swims (or fights) with its mouth closed. There are differences of opinion regarding the surest way to set a hook. Those who use bait often let the fish run a little before yanking back, because a bonefish frequently drops a bait, then picks it up again with increased determination. Lures are sometimes snatched broadside so that the angler's strike puts the barb into the lip or side of the mouth. When a lure is taken head on, the fish usually turns away with it, and the hook can be set best at that instant.

The ones that do not get away average from 2 to 5 pounds. A 7- or 8-pounder is considered large, and anything over 9 ranks as "bragging size" although quite a few 15-pound bonefish are caught every year in the Bahamas and the Florida Keys. The sporting record, 19 pounds, was set in 1962 in South African waters. That fish was almost 40 inches long. The previous record was set in Hawaii and the one before that in Bermuda.

A more typical specimen, 18 inches long, would weigh about 3½ pounds; a 22-inch fish generally weighs about 5 pounds, a 28-incher weighs 8 or 9, and a 32-incher weighs per-

Bonefish.

haps 13. Small ones (2 to 3½ pounds) are often rigged as trolling bait because nothing is more appetizing to a marlin. In some regions the larger ones are eaten. They are considered a delicacy in Hawaii, Japan, and parts of the West Indies. Yet for every angler who has tried the white, dry meat and called it "nutlike," another has likened it to cotton stuffed with bones.

Primarily a shoreline fish, found in shoals and tidal flats, the species is distributed through all of the tropical and subtropical seas. Strays have been collected as far north as Massachusetts, but the range is essentially limited to warm waters. Before Florida attracted large numbers of angling tourists, the excellent game qualities of this strange fish were undiscovered. The first recorded catch on rod and reel took place in 1891 at Biscayne Bay. The angler, J. B. McFerran, described it as "a distinctly new proposition in the piscatorial line . . . a new edition of chain lightning, and that greased." Bonefish frequent the waters of lower California, Baja, and the Gulf of California, but most fishermen on the Pacific coast seem to be unaware of their presence.

In the East, Florida is the only bonefishing state. It has extremely productive flats from Miami southward. The shallows of the Keys are ideal habitat; some of the renowned bonefishing links in that chain are Key Largo, Islamorada, Marathon, and Key West. Excellent bonefish waters are also located in the American and British Virgin Islands, Bermuda, the Bahamas, many Caribbean islands, and along the coast of Central America. The largest Bahamian bonefish concentrations have been recorded from February through May (possibly revealing a spring spawning peak in that area), and autumn fishing is superb in the Keys, but there is no single best season; the only rule is that bonefish come and go with the tide and gather in the greatest numbers when the flats are hot and sunny.

FISH HABITAT & FEEDING BEHAVIOR—ANGLING TACTICS:

Many saltwater game species are still mysterious to biologists, and less is known about bonefish than about most. In Puerto Rican studies, ripe adults were found from November through January and larvae were collected in every month but July. Bonefish may spawn throughout the year in some regions. There is evidence that the eggs and larvae drift with masses of plankton for perhaps five or six months. Spawning evidently occurs far offshore and has little effect on angling.

The larvae grow to a length of 2 or 2½ inches on a diet of minuscule plankton. They look rather like the larvae of some eels —white, transparent, gelatinous ribbons, larger at the rear end than at the front, with a tiny dorsal fin positioned far aft and a small head that is mostly eye. Then, when heat or light conditions are suitable, they metamorphose completely in eight to ten days, thickening but shrinking to about half the larval length, shifting the dorsal fin to a central position, and assuming adult shape and color in extreme miniature. Anglers in protected shallows almost never catch bonefish weighing less than a pound or measuring less than 13 or 14 inches, yet surfcasters occasionally hook 6-inch juveniles while fishing for pompano. Perhaps at this stage the young bonefish stay just beyond the surf; on the flats they would be easy prey for the larger fish hunting the shallows.

It is also possible that most of the fish caught on the flats are males, though science has not yet confirmed this. They rarely contain roe. Perhaps bonefish share a strange characteristic with certain groupers, which spend their first five years as females and then become males for their final few years.

Male or female, they are caught in one of three basic ways: bait-fishing, spinning, and fly-fishing. They do most of their foraging in the very shallow water of harbors, bays, lagoons, and—especially—tidal flats. They feed their way in with the tide, then rest and feed their way out again with the tide. The best fishing almost invariably occurs during the last hour of ebb tide and the first couple of hours of flood tide unless the water temperature drops below 70°. They stop feeding or leave if the water is too cool. Most water more than four feet deep can be ignored except when using bait at channel edges or around creek mouths. The best flats usually have sand or marl bottoms, some vegetation, and visible animal life such as crabs, clams, conchs, snails, sea urchins, sand dollars, shrimp, and small fish.

Some of the best lures imitate shrimp, but only because an artificial clam or crab would be impractical for fishing purposes. Many fishermen have the notion that shrimp are the primary or preferred food of bonefish. On the contrary, clams, crabs, and snails form the bulk of their diet in typical waters. The best baits are fresh pieces of crab (including terrestrial hermit crab, but the aquatic species are better), whole or cut crawfish or shrimp, and pieces of conch. Though fished on or near bottom, bait is most effective with no sinker or only a small split shot. An excellent tactic is to anchor at a channel where the bonefish come to a flat on the rising tide. By arriving at low tide (shortly before the turn) and chumming with bits of conch or crawfish, an angler can decoy hungry bonefish as they come in.

Bonefish forage actively in water from a few feet deep to less than a foot. Often their dorsal fins cut the surface, and when a school is rooting, head down in very shallow water, the tails protrude—sometimes wholly exposed, waving in the air. This activity, known as tailing, is a great help to a spin-fisherman or fly-rodder who wades or skiffs in search of casting targets. Another sign to watch for is mudding—a pale clouding of the water when rooting bonefish stir up the marl. Ordinarily, blind casting is not very productive, but mudded water often conceals a good-sized school of feeders, and the sensible response is to cast into its fringe. Though a guide or experienced bonefisherman may spot an occasional school nearly a hundred yards away if the water is flat and the sun is at his back, bonefish can be difficult to see when they are not tailing. The largest ones feed in small schools or sometimes alone or with only a companion or two. Finding them is somewhat simplified by wearing polarized sunglasses to cut the glare.

Whispering or hand-signaling is unnecessary when stalking this or any fish. The game can hear only about 5 percent of any airborne sound. What must be avoided is sound transmitted through the water—splashing when wading, rubbing a pole on the side of a skiff, shuffling in a boat, or dropping anything. Stanley Babson, a recognized authority on this kind of fishing, believes that nearby bonefish can detect a loudly clicking reel since the vibrations ride down the line.

Wading is safe and silent only on a hard bottom with reasonably good footing, and it should be done slowly. Sometimes a wading angler can stalk within ten yards of a bonefish and make an easy cast. However, he cannot see as well as he could from the elevation of a skiff, nor can he lift his rod as high. Getting the rod high can be important when tension has to be maintained or there is danger of having the line cut by rocks, shells, coral, grass thickets, or mangrove roots. Bonefish often feed around grass and mangroves. And a hooked fish makes an incredibly fast initial run, usually toward deep water or cover.

For many of us, the epitome of the sport is to hunt while standing in the bow of a skiff. At the stern, an experienced guide silently poles, helps to spot fish, and moves the boat into good casting position. A skiff, moreover, can follow a running fish faster and into deeper water than a wading angler can. Each new situation may dictate its precise terms, but a lure should generally drop ten or fifteen feet in front of a bonefish, with little or no splash. If it hits too near or heavily, it will startle the fish into flight. Even preoccupied tailing fish may react with a popping surface-slap of their tails as they whip away. If the lure appears in their path without stampeding them, it can then be drawn before them in a jigging retrieve, hopping a foot or two, pausing and sinking, then hopping again like an alarmed shrimp.

Some anglers can be sufficiently delicate with combination spinner-flies, but most rely on ⅛- or ⅑-ounce weighted, wiggling, jig-type bucktails and streamers. The favorite colors are white, pink, and yellow, though sometimes a brown or even black pattern works better on a light-colored bottom. (The same color recommendations apply to fly-rod streamers.) Spinning lures recommended by Babson include the Wiggle Jig, Dunmore Streamer, Spin Streamer, Snooper, Upperman, Bucktail, and Upperman Hi-Tie, but tackle shops in bonefishing areas often display others that have earned a local following. A good spinning rod for this kind of fishing is 6½ or 7 feet long—something in the 4-ounce class with a medium-stiff action. Monofilament line testing 6 or 8 pounds is sufficient.

A fly rod should be a bit heavier; a 6-ounce, 9-foot rod with a slow action is a good choice for long casts. A floating line is generally used since the water is so shallow; it ought to have about 200 yards of backing and at least 9 feet of leader tapered to a tippet of the same strength recommended for spinning line. Probably the most popular fly dressings are shrimp patterns such as the Phillips Pink Bonefish Fly. The Pink Shrimp introduced by Joe Brooks some years ago is another fine example. No. 4 is an ideal size, though 2's and 6's are also used. Additional recommended patterns are the Dunmore, White and Yellow Maribous, Phillips Bead Head, and Gray Ghost.

If a hooked bonefish jumps, it is probably under attack by a barracuda or shark. There is no choice but to give line and help

the fish escape. Otherwise, some tension but not too much drag should be applied whenever possible. After the fish has run, circled, dodged, created sudden slack by heading for the boat, then switched and run again, it may come to the net exhausted. Unless its size demands taxidermy, the angler usually releases it, yet simply letting the fish go may doom it. Instead, grasp it gently just forward of the tail, with the other hand under the belly to support it, and move it forward and back in the water for a couple of minutes to open and close its gills, forcing water through them. This is the equivalent of artificial respiration. When the fish stays upright by itself and begins to wave its tail, the time has come to let go and wish it well.

Bonito *(Sarda)*, **Little Tuna** *(Euthynnus)*, **& Skipjack Tuna** *(E. pelamis or Katsuwonus pelamis)*

COMMON & REGIONAL NAMES: The misnomer *school tuna*, which properly designates young bluefin or yellowfin tuna, is sometimes applied to bonito and allied species. Other common names, denoting various species, will be included in the descriptions of those species.

Bonefishing the flats.

GAME IDENTIFICATION & LOCATION OF FISHING REGIONS: In size and characteristics, the bonito and a number of similar species are intermediate between the mackerels and the big, deep-bodied tunas. Indeed, they belong to the mackerel-tuna family, the Scombridae, and they look and act so much like young, small tuna—the "school tuna" frequently encountered in dense, voracious feeding aggregations—that many anglers make no distinction. Taken on appropriately lighter tackle than their giant relatives, they stage a slightly different kind of battle; they tend to fight nearer the surface, with abrupt runs, reversals, soundings, and risings. They attack live baits or lures, and are caught by chumming, drifting, casting, or fast trolling.

They are as bewildering to biologists as they are exciting to saltwater anglers. Half a dozen species may be common in American waters, or perhaps there are fewer; ichthyologists have doubts about some varieties, which may be demoted from the status of species to subspecies. They are distributed through most of the world's oceans. Along the American coasts, some of them range from the northern temperate zones to Chile and Argentina, but they are most abundant in warm waters.

North America has two major populations of bonito. The Atlantic, or common, bonito *(Sarda sarda)* travels in large schools on both sides of that ocean as well as in the Mediterranean and the Black Sea. Though occasionally it strays to Nova Scotia, it is more common from lower New England southward and through the Gulf of Mexico. It has the big, conical teeth that characterize its family but, unlike the bigger tunas and some of the small related species, has none on the roof of the mouth. All of the species in this group have wide, dark, lunate tails and two dark dorsal fins. The front dorsal is triangular and higher than the second; the rear one sweeps to the tail and consists of progressively smaller, disconnected segments, or finlets. The anal fin mirrors the rear dorsal. In the case of the Atlantic bonito, the front and rear dorsals are almost joined. It is a handsome fish, blackish on the dorsal surface and dark blue down to a conspicuous lateral line. Below the line, the body is silvery, often with cream, pink, or blue glints; above, a dozen or more black, oblique, wavy lines run forward and down from the back. The average size is 3 pounds, though now and then an angler boats a 15-pounder.

The average Pacific bonito *(S. chiliensis)* is of the same

size and color. It may, in fact, be a separate population of the same species. However, it has a slightly shorter first dorsal fin with no more than nineteen spines, whereas the Atlantic bonito has twenty or more. Other anatomical differences are more easily detected by an ichthyologist than an angler. It ranges from the Gulf of Alaska to Chile, but is uncommon above California and between lower Baja California and Peru.

The little tuna *(Euthynnus alleteratus),* a fish of the Atlantic and Mediterranean, ranges from Cape Cod to Brazil. It is also called little tunny, bonito, frigate mackerel, and false albacore—as are other species of the same genus. (True frigate mackerel and albacore will be described, respectively, with the mackerels and tunas.) It has no vomerine teeth and, like others of the genus *Euthynnus,* no scales except for a corselet in the pectoral area. Its high, deeply concave front dorsal fin is narrowly separated from the rear one. In coloration it resembles the bonito and all the others in the group, but instead of longitudinal or oblique stripes, it has wavy lines—almost vermiculations—and is marked below and behind the pectorals by several dark spots. It averages about 5 pounds. A new rod-and-reel record was set in the spring of 1976 off Key Largo (where the previous record was set in the spring of 1975) by a 39-inch fish weighing 27 pounds.

The black skipjack *(E. lineatus)* usually has several more or less horizontal black lines on its back and upper sides, yet there is speculation that it may be just another race of little tuna. Its size is about the same, and its primary range is from California to Panama.

Some taxonomists classify the globally distributed skipjack tuna as *E. pelamis*—a member of the same genus—while others

Top: Pacific bonito. Right: Little tuna.

designate it *Katsuwonus pelamis*. "Skipjack" is a descriptive term applied to a number of game species; it refers to the habit of surface-skipping in pursuit of prey. This particular skipjack is also known as oceanic skipjack, oceanic bonito, and striped tuna. In the Atlantic, it sometimes ranges north to Massachusetts, but is more common in warmer waters; in the Pacific, it is found off California, South America, Hawaii, Australia, New Zealand, and Japan. It often cruises close to shore in spectacularly big schools, occasionally numbering tens of thousands. Its background colors are like those of its relatives but with a lateral line that dips sharply below the dorsal fin, and it has about four to six intense black stripes sweeping the pale lower half of the body from the pectorals to the keeled peduncle at the base of its tail. Most of the skipjack tuna caught by sportsmen weigh less than 10 pounds, but an occasional catch doubles that. The largest to date was a 40-pounder gaffed in 1971 in the Indian Ocean off Mauritius.

FISH HABITAT & FEEDING BEHAVIOR—ANGLING TACTICS:
Until a couple of decades ago, bonito, skipjack, and the like were
underrated, partly because they were used as strip baits and
whole marlin baits—to most of us, game is game and bait is only
bait—and also because they were most often taken on overweight
tackle, as mere interruptions while trolling for big tuna or marlin.
Their reputation has risen with the development of more limber
tackle, the profusion of small but seaworthy private boats, and the
search for new game by charter- and party-boat skippers as well
as anglers. Now they are actively pursued, together with amberjacks, yellowtail, and school tuna. Our knowledge of their lives remains scant. We know that bonito (and probably skipjack and little tuna) spawn chiefly in spring and summer, but at least some
species in some locales probably breed all year. Evidently the
spawning grounds are fairly far offshore, and the eggs—from half
a million to perhaps six million per female, depending on species
and size—drift for some time with other plankton. And we know
that their primary foods are small schooling fish of all kinds, heavily supplemented by squid and crustaceans.

Schools of some species, particularly the little tuna and
skipjack, frequently cruise near shore; they can be located by
trolling and, when feeding near the top, they can be seen from
a boat's flying bridge or tuna tower. They prefer a surface
temperature between 50° and 80° when actively foraging there,
and some boatmen mount a sea-temperature gauge on the bridge
or stow an outdoor thermometer to test samples dipped up in a
bucket. The traditional fishing season lasts from March to October in many regions. On both the Atlantic and Pacific coasts it
is generally best from spring to midsummer, especially in northern waters, but in warm regions it may be excellent in fall or winter. The best months for Pacific bonito coincide with the warm
party-boat season for California yellowtail (which see), and
schools of the two species often mix. In September, as the Japanese Current veers close to shore, surface-feeding schools appear again at some ports. They swarm in Monterey Bay, providing
fast action just after daybreak. The fishing gets even better in
February at Redondo Beach.

Baits in various regions include live squid, anchovies, sardines, herring, and mackerel. A gold-plated tuna hook from size
1 to 4 is excellent for use with bait. The usual way to hook an an-

chovy is through the snout, but it will stay livelier if the hook is run under and up through the bony area next to the gill cover. A sinker weighing a quarter-ounce or more may be necessary to gain casting distance or to get deep if the fish refuse to come up, but the best weight is none when they feed on top. On a yellowtail boat, quantities of bait are tossed over for chum, and when game boils the surface and someone shouts "Hot rail!" as rods bow on the starboard or port side, forward or aft, 8- to 12-pound bonito may come aboard together with yellowtail. One of the anglers, bored with drifting, may cast a bait or lure into the boil. He feels a cracking strike, relinquishes ten or twelve yards of line before hauling back, and then, with the hook set, may have to yield a hundred yards more before gaining control. As the fish bulldogs near the surface, zigzags, and sounds, he pumps carefully, trying to stay in charge, knowing that a seemingly tired bonito, skipjack, or little tuna can dash under a boat to tangle a prop or cut the line against the keel.

For this kind of fishing, the saltwater authority Frank Moss recommends an 8-foot spinning rod, though some of us prefer a shorter stick on party-boat outings. The reel should have about 250 yards of monofilament testing 20 pounds or better. Some anglers insist on a no. 7 to no. 10 wire leader to withstand teeth, but a shock tippet of 40-pound-test monofilament will suffice.

If crowding is no problem, a 10-foot jigging rod with a star-drag reel can be used to work 5- to 7-inch casting spoons. Favored colors are white, blue and white, purple and white, silver, black, rose, and gold, but it pays to buy whatever is locally popular. The hook is generally about a 4/0 treble. The line should be relatively heavy—up to 40-pound test.

On a chartered or private boat in quiet waters, an angler can try the same fly rod he would carry for bonefish, using floating line to cast to the edge of a surface melee, sinking line or even a lead-core shooting head when the fish are down. Bonito and their relatives are sight-feeders; casts should be directed ahead of them when they are visible. Most frequently, the fastest pos- sible retrieve—hand-over-hand stripping—triggers a charge, but sometimes reluctant takers can be coaxed with a drift or slow re- trieve. The drag should be light, the backing copious, the fly a streamer in the 2½- to 4-inch class. Favorite patterns are white: bucktail, marabou, or polar-bear hair with Mylar strips on a naked hook or with a white chenille body.

On the East Coast, fast offshore trolling is more common (sometimes with a switch to casting when a school is located) and heavier tackle is needed. A logical choice is a roller-guide fiberglass trolling rod with a large star-drag reel and line testing 30 pounds (or 50 where full-sized tuna or wahoo may happen by). A strike will take out quite a lot of line before the boat can stop. Moreover, if several rods are being fished, additional strikes can be induced and a dense school may be held close under the stern if, instead of stopping, the engines are given a little extra throttle for a few moments. This puts considerable strain on rod and line.

In the Southeast and probably other locales, the fish are most often found in green water a mile or two from the beach. The most productive spots seem to vary regionally. An angler or skipper watches for game chasing prey just under the surface or leaping and skimming over it. When the action is farther down it may be revealed by wheeling sea birds, an oil slick, or the same faint melon odor sought by bluefish anglers.

Sometimes a decrepit single-prop tuna smack fares better than the sleek new twin-screw cruisers because it churns a deep, narrow wake that draws schools from a distance. Unlike many fish, tuna and bonito are attracted by the rumble and tumult of engine and wake, perhaps because the churning tosses prey about. Each boat has its own best speed. A twin-screw sport fisherman may get strikes at 6 or 7 knots, while a single-engine vessel outperforms it at 8 or 9.

Baits are used, as on the West Coast, but more often feathers, spoons, and plugs are trolled. The most consistently reliable are the traditional Japanese feather jigs in white, red and white, black and white, yellow, green and yellow, blue, black, and red. Those with some white or yellow are most popular. A variety of colors and sizes should be stowed because what works one day can be worthless the next. Hooks are generally of the Sobey or O'Shaughnessy type, from 4/0 to 8/0, depending on lure size and the size of the fish in the vicinity. Spoons are normally used only if low trolling speeds bring fish, because at high speed they twist line despite the use of a swivel. When tuna and bonito are preying heavily on squid, a small plastic squid is another fine lure. And once a school has been assembled at the stern by trolling or chumming, equally good lures include heavy metal diamond jigs.

Outriggers are not for this sport, because the lures must be kept in the wake. Often, two feather-jigged lines are clipped to the stern with snap-jaw clothespins or outrigger-type snaps to hold the lures only fifteen or twenty feet from the stern; two more are clipped to ride the crest of the second stern wave, about a boat-length back; and two more ride the near slope of the third or fourth wave.

When action is achieved, two additional stratagems can be employed. One is to bleed any bonito, skipjacks, or little tuna that have been put into the stern fish box, then pour in the sea water. As it drains, it creates a blood slick in the wake. The second is to tow a couple of hooked fish under the stern on short lines. Others in the school will gather below and behind the captives. A fairly long, heavy, two-handed gaff is needed because the fish are often large and the reach is long from a sport-fishing cruiser. The game is gaffed behind the head and hauled up with a fast, smooth, two-handed swing. In this as in all else, there is need for timing and cooperation if a frenzied school is jostling at the stern and two or more fish are on.

Cobia *(Rachycentron canadum)*
COMMON & REGIONAL NAMES: *crabeater, sergeant fish, ling, cabio, cobio, lemonfish, coalfish, black bonito, black kingfish*

GAME IDENTIFICATION & LOCATION OF FISHING REGIONS: Lurking around buoys, wrecks, bridge pilings, rocks, and anchored vessels, the cobia appears as a long, slim, fusiform shadow with an indecent resemblance to a remora but without any suction disc atop its head. It does not have the remora's need for attachment to a stronger swimmer. After striking a lure with a jolt or crunching a live crab between the bands of small teeth that stud its jaws, tongue, and the roof of its mouth, it fights stubbornly, making strong runs, occasional jumps, and sudden dives. Long ignored, it is now acclaimed as a gamefish.

With maturity, the squarish tail of a young cobia stretches at the corners, assuming a swept-back, broadly forked contour. The pectoral fins are large and wing-shaped. The first dorsal consists of nine or ten short, stiff, separate spines. The aft dorsal is long and low, almost reaching the tail, with a fairly abrupt rise at the front end, and the anal fin mirrors it in slightly abbreviated form. The head is long and flat, the snout broad, the lower jaw projecting slightly. The body is covered with very small scales, olive-brown on the back and upper sides. A blackish band runs from the snout through the eye and rearward until it tapers and dims at the base of the tail. Below this band is a second, fainter stripe from the pectoral fin to the tail, and below that the body pales to cream or silver. The stripes dim on older fish.

Anglers along North America's southeastern coasts are accustomed to hooking cobia weighing from 2 to 10 pounds. But on the Gulf Coast from Florida to Texas these fish tend to be large and abundant. Gulf fishermen catch 20-pounders often, 50-pounders occasionally. Elsewhere in American waters, large specimens are unusual but not rare. The present world record is held by a fish caught in the shallows of the Indian Ocean, off Mombasa, Kenya, in 1964. Its weight was 110 pounds, 5 ounces, its length 5 feet, 3 inches.

Like the bluefish, the cobia has no close relatives and is classified in a taxonomic family of its own. It is found—though not in great density—in most of the world's warm seas, yet is totally absent along some coasts. It inhabits Indo-Pacific waters but not America's Pacific coast, for example. On the Atlantic coast, a few cobia stray as far north as Cape Cod in summer, and they are common in Chesapeake Bay during the warm months. They are also fairly plentiful in Bermuda's waters and along the lower eastern seaboard, through the Gulf and Caribbean, down into the Argentine Atlantic. May is a prime month for 20- to 30-pound catches in the Gulf States. Warm waters hold some cobia throughout the year, but in most ports the catches are impressive only from spring to fall.

FISH HABITAT & FEEDING BEHAVIOR—ANGLING TACTICS: Little is known about the life cycle of this species but much is known about its feeding habits and habitat, secrets quickly yielded to any interested angler. In the shallow waters of harbors, bays, and inlets, and around the mouths of tidal rivers, cobia fishing is best just before and during high tide. These areas call to the light-tackle enthusiast because they call to a great many young fish. The bigger, older ones are more often hooked a little farther out, in the shallow but more open sea, where the fishing is best at slack tide, especially around underwater obstacles or floating lode-

stones such as buoys and channel markers. Wherever cobia wander, they haunt anchored boats, debris, breakwaters, pilings, and rocks—the abodes of crabs and other crustaceans as well as small fish of all kinds. Crabs, shrimp, and baitfish are their preferred foods.

They are caught from boats, jetties, piers, beaches, harbor bridges. Though they sometimes mill about the feeding spots, they do not really school but travel alone or in small, loose groups. In recent years, many Gulf Coast fishermen have become cobia specialists, using beach buggies to scout the shorelines, or installing towers (small versions of tuna towers) on their boats in order to hunt for groups and lone fish. Sometimes cobia can be spotted at a distance, feeding close to the surface, usually near shore. They scour the bottom for crabs and other crustaceans but rise to raid baitfish schools. The best baits are small live crabs, hooked and worked in the same manner as for bluefish (which see), and various baitfish, which are lowered to every depth from top to bottom; the pinfish is a favorite, especially in the south. An Eagle Claw no. 8/0 hook is very popular for this.

The favorite tackle is spinning gear, most often with monofilament testing from 15 to 25 pounds, though something lighter is certainly appropriate for the small cobia caught in sheltered waters. In consideration of the cobia's teeth, terminal tackle includes about a yard of tough leader—a choice of no. 7 to 9 wire or a monofilament shock tippet testing 60 pounds or better.

The customary method with live bait is to drift or still-fish,

Cobia crowding a hooked companion.

mostly with a sinker to get near bottom, around the pilings, rocks, and other obstructions where crabs and similar prey scuttle. An alternative is to fish near the top around floating objects.

Fishermen who prefer more activity are inclined to cast to the feeding spots instead of trolling or still-fishing, and this often involves lures retrieved near the surface. "Buoy casting" has gained many Gulf Coast adherents. Lures include scaled blue and flashing silver striper plugs as well as spoons. There is also profit in going deeper with 1½- to 3-ounce white- or yellow-skirted jigs. A fly-rodder can use a similarly colored streamer or bucktail if he also carries a spinning rod or has a companion·who casts a surface-disturbing teaser plug for him. The teaser is chugged along near floating objects to raise any lurking cobia. Then the fly is tossed in and retrieved like a darting pinfish.

Cod *(Gadus)*; Pollock *(Pollachius virens)*, & Related Species

COMMON & REGIONAL NAMES: Names in common usage denote one or more species and will be included in the descriptions of those species.

GAME IDENTIFICATION & LOCATION OF FISHING REGIONS:
Cod, pollock, hake, tomcod, haddock—they are all cold-water fishes of the Northern Hemisphere. With the exception of pollock, the many related species in the group are not very strong fighters, but some attain impressive size, several provide sport at times of year when other game is scarce in the same regions, and most have firm, delicious white meat.

Species of the cod, or codfish, family are characterized by fairly elongate but heavy bodies, spineless fins, and large mouths with many small teeth in both jaws. The pelvic fins are set far forward, ahead of the pectorals. Many species have three dorsal and two anal fins; most have a single small barbel dangling from the chin. Among some species, coloration is variable. The Atlantic, or common, cod *(Gadus morhua)* has two principal color phases, red and gray. In the red phase, the upper body is reddish-brown, brick-red, or almost orange; the gray phase varies from black to brownish-gray or greenish. The sides are covered with dark spots and bisected by a pale lateral line that dips somewhat about midway back. The belly is whitish. This is one of the species with triple dorsal and double anal fins. It has a squarish or slightly concave tail and a short chin barbel. The rounded snout projects slightly beyond the lower jaw. Many years ago, 6-foot, 200-pound cod were netted in the North Atlantic, but a weight of 100 pounds is very rare even among deep-sea commercial catches. Near shore, the average sporting catch weighs less than 10 pounds, and in deep, offshore waters the average is only about double that weight, though anglers continue to haul up occasional 40-pounders. Cod and their kin have the reputation of being winter fish, yet some of the largest are caught in the spring. The sporting record for Atlantic cod is 98 pounds, 12 ounces; that fish was caught in June of 1969 at New Hampshire's Isle of Shoals.

The Atlantic cod is present in the cool latitudes along both the American and European coasts as well as far out at sea. In North America, the schools range from Greenland and the Maritimes to Cape Hatteras but vacate the more southerly waters during the warm months. The Pacific cod *(G. macrocephalus)* occurs on both sides of the Pacific; it ranges along the American coast from Alaska to Oregon and occasionally reaches California waters, but it has a smaller following of anglers than its East Coast counterparts. Somewhat smaller than the Atlantic species and with more pointed fins, it is otherwise similar in appearance.

Better game than the Atlantic cod is its close relative, the pollock *(Pollachius virens),* which shares the same range. It has a broad, slightly forked tail and either a very small chin barbel or, quite often, none at all. Its lower jaw projects beyond a somewhat pointed snout. Like the cod, it has three dorsal and two anal fins but is easily distinguished by its jaw structure and lack of spots. Its meat is sometimes sold as "Boston bluefish." A more common name, descriptive of its dominant color, is green cod. Its upper parts are bright olive-green or greenish-brown, its lateral line white, and its lower parts silvery gray. A moderately plump fish, it averages between 4 and 10 pounds when caught and sometimes exceeds 30. The record pollock, taken at Brielle, New Jersey, in May, 1975, weighed 46 pounds, 7 ounces.

Another close relative sharing the Atlantic range is the haddock, included in the *Gadus* genus by some biologists but classified by others as *Melanogrammus aeglefinus.* Its chief claim to excellence is the flavor of its smoked form, finnan haddie. It has a slightly forked tail and a codlike arrangement of dorsal and anal fins, but the first dorsal is high and pointed. It has the cod's barbel and overbite, the pollock's lack of spots. There is one big dark splotch on each side, above and behind the pectoral fin. The belly and flanks are white. The upper parts display several color variations, of which two are common: greenish- or purplish-gray with a dark lateral line and golden brown with a yellowish lateral line. Most haddock weigh less than 5 pounds. Since they gravitate toward the deepest parts of cod habitat, they are usually just incidental catches for anglers.

Tomcods are still smaller relatives, usually no more than a foot long and weighing less than a pound, but they can provide a diversion with ultralight tackle in winter, when they come to inshore areas to spawn. Most species of the cod group spawn far offshore, but tomcods are caught in less than three fathoms from November through February. They enter brackish and occasionally even fresh water, and can be caught by bottom-fishing with clam chunks, squid strips, shrimp, or worms. Their pelvic fins end in long filaments, probably used to feel the bottom for prey. Their three dorsal fins, two anal fins, and tail, all rounded, are mottled or wavily streaked. A small barbel hangs from the chin. The Atlantic tomcod *(Microgadus tomcod),* ranging from Labrador to Virginia, is olive-brown above, pale below, and marked with wavy black streaks and blotches. The Pacific tomcod *(M. proximus),* ranging from Alaska to Point Conception, above Oxnard, California, has an olive-green or brownish back and silvery sides.

A half-dozen species of hake that are common to American waters (and several more that are not so common) grow somewhat larger. A hake has only two dorsal fins and one anal fin; that is, the second and third dorsal segments are fused into one very long fin, usually with a notch or slight indentation where they join, and the two anal segments are similarly fused. The tail is square or slightly forked. The lower jaw projects beyond the upper, and the barbel is vestigial or absent. Most species have very small scales. Schools of hake generally occupy the edge of the continental shelf or waters still farther out, but some come into the shallows, particularly during late winter and spring.

The southern, or Gulf, hake *(Urophycis floridanus)* is a 1-pound reddish-brown, pale-bellied fish with a small dark spot above the eye, several more behind the eye and on the gill cover, and a black lateral line cut by a series of white spots. Its primary range is the Gulf of Mexico, and it lingers inshore from February to May, providing good fishing in the shallows on ultralight spinning tackle. It bites most readily at dusk. Hooks up to 1/0 are right for bait. It will also hit jigs, bucktails, and streamers.

The red, or squirrel, hake *(U. chuss)* is also called ling though it is not at all like the West Coast species of greenling known as lingcod (which see). Distributed from Newfoundland to Chesapeake Bay, this hake is brownish-gray or reddish with dusky mottling and yellowish underparts. Its pelvic and ventral fins end in filaments, and it has a very long filament on its first dorsal fin. It averages 2 pounds, but 30-inch, 8-pound specimens are occasionally caught. Its preferred residence is over a soft bottom, anywhere from the tide mark down to about three hundred fathoms. Like the southern hake, it can be caught on lures, but more readily takes a hook baited with a clam, a squid strip, or a herring strip. A 3/0 hook would be a good choice. Night fishing is best.

FISH HABITAT & FEEDING BEHAVIOR—ANGLING TACTICS:
Winter is the traditional codfishing season off New Jersey, New York, and New England, the most famous regions, for only in winter do cod frequent relatively shallow offshore and inshore waters. They arrive with cold weather, in October or more often November, and in March or April they leave again, going far out to sea. In the southern part of the range the season is shorter, while in the North there are a couple of renowned spots—Montauk Point on New York's Long Island, and Block Island, off Rhode Island—where the currents are cool enough and the food supply rich enough to sustain good codfishing through most of the year. At many points from New Jersey north, the fish come quite close to shore in October but they soon retreat a bit because they prefer to spawn at about twenty fathoms.

Spawning lasts from December to March. A 20-pound female may release five million eggs in a season, while the males spread their milt in the vicinity. The eggs float and drift, as do newly hatched young. Fry are about an inch long before they can swim well. They move into shallow water to find cover and food while growing. With each successive year, they seek deeper water. A three-year-old usually weighs 5 pounds, and such fish are often caught close to shore. On occasion, older cod may feed at any depth from a few yards under the surface to an ocean bed more than a thousand feet down, but they are fundamentally bottom dwellers, traveling in schools just over the ocean floor.

In New England, where most rod-and-reel catches weigh between 6 and 12 pounds but 40-pounders are not very unusual, big ones are very rarely taken in waters less than sixty feet deep. Except during the inshore runs of autumn, the best fishing is usually in water at least a hundred feet deep, over rocks, rubble, ledges, wrecks, debris, or pebble-and-shell-strewn bottoms. Small to medium cod are taken in winter from jetties and by wading surfcasters. Good baits include clams of all kinds, chunks of conch, strips of squid, whole small herring, cunner, sand eel, capelin, crab, and mackerel and hake strips.

Bait is commonly lowered for cod on a 5/0 to 9/0 Sproat, O'Shaughnessy, or Eagle Claw or a standard codfish hook (which has a tarred snell, intended for setlining, but is just as suitable for rod and reel). A typical cod rig consists of a single hook with a long snell or about 2 feet of monofilament or nylon leader, attached with a three-way swivel a foot or so above a sinker. A second dropper can be added about 3 feet higher; some codfishermen bait three droppers, but the uppermost hook should be no more than 6 feet off bottom. When fishing shoals or in a weak current, a 5- or 6-ounce bank or diamond sinker may suffice, but twice as much weight is sometimes needed for deep water or a tidal current. The depth, current, sinker, and an occasional heavy fish put more strain on rod and line than is wanted with spinning tackle. A better codfish outfit is a sturdy surf or boat rod with a star-drag reel and a couple of hundred yards of linen, Dacron, or nylon line testing 36 pounds.

The usual procedure is to anchor or, if wind and current are light, drift slowly while bumping bottom with the sinker. Scraps of bait are tossed over for chum. As an alternative to bait, a 4- to 10-ounce chrome diamond jig with a 5/0 to 8/0 hook can be fished. It is especially effective around wrecks, where the schools assemble to gobble small baitfish. It should be dropped to the bottom, then repeatedly raised 10 or 15 feet and lowered again. A bit of jigging is also advisable with bait, not only to attract the fish but to check that bottom is being touched.

When a run approaches shore in autumn, jetty and surf fishermen spread the news. They generally cast baits, jigs, and

tin squid. The shallows can be trolled slowly, using a bucktail or spinner baited with pork rind or a squid strip. Deeper trolling can be effective with a bright spoon or a metal squid similarly baited.

Catching pollock involves a basically similar approach but with several notable differences. Pollock, too, spawn from late autumn into early winter, yet they move inshore again for a while in the spring, generally in May, and at this time can be taken on lures near or at the surface. Springtime fishing is excellent at Cape Cod, and in upper New England and Nova Scotia it sometimes remains good until early fall. The shallows and surf may be productive during an incoming or high tide, especially at dawn or dusk. Pollock will take the same baits, jigs, and spoons used

Atlantic cod (left) and pollock.

for cod; they also hit big leadheaded bucktail jigs. Some anglers use a bucktail on one dropper and a diamond jig on another.

Pollock are more active feeders than cod. They prey chiefly on small fish (including cod and hake) but also eat mollusks, crustaceans, and annelids, just as cod do. Probably most pollock are taken by trolling jigs and spoons. However, the schools often cruise closer to shore than do cod, and the small to medium fish, in particular, can be caught on big bucktails and streamers in the inshore waters. A sturdy saltwater spinning rod or any surfcasting rod is suitable. Despite a codlike predilection for bottom-feeding, schools often appear at the surface, gorging on menhaden and the like, boiling the water and attracting sea birds in the manner of blues and bonito. An angler can cast into the boil—or through a rip or over a drop-off—to reach feeding pollock. Favorite fly colors are yellow, white, and baitfish hues, but shape and motion probably matter more than pattern. Strikes are garnered by assorted big bucktail or feather streamers such as a Gibbs Striper Bucktail, Bonbright, Strawberry Blond, a long-winged Lefty's Deceiver, or a braided Mylar eel.

Corvina *(Cynoscion)*
COMMON & REGIONAL NAMES: *corbina, sea bass.* (Names denoting various species will be included in the descriptions of those species.)

GAME IDENTIFICATION & LOCATION OF FISHING REGIONS:
Closely related to weakfish and in some respects so similar that they have been called the weakfish of the Pacific, corvina range from lower Alaska to Peru. Most species are uncommon above the Mexican border, but two enhance the fishing in California waters. Though their meat spoils quickly, it is excellent when fresh or made into the pickled delicacy known in Latin America as *seviche.* They strike hard and make one or two strong runs, after which they fight less vigorously but renew the battle briefly upon coming close to a boat or a surfcasting angler. The two species of greatest importance to North American anglers are the white sea bass, or white corvina *(Cynoscion nobilis),* and orangemouth corvina *(C. xanthalus),* also known as yellowfinned corvina. The white sea bass, in particular, is a fine surface fighter. Both species belong to the same genus as the weakfish and about a dozen other varieties; all have moderately fragile mouths—though not

so weak as legend claims—and are usually boated with a net because a hook can tear out as such a fish is hoisted aboard.

They are members of the Sciaenidae, the family of croakers and drums, numbering some two hundred species in tropical and temperate seas. A number of them (including the California corbina, which is sometimes confused with corvina because the similar names are inevitably interchanged) will be described in the section on croakers and drums. A few—corvina on the West Coast, weakfish and seatrout on the East Coast—merit separate treatment because they are caught by different methods.

Young white corvina, or white sea bass.

Though not very colorful, they are handsome fish, slim-bodied and troutlike in conformation. They are distinguished by a very long lateral line which extends onto the tail. The species described here (and most others) have a short anal fin and a short, spiny first dorsal fin separated from a second, longer, soft-rayed dorsal by a deep notch. They are white-bellied, and most have an orange or yellowish tinge on the fins and a metallic iridescence.

The white sea bass is the largest, most abundant, and most popular of the common Pacific species. Most of those caught weigh between 8 and 15 pounds, but now and then someone brings in a much larger one. The biggest yet taken on rod and reel weighed 83 pounds, 12 ounces, and was 5 feet, 5½ inches long; it was caught in 1953 off San Felipe, Mexico. This species has bluish-gray or bluish-tan upper parts, usually with a wash of rust, bronze, or pink, and silvery flanks. A dusky spot marks the base of each pectoral. The young have three to six crossbars that disappear after maturity. The lower jaw is slightly projecting, the tail slightly concave. The upper jaw lacks the canine teeth that characterize several other species. A distinct ridge of scales can be seen on the belly, from the pectorals to the anus. White sea bass are abundant off lower California and Mexico.

The orangemouth corvina looks like a white sea bass but with a yellow-orange mouth lining, canine teeth, a black gill-cover lining, a yellowish tinge on the fins, a squarer tail, and no ridge of belly scales. Indigenous to the Gulf of California, between Baja and mainland Mexico, it is uncommon off the coast of the United States. But in 1950 it was introduced into California's Salton Sea, a great, shallow, artificial lake in the Imperial Valley northeast of San Diego. It has become that reservoir's chief game species, estimated to number in the millions. As a rule it grows to a length of 2 feet or so, but larger catches, including weights exceeding 30 pounds, have been reported at the Salton Sea.

FISH HABITAT & FEEDING BEHAVIOR—ANGLING TACTICS:
Corvina spawn chiefly in spring and summer, and are most abundant off the California coast from May to September. They are taken during the winter in more tropical waters. The young feed on plankton, the adults on fish, crustaceans, and squid.

Orangemouths in the Salton Sea are piscivorous. They generally weigh a little over 2 pounds by their second winter, over

5 by their third, 11 by their fourth. These orangemouths are some-times taken on live or cut baitfish but can be as easily tempted by a trolled or cast gold-finished wobbling spoon. Corvina in gen-eral are caught by still-fishing or drifting with live bait and by troll-ing or casting with deep-running plugs, spoons, and leadheaded jigs. Fly-rodders catch them on weighted white streamers.

All species forage in schools or small groups over sandy bottoms, both inshore and offshore, but the white sea bass is especially fond of kelp beds. Party boats and private craft troll, drift, and still-fish the beds, and surfcasters work from the shores and jetties with feathers, spoons, metal squid, and deep-running plugs. Live and strip baits include herring, sardines, and other commonly abundant species. The schools often follow and plunder hordes of migrating squid, which are sometimes seen near the surface or near shore. At these times a 6-inch live squid is excellent bait. Hooks ranging from 1/0 to 4/0 are used.

Among lures, white jigs and white-painted metal squid are very good, as are soft-bodied plastic squid. Some fishermen use homemade squid jigs both for corvina and lingcod. A 10-inch cir-cle of fish skin is taken from a previous catch, and strips are cut inward from the perimeter toward the center to resemble tenta-cles. The center, or head, of the skin is tied over a hooked jig with a bit of monofilament so that the strips trail. Normally, any rod and reel with monofilament line testing 10 to 25 pounds will suf-fice except for jigging deep kelp bottoms; this can demand test strengths up to 40 pounds. Two rules help to net corvina, regard-less of lure. The first is to jig slowly, on or near the bottom. The second is that even when corvina respond eagerly during daylight they are most gullible and hungry at night.

Croakers & Drums (Sciaenidae)

COMMON & REGIONAL NAMES: Names in common usage denote various species and will be included in the descriptions of those species.

GAME IDENTIFICATION & LOCATION OF FISHING REGIONS:
Some two hundred species of Sciaenidae—croakers and drums—inhabit the world's tropical and temperate seas. Over two dozen enlarge the sport and commercial catches along the Atlantic, Pa-cific, and Gulf coasts of the United States. They include white sea

bass and other species of corvina, as well as weakfish and closely related seatrout—small gamefish of sufficient importance to be covered under the separate headings of Corvina and Weakfish. Red and black drum are the most important among the other major species, which will be treated in detail here.

Those belonging to the genus *Menticirrhus* (the whitings, or kingfish, and the California corbina) are sometimes described as "silent drum." They lack a swim bladder, which, in the other species, serves the secondary function of resonating and amplifying peculiar sounds made by the vibration of a muscle adjacent to the bladder. Typically, croakers croak and drums drum. Some species, at least, probably gain a spawning or feeding advantage from the ability to communicate by means of vibrations that are audible underwater. Often the sounds are audible above the surface, too, indicating the presence of a school.

Certain other characteristics are also shared by members of the family. All have an exceptionally long lateral line that extends onto the tail. Some are humpbacked, but most are rather troutlike in conformation. Most have one or more barbels dangling from the lower jaw. In general, they forage and rest on shallow, sandy bottoms near beaches in bays or lagoons, near estuaries, or in the surf. Some enter brackish waters.

There is, however, only one freshwater species, appropriately if unimaginatively called the freshwater drum *(Aplodinotus grunniens)*. It is also called freshwater sheepshead, grunter, croaker, crocus, jewelhead, and—confusingly—white perch. It is easy to identify by its highly arched back, convex—in fact, bluntly pointed—tail, and large, rough, silvery scales. It is, moreover, the only freshwater fish with a lateral line that reaches the end of the tail. The body is pearl-gray with bronze or silver overtones and a white belly. The spiny forward dorsal fin is short, triangular, and almost separated from the long, soft-rayed hind dorsal. Its jaws are equipped with comblike little teeth. A bottom-feeder like its marine relatives, it is particularly fond of clams and mussels, which it crushes between pharyngeal teeth. It can be caught on the bottom in big, clear rivers and lakes from the St. Lawrence through the Great Lakes and the Mississippi River drainage. A 10-pounder is not uncommon but most weigh less than 2 pounds.

Most of the marine species are similarly partial to bottom-dwelling invertebrate prey, though adults of the larger species be-

come piscivorous. The most common eastern variety is the Atlantic croaker, or hardhead *(Micropogon undulatus)*. Its tail is a wedge, like that of its freshwater relative. A fairly small fish, it has a short, high first dorsal fin, a long, low second dorsal, a convex head, numerous little barbels on the chin, and a generous sprinkling of brownish-black specks on its upper body and dorsals. It is pale silvery gray with a white belly and greenish back, but during its spawning season (early fall to December in the North, slightly later in the South) it acquires a bronze or yellowish tinge that explains why it is sometimes called the golden croaker. Anglers now and then take Atlantic croakers measuring 2 feet long and weighing 6 or 8 pounds, but the average is only about a pound, a 2-pounder being an excellent catch. The range stretches from Texas to New Jersey, and occasionally as far up the coast as Massachusetts. However, overzealous trawling and gill netting have depleted the northern populations. This croaker is most abundant from the Carolinas to upper Florida and along the Gulf Coast. Its primary foods—an obvious key to baits, as with all its kin—are worms, crustaceans, and mollusks.

The silent genus *Menticirrhus* is a group of drums often referred to collectively as the whitings, and any of these species may be known locally by that name. They include the northern kingfish *(M. saxatalis)*, southern kingfish *(M. americanus)*, Gulf kingfish *(M. littoralis)*, minkfish *(M. focaliger)*, and California corbina *(M. undulatus)*. All have a single fleshy chin barbel, and all

Black drum.

but the California corbina are distinguished by an asymmetrical tail with a slightly concave upper lobe and convex lower lobe forming an S-shaped rear edge. All have bands of teeth in both jaws. The northern kingfish, found close to shore from Maine to Florida, is an olivaceous species with irregular black blotches. It averages a pound. The southern kingfish, ranging from New York to Argentina, is a pale fish of the same size with seven dark, oblique bands along its sides. It keeps close to shore over sandy bottoms. The Gulf kingfish, or surf whiting, is most abundant in the Gulf of Mexico but also ranges from Florida north to Virginia. Silvery gray with a white belly, it can be distinguished from the southern kingfish by its lack of bands. It averages a half-pound but occasionally weighs as much as 2 pounds. The minkfish resembles it but has a dark body. It is found only in the Gulf of Mexico. These two Gulf species are the most common drums along the Texas coast. Both can be caught on bottom-fished shrimp, clams, and crabs.

The best game species among the whitings is the California corbina, a prized surf fish found along sandy beaches from Point Conception to Baja and the Gulf of California. Surfcasters sometimes hook corbina on spoons, jigs, plastic or rubber eels, and the like, but these fish are more susceptible to natural baits matching their prey: clams, mussels, small crabs, and worms. A typical corbina weighs a pound; however, anglers have reported 30-inch lunkers weighing more than 8 pounds. Like other whitings, the corbina has a single chin barbel, a convex head, a short, high first dorsal fin, and a long, lower second dorsal. Its tail, however, tends to have a slight fork rather than a pronounced S-shape. A pale-bellied fish with light metallic blue and gray upper parts, it often has dark spots or wavy lines on its sides and a bronze tinge on the fins.

None of these relatively small species, however, can rival black drum and red drum in popularity. The black drum *(Pogonias cromis)* ranges from Cape Cod to Argentina, is common from New York southward, and is found in the greatest concentrations from Virginia to Florida and along the Gulf Coast. In contradiction of the regional name "sea bass," it is fundamentally a shoreline fish, most often caught in shallow waters from private and party boats, from piers, and in the surf. In the Gulf states, most black drum are taken in bays and lagoons, while from Delaware to South Carolina a substantial spring run gives surfcasters an opportunity to haul in numerous lunkers.

The black drum, though less determined in battle than the red drum, is the largest member of the clan. The average catch weighs less than 10 pounds, but anglers beach a great many in the 20- to 40-pound class, and black drum are known to attain a weight of at least 125 pounds and a length of 4 feet. The heaviest yet taken on rod and reel was caught in 1975 off Lewes, Delaware. It weighed an ounce over 113 pounds. The largest species is also the noisiest; often a feeding school can be heard above water, its drumming combined with an odd purring sound. A juvenile specimen, or "puppy drum," is marked by five broad, black, vertical bars that fade away at maturity. The black-finned body of a typical adult may vary from silvery to nearly black, usually with a brassy sheen. After death, the body quickly dulls to dark gray. The chin of a black drum bears a whiskery fringe of short barbels. The body is short and chunky, with a highly arched back.

The red drum *(Sciaenops ocellata)* is at least equally well known as the channel bass or redfish, and is also called red bass or spottail. It has a large, pronounced, black splotch (sometimes two) at the base of the tail. Like the black drum, it has a squarish tail, but it lacks barbels and is elongate in shape. Its body is most often a coppery color that darkens to brick-red after death, but it may also be orange or reddish-bronze. An average catch weighs 5 pounds, yet anything under 15 is considered a puppy drum and quite a few 40-pounders have been beached or boated. The current record was set by a 90-pounder in 1973 at Rodanthe, North Carolina. The range of this Atlantic species is from Massachusetts to Florida and along the Gulf Coast, and it is common from New Jersey southward. A small landlocked population has also been established in a freshwater reservoir near Waco, Texas. In the cool northern part of the range, schools of red drum appear to be seasonally migratory; they are most abundant in spring, when they provide excellent surf fishing and inshore trolling.

FISH HABITAT & FEEDING BEHAVIOR—ANGLING TACTICS:
Most croakers and drums spawn offshore in fairly deep water during spring, summer, or fall—the peak depending on species and locale—but they soon return to the shallows and provide good fishing during the warm months. In southern waters, they provide year-round sport. Apart from those scant generalizations and the

foregoing remarks about seasonal migrations and abundance, not very much is known of their life cycles. What the angler needs to know about their habits and habitat can be summed up briefly: they prefer to feed on the bottom in shallow water. The most common eastern species, the Atlantic croaker, is most frequently caught on clams, mussels, or strips of squid; with the addition of crabs, bloodworms, and sandbugs, the list of choice baits is complete for all species except black and red drum, which also show an avidity for strips of fish, particularly mullet and menhaden.

Some, particularly the whitings, hit small feathered jigs or streamers worked gently through a surf line where they are feeding, but cut bait is more productive.

For the bigger drums, a favorite arrangement of terminal tackle is the fishfinder rig, which consists basically of a pyramid, egg, or bank sinker attached to the line by a sliding ring above a barrel swivel that holds a long leader. This is excellent for surf-

casting. After the rig has settled in the water, the line runs freely through the sinker ring so that the bait drifts over a wide area instead of being anchored. Hook sizes for the larger species range from 5/0 to 9/0. Puppy drum can be handled easily on line testing 6 or 8 pounds, but the big ones demand 20- to 30-pound test strength. A shock leader is recommended, and if sharks are in the vicinity there is no taint of overkill in using nylon-coated braided wire. Rods include the spinning, baitcasting, trolling, and surfcasting types. Puppy drum, like the smaller croakers, are also taken on fly tackle.

The black drum, a sluggish striker but a fairly determined if unspectacular fighter, uses its pharyngeal teeth to crack vast numbers of mollusks and crustaceans; it is, in fact, considered a pest in areas where it ravages oyster beds. Knowing this, an angler may be inclined to fish the beds, baiting a fishfinder rig with clams, mussels, crabs, or shrimp.

The largest red drum usually inhabit the northern part of the fishery—from the Carolinas up to New Jersey—where the sport is best in the spring because the schools move away in winter and often head for deep water in the heat of summer. Famous springtime fishing resorts are at Assateague and Chincoteague, but comparably good places can be found along many of the barrier islands, beaches, and sloughs in Virginia and the Carolinas. These sloughs are shoreline pockets and strips protected by sandbars and similar sea barriers. The red drum, or channel bass, arrive in them through entry channels on the incoming tide, and the channels themselves become prime fishing spots again during the first half of the falling tide, as the schools depart. Strikes are most frequent when the good tide levels coincide with dusk or daybreak.

Although red drum subsist primarily on crustaceans and mollusks, they are very fond of fish, especially mullet, which make excellent bait on a 7/0 hook. A small mullet can be used whole, a big one in chunks or strips. Other popular baits include peeler, shedder, or blue crabs with the top shell removed and the body tied to the hook. Still others are clams, bloodworms, and squid. Shrimp is a favorite in Florida and along the Gulf Coast.

While baits are most efficacious, roaming schools of channel bass hit spoons, deep-running plugs, metal squid, or lead-headed bucktail jigs. Artificials should be fished slowly, bumped

Freshly gaffed channel bass.

and drifted along the bottom, and any rushing of the strike will simply pull a lure away from a taker. Jigs work best if used with a strip of bait and continually moved.

On Florida's grassy flats, puppy drum can be seen as a skiff is poled along. Excellent year-round feeding spots are oyster beds and mangrove edges. In the shallows, foraging drum often tail like bonefish, and a fly-rodder or spin fisherman can also watch for swirls or wakes. After poling into range, he can cast his lure just ahead of the fish, bearing in mind that drum are rather near-sighted. If he is using a crab or shrimp, the drum-will scent the bait and pick it up as it is worked slowly along the bottom. Favorite fly-rod lures include popping bugs and feather, nylon, and buck-tail jigs in red and white, red and yellow, blue and white, or all blue, as well as bonefish-type shrimp flies. Another excellent choice is a bucktail or feather streamer with a wing behind the eye and another over the barb. Some of the same lures can be used with a spinning rod, as can surface plugs and spoons.

Mississippi Sound and other extensive areas of flats to the west along the Gulf can be fished in the same manner, but during summer and fall, when bigger fish are often caught there, many anglers prefer spinning gear with a short monofilament leader testing 30 pounds, a quarter-ounce sliding egg or bank sinker above the swivel, and a 4- to 6-inch live croaker on a 6/0 or 7/0 hook. The bait is cast out and left there. The best fishing in this area occurs from September to November, rather than during the springtime boom that hits the more northerly coast.

Regardless of region, some anglers prefer to troll deeper waters. This can be effective with big spoons moved very slowly in the depths, in the shallower bays at high tide, and near the beaches during tide changes. When a school is found, the lures should be trolled beside or just ahead of it. From a boat or from shore, red drum can be sight-hunted. After dull hours of inactivity, the arrival of a school may tint the water rosy bronze, the color of impending action.

Dolphin (*Coryphaena hippurus* and *C. equisetis*)
COMMON & REGIONAL NAMES: *dorado, mahi-mahi*

GAME IDENTIFICATION & LOCATION OF FISHING REGIONS: An angler's first dolphin is not quickly forgotten. It strikes and fights with explosive speed and power, flails against the gaff, and comes aboard in a suffusion of colors that change, eerily, as the fisherman views his prize. Then, in death, it fades so quickly that the conqueror's exhilaration almost palls with it. In the cobalt waters off the Florida Keys, the author's first dolphin knifed the surface with its low dorsal fin as it streaked after a rigged balao skipping on a fanning swell beside the wake. Its long first run probably reached a speed of 50 miles an hour—for the dolphin is one of the fastest fish in the sea as well as one of the handsomest—after which it leaped high, leaped again, and danced over the surface on its tail. When at last it was close off the port side it looked like a yard-long animated jewel, first bright greenish-blue, then flashing a yellow flank. As sometimes happens, vague dark bands appeared and disappeared.

A dolphin's laterally compressed body tapers sharply from its big, blunt head to the narrow peduncle of its long, very deeply forked tail. Its dorsal fin begins far forward, rising almost directly above the eyes and extending all the way to the peduncle in a lowering taper. Its narrow anal fin is also very long, reaching from the peduncle forward under about half the length of the body. The jaws and roof of the mouth are equipped with small, comblike teeth for grasping the small fish that constitute the bulk of its food. When a male, or bull, nears maturity its head begins to enlarge, and eventually the high forehead rises almost vertically from the mouth—an unmistakable mark of identification quite different from the sloping forehead of a juvenile or female. Until death mutes the colors, a dolphin's dorsal fin and back are usually sea-blue with overtones of sea-green, grading into green on the upper sides and bright yellow from the lateral line to the slim silvery zone of the belly. The sides are sprinkled with dark and light blue and blue-green spots. Typically, the anal fin is silvery or yellow, margined with blue. The tail, pectoral, and pelvic fins generally are yellow, too, often substantially tinged with green, and the pelvic fins are generally edged with blue. From this summary of shape and hues, an angler can instantly recognize a dolphin, yet no description is definitive because the pigments fluctuate strangely. The exquisite meat, once thought to be inedible, is reddish.

Most of the dolphins caught by anglers weigh from a couple of pounds to 15 or so, but 20-pound specimens are not uncommon and fish weighing over 50 pounds are occasionally taken. Off

▲ Bull dolphin jumping. ▼ Dolphin being swung into transom well.

Baja California in 1962, a 73-pound, 11-ounce dolphin was caught; two years later, off Bimini, that record was bettered by 3 pounds, 1 ounce; and in 1968, off Spanish Wells, another fine Bahamian fishing ground, the current record was set by a 5-foot, 9-inch bull dolphin weighing 85 pounds.

The variegation of dolphins at one time led biologists to list over a dozen putative species; the consensus now is that there are only two, the common dolphin *(C. hippurus)* described above and the pompano dolphin *(C. equisetis)*. The pompano dolphin is smaller, rarely exceeding 5 pounds or a length of 2 feet. It is a stubbier, less streamlined fish—more like a pompano—with its greatest depth of body located about midway back rather than at the head; and it has a lower, more sloping forehead.

Dolphins inhabit all of the world's warm seas. In the Atlantic they stray as far north as Nova Scotia and sometimes are caught off New England in August, but are seasonally abundant only from Delaware southward. Following the Gulf Stream that far north in hot weather, they become plentiful off the Carolinas in early summer, when they can be caught in good numbers off Cape Hatteras. Although they are present all year in the Gulf of Mexico and around Florida, spring is the season of greatest action there. Florida, Louisiana, and Texas are probably the best states for dolphin fishing, but the species is also plentiful elsewhere in the warm Atlantic and in the Caribbean. In the Pacific, the species is abundant around Hawaii. West Coast dolphin fishing is worthwhile only from lower California southward.

FISH HABITAT & FEEDING BEHAVIOR—ANGLING TACTICS:
There seems to be no direct correlation between breeding season and good dolphin fishing but there is evidence that in most waters spawning occurs during spring and summer, when the fishing is best. A female may produce from 500,000 to 2½ million adhesive eggs, which cling to weeds and floating debris, hatching offshore.

Dolphins are blue-water fish, commonly hooked by anglers trolling for sailfish or other billfish in the Atlantic, Caribbean, or Gulf of Mexico, and by marlin trollers in the Pacific. Light sailfish tackle or other, more or less comparable trolling rods probably account for most of those caught. But once dolphins are encountered, better sport lies in a switch to light spinning, baitcasting, or even fly-fishing tackle. If dolphins are the principal objective, a trolling line needs to be no heavier than 12- to 20-pound test (depending on whether local waters are producing big fish). The largest bulls tend to hunt alone or in loosely associated groups; the fish in a given school may average 2 pounds or 20, but the bigger the school is (and it may number in the high hundreds), the smaller its members will be. Drag should be fairly light, because a dolphin's mouth is soft enough to let a hook pull out. Many anglers use a nylon leader for school dolphins but switch to wire if there is a likelihood of hooking something big. A fly fisherman will do well with a floating line, plenty of strong backing, and the same 9-foot rod he might use for a number of other saltwater species. Some fly-rodders like the security of a 40-pound shock tippet while others rely on a test strength of no more than 15 pounds.

Some skippers make a practice of "bailing" dolphins—stopping to chum when a school is encountered. Since a hooked fish tends to circle back into the school, instinctively seeking protection among companions rather than making the long, hard runs that are characteristic at other times, a light spinning outfit with monofilament testing 6 pounds is strong enough. The angler has a choice of casting bright wobbling spoons, spinners, diving or popping plugs, popping bugs, feathers, or bucktails. Fly-rodders take dolphins consistently with Honey Blonds, Strawberry Blonds, and various other bucktails and feather streamers. Preferred colors are red, yellow, red and yellow in combination, and white with flashing Mylar strips. Sizes vary from 1/0 to 5/0.

Dolphins feed on small fish, squid, and crustaceans. Juvenile flying fish are their favorite food, but they also pursue filefish, triggerfish, jacks, and other species that haunt sargassum or kelp. When not probing the weed rips, they like to rest in the shade of driftwood and other floating debris or navigational aids. All such spots are worth trying. Sometimes the boat itself attracts dolphins, as these fish are inordinately inquisitive. The first one caught is often tethered behind the stern, because curiosity draws others within casting range of a captive "Judas fish."

Dolphins are also found far from weeds or debris, hunting the open ocean. Where flying fish are seen in profusion, surface trolling at about 6 knots is a good tactic, with baits let back 60 to 80 feet from outriggers. Hook sizes are usually 5/0 to 7/0. Choice baits include small, whole mullet, balao, and flying fish, squid strips, belly strips of flying fish or bonito, and even 10-inch "sea strips" of pork rind. Good trolling lures are big spoons, plugs, Japanese feather jigs, and big streamers. Dolphins hound prey along the surface or dash ahead when a flying fish shoots from the surface on a long glide, intercepting it when it comes down. This requires a speed demonstrated again when a dolphin makes a line hum and twang, a reel smoke, or when it slams across a boat's wake to snatch two surface-skipping baits at a time.

Flounders & Related Species *(Bothidae* and *Pleuronectidae)*

COMMON & REGIONAL NAMES: *flatfish.* (The name *fluke*, an alternate term for summer flounder, occasionally is misapplied to other species. The name *dab* designates several small and medium species. The *turbot* is a European species whose name is also used for several small American species of little angling importance. The name *sole* designates several European and unimportant American species—true soles—plus some American flounders of greater angling significance. Other names designate various species or growth stages thereof and will be included in the descriptions of those species.)

GAME IDENTIFICATION & LOCATION OF FISHING REGIONS: Flounders and their close relatives belong to the order of Pleuronectiformes—the flatfishes—an anatomically strange group of bottom-feeders that spend most of their time lying against the sea bed or partially buried in it, thus escaping the notice of predators and prey. When hooked, they neither jump nor make long runs but some of them offer reasonably spirited resistance. Those that do are popular for additional reasons. They become seasonally abundant (chiefly during the warm months, though winter flounders are a notable exception) in bays, harbors, and estuaries, where they can be caught from beaches, piers, bridges, jetties, and small boats. Easily inveigled by baits moved along the bottom, they sometimes make up in numbers what they lack in verve. And their firm, white meat, bony but simple to fillet, is delicious. Of more than two hundred species in the Atlantic and Pacific, a couple of dozen are common along the North American coasts. Those of angling importance will be described.

A hatchling of any species looks rather like the larvae of other marine fishes, but within a few days it begins to lean over on one side. The eye on the downward side gradually shifts upward and across the head, the skull simultaneously twisting to accommodate this migration. Soon both eyes are on one side, and that side darkens, while the side that will hug bottom remains pale. Lying on the bed or dug in almost level with it, a flounder becomes nearly invisible against the sand, mud, gravel, or vegetation. The color of a single species may vary regionally, matching the dominant background, and some varieties modify their hues individually and quickly, as a chameleon does. With few exceptions, the tail is squarish or rounded; the flat, almost discoid body is fringed with a single long dorsal fin and single long anal fin. Generally, the teeth are small, sharp, and numerous.

Habitat, habits, and appearance lead many anglers to assume that these fish subsist exclusively on invertebrates or carrion, but the larger (or relatively large-mouthed) species capture numerous small fish. Crustaceans, mollusks, squid strips, anchovies, spearing, and killifish make excellent baits.

Flatfish are grouped in four families. The Bothidae are predominantly left-eyed, or sinistral, flounders, while the Pleuronectidae are predominantly right-eyed, or dextral. However, the position of the eyes varies among individuals of some species. The third group consists of Soleidae, the true soles, warm-water inhabitants that sometimes enter fresh water. Most are very round-bodied and have the eyes set close together on the right side. Finally, there are the Cynoglossidae, or tonguefishes—small, left-eyed, oblong fishes shaped rather like tongues. None of the tonguefishes is worth the attention of American anglers.

Summer flounder, or fluke.

On the eastern seaboard, the most common flounder of the coastal shallows—and one of the most important though not the largest—is the winter flounder *(Pseudopleuronectes americanus)*, also called blackback, blueback, black flounder, or mud dab. One that weighs more than about 5 pounds is commonly described as a "sea flounder" (in reference to its liking for water deeper than the habitat of average specimens) or a "snowshoe" (in reference to its size and shape). The species is right-eyed, yet a few individuals are darkly pigmented on the left side. The color varies from dark reddish-brown to a sooty or slate tone—the "blackback" phase. The brown phase usually has a sprinkling of black spots. A fisherman can expect plenty of catches weighing about a pound and measuring no more than a foot long, together with a few 15-inch 2-pounders. However, during a good early-spring run a productive bay may yield a great many 2- to 3½-pounders. The largest winter flounders may weigh 8 pounds.

Though distributed from Labrador to Georgia, these fish are common only from the Gulf of St. Lawrence to Chesapeake Bay. The most famous centers of abundance are in Long Island Sound, opposite the Sound on Long Island's South Shore, and along the coasts of Massachusetts, Rhode Island, Connecticut, New York, and New Jersey. Generally, winter flounders move to the shallows in the fall and retreat to deeper offshore grounds in the spring. But the extreme temperature changes in the best fishing areas induce two excellent shallow-water runs per year, one from February or March (or sometimes earlier) to May and another from September to November. Even a winter flounder of "snowshoe" size, which spends most of its life out in the depths, will now and then feed in knee-high shallows. A muddy sand bottom is preferred, but winter flounders are less selective than some of their relatives.

A fish of roughly opposite seasonal habits and one that is larger and even more popular is the summer flounder, or fluke *(Paralichthys dentatus)*, which ranges from Maine to South Carolina and, in diminishing numbers, down to Florida. Some fluke remain in bays, harbors, and estuaries throughout most of the year in warm latitudes, but during the winter all or most of the medium and big ones move offshore into depths of twenty-five to fifty fathoms. In the spring, good numbers (and good-sized specimens) return to the shallows, where they seek sand or sandy bottoms. The bays are not only summer feeding grounds for adult fluke but nurseries for juveniles. Catches in the early part of the season—that is, June in most regions—average 1½ to 2½ pounds, about the size of winter flounders. By July or August, the average may rise to 4 pounds, with the sport enlivened by occasional 6-pound "doormats," and in September 12- and 13-pounders are sometimes caught.

This is a large-mouthed, left-eyed flounder with an almost round body. Usually gray, brown, or olive with tinges of dark brown, black, and sometimes orange or pink, it has mottlings that vary from pale to dark, interspersed with a dozen or more small, regularly spaced, distinct "eyespots"—dark with pale rims.

From North Carolina southward, the fluke is largely replaced by the southern flounder (P. lethostigma), which ranges down to Florida and through the Gulf to Texas. A foot to a foot and a half long, it averages 2 or 3 pounds. It is closely related to the fluke and resembles it, but the southern flounder's olive upper side has only indistinct, unrimmed spots. It seeks a muddier bottom than the favored bed of the fluke, and in the warm parts of its range it can be caught all year long in bays and sounds.

In terms of popularity and size, the Pacific counterpart of the summer flounder is the starry flounder (Platichthys stellatus), which has patches of shiny, rough, starlike scales. Ichthyologically classified with the right-eyed flounders, it is often left-eyed. The mouth is best-developed on the blind side. The eyed side is mottled brown or black. Alternating blackish and yellowish or orange-white bars on the fins instantly identify the species. It can grow to 20 pounds and a length of 3 feet but, like the summer flounder, is usually smaller. It ranges from central California to the Bering Sea (and on the far side of the Pacific, down to Korea).

Commonly caught species of the West Coast also include the Pacific sand dab (Citharichthys sordidus), butter sole (Isopsetta isolepis), petrale sole, or brill (Eopsetta jordani), and English, or lemon, sole (Parophyrus vetulus). All of them range from Baja or lower California to northwestern Alaska, though the butter sole and lemon sole are not very common in the lower latitudes.

The Pacific sand dab is left-eyed, tan to brown or blackish, mottled with dull orange or darker, sometimes black, splotches. It grows to about 16 inches—a couple of pounds. Not very selective as to the bottom it chooses, it comes to water as shallow as

Starry flounder.

ten fathoms but is more often caught at twenty to forty fathoms. About the same size or slightly larger is the butter sole, a right-eyed denizen of shallow waters and soft, silty bottoms. It is brownish or gray with irregular yellow or pale green blotches and sometimes darker markings. Its rough scales extend onto the dorsal and anal fins, which are usually yellow-edged.

The lemon sole has the shape of a long diamond (or a diamond jig) and, when freshly caught, smells faintly like a lemon. It sometimes grows to more than 20 inches, has a fine, delicate flavor, and forages on both sandy and muddy bottoms, yet it is caught less often on light sporting gear than some of its relatives because it tends to stay at depths of sixty fathoms or more. Its blind left side is white or yellowish with rusty brown tinges, while the eye side is a uniform yellowish-brown. The petrale sole, or brill, is another right-eyed flounder caught in deep habitat. Olive-brown with vague, pale blotches, it attains a length of 20 inches or so and a weight of 6 or 7 pounds.

Largest of the group are the halibuts, whose meat was once traditional fare on holy days and whose name is derived from the Middle English for "holy flounder." Halibut are somewhat more elongate than most flounders. They have slightly concave tails,

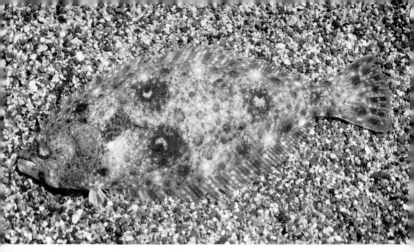

and their dorsal and anal fins widen almost to points about midway back. Of three species in American waters, the California halibut *(Paralichthys californicus)* is most interesting because it is commonly caught in less than ten fathoms of water—chiefly over sandy bottoms but also in channels and in the surf along rocky or sandy beaches. The species is classified as left-eyed, but nearly half the catches are dextral. It is grayish-brown to greenish, sometimes with dark and light mottling. Young ones are often marked with small, pale spots. Though most catches are comparable to summer flounder or starry flounder, the California halibut is known to attain a weight of about 70 pounds. It is common from central California down to Baja.

The Pacific halibut *(Hippoglossus stenolepis)* is a right-eyed flounder that looks much like the California variety but grows to gigantic size—nearly 500 pounds. A deep-water fish ranging from California north to the Bering Sea, it is taken almost exclusively by commercial long-liners. The Atlantic halibut *(H. hippoglossus)* grows still larger; females have been known to reach a weight of 700 pounds, although anything over 300 is rare. It is a right-eyed species, usually brown, gray-brown, or olive, with irregular dark spots or rings; the color sometimes turns blackish with age. It, too, is caught primarily by commercial fishermen, but small specimens—under 20 pounds—are sometimes taken by anglers while drifting baits over the bottom in deep cod waters. Called "chicken halibut," these young specimens furnish better eating than the big ones. The range encompasses northern Europe, Greenland, and America's coast down to Chesapeake Bay.

California halibut, camouflaged on bottom.

FISH HABITAT & FEEDING BEHAVIOR—ANGLING TACTICS:
Most flounders spawn offshore, and the eggs float and drift until
they hatch. An exception is the winter flounder, whose eggs sink
and cling together in masses. Generally speaking, the Pacific species are spring spawners. On the East Coast, halibut spawn from
April to July in fairly shallow areas, which means that an occasional fairly big one may be taken in the "chicken halibut" water
where small ones are present throughout most of the year. Winter
flounder spawn from January to May, with a peak in March and
April, over sand in water from a fathom or so deep to forty fathoms. The summer flounder spawns from late fall to early spring,
depending on latitude; its young drift inshore in the spring—
unlike the pelagic young of Pacific sand dabs and many other
flounders—and they grow at a fast rate through the summer in
the nursery shallows. The reproductive cycle of this species has
a more pronounced effect on fishing than that of other flounders;
and fishing customs have a corresponding effect on the species.
In spring and early summer, fluke fishing is popular in countless
bays because so many summer flounders can be caught. Too
many, probably; and they tend to be small since the population
is composed largely of juveniles.

The young of all species feed on small invertebrates and
probably on vegetable matter. An adult summer flounder eats
crabs, shrimp, mollusks, marine worms, and squid, and is also
well able to catch small fish. The smaller-mouthed winter
flounder is more or less limited to larval fish, but its other prey
is the same, and it moves about a good deal to forage. The southern flounder feeds chiefly on shrimp and on such fish as small
mullet and anchovies—alert, constantly moving creatures. The
Atlantic halibut eats crustaceans and mollusks but feeds primarily on such fish as ocean perch, smaller flounders, mackerel, and
herring. And all of the popular Pacific species feed on worms,
shrimp, clams, small crabs, and fish.

Among West Coast flatfish, the starry flounder is probably
the most sought-after year-round species. It is caught most often
by still-fishing with clams, shrimp, or small live fish such as anchovies, and the baits are jigged or occasionally moved around
on the bottom to attract attention. The other most admired western species, the California halibut, is generally caught by bottom-
drifting with a live anchovy, queenfish, or shrimp, or by slow troll-

ing as for summer flounder.

Anyone who has fished for winter flounder can adapt the same procedures to the other small species of both coasts, while the methods used for fluke—summer flounder—can be applied to the more sizable shallow-water species. The chief differences concern the most productive holding waters—that is, the bottom preferences described above for each variety. Within that framework, any spot that holds small fish or shellfish is promising. Generally, feeding is most active at high tide, especially on flats, but deep holes and channels are worth probing at low tide. And the vicinity of a clam digger or oyster dredge is good since it contains drifting odors and bits of food, as if it had been chummed just for flounders. A 6- or 6½-foot light-action spinning rod with line testing 6 or 8 pounds is quite sufficient for fish the size of winter flounder, though a medium action may be advisable where wind and current require a heavy sinker to keep a bait down on the bottom. Since these fish are gentle nibblers, heavy tackle can prevent a bite from being felt. And since they are small-mouthed, hooks ranging from no. 6 to no. 10 are best. A three-way swivel is tied to the end of the line, and a round or bank sinker is attached to the swivel's bottom eye. (Pyramid sinkers are excellent for casting into the surf, but elsewhere they tend to catch in bottom debris.) A snelled hook is snapped to the swivel's middle eye. This terminal arrangement is basic and traditional; a more popular one in many regions is a two-hook rig with a curved wire spreader.

Excellent baits include bloodworms, sandworms, clams, and mussels. Small pieces should be used for the small-mouthed species. Since food preferences sometimes change abruptly and inexplicably, anglers often carry two kinds of baits for switching or for use in combination. Cracked mussels or clams can be tossed into the water now and then as chum, but a better method is to put them (or ground fish or the canned fish sold for cat food) into a coarse mesh bag. This chum pot is lowered to the bottom.

The same chumming techniques apply to the summer flounder and similarly good-sized species. From June to September, fluke fishermen go out in small boats to ply the harbors, bays, estuaries, channels, creek mouths, eelgrass beds, pilings, rocks, and the shallows around points and the ends of bars. Anglers also line the jetties, banks, piers, and bridges. For winching doormat flounders high out of the water to piers or bridges, a fairly stout rod is needed; 8- to 10-foot surf and bay rods are common. Party-boat fishing also calls for hefty rods, but short ones to avoid tangling with the crowd. In other situations, all sorts of rods are used, some designed for spinning, others employing revolving-spool reels, with line testing 20 pounds or more.

Sometimes the fish come close enough to a beach for surf-casting. At such times, a good terminal arrangement is a conventional fishfinder rig—a pyramid sinker on a sliding ring above a barrel swivel that holds a 3-foot leader. About equally efficient is a surf rig, with the leader attached to the bottom eye of a three-way swivel and the pyramid on a dropper trailing from the middle eye. The basic rig for all fluke fishing is a slight variation on this: a bank or egg sinker substituted for the pyramid and hung on a dropper from the bottom eye, with the leader—which matches the line strength—hung from the middle eye. However, many anglers add

Angler showing real "doormat" and justifiable grin.

a spinner blade or two a little above the hook, and some use a second hook on a snell midway down the leader.

Probably the three favorite baits, at least along the Middle Atlantic Coast, are squid strips, live "mummichog" (killifish), and spearing (Atlantic silversides). On the West Coast, anchovies replace killies and spearings. An excellent two-hook combination is a 3-inch strip of squid mantle together with a 3-inch baitfish hooked through the lips. Long-shanked hooks are best, in sizes from 1/0 for small fluke to 5/0 and 6/0 for doormats.

Grouper *(Serranidae)*

COMMON & REGIONAL NAMES: *sea bass*. (Scientifically, all grouper species are sea basses, but not all sea basses are groupers. Other names in common usage denote various species and will be included in the descriptions of those species.)

GAME IDENTIFICATION & LOCATION OF FISHING REGIONS:
The groupers and other sea basses—over four hundred species of the serranid family—are extremely diverse fishes ranging in size from less than an inch long to half-ton giants 12 feet long. The 150- or 200-pound Nile perch of Africa is a freshwater serranid, as are America's moderately proportioned white bass, yellow bass, and white perch. Most sea basses inhabit tropical, subtropical, and temperate oceans. The freshwater American species are treated elsewhere in this book, and their close relative, the primarily marine striped bass, also merits a chapter of its own. The black sea bass of the East Coast and the giant sea bass of the lower West Coast are covered under the heading of Sea Bass. The kelp and sand basses are included under the heading of Rockfish—a classification that is biologically mixed but homogeneous in terms of angling.

The groupers comprise still another important category among sea basses. Ichthyologists speak of "true" groupers, meaning those belonging to two genera, *Epinephelus* and *Mycteroperca,* but the name is popularly applied to some species in other genera as well. They are broad-headed, thick-bodied, bottom- or reef-dwelling, predatory sea basses with very large mouths, protruding lower jaws, caniniform teeth, and scales that typically extend onto the bases of some or all fins. Most groupers are of medium size—about 8 to 12 pounds—but occasionally grow much larger. Like sea basses in general, they have a heavy-set body conformation resembling that of the unrelated black bass found in America's fresh waters. They have a first dorsal fin armed with pronounced spines; the soft-rayed hind dorsal is usually joined to the first with only a small dip or notch between.

Groupers do not cruise in schools, but they tend to assemble in loose sedentary gatherings, lying on or near a food-rich bottom, under ledges and overhanging rocks, in crevices, holes, and caverns, or amid rubble. They remain rather listless until they detect prey, then rush from hiding with surprising speed. They feed chiefly on fish, mollusks, and crustaceans.

Dozens of species inhabit all the warm oceans, yet in the Pacific, where several kinds of sea bass furnish sport for West Coast anglers, no grouper of any angling importance is common above the Mexican border. In contrast, a great many are available to southeastern fishermen. They share a single general range: around Florida and throughout the tropical Atlantic.

Probably the most common variety in Floridian waters is the red grouper *(Epinephelus morio),* which also ranges through the Caribbean and the Gulf. Its average weight is less than 10 pounds, its maximum about 40; at its top weight it would have a length of 3 feet or so. It has a squarish tail and a brownish-red or rusty head and body, darkly barred and marbled. Often, it has scattered white spots. Small specimens can be caught near shore but they are not especially vigorous fighters. Fairly large ones, which seek rocky bottoms at medium depths a little offshore, perform well on light tackle. They take live or dead baits.

Comparable in size but with a slightly greater maximum weight is the Nassau grouper *(E. striatus).* It, too, is common in Florida but is even more abundant in the Bahamas, as its name implies. An olive or greenish-tan fish with a slightly convex tail, it has broad, vertical brown or blackish bars mixed with paler areas and spotting on its head and body. A very dark band runs obliquely up through the eye, and a black splotch tops the caudal peduncle. This is one of the hardest-fighting groupers. It stays close to shore until fairly large, then heads into medium depths around reefs or coral heads. It responds well to live baits or lures.

The Warsaw grouper *(E. nigritus),* a very dark fish, is sometimes erroneously called black grouper—the common name of another species. The name "Warsaw" is probably a corruption of

▲ Nassau grouper. ▼ Rock grouper.

guasa, a Spanish word derived from a Taino Indian term for grouper. This is one of the larger species. An average catch weighs less than 20 pounds, but 100-pounders are not uncommon and there have been reports of 6-foot Warsaws weighing 500 pounds. Even a small one can be identified by its very large head, squarish tail, and blackish body, usually patched with somewhat paler amorphous areas. Though most abundant around the Florida coasts, it strays to South Carolina in the summer. Caught by bottom-trolling at moderate offshore depths, it occasionally hits a lure but is more likely to take live or dead baits.

The tail of the black grouper *(Mycteroperca bonaci)* tends to curve slightly inward from the tips and outward again to a convex center. The body is olive, bluish-black, or dark gray, sometimes with a reddish cast. It is covered with dark or blackish areas whose interstices form a vague netlike or chainlike pattern. The fins are often black-bordered. Averaging 10 to 20 pounds, it may reach a weight of 100 and a length of 4 feet. It is common in the tropical Atlantic and Caribbean, and in summer even farther north than the Warsaw. Juveniles come inshore, but adults prefer fairly deep water.

The yellowfin grouper *(M. venenosa)* is also called rock grouper, a name that would fit any member of the family. Its preferred name alludes to the yellow along the edges and on the outer third of each pectoral fin. In general coloration, this is one of the more variable species. As a rule, the head and body are marked with red spots and irregular longitudinal rows of dark blotches, and the concave tail is barred and tipped with black. One color phase has a bright red belly. A 3-foot, 30-pound yellowfin grouper definitely qualifies as "bragging size" but cannot be called rare; the usual weight is 5 to 10 pounds. It is most common off southern Florida, where it frequents shallow to medium waters, very often around coral heads. It is taken on lures and live or dead baits.

The most unusual of the Floridian and lower Atlantic array is an elephantine grouper called the jewfish *(E. itajara),* which also inhabits the Pacific from Panama up into the Gulf of California. The origin of its popular name is uncertain, but the size of its mouth prompts the speculation that the title is a corruption of "jawfish." Also called guasa, spotted jewfish, spotted grouper, and giant sea bass, the species is often confused with the true giant sea bass (described under the Sea Bass heading), which shares its Pacific range. Jewfish weighing 100 pounds are almost as common as those weighing 20, and quite a few 200-pounders are caught. The record on rod and reel is 680 pounds; it was set in 1961 at Fernandina Beach, Florida.

Even a small one can be distinguished from other groupers. It has a long, low first dorsal fin, rounded pectorals and tail, and a brownish or dusky body with numerous small black spots, particularly on the upper and forward parts and the head. It usually dwells inshore, in deep holes or under ledges and overhangs in relatively shallow water. Small jewfish and sometimes large ones penetrate estuaries and shallow waterways in the Keys. Enormous ones call for heavy tackle; small ones are caught on trolling, baitcasting, and spinning rods with live or dead bait.

FISH HABITAT & FEEDING BEHAVIOR—ANGLING TACTICS: Evidently, most groupers spawn offshore at various times of year, the peak depending on locale and species. Their reproductive cycle has little effect on fishing, as they are caught in their customary lairs at all seasons. The jewfish and some of the smaller shallow-water varieties can be caught around pier or bridge pilings, in deep channels between a bay and the sea, and in rocky coastal holes, as well as at the reefs, wrecks, and coral heads.

In the Bahamas, charter-boat skippers sometimes treat clients to the prospect of catching very large groupers by trolling baits of appropriate size at depths of 150 to 400 feet. The bait might be a 5-pound barracuda or king mackerel. American an-

Jewfish, or guasa, largest of American groupers, being boated.

glers trolling for jewfish or other big groupers sometimes rig a live grunt, snapper, or crevalle. More conventional—and equally good —offerings are chunked, stripped, or whole rigged baitfish such as mullet, sardine, or balao. Conch, squid, clams, crabs, and shrimp are also excellent. Any of these baits can be drifted, jigged, or trolled over the bottom.

A very good combination, especially for deep trolling over reefs, is a big, bright feather or bucktail jig trailing three tandem hooks on which are rigged the rear half or two-thirds of a mullet. A fine alternative is a large jig with two hooks, the rear one holding a whole dead balao, mullet, menhaden, or sardine.

Among lures, the best are big, deep-running plugs, spoons, baited jigs, and spinners. Spinners are more effective in the shallows than over the deep reefs. A wobbling spoon with a strip of mullet is effective in all waters.

Shorebound fishermen catch groupers from bridges just before and after slack tide, a good time for probing channels and holes as well, because groupers forage most actively when the current is weak. Time is inconsequential in deeper water, where anglers look for rocky points or coral surrounded by sand and for light, sandy patches surrounded by darker, rocky bottom.

Rods for small to medium groupers range from light spinning wands to boat rods with star-drag reels and line testing 20 or 30 pounds. Wire leaders are used to prevent cutoffs on rock or coral. Hook sizes range from 8/0 upward, bank sinkers from a couple of ounces to 12 or more—as heavy as 20 in very deep water. Jewfish and other outsized groupers are commonly caught on the medium trolling tackle used for several kinds of big game.

Grunt *(Haemulon)*

COMMON & REGIONAL NAMES: Names in common usage denote various species and will be included in the descriptions of those species.

GAME IDENTIFICATION & LOCATION OF FISHING REGIONS:
Among the many saltwater panfish, some can be regarded as sunnies of the sea—a description that best fits the grunts. They travel in schools like sunfish and take baits just as avidly. Some are more colorful than the brightest sunnies, their flesh is comparable, and those of angling interest are generally the size of a very

large sunny or small bass. Caught in the shallows close to shore and around offshore reefs, coral heads, and oil rigs, they are spirited fighters when played on ultralight spinning tackle or a fly rod.

The name grunt alludes to the sounds they make by grinding their pharyngeal teeth; these noises are resonated and amplified by a taut swim bladder. All species are bottom-feeders with well-developed pharyngeal teeth—like those of the shellcracker sunfish—and weak jaw teeth, yet they can devour occasional small fish as well as crustaceans, mollusks, and marine worms.

Grunts belong to the family Pomadasyidae, related to snappers and represented by several hundred species that abound in the world's warm seas. In North American waters, the varieties common and sizable enough to be worth catching are all restricted to the Atlantic. With exceptions that will be noted, they range from the Bahamas and Florida—especially the Keys—through the West Indies and down to Brazil. All of them belong to the genus *Haemulon,* and in all but the margate *(H. album)* the inside of the mouth is red, pink, or carmine. They have forked tails, joined dorsal fins, deep, and laterally compressed bodies.

The margate, also called white margate, margate grunt, and margaret grunt, tends to cruise a bit farther offshore than the others and is somewhat less common in Florida. It is worth seeking, however, as it grows larger than its relatives. An average adult is perhaps a foot long and weighs less than a pound, but it can grow to twice that length and a weight of 8 pounds. A big margate is a battler. Its color varies from silvery white to pearl-gray, sometimes unmarked but usually with two or three brown or blackish longitudinal stripes.

The most common and widest-ranging species is the white grunt *(H. plumieri).* The cold-tolerant white grunt, while most abundant in tropical waters, ranges as far north as Chesapeake Bay. A 10-incher weighing less than a pound is average, but 3-pounders are sometimes caught. The head of this species is grayish or olive on top, silvery on the sides, with numerous thin blue lines and a few yellow stripes running rearward. The body is light bluish-gray or almost white, but many of the scales are edged or spotted with yellow, giving it a yellowish-white appearance. A yellow stripe generally runs from gill cover to tail.

The bluestriped grunt *(H. sciurus)* is usually a 10-incher; it may gain another couple of inches and weigh more than a

pound. It is the most colorful of the common varieties, brassy or gold with blue or blue-green stripes from snout to tail.

The cottonwick *(H. melanarum)* and the Caesar grunt *(H. carbonarium)* also average 10 inches or so. The cottonwick's back, the base of its rear dorsal fin, and the upper half of its caudal peduncle are black. The lobes of the tail are black, widely margined with white. The top of the snout is often grayish. The fins are white, the body white with faint yellowish longitudinal stripes. The Caesar grunt is pale gray or silvery with a dark lateral line and bronze or yellow stripes from the rear of the head to the very wide tail. The Spanish grunt *(H. macrostomum)* looks at first glance like the Caesar but is darker and slightly larger. Its body is silvery gray, often with a greenish tinge. A pronounced black stripe runs from the snout through the eye and back to the tail. On the upper sides, weaker black longitudinal lines converge with this stripe at the head and the caudal peduncle.

FISH HABITAT & FEEDING BEHAVIOR—ANGLING TACTICS:
Grunts have puzzled fishermen as well as behavioral scientists by their strange habit of "kissing" their companions. They press their open mouths together and push. As there is nothing aggressive about the procedure, nor does it appear to stimulate spawning activity, perhaps it is a school-bonding mechanism. Evidently grunts spawn inshore and offshore and—like many warm-water fish—have no definite seasonal breeding peak.

They favor clear water, but some species are less selective

White grunt.

than others in their habitat preferences. The white grunt schools in shallow areas. The Spanish grunt has a pronounced liking for the clear waters around coral reefs and heads. The bluestriped variety is abundant near shore in fairly shallow waters and also schools at greater depths around reefs. The Caesar grunt tends to stay nearer shore, entering small harbors, marinas, and even tidal creeks. The cottonwick and the margate both avoid murky areas; in the Bahamas, where the water is exceptionally clear, they can be caught inshore as well as at the offshore reefs, but in Florida they are more abundant at the outer reefs.

Since grunts have fairly large mouths for fish of their size, 1/0 hooks are about right, but tackle should be extremely light—a fly rod or a spinning rod of the sort that would be used for freshwater panfish. The bluestriped grunt and probably most others will frequently strike a small deep-running plug, a jig, or a weighted fly. A white or yellow streamer or a shrimp imitation would be a good choice. But all species are more responsive to bait. They are, in fact, very easy to catch by jigging dead shrimp, cut mullet, or cut pilchard (the small, silvery sardine also known as sprat). Other good baits are marine worms and bits of conch, squid, or crab. Whatever is used, it should touch bottom and then bounce along with brief pauses. An angler who is familiar with grunt generally adds a refinement. By putting a small sinker on a sliding ring above a leader swivel, he fashions a very delicate version of the fishfinder rig used for larger bottom-feeding species.

Bluestriped grunt.

Jack *(Caranx)* **& Jack Mackerel** *(Trachurus symmetricus)*

COMMON & REGIONAL NAMES: The name *crevalle* usually designates a particular jack species, *Caranx hippos,* but is also an accepted term for the entire genus *Caranx* or any species of that genus. (Other names in common usage denote various species and will be included in the descriptions of those species.)

GAME IDENTIFICATION & LOCATION OF FISHING REGIONS:
Exceptionally powerful, dogged fighters, jacks are members of the family Carangidae—together with amberjacks, pompanos, roosterfish, and several other, less important groups. Carangids inhabit all tropical and subtropical seas, and a few species occur in cooler waters.

As with amberjacks (which see), the meat of jacks taken in the West Indies is occasionally toxic, probably as a result of preying on poisonous fish. Elsewhere, the meat ranges from mediocre to good. However, sportsmen normally release anything less than a trophy. The enjoyment is in the battle, not the eating.

American waters hold almost two dozen species of jacks, belonging to half a dozen genera. Some, however, are rare or very small, and a few others are seldom seen because they dwell far out in deep waters or near isolated islands and reefs. Among those commonly caught by American anglers, all but one belong to the genus *Caranx* and properly share the name crevalle—or jack crevalle or crevalle jack—though the same title designates the single most popular (and largest) species in American waters.

Generally speaking, jacks are high-backed fish with rather blunt heads, soft-rayed dorsal and anal fins, long, curving, pointed pectorals, and deeply lunate tails. Additional characteristics distinguish the group from other carangids: a jack has a short, triangular first dorsal, usually with eight spines; a long second dorsal reaching to the narrow caudal peduncle and widened at the front end to form a lobe; a similarly lobed and almost as long anal fin; a lateral line with a long forward segment curving up from the gill cover, around the pectoral, and down to a straight rear segment; and finally, on the straight part of the lateral line, a row of scales modified into big, pointed scutes forming a narrow keel on each side. Jacks of the *Caranx* genus are further distinguished by a particularly high, compressed body and a more or less bluish

back. Depending on species, four to eight broad, dark, vertical bars on each side and a stripe on the back of the head mark the young; these markings persist in some adults but fade after death.

American anglers on the West Coast have at hand only two worthwhile jacks, one of which belongs to a separate genus. It is the little jack mackerel *(Trachurus symmetricus)*, also called Pacific jack mackerel or California horse mackerel. Ranging from British Columbia to Mexico and from inshore waters to the depths six hundred miles out, it is abundant in California waters. More slender-bodied than the crevalles—more like a mackerel—it has scutes along the entire lateral line. Its head is streamlined rather than blunt. Iridescent bluish-green on the back and silvery below, it is often darkly mottled. The largest recorded was 32 inches long and weighed 5 pounds; the average is half that size.

The West Coast crevalle is the green jack *(C. caballus)*, a fish never weighing over 5 pounds, typically weighing less than 1 and measuring about a foot long. It ranges from lower California to Perу and also occurs at a number of Pacific islands. It has forty to fifty-one scutes in the straight part of the lateral line and its body is slimmer in profile, rounder in cross section, than that of most crevalles. It is distinctly greenish above, silvery below.

On the East Coast, a similar fish is the blue runner, or hard-tail jack *(C. crysos)*, so closely related to the green jack that some

Top: Crevalle schooling. Right: Fly fisherman with good-sized crevalle.

biologists consider it to be a very slightly larger race of the same species. However, it usually has more scutes (forty-six to fifty-six) and slightly different coloration. The back varies from blue-green or olive-green to blackish, the fins from colorless to blackish. The sides are gray—often quite dark—with golden glints, and the belly is silvery. Like the green jack, it has a black spot on each gill cover and its body turns blackish when spawning. Runners are uncommon above the Middle Atlantic states; they are caught in the summer in those states, and jack fishing is fine all year in Florida. The blue runner is common in Bermuda and the Bahamas.

The finest gamefish of the group is the one most widely known as the crevalle *(C. hippos),* but also called common jack, jack crevalle, crevalle jack, cavally, cavalla, horse crevalle, and toro. It is common in Bermuda and along the continental coast from the southern United States to Uruguay. It also occurs in the Pacific from Baja to Peru, as well as in Hawaiian and Asian waters. Various races of this species probably have an almost global distribution. The Atlantic race, which has twenty-six to thirty-five scutes, is blue-black or blue-green, silvery and sometimes yellowish below, occasionally with rosy glints. The tail and dorsal fins

are dark, the pelvic and pectoral fins light, the anal fin often yellowish. A black spot marks the rear edge of each gill cover, and a dark blotch marks the lower rays of each pectoral. The head is high and very blunt, with the big eyes located far forward. A sure way to tell this species from others is by examining its breast; from the throat to the area of the pectoral fins it is scaleless except for a small round or triangular breast-patch of scales (which can be hard to see on a very small specimen or an old, large one). A typical catch weighs perhaps 2 pounds, but much larger ones are common. The International Game Fish Association does not list jack records, but 5-foot catches have been documented. The largest one known to the author was a 70-pounder caught in October, 1966, at West Palm Beach.

The horse-eye, or Atlantic horse-eye, jack *(C. latus)* ranks as the second most desirable species. Also known as the goggle-eye jack in some regions, it is common from Brazil to the southern United States and in Bermuda. As with *C. hippos,* there is considerable confusion about the identity of this fish in other seas. Either the same species or a very closely related one occurs in various parts of the Pacific, including the Hawaiian Islands. The Atlantic race (or species) averages between 2 and 8 pounds; 12-pounders have been authenticated and 30-pounders are believed to exist. The popular name describes the eyes—large, placed well forward, and equipped with thick, transparent adipose lids that are easily discernible. The scutes number thirty-two to thirty-nine and the color is dark blue or blue-gray, paling to

Jack mackerel—also known as California horse mackerel.

silvery white or sometimes golden on the sides. The tail is yellow and the tip of the dorsal fin's high lobe is usually black.

The somewhat slimmer bar jack *(C. ruber)* ranges from North Carolina to Panama and probably farther south. It is also caught in Bermuda and the Bahamas. Other names for it are skipjack, runner, and cibi mancho. It has twenty-three to twenty-nine scutes, a dark bluish band along the base of the dorsal fin, and another dark bar on the bottom lobe of the tail. A dark blue or black stripe (which becomes indistinct after death) runs along the blue-gray back from nape to tail. The sides are pale or whitish. The species is usually small, but in the Bahamas it grows to a weight of about 15 pounds.

FISH HABITAT & FEEDING BEHAVIOR—ANGLING TACTICS: Jacks spawn in offshore waters, principally from February through September, and the young of most species linger near sargassum or move inshore, where they evidently feed on plankton. Most adult jacks feed on small fish, shrimp, crabs, other crustaceans, and mollusks. The jack mackerel, which roves farther out to sea than most, subsists chiefly on pelagic crustaceans and mollusks, but closer to shore—where it is usually sought by anglers—it often preys heavily on anchovies, other small fish, and squid. A popular method of catching it is to drift or troll live anchovies, jigs, spoons, or plugs that resemble its inshore prey.

Another species that cruises open, offshore waters more than most (though it occurs inshore, too) is the bar jack. It also patrols isolated islands, bars, and reefs. Usually it is encountered in big schools over deep flats, in channels, or in blue holes—the deep pits and caverns in coral deposits, often adjacent to flats. Blue holes, in fact, are prime grounds for most jacks. Like the others, this species will gobble live bait such as mullet, pinfish, or pilchard, and will usually take cut bait, but there is seldom a need for bait because all crevalles race after lures—popping plugs and other surface plugs, jigs, popping bugs, and streamers.

The green jack and blue runner school in moderately shallow water, mostly in bays, near beaches, and around offshore reefs, and they can be caught by trolling, casting, or sometimes still-fishing. The horse-eye, like the crevalle—that is, like *C. hippos*—schools in deep and shallow waters, around islands, over flats, along beaches, in brackish as well as salt water, and even in coastal streams. But regardless of species, the big schools and the occasional old loners, pairs, or pods of lunkers are almost constantly on the move, often sharing habitat and prey with other gamefish as they pass through. Anglers tend to go prepared for anything from small to medium, easy to tough. Fly-rodders often use tippets testing 10 pounds or better in case they hook something with sharp canines or abrasive gill covers. Spinning outfits are very popular; ideal spinning tackle for most jacks would be a 6½-foot rod with monofilament testing 8 pounds.

When horse-eye or crevalle schools are prowling fairly deep, as they sometimes do, a subsurface plug or a streamer tied on a 2/0 or 3/0 hook should work well. When they are whipping up prey on the surface, a popping plug or bug is better. When mullet, pilchards, or other baitfish approach the beaches, these jacks can be caught in the surf.

Ripples on top or dark patches below can mean that jacks are "balling up" baitfish, herding their prey into a compact mass, then ripping through from all sides, often whitecapping the water. Like some other game species, they can be heard doing this, even from far off—a sound like rain falling.

More often than not, a jack hooks itself, but the angler should strike back for insurance. The fish will run, circle, switch directions, perhaps dive under the boat, thrash, run again, and perhaps just hang there, exerting such strength that for a time it cannot be budged.

Ladyfish *(Elops saurus)*

COMMON & REGIONAL NAMES: *chiro, tenpounder, bigeye, bigeye herring, Lisa, Lisa Francesca, bonyfish, skipjack, springer*

GAME IDENTIFICATION & LOCATION OF FISHING REGIONS: A minor puzzle of saltwater sport is why the ladyfish is faintly praised (or simply ignored) in much angling literature. Though despised as a diminutive, unappetizing bait-thief by some surfcasters and trollers intent on bigger game, it may be a more acrobatic, frantic battler than any marine species of its size.

The misleading nickname "tenpounder" probably has a Bahamian origin, for 8- and 10-pound ladyfish are caught at Andros Island. Along the Florida and Gulf coasts and in the Carib-

bean, the typical adult weight is between 1 and 4 pounds, though 6-pounders are taken fairly often and there have been rare reports of yard-long 15-pounders. The species is common in the Atlantic, Indian, and western Pacific oceans. Unfortunately, it does not occur on the West Coast of the United States. On the East Coast, it is most plentiful from Biscayne Bay down through the Keys.

It is a long, very lean, finely scaled, silvery fish with a black-ish or blue-green back, big, black eyes, a deeply lunate blackish tail, and a single high, triangular, soft-rayed grayish dorsal fin about midway back from the head. The pelvic fins are also far back, under or just ahead of the dorsal, and the pectorals are very low on the body. The mouth is big and toothless, like a tarpon's, but without the pronounced downward slant of the tarpon's mouth.

Fly-rodder with ladyfish.

FISH HABITAT & FEEDING BEHAVIOR—ANGLING TACTICS: Ladyfish prowl the shallows, occasionally alone, more often in small or medium schools, sometimes in schools of hundreds. Very large gatherings usually consist of 1- to 2-pound fish, but even the small ones are stimulating on a fly rod or very light spinning or baitcasting tackle. Some anglers use line testing 4 pounds or less. A tough leader or nylon shock tippet is recommended, because a ladyfish has rough gill covers and sharp jaw bones.

Spawning probably parallels that of tarpon, with millions of eggs dropped in shallow estuarine nursery grounds, chiefly during spring and summer. Ladyfish are caught at all times of year in the Bahamas and Florida but are most plentiful from spring to fall. Preying chiefly on shrimp and other crustaceans and on small fish, they cruise close to shore over sand or mud bottoms and on weedy flats, entering bays, narrow straits, lagoons, tidal creeks, and even fresh streams. They can be caught from shores, piers, causeways, bridges, or boats. A school of big ones may monopolize a choice feeding area—sometimes just a weedy patch in eight feet of water—day after day for long periods, with anglers following suit. Often the fish are seen breaking the surface as they churn up baitfish and shrimp, and sometimes they can be heard at a distance slapping and splashing: a sound like the patter of rain, becoming thunderous as a fisherman nears it. Some ladyfish are always in the shallows. More arrive with an incoming tide, and they become hungriest—or perhaps just hurried —as the tide begins to drop again. The fastest fishing action is at night or in early morning with an outgoing tide.

A ladyfish will seize a shrimp or small fish, but the use of bait is unnecessary—almost shameful—with a game species so eager to attack lures. The most effective offerings are quarter- to half-ounce silver or silver-scaled plugs, small yellow or white jigs, silver spoons, white or yellow popping bugs, and bucktails or streamers of the same colors or with a dash of red. A fine choice might be a Platinum or Honey Blond on a no. 1 or 1/0 hook. Among plugs, surface-disturbing and diving models are right on most occasions, but sometimes ladyfish concentrate on the bottom and respond at least as well to deep-running or bottom-bouncing lures. Conversely, there are times when they snap at almost anything skated or slid in erratic jerks over the surface.

They charge in a sudden, swift frenzy, quite often knocking

a lure out of the water without touching a barb. The frustration of these false or missed strikes is offset by the expectation that a single retrieve may elicit two or three hits from a dense school. Moreover, the problem is overcome to some extent by moving the lure fast enough so that the fish is forced to overtake rather than swat it. With baitcasting or spinning gear, a useful tactic is the whip retrieve used by tarpon fishermen. If, on occasion, the fish follow without taking, they may be coaxed by stopping the retrieve and working the rod tip.

Lingcod _(Ophiodon elongatus)_ & Kelp Greenling
(Hexagrammos decagrammus)
COMMON & REGIONAL NAMES: _greenling, rockfish, rock cod, rock trout._ (Additional names in common usage denote one species or the other and will be included in the description thereof.)

GAME IDENTIFICATION & LOCATION OF FISHING REGIONS:
Lingcod and the closely related true greenlings comprise a small family of bottom-dwelling predators—the Hexagrammidae—found only in the Pacific off the North American coast from Alaska down to Point Conception, California, and in much smaller numbers southward to Baja. They are elongate fish with square or slightly concave tails, pointed gill covers, a fleshy skin flap above each eye, wide pectoral fins, and a single long, low dorsal fin with a deep notch at the juncture of the spiny forward and soft-rayed hind portion. Most species have several lateral lines and most are drably mottled, spiny-looking creatures.

Biggest of the lot is the lingcod, a species unrelated to ling or cod. Other names for it are cultus, cultus cod, and buffalo cod. The species can reach a length of nearly 5 feet and a weight of about 70 pounds; 50- to 60-pound specimens turn up with fair frequency in commercial catches. On rod and reel, however, the average is between 1 and 5 pounds, and a 15-pounder would be considered outstanding. Very big ones are always females. The species is distinguished from relatives by its single lateral line and its massive jaws, filled with big, sharp canine teeth. Its color, generally bluish-gray or greenish-tan with dark brownish mottling, varies to match its environment. The internal color is more unusual, as the flesh usually has a greenish tinge; this does not detract from its wholesomeness or fine taste.

The kelp greenling, often called seatrout in California but known as greenling in the north, is a smaller fish, averaging 2 or 3 pounds, sometimes reaching a weight of 4 pounds and a length of about 18 inches. It has five lateral lines, two on each side and one on the back, and is further distinguished by pronounced sexual dimorphism—the males are bluish with brown mottling, the females brownish with black mottling. Several closely related and rather similar but smaller species occupy the same general range, and more abundantly in a few locales. A couple of hours of fishing can produce a mixed bag of these plus rockfish, surfperch, kelp bass, opaleye, and the like.

FISH HABITAT & FEEDING BEHAVIOR—ANGLING TACTICS: Lingcod spawn in shallow water, chiefly from December through February, and their large egg masses adhere to rocks or lodge in crevices. The males tend these masses, driving off predators, but their aggressive instinct evidently does not sharpen their hunger. Fishing may be good then (and all year) but is best from spring to October in most regions.

Lingcod, kelp greenling, and their relatives seek a common type of habitat, the only important difference being that some—especially big lingcod—often venture a bit deeper than others. All are caught from shore and from small boats, and neither time nor

Lingcod.

tide is very important. Anglers in central California, around Puget Sound, and along British Columbia's coast—the greenling fishing centers—concentrate on bays, coves, headlands, and reefs where there are plenty of rocks and where tidal waters rip and swirl about dense kelp beds or other algal vegetation. Such places teem with greenling foods: small fish and invertebrates.

Kelp greenling feed voraciously, yet cautiously enough so that they are not often duped by lures. The normal and most productive technique is simply to impale a sea worm, chunk of clam, or piece of fish on a fair-sized hook—2/0 is about right.

Where lingcod are biting, a line's test strength may be 8 pounds—or 30 if the fish are running big—and hooks may be as large as 8/0. In deference to the teeth of this species, a wire leader is attached. Most anglers drift a cut sardine, a worm, or a chunk of clam near bottom. Good baits also include octopus or squid, as well as live sardines or herring. Unlike the true greenlings, lingcod quite often take lures—cast or slowly trolled spoons, deep-running plugs, metal jigs, and weighted red-and-yellow yarn, hair, or feather jigs. Of these, a metal diamond jig is probably most reliable. However, the best lure of all is an artificial squid with a moving skirt of tentacles.

Mackerel (*Scomber* and *Scomberomorus*)

COMMON & REGIONAL NAMES: Names in common usage denote various species and will be included in the descriptions of those species.

GAME IDENTIFICATION & LOCATION OF FISHING REGIONS:
Depending on species and locale, mackerel provide both inshore and offshore sport—often at a staccato tempo, since they are schooling fish with hearty appetites. They are not jumpers, but against light tackle they can make 30-mile-an-hour runs, just under the surface or toward bottom, then rest and run again.

Smaller relatives of the tunas, these scombrids are characterized by a spindle-shaped body with a pointed head and a sharp taper to the narrow caudal peduncle. The peduncle itself is ridged, or keeled, on the sides, and the tail is wide and lunate. The spiny and soft-rayed dorsal fins are separated—quite widely on several species. The rear, soft dorsal is a triangle or lobe backed by a series of small, separated finlets ending at the base

of the tail. The anal fin and finlets match the dorsal structure. All species either lack scales or have extremely small ones. Typically, the tail and upper fins are dark, sometimes quite black, and the sea-blue or blue-green back may be almost as dark, shading to silver or silver-gray on the lower parts. Except for the cero and Spanish mackerels, the back is usually marked with definite black, wavy lines running obliquely down toward the lateral line.

Mackerel feed on a wide variety of small schooling fishes as well as crustaceans, squid, marine worms, and nondescript plankton. A few species, notably the small ones, dwell chiefly in cool latitudes. Most varieties inhabit the world's warm oceans, spawning offshore from late winter or early spring to early summer and migrating seasonally into somewhat cooler seas.

Along the Gulf Coast and around Florida, good-sized mackerel can be caught all year. But summer brings the best Gulf fishing—especially off Texas and Louisiana—and summer is the time when mackerel also appear in greatest numbers in more northerly latitudes on the East Coast. In Delaware and New Jersey, the annual run begins in April. Oddly, however, Florida's best mackerel fishing, particularly for the largest species, lasts from September into November. Perhaps the fish congregate there during their return from the North. Similarly, the biggest California run of Pacific mackerel takes place in autumn.

One of the most common species of the eastern seaboard is the Atlantic mackerel *(Scomber scombrus)*, found from the Gulf of St. Lawrence to Cape Hatteras as well as on the other side of the Atlantic and in the Mediterranean. A weight of 7½ pounds has been recorded, but the average catch is less than a foot and a half long and weighs only a pound or two. It can be identified by wavy black lines—two dozen or more—running down each side

Atlantic mackerel.

to the lateral line, and by the double keel on each side of the caudal peduncle. Other mackerels have a single median keel. Both this mackerel and the next to be described have widely separated fore and aft dorsal fins.

The chub mackerel, also called tinker or tinker mackerel, was formerly classified as *S. coliss* but is now recognized as *S. japonicus*, an Atlantic race of the Pacific mackerel. Smallest of the American group, it is generally 8 to 14 inches long, has black blotches below the lateral line, and has fewer stripes than the Atlantic mackerel. It ranges about as far north as the Atlantic mackerel and much farther south—at least to Cuba. The same species in the Pacific, where it grows slightly larger, is called the Pacific mackerel, greenback, striped mackerel, or zebra mackerel. It is found all the way from the Gulf of Alaska to Chile.

Spanish mackerel.

Another species with widely separated dorsals is the frigate mackerel *(Auxis thazard),* whose lunate tail is less deeply forked —more like a tuna's—than that of the other mackerels. Its back has wavy, oblique stripes, but only toward the rear. Its body is scaleless except for an anterior corselet with a narrowing extension along the lateral line. Its average weight is about 2 pounds, its maximum probably 8 or 10. It ranges in American waters from Florida to the Carolinas.

The wahoo (*Acanthocybium solanderi*) is a long, slim, fully scaled fish with a uniquely movable upper jaw and teeth like a barracuda's. It generally weighs 15 or 20 pounds but can grow much larger; a 149-pound record was set in the Bahamas in 1962. Steel-blue or greenish, it has dark, narrow, vertical bars that dim with age but darken with excitement, like the fighter stripes of several game species. Its spiny dorsal fin is long and low, followed by a soft lobe and nine finlets. The anal lobe and finlets match the dorsal structure. The wahoo runs hard, fights brilliantly, and occasionally leaps. Unfortunately, it is truly abundant only off Bermuda, the Bahamas, and Mexico, though fairly common in the Keys. It will hit 1/0 to 5/0 feathers or a rigged mullet or balao trolled on a flat line or drifted. But since it usually hunts alone rather than in schools, it is most often an incidental bonus for offshore trollers fishing for marlin, sailfish, or tuna.

The remaining species, the Spanish mackerel and its close relatives, all belong to the genus *Scomberomorus.* The Spanish mackerel *(S. maculatus)* is sea-blue above, silvery below, and marked on its sides with scattered yellow spots. The average weight is 1½ to 3 pounds, but yard-long specimens weighing 9 or 10 pounds are caught once in a great while. This species ranges from Brazil to Chesapeake Bay and occasionally up to Cape Cod, and also occurs off the European coasts. Most plentiful in the Gulf and around Florida, it has a preference for warm areas, either inshore or offshore. The Sierra, or Sierra mackerel *(S. sierra),* of the West Coast tends to have its yellow spots arranged in several vague rows but is otherwise so similar to the Spanish mackerel that some biologists think it may be the same species. It occurs from Peru to San Diego but is uncommon above Baja.

The cero, or cero mackerel *(S. regalis),* also known as pintada, ranges from Brazil to Cape Cod. It is most abundant in the West Indies and around lower Florida. Along each side of this fish

runs a median yellow or brownish stripe, sometimes ragged or broken, and under it several rows of matching oval spots. Its size and weight are the same as the Spanish mackerel's.

A more common species in the same waters is the king mackerel *(S. cavalla),* largest of the group and by far the best game. Also called the kingfish or cavalla, it has an average weight of less than 10 pounds, but specimens twice as heavy are not uncommon, and occasional monsters are caught. The record king was a 90-pounder, 30 inches around and 5 feet, 11 inches long, caught in February, 1976, off Key West. Like the cero, the king has scale-covered pectorals. A juvenile may be mistaken for a cero since it has yellow spots that fade with maturity. However, it can be identified by its lateral line, which is high at the forward end but drops sharply in the area below the second dorsal. An adult has unmarked silvery sides below a dark blue-green back saddled with wavy black stripes. Ranging from Brazil to Florida and in summer to North Carolina, the kingfish is most abundant in the Gulf during the summer and around Florida in the fall.

FISH HABITAT & FEEDING BEHAVIOR—ANGLING TACTICS: All mackerels like to feed over deep reefs, but they also come inshore. The small varieties, in particular, often enter harbors and patrol close to the beaches in summer. They can be taken by drifting or trolling a sea worm, fish strip, or squid strip. Whereas the large species (especially the king) more often than not go deep to feed, the smaller ones may be anywhere from the bottom to the top, and some anglers watch for slicks or diving sea birds as

Angler with hefty king mackerel.

signs of near-surface activity. It is probably more productive to locate small mackerel by trolling a bait, feather jig, or spoon.

The first catch usually indicates the presence of a school, even if the fish are too deep to be seen. The engine can then be cut and any small, bright lure can be cast. An excellent choice is a metal squid or diamond jig with a no. 10 treble hook. Multiple rigs also work very well; a diamond jig can be attached to a 3- to 5-foot monofilament leader, and above the jig, at intervals of about 8 inches, several small, shiny spoons can be added on short droppers. Or, instead of the spoons, 2-inch lengths of worm-mimicking surgical tubing can be slipped over small hooks. The leader should test about 20 pounds, because even small mackerel can sever lighter line with their many sharp teeth. Light spinning tackle is the popular rule, but the line may have as high a test strength as the leader for deep trolling or larger fish. Many anglers have taken to stowing a light fly rod with their mackerel gear. When the fish are at the surface or can be coaxed up by chumming, they will attack a fast-moving yellow or white streamer.

The larger species also attack feathers or hair if the fly is retrieved fast enough. It takes speed both to attract and hook the fish. Because fast line-stripping can become tiresome, many fly-rodders prefer to troll. Hair (real or synthetic) seems to withstand mackerel teeth better than feathers, but even with bucktails an angler wants to have plenty of replacements on hand. Baitcasting and trolling rods are often used for Spanish mackerel and kings, but they are being eclipsed by light spinning tackle. With a spinning rod, monofilament testing 10 to 20 pounds is the general rule; with revolving-spool outfits the line often tests 30 pounds.

Where Spanish mackerel or comparable species predominate, a light wire (no. 1 to 3) or a monofilament leader testing 30 pounds should be sufficient. Spanish mackerel occasionally become peculiarly selective, demanding very small lures or baits and proportionately subtle terminal tackle. Selective as they may be, however, they sometimes strike a brass swivel, severing a line, so black swivels are *de rigueur.* For kings, a stronger leader is needed—no. 5 piano wire or a shock tippet testing 40 pounds.

Schools of Spanish mackerel cruise offshore, feeding over reefs or merely traveling in search of prey. But during the peak summer fishing months they are just as often caught inshore, especially at high tide, feeding in bays and channels or along the surf line. They can be caught on baits, the best of which seem to be live shrimp or dead but fresh minnows. When mackerel are near the surface, a shrimp can be drifted on a 1/0 hook under a bobber, and when they are near the bottom the bobber can be removed and a couple of split shot added. Minnow baits, depending on size, may demand a slightly smaller or larger hook, but they are used in the same way. Trolling also works, but casting is the favorite method, particularly after a sizable school is found; either way, lures provide more enjoyment than baits. Nylon jigs, feather jigs, and spoons are all effective if moved fast.

Kingfish, more often found in large offshore schools, have become a mainstay of party boats off Texas, Louisiana, and Florida. The choice of hooks is governed by the size of the local fish. Metal jigs are often used, but during the fall run in Florida the favorite lures are 1- to 2-ounce baited, leadheaded jigs in yellow, white, or with a yellow head and white nylon skirt.

Trolling accounts for a disproportionate share of the largest kings, as they rove more than the small or medium ones and often in smaller, looser groups. Good areas include current rips where green inshore water abruptly gives way to blue offshore water, as well as around offshore oil pumps and over deep, rocky reefs.

Big subsurface plugs can be trolled, or live shrimp, or sailfish baits—5- to 6-inch mullet or balao. A favorite in Florida is a blue runner hooked through the head. When the mackerel are very deep, wire line is sometimes used with a heavy trolling sinker and a whole mullet or balao. Sometimes, if the fish are not very active, they can be stirred by trolling several offerings—balao and a couple of heavy feather jigs.

Marlin (*Tetrapturus* and *Makaira*)
COMMON & REGIONAL NAMES: *billfish*

GAME IDENTIFICATION & LOCATION OF FISHING REGIONS: Often, an encounter with a marlin begins when a dorsal fin cuts through swells or wake toward a skipping bait. The marlin's bill, or spear, may cut the surface for a splashy instant as it swats the thing it mistakes for easy prey. The line snaps away from an outrigger clip and streams into the wake. Someone shouts, "Line down!" The skipper may ease off on the throttle for a few moments to increase "drop-back"—for a billfish first swamps its fleeing prey with a slash or wallop of its long, hard bill, and only then, when the victim appears stunned or wounded, does it close its toothless maw around the food. The marlin wheels away, the rod dips low over the stern transom, and the angler, feeling the weight of the fish, hauls back hard while the skipper guns the engine.

The angler does not slow his marlin's initial runs; to try would be futile and might well cause a break-off. All he can do is keep a tight line when the fish bursts from the water in a magnificent spray, twisting, vaulting, shaking its head, dancing on its tail, slapping back into the waves, leaping again. Whether the fish sounds or remains at the surface throughout the fight, what ensues is a long contest between a determined angler, pumping, cranking, wondering if he can gain any significant amount of line before his hands and arms lose all feeling, and an extraordinarily powerful, speedy, agile creature that seems tireless.

The four great marlin species and a couple of smaller, less impressive kin are istiophorids, members of the billfish family, closely related to the sailfish (which see). Though pelagic, they feed and migrate close enough to shore to be a major quarry for trolling cruisers, both chartered and private, and in many regions they are caught from outboard-powered runabouts and skiffs. An adult marlin of any species has a greatly prolonged upper jaw, forming a rounded spear for disabling prey. It also has a long, low dorsal fin with an enlarged front end that rises to an abrupt peak. This fin is much smaller than the dorsal of a sailfish, but high enough just behind the head to create considerable resistance as the fish plows through the water. When a marlin is swimming fast, it folds the fin down flat into a furrow along its back, enhancing the streamlined contour of its deep-shouldered, smoothly tapering body. Aft of the big dorsal fin, near the keeled caudal peduncle, is a second, much smaller dorsal fin, hardly more than a finlet. Directly below this is a roughly matching anal finlet, aft of a fairly large, triangular anal fin. The tail is wide and lunate. The pelvic fins are long, slim filaments, located far forward.

Of equal interest to anglers are several additional characteristics: large size, spectacular leaps, mighty runs, speed, endurance. A marlin is even faster, stronger, more acrobatic than a sailfish. Swift agility is demanded by the basic feeding method of all istiophorids. They either club a single target or streak

through a school of prey, flailing their bills like the swords of glad-
iators, then scooping up casualties. They consume a few crustaceans and a considerable number of squid and octopi, but in
most regions they subsist chiefly on fish: herring, anchovies,
jacks, flying fish, bonito, small tuna, mackerel, bonefish, sauries,
mullet, balao, or any other locally plentiful species.

Like a great many pelagic carnivores, marlin tend to be
blue dorsally and silvery below, but disparate markings identify
the various species. Anglers sometimes speak of "fighter stripes"
or of a billfish "lighting up." The reference is to an intensification
or change in the markings or general color—a nervously stimulated flush that appears when a fish is fighting or sometimes when
it attacks prey or bait.

The silvery white of the white marlin *(Tetrapturus albidus)*
usually begins rather abruptly and rather high—slightly above the
lateral line, which is more distinct than on other marlins. Its back
is greenish-blue, a bit greener than that of its relatives. Pale blue,
lavender, or whitish vertical bars, variable in number and not very
distinct, run down the upper sides. These markings fade away
soon after death (as on all marlin species). The dorsal fin is a
bright, deep blue, often with a violet cast and purple or blackish
spots scattered over it. The tail and other fins are dark and drab,
but the anal fin may be marked like the dorsal fin. The white marlin is the only member of its family with rounded rather than
pointed tips on its dorsal, anal, and pectoral fins.

Striped marlin leaping.

Smallest of the marlins, the white averages 50 to 60 pounds, though 80-pound catches are not at all unusual. The record weight is 174 pounds, 3 ounces. Caught off Victoria, Brazil, in 1975, that marlin was 8 feet, 8⅓ inches long and had a girth of 35½ inches. The species ranges through the Mediterranean, the Atlantic, the Caribbean, and the Gulf of Mexico. All marlins prefer warm regions but migrate in spring or early summer into cooler waters. The white is found from Brazil to Cape Cod and sometimes Nova Scotia; however, even in summer it is common only from New York south to the tropics. One of the largest concentrations is found in September off the port of La Guaira, near Caracas, Venezuela. More convenient for North American anglers are the waters of the Bahamas, the Keys, the Florida coast, and the Gulf, from March or April through June; Ocean City, Maryland (and northward across Delaware Bay to Cape May) from mid- or late July to mid-September; and from Montauk Point to Block Island in August.

The blue marlin *(Makaira nigricans),* though not as abundant as the white along North America's Atlantic coast, has a wider distribution. The species ranges through the world's warm and temperate oceans—the Pacific and Indian as well as the Mediterranean, Atlantic, and Caribbean. In the Pacific, unfortunately, very few blues wander to the coast of lower California, most of them going only as far north as Acapulco. On the East Coast, they range about as far north as the white marlin. They appear in good numbers off the Carolinas in July and August, and are abundant in the tropics during the winter. At the southern extremity of their range, they travel at least as far as Uruguay. From May through July, the fishing for blue marlin is good off the Bahamas, Cuba, Puerto Rico, the Virgin Islands, and throughout the West Indies. It is good in June and July in Gulf and Floridian waters.

Blue marlin average from 75 to 100 pounds; 200- to 300-pound catches are fairly frequent, but the males seldom grow beyond that upper weight. Old females, on the other hand, vie with black marlin as the largest istiophorids.

The biggest blue ever taken on rod and reel was a 1,805-pound specimen caught in 1972 off Hawaii. That one did not qualify as a sporting world record, to be listed by the International Game Fish Association, because a second angler handled the tackle. The official record, set by a 1,153-pound marlin taken at

Guam, has stood since 1969. The Guam marlin was 14 feet, 8 inches long and 6 feet, 1 inch around. The same species in the Atlantic tends to be slightly smaller and is listed separately in the records. The largest to date was a 1,142-pounder taken at Nags Head, North Carolina, in late July, 1974.

A large blue marlin may grow a very long bill, which looks all the longer because after maturity the entire upper jaw grows faster than the lower jaw. However, a blue of average size has a shorter, slightly stouter bill as well as a rounder, less slab-sided body than other marlins of comparable size. It also has a relatively low dorsal fin and deep first anal fin. Its very peculiar lateral line, not usually visible externally, is a chain of irregular hexagons. The back is dark, steely blue, fading to silvery white below and marked with a series of light vertical stripes of variable number. The dorsal and anal fins are cobalt, sometimes with a purplish cast; the tail and other fins match the back.

The striped marlin (*T. audax*) of the Pacific and Indian oceans can be recognized by its high, sickle-pointed dorsal fin; long, slim bill; dark indigo, blue-green, or steely-blue back; silvery-white sides; and distinct, narrow, vertical stripes—usually about twenty, and usually lavender but sometimes pale blue or whitish. The dark-tipped first dorsal and anal fins vary from bright cobalt to the color of the back, and the dorsal may be marked by an irreg-

White marlin at boatside.

ular double row of dark spots. The usual weight is about 200 to 250 pounds, but some waters seem to attract bigger stripers. Fairly large ones come from Hawaii and still larger ones from New Zealand, a nation famous for giant gamefish. The record, set in 1964 in New Zealand, is 415 pounds. Guaymas, on the eastern side of the Gulf of California, is renowned for striped marlin during the summer months. In the United States, the area around San Diego is the mecca. The waters west and northwest of the city, near San Clemente and Santa Catalina islands, yield sizable striped marlin, as does the Gulf of Santa Catalina.

Many big-game anglers rate the species as the most exciting marlin to hook—the most acrobatic fighter of all. North American fishing for striped marlin generally begins in summer, when the water temperature rises above 60°. In the San Diego area it may be good in August but is often better in September.

The largest species of all is the black marlin *(M. indica),* a deep-shouldered giant that reaches a weight of half a ton in a few prime waters such as those off the famous north Peruvian port of Cabo Blanco. The world record was set there in 1953 by a 1,560-pound fish, 14½ feet long, with a 6-foot, 9-inch girth.

Unfortunately for American anglers, black marlin dwell only in the warmer waters of the Pacific and Indian oceans, rarely migrating farther north than the Gulf of California. And although the species is abundant in parts of the Central Pacific, it is scarce around Hawaii. Typically, it has a dark slaty-blue back and silver-gray or paler silvery sides, a relatively short bill, and rigid pectoral fins that jut out from the body—unlike those of other marlins.

FISH HABITAT & FEEDING BEHAVIOR—ANGLING TACTICS:
Large numbers of marlin have been tagged by anglers and ichthyologists in an effort to learn more about their migrations, spawning habits, growth rates, and other details of their life cycles. Despite the recapture of many tagged fish, a great deal remains to be learned. Blue marlin (and perhaps the others) evidently spawn at all times of the year, depending on locale, but with a peak during spring and summer, at least in the Northern Hemisphere. Many spawn during the northward coastal migration or after reaching cooler waters. Breeding activity does not deter them from feeding at or near the surface, where they come to trolled baits and lures.

Like sailfish, marlin probably produce two to five million eggs per female each year. Fertilized somewhat haphazardly in the open ocean, the eggs float with plankton, and relatively few survive. The larvae combine fast growth with slow attainment of adult characteristics. A yearling may be 4 feet long and weigh 30 pounds, but only then does it have a long enough bill and large enough fins to look like an adult.

In the quest for prey, adult marlin probe various depths but are most active near or at the surface. Though blind trolling takes many fish in productive areas, skippers are alert not only for slicks or diving birds but for an occasional dorsal fin cleaving the water. At some ports, skippers troll until they locate fish, then drift and chum. For both trolling and drifting, kite-fishing has become a popular technique. (Balloons had a brief vogue, eclipsed by kites.) The kite can ride the air far astern or to one side, holding a live bait steadily in any desired location. Attached to the kite is a pinned ring, through which the fishing line slips so that it can be adjusted to hold the bait skipping and splashing right at the surface, a deadly temptation to marlin. The blue runner is a favorite Floridian bait for this purpose, as it is very hardy and active in the water. When a fish strikes, the kite's pin works like an outrigger clip, instantly releasing the line. The angler does not concern himself with drop-back; in many cases he does not even have to set the hook, because a marlin usually slaps and gulps the dangled bait very fast.

For conventional trolling, a whole fish or strip bait is usually rigged to ride the surface, though big spoons, plastic squid, and bright Japanese feathers are sometimes used as well. Any of the aforementioned species of preyfish may be a favored bait in a particular port. It can be used with the hook inserted upward through both lips or it may be sewn or wired to the hook—an advisable method with the larger baits—and a charter skipper will have on hand a supply of baits already rigged on hooks. In addition to the usual preyfish, squid make good baits, and so do 12- to 14-inch eels. In some locales, an eel is a popular white-marlin bait, generally rigged on two 7/0 hooks.

Trolling should be fast, as for bonito, but it varies with time and place as well as with the practitioner. There is also a school of thought in favor of trolling assorted offerings simultaneously— perhaps balao on two outriggers plus two other kinds of fish or

a fish and a feather jig on a couple of flat lines.

Marlin tournaments impose their own tackle restrictions, but in unregulated fishing the decisive factor is either the kind of marlin frequenting the neighborhood or, aboard charter craft, the operator's views about what ought to be provided. An angler trolling in his own runabout can handle typical white marlin with a saltwater spinning rod, a reel well loaded with monofilament testing 20 pounds or so, and a 12-foot leader of 80-pound-test monofilament or no. 8 or 9 wire. (Long leaders are common since the whipping tail of a billfish can easily cut a line.) More conventional equipment consists of a fairly short fiberglass trolling rod of the roller-guide type and a level-wind reel with a quadrant lever or star drag; some anglers favor the relatively new lever action, which can be adjusted to a light "strike-drag" (no more than a third of the line's breaking strength) and later switched instantly to a heavier setting. However, most marlin enthusiasts agree that too much drag is a common cause of break-offs. Light tackle is considered to be a 2/0 to 4/0 reel and 12- to 20-pound line strength for white marlin; a 4/0 reel with the same line for striped marlin; a 6/0 reel with 20- to 50-pound strength for blue marlin; and a 6/0 reel with 30- to 50-pound strength for black marlin. For both blue and black marlin, medium tackle would be a 9/0 reel

Black marlin off Baja California.

and 50- to 80-pound strength, while heavy would be a 12/0 reel and 130-pound strength. For whites, medium tackle is a 4/0 to 6/0 reel, 20- to 30-pound strength, and heavy is a 6/0 reel, 30- to 50-pound strength. For blues, medium is a 7/0 reel, 30- to 50-pound strength, and heavy is a 9/0 reel with line testing 80 pounds. Tip weights for tubular glass rods in these categories run from 6 ounces to 30. Monofilament leaders run from 80- to 200-pound test, wire leaders from no. 8 (86-pound) to no. 12 (176-pound). Swivels are stainless steel with small bearings. For large marlin, many experts use a long segment of double line above the swivel—about 15 feet for 50-pound test and twice that for heavier line. The line is run through the swivel above the leader, looped back, secured with a Bimini-twist knot, and held together at intervals with dental floss for easy passage through the rod guides. Hooks depend on the type of bait and rig, but a general rule is 7/0 to 9/0 for whites, 8/0 or 9/0 for stripers, 9/0 or 10/0 for blues, and 9/0 to 12/0 for blacks.

The heft of the usual equipment does not preclude the use of an ordinary 8½- to 9½-foot fly rod when fishing from a private boat or with a very cooperative charter skipper. Fly-fishing for marlin and sails was pioneered by Dr. Webster Robinson and his wife, Helen, in the early 1960's, using only a 12-pound tippet most of the time. These fish seldom venture close enough to a boat for casting, so the Robinsons developed the technique of trolling a hookless teaser bait or feathers and pulling it just out of reach toward the boat when a billfish charged it. When the fish came within casting range, the teaser was yanked away and replaced with a big popper-streamer. The engine was immediately killed while the fly was darted and skipped on the surface. This method is still used, though a teaser bait—preferably a rigged fish or a belly strip of bonito or dolphin—is sometimes dangled from a kite and lifted away at the critical moment.

A Lefty's Deceiver or any similar long-tailed, white, surface-disturbing fly will work. One expert recommends a long saddle-hackle streamer tied on 4/0 tandem hooks. Another dresses a 7/0 hook with a streamer-popper having a square-faced inch-long white styrofoam head trailing 4-inch-long white saddle hackles. Still another stresses the use of a very sharp, upturned 7/0 hook with fifteen to twenty full-length saddle hackles. An angler can pop any of these variations along the top or swim it under.

Blue marlin.

Any moderately long fly rod, up to 7½ ounces, can be used with a matching weight-forward floating line and perhaps 250 yards of strong Dacron backing. The leader ought to be about 9 feet long, tapered from a butt testing 30 pounds down to a 20-pound section, then a 12-pound section, and finally a foot-long shock tippet. Some anglers use a vinyl-coated wire tippet with a breaking strength up to 45 pounds; others prefer monofilament testing as much as 100 pounds.

A marlin hits a fly hard and fast, but does not always dispense with the usual bill-slap before the actual take. A fly-rodder who can remain cool enough waits for the fish to begin turning away before he sets the hook. In conventional trolling with heavier tackle, some anglers throw the reel into free-spool, letting the fish run a couple of hundred yards before the engine is gunned to take up slack and the hook is set with at least one hard strike and often three. But less drop-back is needed with marlin than with some species, such as swordfish. Many anglers dispense with any free-spool run, and Bahamian skippers tend to gun the boat immediately. Either way, the peculiar manner in which a billfish kills its prey means that an occasional marlin is going to be foul-hooked, and a foul-hooked marlin has such an advantage that it may hardly know it is fighting.

There is no point in trying to stop a hard run or trying to tire a marlin by overtightening the drag. After the fish settles into the fight, some anglers merely apply the palm of the cranking hand to the spool while pumping. The hand is raised instantly if the fish surges away. The boat can also be used to help defeat a marlin, though many anglers feel it is more sporting to play the game from a "dead boat," and some tournaments require that the engine be put into neutral when a fish is hooked.

Finally, the marlin is at boatside. If it is to be released, a research tag may be clipped to the dorsal fin. Then the leader is snipped off, as close as possible to the hook, which will rust away harmlessly. If a small marlin is to be kept, it can be taken aboard by "billing" it after first donning cotton fishing gloves. The leader is grasped firmly with one hand; with the other, the bill is grasped near its base, pointed safely to one side, and the fish is swung aboard. A medium-sized marlin usually requires the use of a flying gaff. A big one may require a gaff and a tail rope. A giant black of the sort caught off Peru requires an electric winch.

Permit & Pompano *(Trachinotus)*

COMMON & REGIONAL NAMES: Names in common usage denote one or more species and will be included in the descriptions of those species.

GAME IDENTIFICATION & LOCATION OF FISHING REGIONS:
Permit, or great pompano, and the other, smaller pompanos are warm-water fish that feed in the shallows along the southerly coasts, where they arouse the ardor of all light-tackle adherents. These fish strike fast, can be tricky to hook in some cases, make very long, fast runs, flip their diamond-shaped, flat bodies around in sudden reversals of direction, and have a remarkable stamina that makes for a long, chancy fight. Permit anglers describe their quarry as having the characteristics of bonefish but in excess.

They are carangids, belonging to the same family as jacks and amberjacks (which see) and sharing some of the same habitat, habits, and physical qualities. They are silvery, high-backed, deep-bellied fish, very narrow in cross section, with blunt heads, large eyes, small mouths, shell-crushing dentition for feeding in the manner of bonefish, and wide, deeply forked, lunate tails. As a rule, the first dorsal fin is a short series of about half a dozen small, nearly detached spines. Immediately behind this is a long second dorsal, reaching almost to the caudal peduncle. Its forward end is a high, rearward-sweeping, pointed lobe, and the remainder is a narrow strip. The anal fin matches it but is slightly smaller and fronted by a couple of short, detached spines.

The most abundant, important form is the one most often called pompano *(Trachinotus carolinus)* but also known as Florida pompano, common pompano, and (in a few locales) sunfish. Its back and upper sides are silvery bluish-gray, sometimes with a slight green tinge, shading to light silver below the lateral line and ventrally washed or flecked with yellow. Yellow also tinges the head, throat, and lower fins.

Its range is from Brazil up through the Caribbean and the Gulf and northward to Bermuda and Massachusetts, but it is seldom abundant in cool waters. Florida and the Caribbean have the best pompano fishing. The average size is a pound or two, but 4-pound specimens are caught rather frequently, 7-pounders occasionally. Any larger catch is probably an Atlantic permit *(T. falcatus)*, a species for which the common pompano is sometimes

mistaken. In a few regions, any large pompano is called permit.

Young Atlantic permit also go by the name of round pompano, and large ones are often called great pompano. Though the average weight of those caught is 10 to 20 pounds—about twice the size of bonefish—a good many 30-pound and a few 40-pound permit are taken. The current record is held by a 50½-pound Key West specimen caught in 1971. This species ranges through the same waters as the common pompano, appearing in greatest abundance in the Bahamas and Florida. The world's best permit fishing takes place from Key West to the Dry Tortugas during April and May, August and September.

Sometimes a young permit is almost all black, sometimes mostly silvery, sometimes darkly tinged with red, and it can modify these hues a little more efficiently than most pompanos to achieve protective coloration. Usually an adult is grayish or bluish along the narrow band of its back, the remainder of its body being silvery or almost white. Aged lunkers often acquire a blue tinge.

The Pacific permit *(T. kennedyi)* is also known as palometa —the correct name of a small, long-finned Atlantic species—and as Culver's pompano. It is very closely related to the Atlantic permit and is similar in appearance but smaller—generally under 2 feet long. It ranges principally from Ecuador to Baja, with a few strays wandering up to southern California in the summer.

Young Florida pompano.

The true palometa *(T. goodei)* has the same range as the common pompano. It can be quickly identified by the very long, backswept rays at the front of its falcate, or sickle-shaped, dorsal and anal fins. Alternate names for it are longfin pompano and gafftopsail pompano. It is dark silver on the back, with silver or pale golden sides marked by dark, narrow, vertical bars. The belly is yellowish, the breast orange. This species never exceeds 3 pounds. Probably its closest relative is the slightly larger gafftopsail pompano *(T. rhodopus)* of the Pacific, which occasionally grows to a length of 2 feet. A silvery species with faint yellow vertical bars, this one ranges from Peru to Zuma Beach, in southern California. A few additional, smaller pompanos inhabit the Atlantic and Pacific, but only those described here are of angling interest.

FISH HABITAT & FEEDING BEHAVIOR—ANGLING TACTICS:
Pompano of all varieties feed chiefly on bottom-dwelling invertebrates found in the shallows. The Florida, or common, pompano and probably most of the others prefer bivalves and small crustaceans, for which they root in the sand. A large pompano or permit will supplement this diet with a few small fish, but no pompano is sufficiently piscivorous for an angler to rely on the use of baitfish or baitfish imitations. Small crustaceans are the favorite baits.

Spawning occurs quite far offshore. Much of the breeding activity of Atlantic permit is thought to occur in the Gulf Stream and the Florida Current. It continues from December to September. Common pompano evidently spawn from March to September, at least off the southeastern United States.

The details of the life cycle are thought to be the same for the various other species as for common pompano, though spawning peaks may differ regionally. In the southerly waters where concentrations are heaviest, pompano are present all year but most plentiful from late summer or early fall through spring; the fishing is best in spring and fall. In part, this is because many pompano migrate. However, spawning may be another factor in the summer fishing lull. In southern Florida during June and July, permit are observed to congregate offshore, perhaps to spawn. When the permit begin returning to the shallow flats in August, the fishing is greatly improved.

Common pompano and the smaller species run in schools. They are abundant around bays or inlets and near sandy beaches. Because they often move in and out with the tide, a rising tide is best for fishing the surf or shallows, but there may be good action again on the falling tide at the drop-offs and channels.

Permit differ from the others in several ways. The young ones run in schools—relatively small schools—but mature ones tend to be almost solitary except when they assemble on the food-rich flats. They are most abundant and most often caught on precisely the same flats where an angler would seek bonefish (which see). During low water they remain close to shore, in channels, holes, or the deeper parts of inlets. When the water rises, they move onto the flats to feed. On a typical grassy flat, the best time to waylay them is just after low water, at the start of the rising tide. But if the flat has very shallow banks over which the fish must pass, the best time may be nearer to flood tide. Permit, after all, are twice the size of bonefish, and their deep hulls draw more water, so they need an extra few inches of depth to navigate. Permit sometimes glean shrimp on an outgoing tide around docks and buoys. A bait can be dropped to them in such spots.

On any coast, there are three good ways to catch any pompano except the permit. The first is surfcasting—or beach-casting —with live sandfleas (the long-antennaed little burrowing crustaceans, also known as sandbugs and mole crabs, that colonize

Palometa.

both Atlantic and Pacific beaches). These baits can be used alone or on the hook of a small, leadheaded nylon jig. A jig by itself works admirably when migrating schools arrive in late summer or fall, but the best offering as a rule is a sandflea on a nylon jig with an enticingly short skirt, snipped off at the bend of the hook.

Surf fishermen often need long casts, because pompano like to feed just beyond the nearest sandbar to shore. Both spinning and revolving-spool outfits are used. A popular choice in Florida is a fiberglass surf rod, 11½ to 13½ feet long; it should be limber but capable of handling a 3- to 5-ounce sinker. For skiff-fishing, a shorter, lighter spinning rod is much sportier. The reel can be spooled with monofilament testing 6 to 10 pounds. A small baited or unbaited jig or feather, or a small hook with a sandflea or bit of clam is tied to the end. Since pompano are soft-mouthed, many fishermen dispense with a leader.

The second basic way to catch pompano is to still-fish with a bait on a sliding-sinker fishfinder rig with a single hook or several. An alternative of equal merit is a surf rig, utilizing two or three hooks on droppers above a pyramid sinker.

The third way is to cast or troll from a skiff, preferably with a sandflea-baited jig. After a cast lure touches bottom, a jigging retrieve is made. Some anglers prefer a small, baited wobbling spoon with a light teardrop sinker. Since the spoon has built-in action, there is no need to impart any. In this case, a 6-foot leader is used, with the sinker attached to the swivel or just above it.

Any pompano is a skittish creature, quick to panic. This is particularly true of common pompano during the spring. In the shallows, they often dash about as a boat approaches, some of them skipping across the surface.

Since permit are comparable alarmists, and they must be stalked on the shallow tidal flats where they feed, they can be trickier to approach than bonefish. Partly for this reason and partly because it is hard to pique a permit's interest with a bucktail or streamer, the species usually eludes fly fishermen—including veteran bonefishing zealots who are likely to be using a small bucktail or marabou streamer, a shrimp imitation such as the Phillips Pink Bonefish Fly, or a tarpon fly such as the Keys Tarpon Streamer. The problem is complicated by the fact that permit are hulking creatures, forced to root for their crustaceans on a deeper bottom than bonefish need. A fairly large, heavy fly is best, some-

thing tied on a 4, 2, or even 1/0 hook. Yet it must be presented delicately, without letting line or a shadow fall across a member of a school. This presentation must be almost under the target's nose. Unlike bonefish, permit do not watch for distant prey.

Lures other than flies—small baited spoons or leadhead jigs—will capture a permit's attention more easily. Many experts choose a quarter-ounce light tan pop-eye jig (which resembles no shrimp, much less a crab, but for all anyone knows it may look to a permit like a tasty mollusk). It is cast ahead of the target and, whether a baitcasting or spinning rod is used, it should skid as it touches the water.

Good-sized permit.

Baits are more reliable. The very best is a small blue or spider crab, about the size of a silver dollar. It is fished live, with a very sharp 2/0 or 3/0 hook skewered up from underneath, through one of the pointed, winglike edges of the carapace. Almost as good (or just as good at times) is a big live shrimp, either hooked through the tail in normal fashion or under the head, in front of the large dark spot. With lures or baits, a good choice of tackle is a 6½-foot medium-action spinning rod. The line need not have a test strength of more than 8 pounds but the reel should have a large capacity; a permit's first run often takes 200 yards.

If a small permit takes the bait, an experienced angler waits a second before setting the hook; in the case of a large one, it is better to count off three seconds, as big permit take time to work crustaceans into their mouths. Wait no longer, however, or the fish can crack a crab and spit out the hook. Strike the fish forcefully, at least three times, for a permit's mouth is like hard rubber. If the hook is set, the fish will make a run that leaves no doubt, often toward deep water. Just as often, it will stop momentarily to twist and rub against the bottom, trying to rid itself of the hook. A tight line must be kept for that reason and because a permit may double back. It will run again, perhaps over the rubble-strewn transitional zone between deep and shallow water. The rod should be held high to lessen the chance of cutting or tangling. When a permit begins to tire, it frequently turns its broad side to the direction of the angler's pressure, and pulling mightily, runs again.

Porgy, Scup, & Sheepshead (Sparidae)

COMMON & REGIONAL NAMES: Several species—but no important ones in American waters—are called *bream*. Other names in common usage denote various species and will be included in the descriptions of those species.

GAME IDENTIFICATION & LOCATION OF FISHING REGIONS: The porgies familiar to American sportsmen are small to medium-sized bait-thieves, a nuisance during a bottom-fishing quest for bigger, nimbler, or more pugnacious game. On the other hand, they are strong fighters for their size and, being omnivorous school fish, are easy to catch when locally abundant. Only a jaded, snobbish, or hypocritical angler would sneer at what used

to be called "a good mess of porgy." The American varieties are all of the sort that can be handled with spinning equipment and 6-pound-test monofilament—unless, on occasion, the use of a heavy sinker prompts a conversion to stouter line.

Like grunts, porgies have their eyes located high on the head, and their spiny and soft dorsal fins joined. In shape, too, they resemble grunts, but are even more high-shouldered and laterally compressed. The anal fin and soft-rayed dorsal are fairly large, the tail forked or crescented. Most species are relatively drab but can change the intensity of coloration or can gain or lose blotching to enhance their camouflage. Some have small incisors, but many are equipped with blunt front teeth backed by molars, for cracking shells.

In American waters, porgies are primarily inshore fish, though elsewhere some species roam farther out. There are Pacific porgies, but the common and comparatively sizable ones occur along the Atlantic and in the Gulf of Mexico. They include scup and sheepshead, listed separately above this entry because some fishermen do not realize they are true porgies.

The scup *(Stenotomus chrysops)* occurs principally from Cape Cod to the Carolinas but shifts northward in summer, southward in winter, occasionally reaching Nova Scotia at one extreme and Georgia or Florida at the other. Along some stretches of that

Scup and sheepshead.

range it is seldom called anything but scup, yet in parts of the North (and in far-flung fish markets) it is never called anything but porgy. Typically it weighs less than a pound and barely reaches 10 inches in length; every so often, however, a fisherman catches one twice as long and weighing 3 or 4 pounds. The tail is lunate—more of a crescent than a fork. Coloration varies from dull silver to brownish, dark above and light below.

Whereas the scup and others of its genus have incisors, the jolthead porgy *(Calamus bajonado)* belongs to a genus with conical front teeth and molars. Its common name refers to one of its feeding tactics: the use of its blunt, high-domed head to bump clams and other mollusks loose from their beds. The jolthead is one of the larger American porgies, averaging about a pound but sometimes attaining a length of 2 feet and a weight of 8 pounds or more. It has a forked tail and a yellowish-brown or gray body with a silvery sheen and bluish overtones. When living over a mottled bottom, it becomes duskily blotched. The eyes are exceptionally high on the head, with a blue streak under and sometimes over them. Occasionally the body has faint blue longitudinal stripes. This species may be the most common porgy of the western Atlantic. It ranges through the Caribbean, around southern Florida, and sometimes, when drawn northward by the Gulf Stream, as far up as Bermuda or along the coast to Rhode Island.

Largest of the American porgies is the sheepshead *(Archosargus probatocephalus).* Its average weight is only a pound or two; however, it occasionally spans 3 feet from its blunt head to its forked tail, at which length this deep-bodied fish may weigh 25 pounds. It is thick-lipped and has broad, almost conical incisors. It is sometimes called the convict fish, an allusion to markings reminiscent of an old-fashioned striped prison uniform. Its fins are black; depending on the viewer's bias, its head and body can be described as black with broad, vertical silver bands, or silver with black bands. At one time the sheepshead ranged from Texas to Florida and northward as far as Massachusetts. It is now common only in southern waters.

FISH HABITAT & FEEDING BEHAVIOR—ANGLING TACTICS:
Porgies find their invertebrate prey in abundance around reefs—chiefly inshore reefs—and around rocks, jetties, piers, pilings, and drop-offs, as well as in bays, channels, and tidal creeks. They

move far offshore from these convenient fishing areas only to spawn. Their life cycles have not yet been thoroughly studied, but there is evidence that many species breed in late fall or winter although the scup and probably a few others do so in spring. Their prevalence near shore may be more dependent on temperatures than on their reproductive habits. The sheepshead, which is easily the favorite of anglers, can be caught all year long in Florida. This also holds true for the slightly cooler Gulf Coast, but there and to the north the sheepshead fishing (and other porgy fishing) is best from early spring through summer.

In Florida, the little crustaceans called sandfleas are often used as bait. There and elsewhere, the most common baits are clams, shrimp, pieces of crab, chunks or strips of fish, and strips of squid. Some species have minor preferences; the best jolthead bait is shrimp. The same bait is a favorite for Texas sheepshead, while in Florida the most common sheepshead bait is fiddler crab.

Porgy bait is most often hung on a 2/0 Sproat or Carlisle hook with a short wire leader (because the shell-cracking teeth of sheepshead and some others can cut monofilament). The remainder of the tackle may be anything suitable for working the bottom with a fishfinder or other slip-sinker rig.

All species are taken from private and party boats as well as bridges, piers, causeways, jetties, and shores. Though porgies do·not move around much once they locate a natural food source, they can be attracted in good numbers by chumming, especially with clams, crabmeat, or shrimp. They seem to feed most actively in quiet water or during a slack tide.

Rockfish & Scorpionfish (*Scorpaenidae*); Kelp Bass & Sand Bass (*Paralabrax*)

COMMON & REGIONAL NAMES: On the Pacific coast, rockfish and scorpionfish are called *rockcod;* kelp bass and sand bass are called *rock bass*. (Other names in common usage denote various species and will be included in the descriptions of those species.)

GAME IDENTIFICATION & LOCATION OF FISHING REGIONS: There is no biological basis for intruding kelp bass and sand bass into a guidebook entry on rockfish, yet the grouping will appear logical—almost inevitable—to anyone who has bottom-fished rocky, kelp-bedded inshore waters from a party boat, barge, or skiff on the West Coast. If there were no danger of confusion or verbosity, the entry might also include lingcod, sculpins, and surfperch, which are treated in separate sections. All of these fishes inhabit the same general range and the same general habitat, where they feed in pretty much the same manner and are often caught in a mixed bag by the same general methods.

About three hundred members of the family Scorpaenidae —rockfish and scorpionfish—are distributed through the world's tropical, temperate, and cold seas. However, only one species of the scorpionfish genus *Scorpaena* occurs on the Pacific coast and it is popular among fishermen of the shallows. About sixty other members of the family, belonging to the rockfish genus *Sebastes,* dwell along that coast. (Since kelp bass and sand bass are Pacific sea basses, the fishing described in this section is exclusively a West Coast diversion.)

Some scorpionfishes look almost like pincushions and others have filamentous collars of fins and barbels resembling lions' manes. The game species of scorpionfish and the various rockfishes are less bizarre but share several peculiar characteristics. All have armored heads, equipped with a bony cheek plate that begins under the eye and runs back to the gill cover; on some it is edged with points or spines, or stands out almost like the visor of a medieval helmet. The eyes are set high on the head. The tail is square-tipped, slightly rounded, or slightly notched. The mouth is big, the lips thick, the lower jaw of most species projecting and in some cases knobbed at the tip. On many species, ridges, spines, or both adorn the head or snout, giving it an almost corrugated look. The fore and aft dorsal fins are joined, usually with a deep notch at the juncture. The spines of the first segment are sharp enough to inflict a wound if a catch is handled carelessly.

The majority of rockfishes forage close to shore but in deep water. However, the varieties caught on rod and reel dwell for the most part in the shallows. They hide amid rocks or in kelp and similar vegetation in order to ambush small fish and crustaceans. They are nonmigratory, and where rockfish of any species occur they tend to be abundant. Unlike most fishes, they reproduce by internal fertilization and bear live young rather than eggs. As rockfish do not fast or leave for distant spawning grounds when repro-

ducing, the angling remains good all year; it is best in winter and spring from Washington to lower California. And when it slackens a little in California, it is reinforced by the "rock bass" fishing, which is best from April to October, with a peak in August.

The *Scorpaena* genus is represented on the West Coast only by the California scorpionfish (*Scorpaena guttata*). Californians, being as casual as easterners about mixing up the names of unrelated species, often call it sculpin. The species ranges from central California to the tip of Baja. A relatively small fish, it sometimes grows to a length of 15 or 16 inches but rarely much more. It has two or three spines at the front of the anal fin and a dozen sharper ones in the first dorsal fin. It should be handled gingerly because the dorsal spines can cause a severe infection. This scorpionfish has a rounded tail, big rounded pectorals, and a ridged, spiny-looking head rendered the more grotesque by several cirri—small barbellike growths. The head and body are reddish-brown, with small brown, olive, or purplish spots and mottling, grading to pink below.

The blue rockfish (*S. mystinus*) grows slightly larger, sometimes reaching a length of over 18 inches. Also called priestfish, black bass, black snapper, or neri, it is a spiny but very basslike variety with a slightly concave tail and a body evenly curved above and below. It is slaty blue or blue-black on the upper surfaces, lighter below, blotched with gray, and white-bellied. Its young, often found in tidepools, are brick-red but begin to assume adult coloration when they are about 6 inches long. Small and medium blues may be caught anywhere from the shallows to depths of perhaps three hundred feet; the biggest ones go deeper and are not often boated. The species ranges from Alaska to Baja California.

Blue rockfish.

The bocaccio *(S. paucispinis)* is named for its protrusive lower jaw—*bocaccio* means "bigmouth" in Italian. Also called grouper or spotted rockfish, it is often blotched or spotted with black. The color of its back, varying from light olive-green to dark brown, is tinged with red and grades to reddish or orange on the sides, pink or white on the belly. Because its body is fairly slender and its head more pointed—or less blunt—than that of other rock-fishes, it looks vaguely like the sand and kelp basses. It grows rather large; once in a great while, someone catches a yard-long bocaccio weighing nearly 20 pounds. It is usually taken in deep water but not far from shore. Most abundant off the lower half of California, it ranges from Alaska to northern Baja.

The canary rockfish *(S. pinniger)* is common from upper British Columbia to upper Baja and, although it is not one of the largest, is probably the most important commercially. Its tastiness makes it a particularly welcome catch to anglers, a few of whom refer to it as the orange rockfish. It could easily be mistaken for a spiny, overgrown goldfish mutation—entirely orange on head, body, and fins, with three brighter orange streaks across the head, another along the lateral line, and above that a network of them. It has a knobbed, slightly projecting lower jaw, small spines atop its head, and a slightly notched tail.

From the Gulf of Alaska to Baja, the same waters yield quill-back rockfish *(S. maliger)* and rosy rockfish *(S. rosaceus)*. Both are ready biters. The quillback, sometimes called orange-spotted rockfish or yellowback rockcod, is yellowish to brownish —often yellow or yellow-orange on the forward portion of the body and dark brown to black on the rear portion. Generally it is marked with orange or brown spots. Pale brownish stripes radiate from the eyes, and sometimes a yellow wedge runs from the first dorsal fin to the lateral line. The membrane joining the long spines of the first dorsal fin is so deeply incised that the spines look almost like quills. The fins are black, the head blunt and spiny, the jaws nearly equal in length. Whereas a quillback can attain a length of perhaps 2 feet, the rosy rockfish—also called rainbow rockfish or corsair—is no more than half that size. It is yellow or orange, with a blood-red cast on the back and along the lateral line; a young one is generally yellower, an old one redder.

Both of the "rock bass" sharing rockfish habitat are distrib-uted from central California down into Baja waters and are most plentiful south of Los Angeles. They are caught together so commonly as to arouse confusion, the kelp bass *(Paralabrax clathratus)* sometimes going by the name sand bass and the true sand bass *(P. nebulifer)* sometimes dubbed kelp bass. It is true, however, that the kelp bass has a slightly more pronounced preference for kelp beds while the sand bass is a trifle more partial to sandy bottoms. Both are also caught over rocks and around piers.

The sand bass, sometimes called Johnny Verde, has a muddy greenish-gray back, paler sides, and a whitish belly. It is mottled, particularly on the head, which has vague dusky bars and small brownish spots. It grows to a length of about 18 inches.

The kelp bass is also called cabrilla, bull bass, or calico bass (a name more often applied to a freshwater species). It slightly surpasses the sand bass in tastiness as well as scrappiness, and it grows a trifle larger—up to about 24 inches. It is no heavyweight, however; the usual size is a pound or two, and a 5-pounder would be an outstanding catch. It has a dark gray or brownish back, mottled with darker brown and paling progressively to the yellowish belly. The fins also tend to be yellowish.

FISH HABITAT & FEEDING BEHAVIOR—ANGLING TACTICS:
The California scorpionfish, like all of the rockfishes, is most often caught on cut or live bait still-fished on the bottom from piers, jetties, skiffs, barges, and party boats. Every rockfish species responds readily to a small, live anchovy, herring, or similar fish, a fish chunk or strip, or a chunk of crab or clam. Hook sizes range from no. 1 all the way to 6/0, depending on locale, prevalent rockfish species (all of which are fairly big-mouthed for their size), and the likelihood that other kinds of fish will take the bait. Rock bass, for example, can be handled nicely by a no. 1 hook.

Occasionally, a rockfish of any sort will hit a slowly, deeply trolled spoon but, aside from baits, a metal jig is the surest enticement. A few species are more lively and less selective than most in their foraging; the bocaccio can be caught by trolling or jigging in deep water, and will take a metal jig or a herring skin as well as the more conventional cut baits. And the quillback, one of the better fighters, will grab a herring, dead or alive, or a metal jig.

The best still-fishing, drifting, and jigging spots are the inshore holes around rocks and pilings and the moderately deep waters with rocky bottoms or kelp beds—the spots where kelp and sand bass are often caught. Stiff rods are needed only for rock-fishing in the deeper waters where a heavy sinker must be accommodated. In such areas, line testing 15 or 20 pounds is useful, not only for managing the heavy terminal but for turning any fish —particularly a bass—away from rocks or kelp thickets.

Even though sand bass are often caught over the kind of bottom indicated by their common name, the basses resemble the rockfish in their liking for hiding places that are hard to penetrate by trolling or casting; again, still-fishing is most productive. All the same, kelp and sand bass respond to lures—chiefly small, deep-running plugs and feathered jigs of the same sort that catch freshwater bass. In addition, metal jigs take kelp bass. Though they sometimes snatch lures or bait near the surface, jigging is a favorite tactic. With the basses, all depths should be probed. They will go for a live anchovy, herring, mackerel fry, squid, chunk of fish—or, in fact, any conventional bait.

For the basses especially, night fishing with a bright light is a very reliable tactic. The light attracts mobs of forage fish, which in turn attract bass. Kelp beds are fine for this technique.

Roosterfish *(Nematistius pectoralis)*
COMMON & REGIONAL NAMES: *papagallo, pez de gallo, gallo*

GAME IDENTIFICATION & LOCATION OF FISHING REGIONS:
Both in English and Spanish, the roosterfish is named for its strange first dorsal fin, which looks to some observers like a cock's comb and to others like a rooster's flowing tail. Temperamentally, an even closer parallel exists between the fish and a fighting cock.

The species is generally regarded as a carangid—like jacks, amberjacks, and pompanos—but is relegated to a family of its own by some biologists. Its thick, tapered body, sloping forehead, and deeply lunate tail are like that of an amberjack (which see), and it has the same dark nuchal band—an inverted V that runs obliquely from the upper jaw to the first dorsal fin. However, it lacks the keeled scutes that mark the sides or caudal peduncle of a typical carangid, and its first dorsal fin is a unique plume of seven extremely long, completely separated spines, sweeping up and back. They rest in a groove along the back when the fish is traveling or hunting but rise when it becomes excited, as when

it chases prey or fights a rod. They are blue-black or blue-green, usually with whitish bands.

The tail and other fins are dusky. A long, low second dorsal fin, separate from the first, reaches the caudal peduncle. The anal fin does not run as far forward from the peduncle; it is narrow, with a somewhat widened lobe at the front. The pectoral fins are long, pointed, and marked with a black basal spot. The back, close to the fins, is black, dark blue, or blue-green. The sides grade from silvery blue to silvery white, sometimes with a golden wash, often with gleams of pink. Usually the head and the shoulder forward of the dorsal fin are saddled with two blackish stripes, and two longer stripes curve down and rearward from the base of the first dorsal fin. These bands fade away after death.

Roosterfish.

Roosterfish caught in the surf or near it generally weigh from 5 pounds or less to perhaps 15. Those caught a little farther out average closer to 30. At places noted for dense concentrations of big roosterfish—for example, La Paz, near the tip of Baja California—40- and 50-pounders often circle the boats. The current record was set by a fish caught at La Paz on June 1, 1960; taken on line testing 30 pounds, it weighed 114 pounds.

The species is found only along the western coasts of the Americas, primarily from Peru to Baja, with the greatest numbers dwelling off Ecuador. In spring and summer, a northward shift brings small populations of roosterfish to southernmost California. In more tropical waters, they can be caught all year, but with seasonal peaks. Loose schools or aggregations, sometimes numbering in the hundreds, appear off Baja in October, become most plentiful in January and February, and begin to leave in April, some of them moving farther north.

FISH HABITAT & FEEDING BEHAVIOR—ANGLING TACTICS:
Since roosterfish larvae have been collected off Costa Rica in July, the species probably breeds in spring or early summer, among other times. Apart from that, virtually nothing is known about its life history. The young travel in rather tight schools, the adults in looser groups. They feed on small fish, often in the surf, and are most abundant over sandy bottoms from the surf zone out to moderate depths. While chasing schools of prey along the top, they leap and skim over the water like skipjacks or dolphin. A roosterfish in hot pursuit of a fleeing victim erects its dorsal spines—or "flashes its comb," as coastal fishermen say.

To locate roosters, trollers and sometimes shore fishermen watch for surface activity and wheeling, diving sea birds taking advantage of harried bait schools. If roosterfish are in the vicinity, they may be as close to shore as the breakers and are seldom more than half a mile out. Within casting distance for waders, the most productive areas are bays and stretches of mild surf. Better fishing is likely a little farther out. Though the action is fastest in early morning (regardless of tide), it can be good all day.

Off southern California and a few Mexican ports, a common method is to troll a grunt or any abundant fish of like size—about half a pound, or 9 inches long—on a short-shanked 6/0 hook. (Grunt species on the Pacific coast are too small to qualify as desirable game, but they make excellent baits.) Various strip baits are also used. But in most Mexican waters, artificials are trolled, drifted, or cast. Lures include plugs, wobbling spoons, and feathers. Fluorescent red-and-silver-finished wobblers are effective, as are pearly-headed feather jigs.

Few rooster fishermen have used a fly rod to skip a streamer or popper-streamer, but there is no reason not to use the same fly tackle that would be appropriate for yellowtail or other species of amberjack (which see). However, for anyone who has not encountered roosters—or at least played dolphin on very light tackle—marlin equipment with line testing 50 pounds might be more advisable. Experienced roosterfishermen like to troll with spinning rods and monofilament testing 15 or 20 pounds; for casting in a gentle surf, they reduce the line test by about half.

When feeding roosters are found, the boat can circle them, trolling at 6 knots or faster. A more exciting method is to approach them slowly, then drift in from upwind. During the brief period before the roosters move on, cast or drifted offerings get immediate strikes. Since the fish need time to turn food around into their relatively small mouths, a little slack is yielded after the strike. The hook is set forcefully when a fish begins to move off, carrying line. After several hard, leaping dolphinlike runs, it may sound. At that point it is as near to surrender as was the captain of the *Bonhomme Richard* when he had not yet begun to fight.

Sailfish *(Istiophorus platypterus)*
COMMON & REGIONAL NAMES: *billfish*

GAME IDENTIFICATION & LOCATION OF FISHING REGIONS: By the time an angler has caught a few sails, he may begin to think he knows their ways. He is no longer startled to see a high, glistening dorsal fin loom behind a rigged mullet skipping astern, or feel the panicky jerking of a live subsurface bait—a blue runner darting frantically before the inevitable. With the reel's drag on a properly light setting, perhaps he grins confidently if he sees the long, slender spear of the billfish pierce the air and slap down. Experience entitles him to believe it is the familiar bill-slap of a sailfish, the awaited move, to be parried by drop-back. He is ready to throw the reel into free-spool, count ten while the sailfish picks up the stunned prey and moves off, then brake the reel and set the hook.

Maybe he is right, maybe not.

Sometimes a sailfish swats a bait in playfulness rather than hunger, and picks it up (if at all) only in response to teasing. Tense expectation can subside into exasperation. And every so often a hungry sail "crash-strikes"—grabbing a slowly or steadily moving bait without any preliminaries. Caught off guard, the angler has hardly begun his countdown when the turning spool abruptly accelerates and—if the fish has not hooked itself—the time to strike is now. If the barb is driven in, the sail will leap and run.

The species is a relatively small istiophorid, one of the sleek billfishes of the warm seas. For many years biologists believed it to be three species rather than one—an Atlantic sailfish, an eastern Pacific sailfish, and a third variety in the Indo-Pacific area. The sails caught along the lower Pacific coasts of the Americas were designated *Istiophorus greyi.* But now all races are recognized as *I. platypterus,* a single species, regionally differing only in size and, to a slight degree, in the intensity of coloration. The Atlantic breed, ranging through the Gulf of Mexico, the Caribbean, and along the Atlantic coast from Massachusetts to Brazil, is fairly common from the Carolinas to Venezuela and most abundant in the warm waters edging the Gulf Stream. It also occurs (less plentifully) in the eastern Atlantic and Mediterranean. Fine sailfishing areas include the Gulf, Florida, Puerto Rico, Bermuda, and—during the warm months—Cape Hatteras. The best fishing can be had in December and January off Florida's east coast.

However, some of the largest sails are caught in more exotic waters. The sporting record for Atlantic sailfish was set in March, 1974, off Angola, by a specimen weighing an ounce over

Pacific sailfish.

128 pounds and measuring 8 feet, 10¼ inches from tail to spear tip. The average length in American waters is about 4 to 7 feet, the average weight 25 to 60 pounds or so. Because the Pacific form tends to be about twice as large, the International Game Fish Association lists it separately. The Pacific record, dating back to February, 1947, is 221 pounds. Caught off the Galapagos Islands, that fish was 10 feet, 9 inches long. In the American Pacific, sailfish range from Peru to Baja, with strays appearing to the north.

In appearance, the most impressive characteristic of any sailfish is its sail. This enormous first dorsal fin rises just behind the head and extends most of the way back toward the caudal peduncle. Though the first spine is long, the fin does not peak there, nor does it curve or taper evenly. As a rule it dips a little, then rises to its highest point about midway back before dipping irregularly to a terminus just a bit ahead of a second, very small dorsal fin. For most of its length, it is substantially higher than the body is deep—at least half again as high at the apex. When swimming fast, the fish reduces surface drag by lowering this black-speckled royal-blue sail, folding it down into a long furrow at its base. But the sail rises again reflexively at moments of excitement, when the fish also "lights up"—becomes more brilliant in color.

Its bill is long, slender, and sometimes slightly down-curved, its mouth large and toothless, its body a long, thin slab with a prominent lateral line, its tail wide and lunate. Its caudal peduncle has a double keel on each side. Its pectoral fins are fairly long and pointed, its pelvic fins extremely thin and longer than those of any other billfish. It has two widely separated anal fins, the rear one little more than a finlet. The back is dark blue, ranging from cobalt to blue-violet. The sides and belly are silver or silvery white. Pale bluish spots usually run down the sides.

FISH HABITAT & FEEDING BEHAVIOR—ANGLING TACTICS:
Foot-long sailfish, miniatures of the adults, are common on Florida's coasts from August to October. Sails spawn in the open sea from spring to fall, and a good-sized female may release up to four million floating eggs, perhaps more. The surviving hatchlings, a small fraction of that number, are stubby animalcules, about an eighth of an inch long, with big spiny heads and short jaws. When these larvae reach about an inch in length, their sails and disproportionate upper jaws begin to show, though at that stage they still

have teeth. Their growth rate is extremely fast. An angler who catches a skinny 4-foot sailfish can assume that he has encountered a healthy yearling. He should, of course, release it. Most sailfish are released unless they are of trophy size.

In Florida's waters, where sails have been rather extensively studied, almost a fifth of their diet consists of squid and other cephalopods, particularly the paper nautilus. Discounting insignificant items, the remainder consists of fish.

There is a fairly widespread misconception that all billfish hunt primarily at the surface. Sails often do—especially along reef edges where the water is relatively shallow—yet they probably spend equal time foraging both in the middle depths and close to the bottom. All the same, methods for catching sailfish are those that catch marlin (which see) but with several variations. In either case, trolling from charter boats and private cruisers is most often a social activity, with two lines clipped to outriggers at port and starboard, two flat lines trolled from the stern between them. Sometimes a stern clip holds a bit of flat line slack to achieve the same drop-back provided by an outrigger when a fish slaps and then retrieves a bait. An experienced sailfisherman

Atlantic sailfish.

may use a fighting chair only as a comfortable base for watching baits, consuming refreshments, and sunning himself. Even in the Pacific, where sailfish tend to be big, skilled anglers prefer to leave the chair and stand up while playing a sail in order to gain greater mobility and rod control. They are likely to don a gimbaled or socketed fighting belt to hold and brace the rod butt. They are also likely to request no assistance—no boat maneuvering.

For average clients (those he calls tourists), a skipper usually has trolling rods with 4/0 reels and line testing 50 pounds. Light tackle, for the more adept, typically consists of a 5½-foot fiberglass trolling rod with a 6-ounce tip, a 3/0 revolving-spool reel utilizing a star or quadrant-lever drag, and about 300 yards of Dacron or monofilament line testing 20 pounds, spooled over another couple of hundred yards of backing.

Leaders are usually wire. Among fishermen who release their sails quickly by snapping rather than snipping the wire, no. 7 is favored; no. 9 is more reliable in summer, when blue marlin may seize a bait. Leaders tend to be long—about 15 feet of wire at the end of a substantial loop of doubled line, rigged as for marlin. A bit of the wire is used to rig the bait on a 7/0 to 9/0 hook.

Though spoons and feathers are occasionally used, natural baits take far more sailfish. Sometimes a strip of tuna belly or a tail-and-belly strip of mullet is skipped along the surface. However, the most popular surface technique is to troll fairly fast with a whole dead 6-inch mullet or balao.

Either of these baits, properly rigged, will skip naturally along the top, yet sailfish sometimes shy away from surface-skippers in heavily fished waters. Apparently, released fish remember their mistakes. Slower, subsurface trolling with live baits—primarily blue runners—has therefore gained great popularity.

So has fly fishing with the same rod, reel, backing, line, and leader recommended for marlin. Flies run the gamut from bonefish types to flowing plumes on tandem hooks. Though neither the color nor the size seems to be very critical, one general type has accounted for a great many catches in most locales—a white streamer of 6-inch saddle hackles with a few flashing strips of Mylar, tied on a very sharp 5/0 hook. As with marlin, a hookless teaser is trolled (or dangled from a fishing kite). The most effective teaser may be a surface bait or a 10-inch rubber or soft plastic squid, and two of them trolled at once double the attraction. When one is charged, the other is hauled in. The one under attack is yanked just out of reach, tauntingly, until the fly can be cast. The sailfish usually seizes the fly without slapping it.

Assuming the angler has made a good cast, he must now set the hook hard, several times, and then give a lot more line without tangling it. Even with a hefty trolling rod he would make no foolhardy attempt to slow an early run; unless flustered, he would virtually ignore the reel and enjoy the spectacle, working only to grant no slack. Later—twenty minutes or three hours later —he should be able to bill and release his sailfish.

Sculpin (Cottidae)

COMMON & REGIONAL NAMES: Names in common usage denote various species and will be included in the descriptions of those species.

GAME IDENTIFICATION & LOCATION OF FISHING REGIONS: To most inland fishermen, a sculpin is a spiny but minnowlike model for a number of streamers and other baitfish imitations. Most freshwater species are only 2 to 4 inches long, but a few saltwater cottids—members of the sculpin family—commonly weigh 2 to 5 pounds and occasionally grow to 25 pounds and a length of 2½ feet. Primarily carnivorous bottom fishes, most of them inhabit arctic waters but some extend the range to the tropics. Those that have any sporting significance are most abundant in California's inshore waters.

They are strange-looking creatures, rather like the rockfishes (which see), and distinguished by a number of features: big, toothy mouths; a bony plate from the cheek to the eye; one or more spines on the preopercle—the facial bone at the forward edge of the gill cover; a large head, usually broad and flat, with the eyes set high and close together; fleshy cirri or papillae on the bodies of some species; a large anal papilla marking the males of a few species; protectively mottled, variable colors, strongly modified by environment, and with sexual dimorphism in a few sculpins; a complete or partial absence of scales on some; fairly large dorsal fins, with a deep notch or complete separation between the spiny and soft-rayed segments; large, winglike pectoral fins; and a large anal fin with no spines but with a spiny appearance because of its deeply scalloped membrane.

In the North Atlantic, from arctic regions down to New England and sometimes farther south, is a species called the shorthorn sculpin *(Myoxocephalus scorpius),* which can attain a length of 2 feet or so. It is a drab fish with a square tail, a large anal fin and high dorsal fins, short spines—"horns"—on the snout, cheeks, and head, papillae on the sides and at the male's anus, pale spotting and mottling, and a pale streak along the thorny-looking lateral line. Like most sculpins, it subsists chiefly on crustaceans and small fish. It spawns in fall and winter, in deep water, but during the summer becomes an inshore resident and is occasionally taken on cut bait.

On the West Coast, too, spawning takes place from autumn to spring, but has little effect on the sculpin fishing, which remains good all year, especially in the waters off Monterey and Santa Barbara. The most important game species is the cabezon *(Scorpaenichthys marmoratus),* which deposits a mass of greenish eggs sometimes numbering 100,000. The roe of the cabezon (and some other sculpins) is toxic, but its flesh is excellent.

"Cabezon" (sometimes spelled "cabezone") is an apt name meaning "large head." The species is also known as bullhead, marbled sculpin, giant marbled sculpin, and blue cod. It is one

Cabezon.

of the big sculpins, averaging 2 to 5 pounds and with a potential weight of 25. Its tail is slightly rounded, its pectoral fins very large and wide-based. Its skin is thick and scaleless, with wrinkles or flaplike cirri on the snout and above the eyes. Spines adorn the preopercle and the broad head. The mouth, big and toothy even for a sculpin, has a translucent blue-green lining. Body color, depending on the local environment, varies from green or gray to reddish-brown or sometimes red, with black mottling and big, pale marbled areas. This species ranges from lower Alaska to central Baja. It is always found on or very near the bottom, from the inshore shallows to depths of thirty or thirty-five fathoms.

A fish of similar size—though slimmer and rarely as heavy —is the great sculpin *(M. polyacanthocephalus),* which ranges from Washington to the Bering Sea, off western Alaska, and is regionally known as the bull sculpin or barred sculpin. It has a slender tail, squarish or slightly rounded, and short, blunt spines on the snout and preopercular bone. Small, fleshy papillae are scattered over the body, which is dark olive to blackish above, paling to cream or white below, with creamy bands across the back, black mottling or bars on all the fins except the pelvics, and usually some mottling on the sides.

FISH HABITAT & FEEDING BEHAVIOR—ANGLING TACTICS: In sculpin fishing, what is good for cabezon is good for any other locally available species. The cabezon is a fair fighter and capable of fast, darting movement when escaping danger, but normally it is a sluggard that lies in wait for prey instead of chasing it. Though it prefers to hug a rocky or sandy bottom or to hide in an algal thicket, it is not very selective regarding topography. Every so often, a big cabezon is taken in deep waters by an angler trolling for other game. As a rule, still-fishing or drifting is more productive. It is done throughout the tidal zone and at kelp beds, where lingcod, rockfish, and other bottom-dwellers are caught.

The type of tackle is unimportant; it includes baitcasting, surf, and trolling rods, light spinning gear, and even handlines. Neither is there any rule regarding hooks, except that they ought to be fairly large since a sculpin of any sort has a sizable mouth. The only tackle requirements are a sinker to put the hook near bottom and a wire leader to withstand the teeth of these and other bottom-dwellers. Because a sculpin can puncture an angler's fingers with its teeth or spines, it should be handled carefully.

Some fishermen jig live or whole baits, mainly because any fair-sized fish in the habitat may come to them. Some dance a metal jig about, and this, too, will take several species including cabezon. However, cut bait is best. The most reliable offering is a piece of crab, mussel, clam, fish, or a sea worm, jigged indolently to awaken the hunger of relatively torpid fish.

Sea Bass *(Centropristis striata* and *Stereolepis gigas)*
COMMON & REGIONAL NAMES: Names in common usage apply to one species or the other—or to one growth stage of one species—and will be included in the description thereof.

GAME IDENTIFICATION & LOCATION OF FISHING REGIONS: The name sea bass can be used to denote any of the numerous saltwater serranids—groupers, kelp and sand bass, stripers, and so on. The varieties treated in this section are the black sea bass *(Centropristis striata)* of the Atlantic and the giant sea bass *(Stereolepis gigas)* of the Pacific, the two species most commonly called sea bass. In some locales, the black sea bass is also known as blackfish or black will. Anglers often refer to small ones, weighing up to a pound or so, as pin bass; large male blacks develop a pronounced shoulder-rise just behind the head and are nicknamed humpbacks. If the black sea bass and the giant variety were not separated by a continent, popular nomenclature might cause confusion in printed references, for the giant sea bass is also called black sea bass by some anglers and writers. Others call it California jewfish.

In appearance, there is no cause for confusion between a black sea bass and a giant sea bass. The former averages 1½ to 2 pounds, and seldom weighs more than 5. Among the mature giant sea bass caught on rod and reel, the average weight is between 70 and 90 pounds, and the species grows much larger.

Yet the black sea bass has a greater following and is a better gamefish, at least in the traditional sense. It is fairly plentiful, inhabits accessible waters, strikes jigs or baits eagerly, fights well on light tackle, and provides delicate white meat for baking, poaching, steaming, or deep-frying. Ranging from Massachusetts to Florida, most abundantly from New York's Long Island to North Carolina's Cape Hatteras, it is one of the most popular bot-

tom-fishes of the upper Atlantic coast. It winters in deep offshore waters (where it is harvested by trawlers) but passes the warmer months inshore. The run to the coasts, sounds, and bays begins in May. By midsummer the inshore population of sea bass is at a peak; it disappears by October or early November. The greatest numbers are caught off Cape Cod and along the shores of Long Island, New Jersey, Delaware, and North Carolina.

The black sea bass has a moderately stout, typically ser-ranid body; large, almost pendulous anal and pelvic fins; broad wedge-shaped pectorals; and copious dorsals. The forward dor-sal, armed with stiff, sharp-tipped spines, dips to a juncture with the soft-rayed segment. The topmost ray of the rounded tail is very long, often becoming a trailing filament that gives the edge of the tail an S-shape. Both jaws are equipped with canine teeth. The mouth is large, the snout flat-topped and slightly pointed. A single sharp spine grows near the pointed edge of each gill cover. The upper body is dark gray or dusky brown, often appearing blue-black as it comes glistening from the water. It pales somewhat below, and the bases of the scales, being lighter than the edges, sometimes form pale spots or bars. The maximum size of this fish is probably about 2 feet and a weight of 8 pounds.

The giant sea bass reaches a length of about 7 feet and a weight of more than 550 pounds. The largest specimen taken on rod and reel was a 563½-pounder caught off southern California's Anacapa Island in 1968. This species ranges primarily from the

Black sea bass.

Gulf of California south to Humboldt Bay and Guadalupe Island, with small numbers wandering north to lower California. Because the fishing is exceptionally good about halfway down the outer Baja coast, large and luxurious party boats out of San Diego and neighboring ports make five- to eight-day trips to renowned spots like Uncle Sam Bank, which lies 495 miles down the peninsula and 44 miles out from shore. The vessels generally carry twenty-eight to thirty-eight passengers, and a trip is counted successful if the anglers bring back forty to one hundred giant sea bass—a few of which may weigh 100 pounds or more—plus large numbers of yellowtail, corvina, barracuda, and assorted other game. June is the best month; the fishing is good from May through July.

A typical adult giant sea bass, weighing 70 or 80 pounds, has the thick contours and joined dorsals that characterize groupers (which see). It is a blackish or dark greenish-brown fish with a white patch on the throat and a smaller, vaguer one under the base of the more or less square tail.

FISH HABITAT & FEEDING BEHAVIOR—ANGLING TACTICS: When black sea bass come to the Atlantic seaboard's inshore zone in spring, most of the small and medium ones forage in bays and sounds. The bigger ones are usually caught in more open seas, around rocky heads, ledges, banks, and offshore reefs. They prefer a hard bottom strewn with rocks, wreckage, or comparable objects that accumulate barnacles, mussels, and other mollusks—a primary food source. For the same reason, they gather around pilings and piers, even though they normally like clear, fairly deep water. In channels and bays they are caught where the depth is at least fifteen feet; in the open waters where anglers speak of "deep-sea fishing," they are taken off rocky beds as far down as sixteen or seventeen fathoms.

In the bays, a fine-wire hook is often baited with a large, live "mummichog" (killifish) hooked upward through both lips and still-fished or drifted. Equally common baits for "pin bass" or slightly larger ones include a bloodworm, sandworm, or piece of clam, squid, or shedder crab. For ocean-run fish, the best bait is a "skimmer" (sea clam), hardshell clam, or piece of shedder crab. As the sea bass is large-mouthed, a fairly big chunk is impaled on a sizable hook—1/0 in the bays, 2/0 to 5/0 offshore. As a rule, one hook is attached to the line just above the sinker and another a little higher. For big fish, some anglers use wire leaders; but many sea-bass fishermen merely attach snells or unsnelled hooks directly to the line. If the bass become locally rig-shy, 2-foot leaders are attached, 12 to 18 inches apart.

Quiet water or a slack tide quickens the feeding activity of black sea bass. Still-fishing or slow drifting is the favored method in protected as well as open waters. Quite a few bass are caught from piers. Sometimes a 3- or 4-ounce chromed diamond jig produces as many strikes as bait. It should have a 3/0 or 4/0 hook.

In the bays, where a 3-ounce bank sinker is usually sufficient to keep a bait down, all kinds of tackle are used. Light spinning gear is, of course, the choice of those more interested in sport than in hauling up meat as fast as possible. Where the tide is strong or the water deep, however, sinker weights of 8 ounces or more may be required. To avoid the loss of sinkers or whole rigs in bottom debris, some anglers substitute sandbags tied on with string. The weight of the terminal tackle plus the hoped-for weight of a big fish calls for a medium spinning or baitcasting outfit. The line's test strength generally runs from 8 to 15 pounds.

A large black sea bass is likely to strike hard enough to hook itself. For that matter, so will a pin bass attacking a live mummichog or a jig. But the small and medium bass in the bays tend to nibble at cut bait, toying with it. The angler, feeling a series of twitches, keeps his line almost taut, letting it out as needed until he feels the weight of the fish, then giving the rod a short yank.

The technique for giant sea bass is rather more exotic. Since a typical party boat lacks the fighting chairs of chartered craft, the passengers often wear shoulder harnesses and socketed rod belts. The rod is long and hefty, the reel a 4/0 to 6/0 revolving spool with the drag set tight, carrying plenty of 80-pound-test line. Some anglers prefer to use no leader, but others attach 6 feet of nylon-coated braided wire testing about 100 pounds. A pound to a pound and a half of sinkers or seine weights may be needed. A bait weighing up to 5 pounds is impaled on a big tuna hook—8/0 to 10/0. Sometimes a live Sierra mackerel is used, but the fore or aft end of a barracuda is just as effective.

Early morning may bring the fastest action, yet anglers on party boats can fish day and night if they have sufficient stamina. The bait is held just off bottom, usually at 60- to 150-foot depths. During the warm months, giant sea bass move from deeper water to spawn at reefs and banks. With fathometers and flag buoys, the boats locate and mark the high points of the banks, for most strikes come at distances of 50 to 80 yards from these points. A strike is usually felt as a thump followed by a couple of sharp raps and then a tremendous pull. If the angler can budge his rod, he sets the hook forcefully several times. The runs are not fast, just powerful. The contest would appeal to a weight lifter. Undeterred by excess weight, an angler on a small private boat now and then hooks one so heavy that he must tow it to port.

Sharks *(Selachii)*

COMMON & REGIONAL NAMES: Names in common usage denote various species and will be included in the descriptions of those species.

GAME IDENTIFICATION & LOCATION OF FISHING REGIONS:
Though their danger to man has been exaggerated, sharks are a menace in some waters and, whenever encountered, they exemplify the sea's primordial violence. A drop of blood in the water may be enough to bring them, circling, often ravenous even if they have just fed. They are all muscle and hunger and teeth, band behind band of teeth. Yet sharks are held in contempt by many anglers who have never deliberately fished for them with appropriate tackle. Few sharks are a fighting match for stout broadbill or tuna-trolling gear. To sportsmen seeking marlin, swordfish, tuna, or tarpon, they can be a bait-mangling nuisance; far worse, the distress of any hooked gamefish is a stimulus to attack, and a fair-sized shark can chop a hooked tuna in half.

Shark fishing for its own sake can be intensely thrilling, especially if light tackle is used. In recent years, its growing popularity has nurtured an awareness that sharks are valuable predators and scavengers, desirable components of a balanced marine ecosystem. Many of the sharks caught today are released unless they are wanted as trophies or for meat. The flesh of a few species is toxic, but that of the common varieties taken off the American coasts is wholesome and tasty. In some cases it has a high urea content that imparts an odor of ammonia, but this evaporates if the meat is skinned and stored in a cooler for a few days.

About 250 species comprise the order Selachii, an ancient, primitive group distinguished in part by a cartilaginous skeleton

rather than true bone cells, and by a rough skin with tiny placoid scales whose structure resembles that of teeth. They have no swim bladder and, unlike the "higher," or bony fishes, no cover over the gill clefts. Most have large, very sharp, more or less triangular incisors, in many cases with serrated edges, set in several series.

A few species are as flat-bodied as skates. Some are tapered like the mackerels. Most are torpedo-shaped. They have high, short first dorsal fins, usually about midway back, and small second dorsals set far aft. The tail generally has a lunate curve but is asymmetrical, the upper lobe being longer than the lower one. On the rear or underside of the upper lobe, near the tip, there is usually a notched flap or enlargement—like a small auxiliary rudder. The snout projects far beyond the large mouth and it has two nostrils, which do not connect with the mouth. The many species vary in size from 2-foot cat sharks and dogfish to the 50- or 60-foot whale shark, which outweighs all marine creatures except some whales. A few sharks are fairly colorful, but most are gray or brownish with pale or white undersides. Their eyesight is poor (and limited by a frontal blind spot between the widely placed eyes), yet they are magnificently equipped for their specialized way of life. Some pelagic species are fairly adept at sight-hunting, but their chief prey-locating endowment is an acute sense of smell. By odor alone, they can trace prey and aim their open jaws unerringly as they spurt after it. They also hear low-frequency vi-

Shortfin mako shark.

brations and additionally sense them via nerves in the lateral-line system. Any shark, even a small one, should be treated cautiously.

Most sharks—and particularly those that can be considered gamefish—are fierce predators that devour fish, crustaceans, squid, sea birds, turtles, and seals, as well as carrion. Some also eat other shark species or their own kind. Most are exclusively marine, but bull sharks have been caught 160 miles inland from the Gulf of Mexico, in Louisiana's Atchafalaya River, and several other varieties enter large African and Asian rivers. One species is landlocked in Lake Nicaragua. Distribution is worldwide, though the majority of species inhabit the tropical-subtropical belt. Of the many varieties caught in American waters, seven will be described here. They are the ones recognized as game by the International Game Fish Association and listed in the association's compilation of world records.

Best by far in terms of sporting qualities is the mako, or shortfin mako *(Isurus oxyrhinchus),* also called the bonito shark or sharpnose mackerel shark. It is the fastest shark in the sea, and the only real jumper when hooked. Often it is seen at the surface, deceptively indolent as it basks with its dorsal fin above water, but it is swift and powerful enough to fill its belly with swordfish, tuna, and bonito, as well as mackerel and herring. Though reported in thirty-foot depths off Cat Cay in the Bahamas, it prefers the deeper blue offshore waters. Most of the shallow-zone sightings have been cases of mistaken identity; in color and conformation the mako shark looks rather like the porbeagle, and it has long, slender teeth that protrude from the mouth like those of several sand sharks. Its back and upper sides are blue or blue-gray. Below a rather abrupt demarcation, the sides are light, almost silvery, and the belly is white. The snout is sharply pointed. As with all of the family Lamnidae—the mackerel sharks—the body has a mackerel shape with a fairly slim peduncle, keeled on each side; a large tail with the upper lobe only slightly larger than the lower; a high first dorsal fin about midway back; and wide, sickle-shaped pectoral fins. Of all shark meat, mako is best. Mako steaks have sometimes been sold as swordfish steaks.

Makos are caught in all warm and temperate oceans. Fishing for them has become popular as far north as the New Jersey coast and Montauk, New York, though really big specimens are usually caught in warmer regions. An average adult is 6 to 8 feet long. The species can grow to more than 12 feet and weigh over half a ton. The largest yet caught in the Atlantic was a 786-pounder taken near Bimini. The world record was set in New Zealand waters in 1970—1,061 pounds, 12 feet, 2 inches long.

The closely related white shark, or maneater *(Carcharodon carcharias),* is the largest of the game species and the most dangerous of all sharks. An average white is the size of the biggest mako. The record on rod and reel has stood since 1959, when it was set off South Australia by a 16-foot, 10-inch fish weighing 2,664 pounds. The largest ever authenticated was another Australian fish, 36½ feet long. Just inside the Fourteen-Mile Bank near Oxnard, California, an 18-foot, 2-inch white shark, estimated at 4,100 pounds, was harpooned in 1976. Its name notwithstanding, a white shark is likely to be slate-blue, lead-gray, brownish, or almost black above, shading to dirty white below. The tips of the pectoral fins are blackish, and some specimens have a dark spot just behind each pectoral. The teeth are broad, serrated triangles. White sharks roam all warm and temperate oceans but are not common anywhere.

A member of the same family is the porbeagle shark *(Lamna nasus),* also known as the mackerel shark or the blue shark. It is not much of a fighter by comparison with the mako. It sometimes hunts in waters as deep as eighty fathoms but, unlike the mako, it may idle close inshore during the summer. With a blue, bluish-gray, or blackish body paling to gray and then white, it looks much like a mako but its second dorsal fin is directly above the anal fin, whereas the mako's is set slightly ahead of the anal fin, and the porbeagle has narrower teeth, with a sharp cusp at each base. A typical adult is 5 or 6 feet long. A record of 369 pounds was broken in 1969 off England's Channel Islands by an 8-foot 430-pounder.

The name blue shark, or great blue shark, a misnomer for the porbeagle, properly applies to *Prionaca glauca,* a member of the largest family in tropical and temperate seas—the Carcharinidae, or requiem sharks. These fish have a side-keeled peduncle, a big first dorsal fin set far forward of the pelvic fins, and an extremely asymmetrical tail whose upper lobe is a long, fleshy sickle two to three times larger than the lower one and with a pronounced notch near the tip. They are relatively slim, long-bodied, long-finned sharks with pointed snouts. The blue, in particular, has extremely long, flipperlike pectorals. Its first dorsal is set roughly amidships—farther back than that of other requiem sharks. Its teeth are serrated. Its tail, fins, and upper parts are a vivid blue, its belly white. At maturity it is 7 or 8 feet long, but there have been reports of 20-foot blues. Two 410-pounders, both caught off Rockport, Massachusetts, are listed as a tie for the record. The first, taken on September 1, 1960, had a length of 11 feet, 6 inches, a girth of 4 feet, 4 inches; the second, caught on August 17, 1967, was 4 inches shorter and a half-inch stouter. Blue sharks inhabit tropical, subtropical, and temperate seas, both far out and in continental waters. Often they are seen at the surface—especially in the northern latitudes—swimming slowly, with their dorsal fins and long tails showing.

Most requiem sharks are not as aggressive as their family name implies, but the blue is dangerous and the tiger shark *(Galeocerdo cuvieri)* is notoriously so. Ranging through the world's warm and tropical oceans, it is all the more menacing because it is a coastal species that often invades the shallows. The upper lobe of its tail is thick and long, the keels prominent, the snout short and pointed, the teeth recurved, serrated, and notched at the inner margin. The color is brownish-gray above, lighter gray below, and the fins are almost blackish. A young tiger shark, up to 5 or 6 feet long, has dark blotches and tiger stripes on the sides and back, often extending onto the fins and tail. The stripes dim with age. The record tiger, caught in 1964 at Cherry Grove, South Carolina, was a 1,780-pounder, 13 feet, 10½ inches long.

Even longer-tailed than the requiem group is the thresher family, Alopiidae, numbering only two members and only one in American waters. The thresher shark *(Alopias vulpinus)* has a thick, fleshy, upper tail lobe that sometimes exceeds the body length of a fairly young specimen. Ranging through the world's warm oceans, they sometimes stray north in summer. Good fighters, they often weigh over 500 pounds—enough to warrant swordfish tackle.

The upper body of a thresher is gray or brownish, sometimes with a blue tinge and sometimes blackish but very uniform. The belly is white, occasionally mottled with gray. The pectoral fins are very large—both long and broad. The record thresher was a 739-pound fish caught off New Zealand in 1975.

In 1974 the International Game Fish Association added hammerheads to its list of game sharks, stipulating no particular varieties but only the family designation, Sphyrnidae, because the number of species is in dispute. One large species and several smaller ones frequent American waters. Hammerheads are gray, grayish-brown, or brown with pale or whitish bellies, broad pectoral fins, high first dorsals, and bodies and tails much like those of requiem sharks. Their heads, however, are grotesquely unique —flattened and extended to the sides in the shape of a mallet or double-headed hammer. The eyes are located on the outer sides toward the front, the nostrils on the front edge, the mouth underneath and at the rear. What advantage spurred the evolution of this structure is unknown, but it does widen a hammerhead's peripheral vision (while also increasing the frontal blind spot) and it tightens the shark's turning radius, perhaps enabling it to whip around faster to snatch prey.

Gloved crewman handling leader on hammerhead.

The record hammerhead, caught in 1975 off Jacksonville, Florida, had a length of 14 feet, 4 inches and a weight of 703 pounds. Though the IGFA omitted any species designation, Floridian shark fishermen knew it to be a great hammerhead *(Sphyrna mokarran),* the largest variety—the only one known to reach a length of 15 feet. It is common in the Atlantic as far north as Cape Hatteras and in the Pacific up to Point Conception, California.

FISH HABITAT & FEEDING BEHAVIOR—ANGLING TACTICS:
Sharks grow slowly and bear few young, yet they remain plentiful, in part because they have not been depleted by overharvesting or other human activities and in part because their large, precocial young have a high survival rate. Sharks reproduce by internal fertilization. At the inner edges of the male's pelvic fins, paired sexual organs called claspers are inserted into the female's cloaca. Some species are viviparous; that is, the young are born live after placental nourishment. In oviparous shark species, the females eject eggs that have filamentous tendrils to clutch grass, algae, or debris. Most species are ovoviparous; the young are born live after hatching from eggs within the mother. Broods are small, individual embryos large. Spawning seems to have no effect on fishing, but in northern waters sharks tend to be abundant only in summer.

At mako-fishing centers such as those at Montauk and along the Jersey coast, charter skippers and private boatmen usually attract sharks by chumming. If no particularly productive area is known, they may simply try their luck in waters of about fifteen fathoms. However, a good location is one that holds bonito, school tuna, or mackerel. In other regions, the best waters may be over concentrations of bottom-feeders. If sharks are seen "finning," a tactic worth trying is to drift or slowly troll a strip or whole menhaden, mackerel, or bluefish. Whole squid is also good.

But chumming beforehand is the surest way. The chum can be scattered chunks of squid, a trail of live shrimp, or, best of all, ground menhaden—more familiar as "bunker" or "moss-bunker" on the upper Atlantic Coast. In some ports, five-gallon tins of frozen ground bunker are sold.

Only for the largest sharks in exotic waters does one need massive trolling rods and reels and cable-strong line. For the common sharks, American fishermen now use ordinary boat rods with line testing 50 pounds where very large fish may hit, 20 to 30 pounds where typical makos or anything comparable can be expected. To withstand shark teeth (and the abrasively granular skin of sharks) a 15-foot leader is recommended—something on the order of piano wire testing 190 pounds. Light marlin tackle does nicely with a 9/0 to 12/0 hook.

The bait must not sink far beneath the chum. To buoy it up, some anglers use a foot-long slab of cork with a shallow slit cut lengthwise so that the line can be pressed in. It is attached about 5 feet above the swivel. When a shark begins running and fighting, the cork usually pops away and bobs to the surface.

After grabbing a bait, a shark usually plays with it while swimming in circles or continues to feed through the chum slick. On rare occasions an angler can see the jaws close firmly, and then a quick, hard yank or two jaw-hooks the fish. Otherwise, the procedure is to let the shark take line for at least thirty seconds.

A confirmed shark fisherman plays a mako as he would play a sailfish, standing up and wearing a rod belt. In half an hour, he may bring a 100-pounder close enough so that he can see his swivel. But the shark may be more annoyed than exhausted. An angry shark is capable of leaping aboard if struck with a gaff too soon. A knowledgeable angler or skipper waits for the fish to roll on top before trying to release or gaff it. At that point it can be tagged—carefully, of course—and released by cutting the leader. The hook will rust away harmlessly. Or it can be brought in by using a flying gaff with a solidly snubbed rope. Gloves should be worn to prevent rope burn or leader cuts, and the gaff should be sunk deep into the fish in the pectoral area. A second gaff can then raise the tail, over which a rope can be looped. Sharks have been subdued by shooting them, clubbing them, or slitting their bellies. A safer method is to tail-loop and drag a shark backward, forcing torrents of water through the gills. It can then be hung from a gin pole and trussed securely.

These cautions are not meant to imply that there is any great danger in poling or wading for sharks on the southern tidal flats—unless the fisherman is dripping blood from a fresh cut. In the extreme shallows, the sharks are usually small, 50 pounds or less. Their fins and tails are easily spotted, and in slightly deeper water they can usually be seen even when completely submerged. They will hit a plug or fly if it is cast within a couple of feet from their heads—and moved in short strips past either eye. Spinning tackle will do, or an 8½- or 9-foot fly rod with a slow action for accurate casting. It ought to have at least 150 yards of Dacron backing on the reel, and a leader at least as long as the rod, tapered from a nylon butt section testing 30 or 40 pounds to a 12-pound section and then a wire shock tippet; customarily, the wire tests 18 or 27 pounds and is a foot long. Sharks will snap up large popping bugs and fluffy white silver-flashing 4- to 6-inch bucktails or streamers tied on 4/0 hooks.

When a shark takes a lure, it closes its mouth quickly on what it perceives as small prey, but it should be allowed to turn away before the hook is set. Timing is critical, since it should not be allowed to swallow. After that, one keeps a tight line but a light drag, increasing it only after the fish begins to tire. Under these circumstances, a shark can be released by popping the leader. Landing it can pop one's nerves instead. With the aid of a long-handled, swivel-headed gaff and a heavy club it can be boated. But if a man is wading, he had best walk his shark ashore.

Snapper *(Lutjanidae)*

COMMON & REGIONAL NAMES: Names in common usage denote various species and will be included in the descriptions of those species.

GAME IDENTIFICATION & LOCATION OF FISHING REGIONS:
Snappers are schooling bottom-dwellers with an enormous appetite for crustaceans and other prey found on or near the sea bed. Most species are quick to take natural baits though not easily tempted by lures. Even the small ones are exciting light-tackle fighters, and all are tasty. The fun of most snapper fishing lies in one basslike strike after another, but there are a few species, notably the gray snapper, whose appeal lies in their wariness. Over two hundred species populate the world's warm seas. On the West Coast, where several unrelated fish are called snappers, no true snappers enter United States waters. But more than a dozen frequent the Gulf of Mexico and the lower Atlantic coast.

Several inhabit very deep water where they are caught only occasionally by wire-line trollers, but some of the largest snappers are caught at moderate depths. A few of the big ones also come to the shallows, and many small-to-medium snappers are caught from docks, causeways, shorelines, and skiffs, especially in Florida and along the Gulf Coast all the way to southernmost Texas. Though most species average from 1 to 3 pounds, a few can attain a length of more than 30 inches and a weight of 30 or 40 pounds. One species grows still larger.

They resemble grunts and the smaller groupers (both of which see) and are often found with those bottom-feeders. They are most easily distinguished not by any single feature but by several in combination: pointed pectoral fins; a ten-spined first dorsal fused to the soft-rayed hind dorsal with little or no dip at the juncture; two or three spines in the anal fin; a slightly concave or forked tail; a large mouth; prominent eyes set high on the large head; bright colors; a distinct lateral line; and large scales. Some are toothier than others, but in general they have sharp, strong teeth in the jaws and smaller ones on the tongue and roof of the mouth. A number of snappers are hard to tell apart, and some of the predominantly reef-dwelling varieties can change color.

Most common in Florida's shallows, in the Bahamas, and along the Gulf Coast is the gray snapper *(Lutjanus griseus)*. To those of us who have fished its favorite Floridian abode it is better and more aptly known as the mangrove snapper. It does, however, frequent deep reef water as well as shallow mangrove tangles. It is abundant through the Caribbean and down to Brazil, and in the warm months sometimes ranges north to the Carolinas. A typical mangrove snapper weighs a pound, an occasional big one 3 pounds. Reports of rare 15-pounders generally involve fish caught in deep water, and in some cases may refer to another species mistaken for the gray. When inhabiting the shallows, this fish is gray, grayish-green, or slightly blue-tinged, with broad dusky bars running down its sides. The eyes are red, the anal fin rounded, the tail and dorsal fins gray, the lower fins pink or reddish. In deeper water, the body acquires a reddish tinge.

The largest is the cubera, or Cuban, snapper *(L. cyanopterus)*. It ranges from Florida to Brazil, with the greatest concentrations in Cuban waters. Cuberas weighing 50 pounds are not rare (though not very common, either); 80-pounders have been caught off southern Florida. The species is a toothy, dusky gray or greenish fish with a rounded anal fin, dark red eyes, and sometimes a reddish tinge. A small one is easily confused with the gray.

The mutton snapper, or muttonfish *(L. analis),* which sometimes strays north to Massachusetts and south to Brazil, is very common around Florida, in the Gulf, and through the Caribbean. The fishing for it is best in Texas and Florida. It averages 3 pounds and grows to a maximum of about 25. This one, primarily a reef-dweller, can change color somewhat. Basically, it is olive-green on the back, shading to orange or red on the sides, with seven broad, vertical bands that are darkly prominent when the fish rests on bottom or in cover but become dim or vanish when it swims in the open. Thin blue facial lines stream rearward from the snout and a black splotch adorns the lateral line below the hind portion of the dorsal fin, which is yellowish-olive with a reddish margin. The tail is red, sometimes turning olive on the upper lobe, and the other fins are red. The anal fin is pointed. Because this species is toothy and has sharp gill covers, a foot-long, inconspicuously brown, no. 1 wire leader is recommended.

Because the white flesh of the red snapper *(L. campechanus)* is so delicious baked or broiled, it is probably the most famous variety, certainly the most important commercially. Snapper boats operating out of Florida and Gulf Coast ports sell fishing places to anglers and then buy their catches. The red snapper ranges up to the Middle Atlantic states but is common only from Florida and the Gulf south to Brazil. It averages 5 pounds and

School of snappers.

fairly often exceeds 15; an occasional 30-inch lunker may weigh 35. The body, fins, and eyes are bright red, the belly pink. Sometimes the back has a bluish-green tinge. The anal fin is angular, the pectorals large. On the pectoral bases is a dark splotch.

FISH HABITAT & FEEDING BEHAVIOR—ANGLING TACTICS: In spawning and foraging behavior, snappers roughly resemble grunts. They enliven the winter fishing lull and provide good sport all year. Relatively small ones abound at the shoreline, penetrating bayous and tidal streams. Any kind of tackle can be used—the lighter, the better—whether fishing the shallows or the banks and reefs. A short wire leader is generally desirable, especially for the larger and toothier varieties, but mangrove snappers are too skittish for wire; they are often spooked by anything coarser than monofilament, and nothing much can be done about it except to inspect the leader and replace it when it frays. Hook sizes range from no. 6 or even smaller to 6/0 or even 8/0 when still-fishing with mullet or squid for big red snappers on the banks.

Night fishing is especially good for grays and chumming attracts all kinds. Still-fishing, drifting, or jigging with bait is always effective. Small, live baitfish of any locally plentiful kind will take snappers, but whole dead baitfish, cut baits, live shrimp, and pieces of crab or squid seem to be at least as productive.

Refinements depend on the locally prevalent snappers. Grays respond most eagerly to a live shrimp on a small hook,

Mutton snapper taken on jig.

though they will snatch a piece of hermit crab or any cut bait still-fished in the mangroves or over a reef. They will also take small spinners and pale or shrimp-colored flies moved slowly but jerkily near bottom. The mutton snapper, a very strong fighter, responds best to bottom-fished shrimp or cut mullet but also takes plugs, bucktails, streamers, and jigs. Plugs with silver flash are excellent. Unless the snappers have been raised with chum, lures should bounce bottom and be retrieved jerkily or trolled slowly. Casts must be long because mutton snappers tend to be boat-shy. Good spots include blue holes, reefs in fairly deep water, coral heads, rocks in the shallows, and channels or creeks with depths of ten to thirty feet. Sometimes snappers—particularly of this variety—forage on the flats and tail like bonefish (which see).

The cubera snapper, another strong fighter, enters surprisingly shallow water for a fish of its size. It is caught in coastal stream mouths and canals as well as in the ocean, and from depths of a few feet to twenty fathoms. It accepts the offerings that catch mutton snappers and is often taken by bottom-trolling.

The red snapper prefers twenty to sixty fathoms, sometimes more. As a rule, only small ones come to the shallows. Most of the Texas snapper banks are some thirty miles offshore, and in parts of the Gulf the best grounds are farther out. Fishing boats use fathometers to locate schools, though an angler trolling for other species may hook a big red snapper and discover an underrated battler. Red snappers are seldom fooled by artificials but will take any dead bait.

In the shallows, many small and medium snappers, even including the wary mangrove and mutton varieties, will pluck a weighted streamer or jig, a bonefish fly, almost any pale tuft of fur, and even steelhead flies.

Snook _(Centropomus undecimalis)_
COMMON & REGIONAL NAMES: _snuke, common snook, robalo_

GAME IDENTIFICATION & LOCATION OF FISHING REGIONS:
Angling writers unavoidably echo one another in describing the snook as a silvery saltwater counterpart of the southern largemouth bass. It strikes hard, fights harder, jumps, bores for the bottom, and plows in among mangrove roots or other obstacles to snarl or cut a line just when the angler thinks he is gaining con-

trol. In Florida, where snook are most plentiful, the limit is four a day and the minimum length 18 inches.

When fishermen speak of snook they mean the common snook, largest and most abundant member of a small family inhabiting the world's warm seas. It ranges primarily from central Florida southward along the Atlantic, Gulf, and Carib coasts and down to Brazil. Though strays appear as far north as Delaware, snook are so cold-sensitive that only the tropics furnish congenial habitat. The lower Texas coast has good snook fishing, but Florida's eastern side may have the biggest specimens and its western side has the greatest numbers—especially in the mangrove jungles edging the Everglades from Marco to Flamingo. The species thrives in the Pacific but not as far north as the United States.

The fisherman's snook is a fork-tailed creature with a shape resembling a walleye's but thicker and more basslike in the midsection. It has a depressed snout, two separate but closely spaced triangular dorsal fins, and a pronounced black stripe running along the lateral line from the gill cover all the way to the fork of the tail. Apart from the black stripe, by which a snook is instantly recognizable, color varies slightly with habitat. The back may be gray, olive, or golden-brown, and the body may have a pale blue or olive cast, but the sides are always silver, the belly pale or white. Though the teeth are too small to be of concern, the edges of the gill cover and the preopercle in front of it are sharp enough to call for a strong leader as well as care in handling a catch.

A typical adult snook weighs 5 pounds or less, yet a great many 15- to 30-pounders are caught in Florida, and several weighing more than 40 have been taken there. Ironically, the record was set in the Gulf of California, off La Paz, Mexico. There, in 1963, Jane Haywood caught one that measured 4 feet, 1 inch, had a girth of 26 inches, and weighed 52 pounds, 6 ounces.

FISH HABITAT & FEEDING BEHAVIOR—ANGLING TACTICS:
Strong, fast predators of the shallows, snook feed on assorted small fish, supplemented by shrimp, crabs, and other crustaceans. Like the tarpon populating the same regions, they are caught not only along the coasts and in bays and estuaries but in streams, creeks, and drainage canals, often far enough inland to be found in fresh water. They forage in channels and bays, around pilings, in creek mouths as well as farther upstream, on

tidal flats, on the seaward or downtide edges of oyster bars and sand bars, under banks, in deep holes surrounded by shallows or edging a current, next to drop-offs and island shelves, and— perhaps most of all—amid the tangled, shell-festooned roots of mangroves. All such settings are the "snook holes" sought by Floridian guides and anglers. Because the mangrove shorelines are prime snook nurseries as well as feeding grounds, these fish are constantly threatened by coastal development. They mature at about three years of age, live at least seven in proper habitat, and spawn chiefly from June to November. Though they are caught throughout the year, the spawning season is the best fishing season; when the water cools, they become sluggish, inclined to ignore baits or lures, and they take shelter in deeper waters.

Even in summer, they are moody feeders. A mature snook may be found cruising alone or traveling and resting with others in a school so dense that a cast is bound to touch a fish. In either event, every offering may be steadfastly refused or attacked furiously. Generally, a high, fast-falling tide whets their appetites.

A confirmed snook fisherman lives in hope of visible casting targets cruising the flats, creeks, canals, and mangrove fringes, pushing up low swells as they scout the surface or crashing through baitfish schools. But blind casting or trolling is a necessity more often than not. Deep holes can be effectively trolled with 4-inch spoons at least 75 feet behind the boat. However, spoons and spinners fool snook less regularly than plugs, jigs,

Trio of snook caught on spinning tackle.

and baits. Among baits, a small live mullet is most popular, followed first by a live shrimp (usually drifted) and then by a hind half of mullet. Either of the latter baits is especially good for night fishing off bridges, where plugs and jigs are also excellent. Baits are usually fished on big hooks—5/0 to 7/0—with sinkers weighing from a half-ounce to 3 ounces. In the surf, a live mullet may be the surest seduction, but jigs, plugs, and spoons are also used.

For other forms of snook fishing, monofilament or braided line testing 10 to 20 pounds is fine; 18-pound braided line is a favorite. Where 20-pound snook are a distinct possibility, most anglers tie on a 2-foot leader of no. 6 stainless wire (testing 58 pounds) for underwater lures and baits. The length is reduced to 8 inches or less with surface plugs to avoid dragging their noses down. In either case, the leader is twisted to the lure's eye without a snap-swivel. Where snook are unlikely to exceed 15 pounds, a 12-inch leader of no. 3 wire (testing 32 pounds) can be used both on the surface and under it. In narrow canals and mangrove-bordered creeks, ordinary bass rods are ideal, but for line control, plug-handling, and hook-setting in open, windy places, a slightly heavier, longer, stiffer-tipped rod is needed.

In cool weather, when snook sulk in deep holes, jigs or deep-running bass plugs work well. Yellow nylon, feather, or bucktail jigs tipped with a bit of shrimp are most strongly recommended. Under bridges and in the deeper parts of bays, channels, and inlets, big-lipped, wobbling, flashing, diving plugs may be equally good. The most appetizing plug color is silver with a touch of red, blue, or green to suggest prey, and a deep retrieve is jerky, with slow sweeps and faster darts. But classic snook fishing is shallow-water casting, so close to the mangroves that a few plugs are almost certain to be lost despite efforts at accuracy. Here, the plugs of choice are poppers and cigar-shaped surface-disturbing bass models, the most seductive color silver or yellow. A tarpon-style whip-retrieve is needed, faster than for bass, with almost imperceptible pauses between long, violent darts.

With a fly rod, comparable line-stripping is taxing but worthwhile. Yet fly fishing is most rewarding when an angler sees a snook on a flat or in a canal, heads it off, and teases it into striking by slowly, repeatedly swishing a fly in front of its snout. For creeks and canals, a 7½-foot rod serves well, but an 8½-foot rod is better on open water. The leader need not be any longer than the rod; it should taper to about 6-pound strength above a foot-long wire or a stiff monofilament tippet testing about 40 pounds. The favorite flies are popping bugs and 1- to 3-inch white or yellow bucktails and feather streamers tied on 1/0 to 3/0 hooks with at least four Mylar strips on each side for a pronounced tinsel flash.

Pressure must be applied to keep the fish out of the root tangles that so often cut or snag a line, yet this species has a soft mouth that lets a hook pull out easily. Far more snook are lost than boated.

Striped Bass *(Morone saxatilis)*

COMMON & REGIONAL NAMES: *striper, linesides, rockfish, rock bass, squidhound, greenhead*

GAME IDENTIFICATION & LOCATION OF FISHING REGIONS: At dusk or dawn of a summer's day or when an iron-dark sky heralds squally weather, long surf rods in sand-spike holders flag the beaches of the Atlantic and Pacific coasts. Lanterns flicker through the night on rocky breakwaters. Boats troll the deltas and bays as well as big landlocked reservoirs, and fly-rodders wade the tidewaters of rivers. The object of this attention is the striper—linesides—most famous species of the sea-bass family, Serranidae. Ichthyology being in constant flux, the striped bass and other members of the genus *Morone* are also classified in a separate family, the Percichthyidae, together with the giant sea bass and the wreckfish. In the estimation of many anglers, the striper merits an exclusive classification, a higher rank. School stripers weighing 5 to 10 pounds or so furnish brisk sport with light spinning tackle or a fly rod, while the old bulls and cows battle stubbornly against stouter gear.

The species, indigenous to the Atlantic, was so popular among nineteenth-century surf fishermen that, beginning in 1879, it was introduced to the West Coast. Today the Pacific population of striped bass is estimated at about two million.

Stripers sometimes become landlocked during their spawning runs, and biologists have successfully stocked them in fresh water. Because such habitat lacks the strong current needed for striper eggs to hatch, the populations in impoundments are generally hatchery-bred, yet freshwater management of the species has been very successful and the fishing is excel-

lent in such renowned waters as North Carolina's Kerr Reservoir and South Carolina's Santee-Cooper. Recently, waters farther west have been earning a reputation for big stripers. In 1976 Lake Havasu, on the Arizona-California border, yielded a 50-pound, 4-ounce mammoth. It is thought to be the biggest freshwater striper taken anywhere so far.

In salt water, stripers are abundant from Massachusetts to South Carolina, and occur in smaller numbers as far north as the St. Lawrence, as far south as Florida and the Gulf of Mexico. In the Pacific, they range from the Columbia River in Washington to the Los Angeles area, most plentifully from Oregon's Coos Bay to the Sacramento-San Joaquin Delta. Along that coast, the largest ones are generally caught in the area of Coos Bay itself, the Umpqua, Rogue, Coquille, and Alsea rivers, and the delta waters around San Francisco. In the Atlantic, the waters from Cape Cod to northern New Jersey yield the biggest bass.

The record was set at Cuttyhunk, Massacushetts, in 1969, by a 72-pound cow bass with a length of 4 feet, 6½ inches; a girth of 2 feet, 7 inches. The cows outgrow the bulls, and the largest of them are usually taken in summer and fall in the upper part of the Atlantic range. Though 30-pounders are not especially rare, a 10-pounder measuring about 2½ feet is closer to average.

The species is easily identified by the six to eight black longitudinal stripes or lines along its olive-gray and silvery sides. Its back is dark olive-gray, blue-gray, or sometimes almost black,

School-sized striper.

shading to silver flanks and a white belly. A yellow tinge frequently appears on the head, pectoral fins, and slightly concave or moderately forked tail. A pronounced green tinge may also appear on the back and the long, flat head. The fish has a projecting lower jaw and separate but closely set triangular dorsal fins.

FISH HABITAT & FEEDING BEHAVIOR—ANGLING TACTICS:
The striped bass is fundamentally an inshore fish, seldom caught more than a few miles from a coast or estuary. It feeds in bays, around river mouths, and in the surf, moving into fresh water to spawn in spring and early summer. In some waters—the Chesapeake area, for instance—stripers can be caught throughout the year. But because they tend to shift northward during the warm months and southward during the winter, the fishing is best in summer and fall along the coasts of New Jersey, New York, and New England. Pacific stripers winter principally in fresh water, and in spring they move down over the deltas and tributaries. After spawning, they move out into brackish and salt water.

Preferred spawning grounds are not far inland, though in brackish or fresh water. The sites are in strong current over gravel, rocks, or sand. Anglers have described "rock fights" that look like battles among rivals but are merely a courtship ritual performed by several males accompanying a female. A four-year-old cow, spawning for the first time, is likely to weigh 4 to 6 pounds, measure 18 to 24 inches, and produce about 65,000 eggs. A few years later, when she weighs 20 pounds, she may release a million eggs—and up to five million if she reaches 50 pounds.

Stripers are voracious predators of assorted small fish and invertebrates. Their preferred foods, which vary somewhat with locale, include herring, menhaden, flounders, mullet, eels, squid, shad, anchovies, clams, mussels, sea worms, crabs, and lobsters. Unfortunately for the angler, while they are gorging themselves on a given kind of prey they sometimes ignore all others. Many fishermen stow at least one kind of bait plus two rods rigged with two different lures, ready for instant use. Favorite live baits include small mackerel, herring, sardines, alewives, eels, anchovies, mullet, bloodworms, and long, flat sandworms (known on the West Coast as musselworms or pileworms). A 7- to 14-inch sand eel, rigged on a couple of hooks or a single big hook (8/0 to 10/0) is excellent for slow trolling or drifting in a current, over weedy ledges, and around inlets. Live baitfish are mostly attached through the lips or back on a 4/0 or 5/0 hook without a leader. They are fished deep, often with a split cork to hold them off bottom. Any supple rod will do, but where large baits are used and the stripers tend to be heavy, monofilament or Dacron may test 20 to 40 pounds.

Probably the best cut baits are strips of squid or fish and pieces of crab, clam, or shrimp, all of which are especially good for summer still-fishing or drifting. A standard bait rig calls for a pyramid sinker (or an egg or bank sinker where pyramids snag too regularly) attached by a short cord or link to a three-way swivel. The swivel's second eye holds a foot-long monofilament leader of the same strength as the line, while the third eye, of course, attaches to the line. Hooks are usually 3/0 or larger. For fishing the surf—or wherever an angler wants his bait wafted around by the current—many of us prefer the sliding-sinker arrangement of a fishfinder rig.

On landlocked waters, live gizzard shad are often still-fished or drifted, though they are less hardy on the hook than minnows. Because 20- to 30-pound bass are occasionally taken, fairly heavy spinning or baitcasting gear is popular. Trolling for inland stripers is much like summer trolling for deep-lying largemouths, using leadheaded jigs, deep-running plugs and spoons, and plastic worms or eels with spinners at the fore end. But in spring and again from late summer through fall, landlocked stripers often hound shad schools at the surface. These are times for popping plugs and light spinning gear with line testing 8 or 10 pounds. And fly-rodders can make use of popping bugs or streamers. The technique is jump-fishing as for white bass.

In salt water, too, baits and lures are trolled, cast, still-fished, and drifted. For working the big schools that cruise the rivers, bays, and estuaries, light spinning gear with line testing only 4 to 8 pounds is adequate. The fish are likely to weigh less than 15 pounds, and the angler can troll or make fairly easy casts with lures not often weighing much more than a half-ounce. Some fishermen hunt the dense schools, others ignore them because stripers travel with companions of like size and the bigger a school is, the smaller its members are. When using 1½-ounce lures for somewhat larger fish, a line with a 15-pound breaking strength is more reliable.

The really big stripers are attracted to big lures, and they prefer to forage near bottom. An angler may troll for them in twenty-five-foot water, using a trolling rod and a star-drag reel loaded with line testing 50 pounds, and there he can use an ordinary trolling sinker to probe the holes and channels. Or he may go deeper, imitating the Great Lakes fishermen who take coho (which see) on wire or lead-core line or with downriggers and planers or sash weights to keep the lure at least three-fourths of the way to bottom. Trolling should be slow. Popular lures include big plugs and spoons; surgical-tubing eels; metal, feather, or nylon jigs (an orange nylon squid has worked well for the author) tipped with a pork-rind strip; and homemade or bought eelskin rigs.

For fly casting—which is most exciting on wadable grass in tidewaters during an incoming tide, especially at night—big popping bugs and bucktails are used. The favorite pattern, at least on the East Coast, is the Gibbs Striper Bucktail. But an Imperial Supervisor will also get strikes, and so will coho flies. A fairly long rod is needed with a big saltwater reel carrying plenty of backing, a weight-forward sinking or sinking-tip line, and a light, tapered, fairly short leader.

But surf fishing is, of course, the classic approach. Both spinning and revolving-spool outfits are used. For prospecting

Striped bass.

close to shore, a light, short rod with line testing 10 or 12 pounds will suffice. However, for the long casts that are more often needed to reach big stripers, an angler wants somewhat heftier line and a long, fairly stiff two-handed casting rod—frequently up to 12 feet long. The favorite baits are sea worms, clams, squid, and small fish. The lures recommended for trolling also catch bass in the surf. On occasion, so do popping plugs and other surface-disturbers as well as barely subsurface swimmers and darters with built-in action. But deep-runners work most of the time. An excellent choice is a flatfish-style chromed squid with a bucktail dressing on its treble hook. Another excellent choice is a feather or bucktail jig, the favorite being the Upperman Bucktail.

Casts are made from the beach, rocks, jetties and other breakwaters, or while wading the surf. An effort should be made to shoot every offering out behind the incoming waves so that, instead of being washed in, it is pulled farther out by the undertow. The bait or lure can be left there for a while, and the rod is often rested in a sand-spike holder. The skill is not in the eventual slow retrieve but in making long casts and finding the right places at the right times. There is more to it than fishing the shallows at high tide and the deeper pockets at low tide. For one thing, stripers feed half-heartedly if at all in slack water; they bite best during periods of fast rise and fall. For another, they feed most avidly at daybreak and again from dusk through the night, and they are stimulated by rough weather.

Where creeks or breechways link saltwater ponds to the sea, the outlets are worth fishing on an ebbing tide, when prey is flushed down from the ponds. Bass like deep water near shore, and they like a turmoil that swirls prey about.

Surfperch (*Embiotocidae*) **& Opaleye** (*Girella nigricans*)

COMMON & REGIONAL NAMES: Surfperch—especially the deeper-dwelling ones—are also called *seaperch*. Other common names denote various species and will be included in the descriptions of those species. Opaleye are called *Catalina perch, button perch, green perch, blue-eyed perch, blue-eye, Jack Benny*.

GAME IDENTIFICATION & LOCATION OF FISHING REGIONS:
Surfperch are among the West Coast's most important saltwater

panfish. They put up a sprightly though brief fight, turning side-ward to the angler's pull in the manner of many slab-bodied fish, and they make tasty deep-fried fillets. They are the "porgies" of Oregon and the stars of many California fishing derbies. The twenty-three species vary in size from less than 5 inches to about 18. The popular ones average from 8 to 14 inches and a half-pound to 1½, with an occasional catch weighing over 2 pounds and one species sometimes weighing 4.

They are bottom-dwelling school fish that prey on assorted small crustaceans—particularly sand crabs—and on fish eggs, small fish, and mollusks. Some are motley but in general they are silvery, with a laterally compressed, oval body, a forked or con-cave tail, joined dorsal fins, a fairly long anal fin, a small head and mouth, and a lateral line that rises high on the forequarters. A few varieties inhabit waters as deep as three hundred feet but most—even including those commonly called seaperch—prefer moderate depths or the shallows of bays, coves, estuaries, and the surf along rocky or sandy coasts.

Most important of the clan is the barred surfperch *(Am-phistichus argenteus).* Ranging from central California to Baja, it is especially abundant around Oceanside, a little above San Diego. It averages less than 10 inches long but has been known to reach 16. It has a gray or olive back and silvery or almost white

Redtail surfperch.

sides, vertically barred with bronze or a dark brassy color. Between the bars are matching spots. The moderately forked tail and the fins match the bars or may be dusky. The belly is white.

Unlike other species, the calico surfperch *(A. koelzi)* has a slightly projecting lower jaw. Higher-backed than most, it is also called humpback perch. It grows to a length of about 12 inches. The color is olive or silvery with brownish or reddish specks and small bars. The fins are duskily tipped, and the belly and head are sometimes coppery. The tail is wide and only slightly forked. This species ranges from northern California to Baja. The range of the redtail surfperch *(A. rhodoterus)* is slightly farther north, from Washington to central California. It is sometimes called Oregon porgy or—in reference to an angular peak where the dorsal fins join—humpback perch. Fishing for the redtail is best in Oregon and around Eureka, California. The same size as the calico,

Surfperch caught with spinning gear in rocky cove.

it has a rosy tail, anal fin, and pectoral fins, reddish vertical bars on its silvery sides, and a light green back.

Almost as popular as the barred surfperch is the wider-ranging walleye surfperch *(Hyperprosopon argenteum)*, which occurs from lower British Columbia to Baja and is sometimes called silver perch, white perch, or China pompano. Its most common name refers to its unusually large eyes. Another 12-incher, it has a steel-blue back, bluish-silver sides often marked by vertical golden or dusky bars, and a white or silvery belly. The last spines of the dorsal fin's forward segment are higher than the soft rays, and the tail, anal fin, and pelvic fins are black-tipped.

Another popular one, especially around Monterey, is the rubberlip seaperch *(Rhacocilus toxotes)*, also known as rubbertip seaperch, liverlip surfperch, or buttermouth. It is the largest of all—up to 18 inches and a weight of 4 pounds or so—and might be the most popular except that it is abundant only in central and southern California. Its names allude to its very thick white or pinkish lips. It has a bluish-black back and whitish-silvery sides clouded with smoky pigment. Juveniles display one or two dusky vertical bars. The pectoral fins are yellow. Sometimes the other fins are also yellow, but they are dark-tipped.

Prominent among the unrelated panfish sharing the rocky, algae-carpeted shallows and the kelp beds from Monterey to Baja—most plentifully off southern California—is the opaleye *(Girella nigricans)*. Several of the alternate names listed at the head of this entry refer to it as a perch. Indeed, it looks rather like a surfperch but with a longer (fourteen-spined) front segment of dorsal fin, a rounded anal fin fronted by three short spines, a blunt or slightly lunate tail, and no scales on the gill covers or top of the head. A typical opaleye is under 10 inches long, but rare specimens grow quite large. The biggest recorded catch on rod and reel weighed 6 pounds, 2 ounces and measured 19¾ inches. The eyes of this species are a bright, lovely, opalescent blue. The body is green, dark and sometimes olivaceous above, lighter and sometimes grayish or brownish below. Juveniles and young adults are marked by a white or yellowish spot below the soft rear segment of the dorsal fin. The opaleye belongs to the family Girellidae, commonly and aptly called the nibblers. A grazer of algae, it forms large schools in kelp and along rocky or weedy shores. It is not purely vegetarian, and is often caught on surfperch baits.

FISH HABITAT & FEEDING BEHAVIOR—ANGLING TACTICS:
Now and then, as an angler unhooks a surfperch, the fish startles
him by giving birth to a handful of fry. These fish bear live young,
1- to 2-inch miniatures of the adults. Among some species,
broods are as small as half a dozen to a dozen, while others have
broods occasionally numbering over one hundred. The gestation
period is unusually long—half a year or more in some species.
Walleye surfperch mate in late autumn but most others do so in
spring or summer. They can be seen in the shallows, over sandy
bottoms, lying on their sides vent to vent. Birth takes place chiefly
from March to August. Since surfperch continue to school and
feed during this period they provide year-round sport, but the fishing is best in winter.

    A no. 10 hook ought to suffice for opaleye and the smaller
surfperch, and it should be set firmly at any indication of a bite,
for these gentle nibblers do not forcefully telegraph their inten-
tions. Surfperch in general are caught on small to medium hooks.
Some anglers elicit bites from opaleye with a bit of moss balled
onto a thin-wire hook in the same manner as for carp (which see).

    Both opaleye and surfperch are indifferent to lures. Surf-
perch will take shrimp, pieces of clam, very small crabs or pieces
of crab, mussels, or fish. All species accept live minnows and
sandworms—better known on the West Coast as pileworms.

    The common method is to still-fish or drift bait along the
bottom in the surf, in a tidal current, or along the lip of a drop-off
or ledge. No leader is necessary over sand, but for sharp rocks
or debris a short wire or stiff monofilament leader can forestall
fraying. The bait can simply be cast beyond the surf line and left
there until a bite is felt. It is easily done from rocky shores,
beaches, breakwaters, piers, and boats.

Swordfish *(Xiphias gladius)*
COMMON & REGIONAL NAMES: *broadbill, broadbill swordfish*

GAME IDENTIFICATION & LOCATION OF FISHING REGIONS: A
350-pound swordfish at first fails to notice the pull of hook and
line. When it does notice, it streaks away in alarm and then, as
fright turns to rage, makes stupendously powerful runs, leaps repeatedly, sounds, rolls and writhes, twining yards of leader
around its body, and hangs motionless but almost immovable as

▲ White shark. ▼ Tiger shark.

▲ Surf fishing.   ▼ Atlantic striped bass.   Pacific striper. ▶

▼ Snook. ▲ Snappers—from top, mangrove, lane, red. ▼ Wahoo.

▲ Hooked tarpon, leaping. ▼ Tarpon caught on fly.

▲ Spotted sea trout.   ▼ Blackfin tuna.

▲ California yellowtail.

▼ Sheepshead.   ▲ Rubberlip surfperch.   ▼ Striped surfperch.

it regains energy for a battle that may last hours. When an angler has sighted scores of swordfish, managed to entice and hook only three or four, and lost them all, he desperately wants the one he is playing, yet he must control his fervor or he will merely pull the hook from the broadbill's soft mouth.

Most sportsmen regard the species as a large variety of billfish, but it is scientifically classified in a family of its own, differing from the istiophorids—the true billfish—in its lack of scales or pelvic fins and in less apparent anatomical features. Its first dorsal fin is a high, soft-rayed, permanently erect sickle rising just behind the head. The second is a small finlet at the rear of the body. The anal fin is a sizable lobe, also sickle-shaped, backed by a finlet that matches the hind dorsal finlet. The large pectoral fins droop below the body. A single keel protrudes on each side of the caudal peduncle. The tail is wide and lunate. The bill, or sword, is broad, flat, and long. Color varies with locale and among individuals. The back and upper sides are usually dark bronze but may be gray-blue or blackish, and the sides may have blue or lavender glints. The lower sides and belly are pale gray or whitish.

Most of the swordfish caught on rod and reel weigh between 150 and 400 pounds, but much larger ones are not unusual. They grow especially big along South America's western coast. The record was set in 1953 off Iquique, Chile, by a fish weighing 1,182 pounds. It was 14 feet, 11¼ inches long.

Swordfish range through the world's tropical, subtropical, and temperate seas. On North America's Atlantic coast, they occur from Newfoundland to Cuba and probably farther south; on the Pacific coast, they are found from California to Chile but are not abundant much farther north than lower California's coastal islands. At the onset of winter in the cool latitudes they move rather far offshore, into deep water, and some populations evidently migrate southward as well. Those of us who cannot afford a quest for gigantic Chilean trophies find American swordfishing best in the Atlantic—off Nova Scotia's Cape Breton from midsummer to the end of August; and, especially, off Hampton Bays and Montauk on Long Island, Point Judith and Newport in Rhode Island, and Cuttyhunk, Menemsha, Edgartown, Falmouth, and Nantucket in the Massachusetts Cape and Islands area from mid- or late June to mid-July. As early as April and May the swordfishing is sometimes fairly good off the lower Atlantic states. Off southern Florida, broadbills seem to be more nocturnal than elsewhere; they were thought to be scarce until anglers recently discovered that they feed heavily at night in the Gulf Stream.

On the West Coast, swordfishing is a newer sport but is rapidly gaining adherents. Southern California's major broadbill ports are at Balboa, Newport Harbor, Catalina, and Costa Mesa. Swordfishing in that region begins in late spring, improves through the summer, and reaches a peak in September.

FISH HABITAT & FEEDING BEHAVIOR—ANGLING TACTICS:
Small swordfish are sometimes caught at or near the surface in the warmer regions occupied by the species. But the adults seem to require cooler water. In the warmest tropics they avoid the surface and near-surface strata where angling for them is most practical. Since they are summer spawners, and breeding activity evidently takes place chiefly in the offshore tropics, this could be unfortunate for anglers if it were not for the fact that adult broadbill populations always appear in relatively cool latitudes during the warm months. It is believed that they do not breed every year.

In their feeding habits, they resemble true billfish. Though squid is their favorite food in most areas, they eat large quantities of whatever small fish are available—mackerel, menhaden, bonito, school tuna, bluefish, herring, whiting, and so on.

Until recently, tackle for this aloof and powerful quarry was invariably heavy in the extreme—typically a roller-guide rod with a 26-ounce tip, a 14/0 star-drag reel, at least 800 yards of 39-thread linen line, and a 25- or 30-foot leader of stainless-steel cable with a strength of 450 pounds. The length of leader remains unchanged because swordfish roll in it and hit it with their tails and swords. And roller-guide rods are still best because they reduce line-weakening friction, but the trend is toward lightness. Though some anglers prefer a leader of no. 12 stainless-steel wire, the best is probably 200-pound-test monofilament. A charter skipper will spool reels for average fishermen with line testing 130 pounds, but experienced broadbill anglers use 80-pound tackle in North American waters. Their outfits duplicate the medium to heavy tackle recommended for marlin (which see). Hooks range from 10/0 and 12/0 in the Atlantic to 14/0 and 16/0 off Chile.

Lures more often alarm than fool a swordfish. Whole dead baits are the general rule, and good ones include mackerel, squid, eels, balao, mullet, skipjack tuna, school tuna, and bonito. The most popular are mackerel and squid. Favored rigs often employ two hooks, one inserted through the head or below the gills and another partway back or near the tail. If broadbills are definitely known to be in the vicinity, live baits may be still-fished or dead ones trolled very slowly at various depths—often four hundred feet down—but at the same time everyone aboard watches the surface, because still-fishing or blind trolling is sporadically productive at best. Off southern Florida, broadbills are caught by drift-fishing at night, and squid make excellent bait for this purpose. Elsewhere, the most common method is to cruise the blue waters offshore in daylight, scouting in the manner of nineteenth-century whalers. Swordfish are often spotted as they swim several feet below the surface. Perhaps just as often, their high, curved dorsal fins and tails are seen above water.

A rod is kept in a holder, ready for instant use. When a fish is discovered, an angler grabs the rod, settles into the fighting chair, adjusts his harness, and lets out a couple of hundred feet of line. The mate or an experienced companion takes light hold of the line below the rod tip while an additional length of 75 feet or so is let out in a slack loop, to be released at the moment of the strike. The angler keeps the reel on free-spool, resting his fingers against it to maintain some control and prevent a possible backlash without hindering drop-back. The fish must be approached stealthily. Broadbills are easily spooked and will sound when a boat comes near. If this happens, it pays to remain in the area for some time, as the fish is likely to surface again in the general vicinity.

The bait should be trolled about two feet underwater and very slowly—at about three knots. It must be drawn twenty or thirty feet in front of the fish. If it is not taken, the process is repeated until the broadbill becomes aroused and strikes it or becomes nervous and disappears.

The hope is that at last the swordfish will propel itself forward with a powerful swish of its tail and dive for the bait. The mate watches tensely, his fingers on the line. If the fish takes, he shouts, "Strike!" and releases the line or strips out more while the boat's engine is put into neutral. The angler can feel a change from the normal trolling pull of the line and the initial drop-back to the steady, stronger pull of a departing fish with the bait solidly in its mouth. After signaling the skipper to get the engine in gear and start forward, he switches on the reel's drag and strikes hard, again and again.

Very often a swordfish is foul-hooked or only lightly hooked, and too tight a drag or overenthusiastic, jerky horsing can easily rip the barb loose. The fight must be smooth, steady, and tenacious. Assuming the angler's stamina, strength, and skill bring success, the boat's gear had better include a heavy flying gaff with 10 yards of cable or stout rope, a gin pole or similar device, a tail rope, and spliced lifting grommets.

Tarpon *(Megalops atlantica)*
COMMON & REGIONAL NAMES: *silver king, tarpum, sabalo real, cuffum*

GAME IDENTIFICATION & LOCATION OF FISHING REGIONS: If a fish had evolved just for the delight of anglers, it would be very much like the tarpon—big, powerful, handsomely silver, found in the shallows close to shore, sometimes eager to strike but not always easy to dupe, and capable of twisting, hook-throwing leaps mixed with motionless sulks and 300-yard runs.

It is the largest member of the family Elopidae, a small, primitive group that includes the ladyfish and in many anatomical features resembles the ancestral stock from which all bony species developed. It has soft-rayed fins, a wide, deeply forked tail, pelvic fins set far back under the body, a single, triangular dorsal fin about midway back, and a single large anal fin. The last ray of the dorsal is a long, swept-back filament that sometimes wears off with age. The sides of the body are flat, the head short, deep, and flat-topped. The big, toothless but sharp-jawed mouth is upturned and has a protruding, upward-thrusting lower jaw, as if the fish always attacked from below. Its back is usually dark blue or greenish-black. The tail and dorsal fin are comparably dark, but the lower fins may be dark or pale. In fresh inland waters a tarpon may acquire a brassy wash, but in typical habitat its sides and belly are bright, light-reflecting silver. The scales of an adult may be as large and shiny as a newly minted silver dollar.

"Baby" tarpon—the juveniles often caught in canals and streams—are defined by some anglers as those weighing up to 20 pounds or so and by others as anything under 50. Actually,

mature tarpon have an average length of about 5 feet and an average weight somewhere between 25 and 30 pounds. Yet 70- and 80-pounders are quite common, and occasional catches weigh more than 125. The record fish on rod and reel was a 283-pound tarpon caught on Venezuela's Lake Maracaibo in 1956.

The species is an Atlantic denizen of warm coastal waters, ranging as far south as Brazil or sometimes Argentina, straying as far north as Cape Cod, and also occurring off northwestern Africa. The region of abundance in American waters is relatively restricted—around Florida and along the Gulf Coast to Texas and Mexico. The range is slowly spreading, as tarpon have wandered through the Panama Canal to the western side of Central America. In the tropics and subtropics, they are also found in fresh water; they roam a hundred miles or so up rivers. They seek the shallow hunting grounds and low salinity of estuaries and river mouths.

Tarpon attempting to throw hook.

Tarpon prefer a water temperature of about 75°. Cold inhibits their feeding and prods them out of the mangroves and off the flats into the Gulf or other deep water. They can be caught in any month along some of the warmer stretches of the Gulf Coast, but spring or summer generally improves the fishing. They begin returning to Floridian waters in good numbers toward the end of winter, and the population peaks by early summer. In the Keys, tarpon fishing is best from mid-May to mid-June.

FISH HABITAT & FEEDING BEHAVIOR—ANGLING TACTICS:

Tarpon are school carnivores, patrolling the shallows in loose packs to find such prey as blue crabs, shrimp, mullet, silversides, pinfish, and marine catfish. When a school is plundering in only a few feet of water, fishermen are sometimes able to locate tarpon by the lathered surface or the sound of their noisy splashing. Shallow feeding grounds also serve as nurseries. Tarpon are among the most prolific marine creatures; a big female may hold more than twelve million eggs. In Florida's famous estuarine waters, spawning occurs chiefly from May to September. The young pass through an eellike larval stage roughly similar to that of ladyfish and bonefish, after which they grow slowly, probably reaching sexual maturity at six or seven years of age, when they are about 4 feet long. A 100-pounder is at least thirteen to sixteen years old.

Young tarpon are commonly caught in small brackish and fresh ponds, streams, and canals. As they grow older, they move into bigger streams and out into estuaries, bays, mangrove banks, flats, and other coastal shallows adjacent to channels or deeper waters. Fishing for small ones is wonderful sport with light spinning or fly tackle. The capture of baby tarpon does no harm, partly because the species is so fecund and partly because tarpon of less than trophy size are almost invariably released. Though the roe is excellent sautéed, the flesh is rated by most North Americans as barely edible.

For larger tarpon, tackle of several kinds is used. At some of the Gulf Coast and Florida harbors, charter boats carry trolling rods equipped with line testing 50 pounds to troll slowly with big plugs, spoons, and feathers as well as mullet, pinfish, or squid baits. Such rigs usually employ a short no. 9 stainless-steel leader testing 104 pounds to prevent fraying or cutting on a tarpon's rough body or sharp gill covers and jaws. Unless sharks are prev-

Fly-rodder with tarpon.

alent, experienced anglers prefer to troll with line testing 20 pounds or less, but trolling plugs should be fairly big. A 1½-ounce, 6-inch model would be about right. Swimming and diving plugs are popular, as are big spoons and feathers.

For plugging, drifting, and still-fishing, a good baitcasting rod would be a stiff-tipped 6-foot model, its reel spooled with 250 yards or more of 15-pound-test monofilament or 18-pound-test braided line. A good spinning rod would be a 6½- or 7-footer, carrying 12- or 14-pound-test monofilament and capable of handling plugs weighing over a half-ounce. Opinions about leaders differ drastically. Some fishermen use the aforementioned wire or splice a foot or so of 100-pound-test cable through a sleeve to 5

feet of monofilament testing 40 or 50 pounds. Others prefer a tapered monofilament affair—15 inches of 20-pound butt, then 15 more of twice that strength, and 30-inch tippet of 40-pound test.

Delicate split-bamboo fly rods are not for the likes of tarpon. In ponds and canals where babies under 20 pounds prevail, an 8- or 8½-foot bass-bugging rod can be used to cast relatively small streamers and bucktails. (Tarpon up to about 5 pounds will take streamers as small as no. 8 or 10 as well as wet flies and even panfish bugs.) But for big tarpon, one wants a heavy-tipped 9- or 9½-foot fiberglass rod that is stiff enough for an angler to strike his fish very forcefully and set a 3/0 to 5/0 hook in a bone-hard jaw. The backing should be at least 250 yards of 27-pound test, and the reel should have a strong drag and brake, because a tarpon has to be worn down by pressure; it is a fish that can haul a skiff several miles. Tarpon competitions generally stipulate the use of a 12- to 15-pound-test tippet, but ordinarily a fly caster may want a 12-inch length of monofilament testing 60 to 100 pounds.

A common tactic, though it lacks the glamour associated with tarpon, is to use a spinning or baitcasting rod to still-fish or drift live or dead bait about 8 feet under a big bobber. Good baits include mullet, pinfish, and squid. The best is a small live crab with its large claw removed and a 4/0 or 5/0 hook impaling it from the bottom through the winglike tip of its shell. Next best is a shrimp on a similar hook. Still-fishing is not always a lazy diversion. Sometimes an angler reels in fast—having seen a tarpon within casting distance—and removes the bobber. He tosses a shrimp or crab four or five feet in front of the fish. A shrimp should be skittered over the surface for a few feet before it sinks. A crab should be swum across the surface, with the rod held high, and if that fails it should be allowed to sink. A tarpon keeps moving after capturing prey, and it must be allowed to run a short way with a bait before it is struck.

With lures, an angler may alternately jig, cast, and troll. On the flats and banks and along the mangrove shores where deep water is close, trolling is sometimes more effective with surface-disturbing plugs, sometimes with sinking swimmers, spoons (unbaited or with a strip bait), and feather or bucktail jigs. Surface lures generally work best in the shallower waters. Both on top and underwater, a favorite color combination is red and white, but orange or yellow or both will also take fish. Another excellent lure

Guide and angler with bragging-size tarpon.

on the flats is an orange or yellow plastic worm, fished with a slip-sinker as for largemouth bass. Whatever is used, the hooks should be kept very sharp if they are to penetrate a tarpon's jaw. For surface or shallow-diving lures, a whip retrieve is recommended. But when the fish are feeding down below, a somewhat slower though active bottom retrieve will attract them.

For fly fishing, splay-winged streamers with 3- to 5-inch hackles are ideal. They sink slowly and their wings "breathe," or pulsate, during a relatively slow retrieve. This animates them with little more effort than the rod-tip movement imparted by line-stripping. The most productive colors are yellow and orange, yellow and red, all yellow, all white, or white with a touch of red. Popular patterns include the Red Grizzly, Ray D's Lemon Lasher, Keys Tarpon Streamer, Lefty's Deceiver, the Stu Apte Fly, Cockroach, and Standard Yellow-and-Red. For tarpon up to about 25 pounds, a 3-inch wing and a no. 2 to 2/0 hook will suffice. For bigger game, a 4- or 5-inch fly on a 3/0 to 5/0 hook is recommended.

A fly should be cast about a yard in front of a tarpon's snout (or farther out if the fish is deep and more time is needed for the fly to sink and intercept the target). Then it must be brought back with a jerky but not too fast retrieve. Unfortunately, cruising tarpon sometimes stay in range only long enough for a single cast, even when a school moves in a drifting circle with its members strung out in a piscatorial daisy chain—a frequently observed phenomenon.

Another common phenomenon, one that can be much more frustrating, is surface rolling. Tarpon possess an air bladder that operates as a primitive lung, enabling them to flourish in water with too low an oxygen content for their gills to function with optimum efficiency. When they roll at the surface, they may or may not be feeding. They are rolling to take in air, not to capture surface prey in the manner of a rising trout. Novices tend to cast repeatedly into a rolling but unresponsive school.

Tarpon are caught from bridges, causeways, jetties, and canal embankments, but the greatest enjoyment is in scouting the tidal banks, flats, and mangrove edges with a skiff. Shallow water—say, five to ten feet—is best of all. In water more than about fifteen feet deep, hooked tarpon make fewer sensational jumps; they still wage an astonishing battle, but a sounding one. In some regions, the fly-rodder's scouting approach is known as "tarpon-jumping." An angler or guide watches for moving shadows underwater as well as rolling fish, bubbles, or occasional swells and wakes at the surface. Sometimes, if no fish can be located, the boat is staked next to a hole or channel. These techniques are best at high tide.

A large tarpon's strike may be hardly more than a light bump. Typically, the fish rolls up onto a lure rather slowly and clamps its jaws on the way down. Some strikes will be missed, regardless of technique, but the surest hook-setting method is to hesitate momentarily and then strike hard, several times.

A tarpon must be played out before it can be released or gaffed (assuming it has not released itself by throwing the hook, as so often happens). It will at last slow down, wallow, and perhaps bubble at the surface, yet it will be unharmed if released by slipping a hand-gaff up under the lower jaw at the gill opening to hold it while the hook is removed with pliers.

Tuna *(Thunnus)*

COMMON & REGIONAL NAMES: Names in common usage denote various species or growth stages thereof and will be included in the descriptions of those species.

GAME IDENTIFICATION & LOCATION OF FISHING REGIONS:
Tuna fishing is two contrasting kinds of sport. Catching small ones—school tuna, albacore, or blackfins—is potentially a matter of hooking and playing one fish after another. An aura of gleeful frenzy pervades a charter boat or private runabout surrounded by ravenous fish. Even the smallest tunas have been known to die fighting and sink toward bottom, but as a rule they are boated after a relatively brief though powerful struggle. With the larger tunas, glee awaits the flying gaff and is preceded by grim determination. After the initial run, when the quarry sounds, a tuna fisherman pumps and hauls, maintaining constant pressure.

Large or small, tuna can cruise effortlessly at 30 miles an hour, attacking and devouring any small fish, squid, or crustaceans they come across. They belong to the genus *Thunnus* of the sharp-toothed family Scombridae. There are about seventy-five widely distributed scombrids—mackerels and tunas—and they are still being classified. With their pointed snouts, spindle-shaped bodies, narrow caudal peduncles, and lunate, saber-

curved tails, they are perhaps the most streamlined of all fishes. They are further characterized by very small scales or none at all, a side-keeled peduncle, separate spiny and soft-rayed dorsal fins, an anal fin positioned beneath the soft dorsal and more or less matching it, and a series of dorsal and anal finlets.

Although every species provides good eating, the law permits only one to be commercially labeled "white meat tuna." It is the albacore, or longfin tuna *(T. alalunga),* a small variety whose sickle-shaped black pectoral fins are so long that they usually extend beyond the bases of the anal and soft dorsal fins. The average size is about 10 pounds, but albacore of twice that weight are caught with fair regularity. The record fish was a 1973 catch weighing 74 pounds, 13 ounces; it was 4 feet, 2 inches long and 2 feet, 10¾ inches around. The site was the Canary Islands. However, the species is far more abundant in the Pacific than the Atlantic, and North American albacore fishing is strictly a West Coast sport. The longfins of that region migrate between American and Japanese waters as well as southward. Off California, runs occur from late spring through early autumn, and the fishing is generally best from July onward. Albacore are caught (primarily) 50 to 100 miles off San Diego, around San Clemente Island, 5 to 40 miles off the Channel Islands, and north of Morro Bay and Avila Beach. This species has a blue back, greenish toward the tail, and is silvery below. When alive, it has an overall metallic bronze sheen. The anal fin is almost colorless, the dorsal and pelvic fins are dark, and the tail has a white margin.

Angler holding 35-pound albacore.

The blackfin tuna (T. atlanticus) has the smallest size—usually under 10 pounds and rarely exceeding 25. The record on sporting gear is a tie between a 1970 Bermuda catch weighing 38 pounds, with a length of 3 feet, 3¼ inches, and a fish of the same weight—just a trifle longer and slimmer—taken at Islamorada, Florida, in 1973. This is a dark-finned, dark-bodied tuna, blackish above, grading to blue and silver-gray below. It often has vague bronze or dusky bands running down the sides. Found only in the Atlantic, from Cape Cod to Brazil, it is frequently eaten by blue marlin. The fishing for it is good only in Florida and the West Indies, and is best during the warm months.

The yellowfin, or Allison, tuna (T. albacares) is of medium size. The average is from 15 to 25 pounds, and weights exceeding 100 pounds are not rare. The record was set in the winter of 1973 at Mexico's San Benedicto Island by a 7-foot yellowfin weighing 308 pounds. Widely distributed in tropical and subtropical seas, this species travels as far north as Maryland and New Jersey in late summer and fall. It is also caught off central and southern California, with a peak in early fall. Yellowfin fishing is good in the Gulf of Mexico even during a good part of the cooler season; the species remains in the Gulf Stream throughout the year, and during the warm months it often comes close to shore. It looks somewhat like the blackfin, but has long, bright yellow pectoral fins and an even longer anal and second dorsal fin, both yellow and edged with black. The finlets are the same color but less bright. A yellow stripe, extending from snout to tail, fades soon after the fish is taken from the water.

The giant of the group, sometimes called great tuna, is the bluefin tuna (T. thynnus). Even young ones, encountered in huge schools, very often weigh more than 20 pounds. Mature bluefins, traveling in small schools or occasionally alone, average more than 100 pounds. In October, 1973, a 1,120-pounder was caught at Prince Edward Island, above Nova Scotia. It had a length of 10 feet, 2 inches, a girth of 7 feet, 1½ inches, and it broke a 977-pound record that had been set in the same region.

The term "school tuna" is most commonly applied to bluefins weighing from 8 to 100 pounds—but the same term often designates 10- to 20-pound yellowfin tuna and, for that matter, some anglers and charter- or party-boat operators apply the name to any small tuna found in large schools. The opposite term, "giant tuna," is obviously a description of any bragging-size catch, but is usually applied to bluefins weighing over 100 pounds.

The bluefin is a cosmopolitan species, wintering in warm seas, migrating to cool zones in summer. Tagging has demonstrated that it also crosses the Atlantic from America to Europe. It appears off the Bahamas in late April or early May, when spawning is still in progress. As the schools slowly work their way northward they feed gluttonously; by late summer, when they reach Nova Scotia, a bluefin may have gained 200 pounds or more. Major tuna tournaments are held in New England waters, but Nova Scotia is the site of the most famous one, the Annual International Tuna Cup Match held in late summer or autumn. On the West Coast the species ranges from Baja to the Gulf of Alaska and is caught chiefly off California from spring to December, with a midsummer peak. On the East Coast the best fishing is from July through October between lower New Jersey and Massachusetts, and from August through October farther north.

The bluefin is dark, steely blue above, often with green glints, and silvery or silver-gray below. It has an indistinct yellow streak along the body from the snout about halfway back, but this fades quickly after death. It has a retractable first dorsal fin and shorter pectoral fins than other tunas. The anal fin and finlets are yellowish. The pelvic fins are sometimes pale, but the other fins are dark. Young bluefins have white spots on the lower sides.

The bigeye tuna (*T. obesus*) is a denizen of deeper water and therefore caught less commonly than the others. It has a worldwide distribution in tropical and subtropical seas. Its size is comparable to the yellowfin's. The record Atlantic bigeye, caught in 1975 at the Canary Islands, weighed an ounce over 335 pounds. In the Pacific, where the species tends to grow larger, the record is held by a 435-pounder caught off Cabo Blanco, Peru, in 1957. This tuna resembles the bluefin but it has very large eyes and its finlets are yellowish-brown eged with black.

FISH HABITAT & FEEDING BEHAVIOR—ANGLING TACTICS: If the greed of the canned-tuna industry does not soon put the bluefin on the endangered-species lists, the current angling record is unlikely to stand for many years. Like other tunas, this is a prolific, fast-growing, long-lived species. Though the spawning grounds have not been thoroughly defined, it is known that bluefins breed

in the Antilles, the Straits of Florida, and the Bahamas from April to early June, and in warmer latitudes the spawning season is probably longer. The fish begin to head northward while spawning or immediately afterward. A typical female may shed a million eggs or several million, and each surviving hatchling is likely to be 8 or 9 inches long by July. The following summer it will be a hard-fighting school tuna; a four-year-old is nearly 4 feet long and weighs about 70 pounds. At ten years, a bluefin has added close to 300 pounds. And that weight can almost double in the next four years.

The yellowfin grows still faster, though its top weight cannot compare. A four-year-old should weigh about 140 pounds—twice as much as a bluefin of the same age. Studies in the Pacific have shown that a healthy female yellowfin casts from a million to several million eggs at least twice annually. Other species, regardless of size, produce the same number of eggs at least once annually. They all breed in warm regions, principally in the warm months. Spawning activity seems to have little effect on their appetites, but the biggest fish are caught afterward.

Among the small species, albacore are the starring performers of the lower West Coast. They have much in common with the California yellowtail, a highly esteemed amberjack (which see), and, in fact, the two species sometimes compete for bait. From early July to mid-October, albacore abound—at first 8- to

Blackfin tuna.

12-pounders and later fish weighing 30 or even 40 pounds. They bite most eagerly in 60° to 66° water, but finding them is not exclusively a job for the thermometer since great expanses may have the requisite temperature. They are located by trolling at 7 or 8 knots—preferably over known feeding areas—with 6- to 8-inch bullet-headed feathered or plastic-skirted jigs carrying single or double hooks. Bone and metal jigs also work, as do spoons, though they are not as popular. Sometimes the fish feed on the fringes of kelp paddies and over ledges and ridges. Big, loose schools roam the blue offshore waters. While trolling, the anglers watch for diving sea birds or the boiling of marauded bait schools. Albacore are more boat-shy than school tuna, but a lure ought to be no more than 100 feet astern because the first one hooked will be followed at least partway by others in the school if it is brought near the boat fairly fast.

A school is coaxed to stay by chumming, often with live anchovies—which are excellent bait in 3- to 6-inch size. Other good baits are live herring, sauries, or sardines, both on the surface and submerged in the chum line. Casting can also be done with squid, spoons, plugs, and jigs. The reel is left on free-spool, and just a little drop-back—a fast count to five—is allowed before setting the hook hard. Some anglers insist on a yard or more of wire leader testing 30 pounds, but more often it is best to tie the hook directly to the line. Hook sizes range from no. 2 to 2/0. While many fishermen prefer revolving-spool gear with line testing 50 pounds —admittedly an asset on crowded party boats—others use short spinning rods with monofilament testing 20 or 25 pounds.

As albacore are to yellowtails, so the other small species and school tuna are to bonito (which see). Far from being boat-shy, they are attracted to the bait-churning prop wash, and some skippers polish their propellers or add teasers to the trolled offerings to draw a school. These fish gather in large numbers from June to October off California and Oregon and between Cape Cod and Maryland. They can be caught by trolling fast with Japanese feathers, spoons, or metal jigs, and by trolling or drifting baits.

Traditional tackle would be a trolling rod with a 4/0 revolving-spool reel and 500 yards of 30-pound-test Dacron line or comparably heavy spinning tackle. But fly fishing, which originated as a stunt for experts, has been gaining popularity for small yellowfins, blackfins, and even bluefins. It also works with albacore.

Normally, the fish are chummed to the surface. In the case of blackfin tuna, however, the fish often linger twenty feet down in the sinking chum and a fisherman may keep one rod ready with a sinking line and another with a floating line. A shooting head is often necessary, as casts may be long. A heavy salmon rod—or any 9-foot, stiff-tipped rod—serves nicely. At least 6 feet of leader is used, and it tapers to a 12-pound test above a light wire or heavy nylon shock tippet. The backing is 300 yards of Dacron testing 30 pounds. The best fly is a white feather or polar-bear-hair streamer with Mylar strips and a touch of color tied on a 1/0 hook.

For big tuna, especially giant bluefins, trolling is the exclusive method in some regions, yet chumming from an anchored or drifting boat may well be the most productive tactic. Anchored chumming is feasible only in relatively shallow inshore waters, of course, but big tuna congregate in such waters off some of the northern coastal ports as well as in the Bahamas. At deeper gathering spots in the open sea—off Block Island, for instance—the boat is drifted. The best chum is a soupy gruel of chopped and chunked menhaden, and the best baits (often obtained by jigging beforehand) are live whiting, mackerel, small cod, or ling. A good idea is to fish two lines, one with the bait about 30 feet down and the other on bottom. Each rod is left in the holder of an unoccupied fighting chair, with the reel in free-spool but with the click engaged for audibility. When a tuna takes the bait, the angler grabs the line and uses it, rather than the rod, to strike the fish. Then he gets into the fighting chair, adjusts his harness, and engages the reel's brake. The drag should be set at about 45 to 50 pounds. If the boat is anchored, the crew hoists the anchor fast during this procedure. After the first run, the fish will sound. It must be given no rest. The boat may be maneuvered to add drag for several hundred feet and then put into reverse while the angler cranks the reel to gain line.

In deep water, a hefty roller-guide trolling rod is used with a spool loaded to capacity; that is, a 12/0 reel may carry 550 yards of 39-thread linen or Dacron testing 130 pounds. In shallow waters, a lighter outfit can be used with a 9/0 reel, carrying the same yardage of 24-thread linen or 80-pound Dacron. It is doubled at the end, as for marlin. The leader is generally about 15 feet of no. 12 to 15 stainless-steel wire or comparable braided cable, and a 12/0 hook is typical.

Bluefin tuna.

In clear waters where tuna can be spotted migrating—or "finning" and raising swells as they feed at the surface—there is more enjoyment in trolling from a boat equipped with a tuna tower or high enough flying bridge to be used for scouting. In this situation, the angler sits in the fighting chair and holds the rod. No drop-back is needed; he will set the hook in the conventional manner, fast and hard. The brake is left on, again with the drag at 45 pounds or so. Unlike school tuna, the big ones are boat-shy, so the bait or lure is let back about 100 yards. Japanese feathers, spoons, and occasionally even plugs are used but (at least in the author's opinion) live or dead bait draws more strikes. It can be mackerel, mullet, or squid. Boat-maneuvering can substantially reduce the back-flexing and cranking to gain line on a tuna that instinctively uses all its weight to resist. But when a big tuna is hooked from a small private craft, it may draw the boat on the kind of rollicking course that whalers called a Nantucket sleigh ride.

Weakfish & Seatrout *(Cynoscion)*
COMMON & REGIONAL NAMES: Names in common usage denote various species and will be included in the descriptions of those species.

GAME IDENTIFICATION & LOCATION OF FISHING REGIONS:
Wherever weakfish or related seatrout occur, they can often be caught in good numbers by an angler who knows their preferences regarding tides, temperatures, habitat, and foods. They respond to lures as well as baits. At the surface they can strike hard enough to startle an experienced fisherman, yet when feeding on the bottom they sometimes bite gently enough to test his timing and hook-setting skill. They are not spectacular battlers or leapers but they fight vigorously, generally beginning with a strong run or two followed by erratic reversals, dashes, and circles. Occasionally they thrash at the surface. They tend to quit after a short tussle, but when a weakfish is about to be netted it may suddenly renew the struggle.

A net is essential whether boating or landing one, for the fish takes its name from its fragile mouth. That angling lore has somewhat exaggerated the fragility does not alter the likelihood that the hook may tear out if the fish is lifted without a net. The delicate mouth also enhances the challenge of hooking and playing one without losing it. The meat spoils quickly but when fresh it is delicious baked or broiled.

In the Northeast, the gradual comeback of the weakfish population after a long decline has been a cause for celebration among inshore fishermen. In the South, particularly on the Gulf Coast and in Florida, the spotted seatrout is probably the most popular bay fish. These handsome species and a couple of smaller relatives are Sciaenidae—members of the large family of croakers and drums, many of which are treated in another chapter. Together with about a dozen closely related drums, they are classified in the genus *Cynoscion,* represented on the West Coast by the white sea bass and other varieties of corvina, also described in another chapter. The weakfish and seatrout merit separate treatment on the basis of specialized fishing techniques.

They are schooling fish, usually found in shallow waters over sandy bottoms. The older, larger ones, survivors of a dwindling age group, often appear alone or in small gatherings. They are characterized by a slim, troutlike body and an exceptionally long lateral line that extends onto the slightly concave or squarish tail. The spiny and soft-rayed dorsal fins are set close together but separated by a deep notch. The lower jaw projects slightly. The thin-walled mouth is large and toothy, but the canines are not big or sharp enough to require the use of a wire leader.

The weakfish *(C. regalis)* is regionally known as sea trout, gray trout, squeteague, yellowfin, and tiderunner. Ranging along the Atlantic Coast from Massachusetts to Florida and occasionally into the Gulf of Mexico, it is abundant from New York to the Carolinas. The best fishing regions are Chesapeake Bay, Delaware Bay, the New Jersey coast, and the bays of Long Island—especially Peconic Bay and its environs. The greatest numbers are caught from April into October or November in the Chesapeake area, from May into October in New Jersey and New York, and from June into September in New England. A typical weakfish weighs a pound, though quite a few weigh 3. The record fish was caught not in a famous Atlantic haven but in Trinidad. A 19½-pounder caught in 1962, it was a well-fed specimen measuring 37 inches.

A weakfish is dark olive, greenish, greenish-blue, or grayish above, silvery or silver-gray below, and peppered with small, indistinct spots that tend to run in undulating waves downward and forward from the back. Usually the sides are tinged with copper or gold as well as faint gleams of blue, green, or lavender. The tail is dusky or olive, and sometimes yellowish along the lower edge. The other fins are yellowish or dusky with a yellow tinge.

The spotted seatrout *(C. nebulosis)* is also known as speckled seatrout, speck, or spotted weakfish. Most commonly caught along the Gulf Coast and around Florida, it is abundant as far north as Chesapeake Bay and sometimes strays to New York. Though the fishing is excellent in the Carolinas and in many bays of the Gulf, the biggest seatrout are caught on Forida's east coast, particularly at Cocoa, Melbourne, Vero Beach, and Fort Pierce. At Fort Pierce in January, 1949, a record was set by a 15-pound, 3-ounce spotted seatrout measuring 34½ inches. In May, 1969, the record was officially tied at Jensen Beach, Florida, by a slightly shorter, stouter specimen weighing 3 ounces more. The average size is between 1 and 4 pounds, but a seatrout has to weigh 7 pounds or more to impress anglers on the southern flats.

Whereas ideal water temperatures for weakfish are between 60° and 65°, spotted seatrout prefer a little more warmth— from the mid 60's to the mid 70's. Both species move out into deeper water when the temperature drops significantly, and the seatrout also seeks the insulation of deeper water during intense summer heat. Therefore, although seatrout can be caught all year in the southern part of their range, the fishing is best in late spring and again in fall. Winter fishing can be excellent even in cooler latitudes at spots where deep pockets lie close to banks, flats, or shore. In the holes at North Carolina's Core Banks, for example, plenty of seatrout are caught from November to February.

The markings on a spotted seatrout are unmistakable. Dark gray or olive-gray above and silver below, the fish is paler than its northern relative and has big, round black spots scattered over the back, upper sides, tail, and dorsal fins.

FISH HABITAT & FEEDING BEHAVIOR—ANGLING TACTICS:

Many experienced northern anglers accept the notion that weakfish refuse to bite until after they spawn. On the contrary, fish of the genus *Cynoscion,* unlike some game species, feed voraciously during the breeding period. They are merely hard to locate until the water warms up. They arrive in Long Island's shallows, for example, about mid-April, when the water temperature is be-

tween 55° and 65°, and they quickly find four- to eight-foot depths with a temperature of about 60° or higher where the tides bring them food: shrimp, small crabs, mollusks, sand lances, squid, sea worms, and small fish such as young menhaden, killies, silversides, or butterfish. The crustaceans are most important. An ideal spot, therefore, would be a warm channel of the right depth, draining an expanse of flats or shoals, since it carries prey from the adjacent shallow water on the falling tide. Similarly, troughs and creek outlets are prime early-season spots. Only later, after spawning on the flats, do the weakfish disperse into the bays.

Depending on region, habitat, and the characteristics of local weakfish, spawning may last a few days or a month. In Massachusetts, it occurs in late June, in New York from late May to June, in New Jersey a few weeks earlier, and down in the Carolinas from March through May. Weakfish spawn in 60° to 65° water on grassy flats. Spotted seatrout spawn in warm, shallow bays and lagoons from March to November, depending on region.

In most respects, the habits and habitat of weakfish and spotted seatrout are alike. Weakfish are caught in sounds, inlets, bays, estuaries, sloughs, and saltwater creeks. They forage prin-

Spotted seatrout caught by wading grassy flats.

cipally over sand in tide-rips, channel flows, the surf zone, and over ledged or shelved bottoms. Prey-collecting pockets at jetties, bridges, piers, and causeways are also productive, especially from dusk through the night, and salt-marsh creeks are particularly good in autumn. The best times of day vary locally but, generally speaking, the most weakfish are caught from about an hour before flood tide through the first two hours of ebb. (In some southern bays it is better from two hours before flood through the first hour of ebb, and best of all if the tide begins to fall very early in the morning.) A new moon or quarter-moon also seems to help.

Depending on what prey is plentiful at a given time and place, weakfish may feed anywhere from the bottom to just under the surface. Shrimp drift with the tide near the surface, and sometimes small baitfish collect at that level in creeks or over sandy or grassy flats. Anglers cast into the surf, and to probe the other aforementioned spots they still-fish or troll the surface and the middle depths, drift or still-fish the bottom, and jig both on the bottom and in the middle depths.

Along the beaches, light and medium 8- to 10-foot surfcasting rods are used, generally with line testing from 20 to 36 pounds. The tackle that prevails in a given place is governed by the size of the local fish, the distance needed to cast to them, the best local depths, and the strength of current and wind. Beyond the surf, long, limber "bay rods" and short baitcasting outfits remain popular but are overshadowed by spinning rods employing monofilament line of 6- to 10-pound breaking strength.

The best bait is shrimp, alone or in combination with a piece of sandworm or bloodworm. A worm alone is also good, as is a squid or fish strip, a piece of crab or clam, a small live crab, or a live killy. Sometimes weakfish become selective, and a two-hook rig with two different baits may reveal what they are eating.

A good rig for fishing just under the surface is a sinkerless hook on 2 or 3 feet of monofilament leader with or without a barrel swivel. If a strong current holds it up on top, it can be sunk slightly with split shot; if it sinks too far or is too heavy to drift away from the boat, a small bobber can be added. Hook sizes range from no. 1 where the fish are running fairly small to 2/0 for 5-pounders and up to 6/0 where there is a chance of catching lunkers. Both for this subsurface fishing and for prospecting the lower strata from a boat, chumming helps immeasurably. The boat should be anchored quietly, because weakfish are easily put off by unfamiliar disturbances. A mild current and a lack of boat traffic constitute ideal conditions. The best chum is grass shrimp (though other kinds work well) served a few at a time to drift out with very short spaces between servings. Three quarts can be used up in the best three hours of the tide change. Other good chum ingredients include ground menhaden or other fish, clams, or mussels. Ground chum can be stretched with bread crumbs or boiled rice and used more sparingly than shrimp. If no action is elicited by a bait drifting in the chum perhaps 100 feet from the boat, a couple of alternative tactics are available. One is to weight the offering to try different levels. The other is to jig a baited lure such as a metal squid or mackerel jig.

For bottom-fishing, a two-hook high-low rig is efficacious. A swivel-equipped egg or round sinker moves nicely with the current if it is just heavy enough to stay down; the high hook goes on a 4- or 5-foot leader attached several feet up, the low one on a 2- or 3-foot leader a few inches above the sinker. Both hooks can be baited for weakfish, or the low one can be baited for locally prevalent bottom-dwellers to improve the chance of frequent bites. A lighter version, utilizing one or two hooks on shorter leaders, lends itself to drifting. Where fish are concentrated, slow trolling also brings strikes. Surface and diving plugs, bucktails, small tin squid, and jigs are used. A spinner designed for use with bait is excellent; the author's choice would be a June Bug or Cape Cod spinner with a sandworm.

Surf-fishing is often done on the bottom with a sea worm, shrimp, sand eel, or piece of squid, crab, or fish. A standard rig employs a three-way swivel to connect the line, a pyramid sinker, and a 1½- to 2-foot leader. However, many of us prefer the sliding-sinker arrangement of a fishfinder rig. Either way, a small cork on the leader will buoy the bait up above grasping crabs. Surf lures are also effective. The most traditional is a shiny lead or chromed squid (sometimes painted white or yellow, sometimes bent to approximate local baitfish) dressed at the rear with a bucktail, feather, or pork rind. Other good surf lures are jigs, small, flashy spoons, and small wobbling plugs.

One of the best boat tactics is jigging, either while drifting or anchored. Small diamond jigs are often used, but the newer leadheaded plastic jigs that imitate shrimp are so enticing to weakfish that they have all but replaced bait for some anglers.

Much of what has been said about weakfishing can be applied to spotted-seatrout fishing, but the little differences are important. When shrimp are plentiful, seatrout may feed on them almost exclusively, and other baits may be of no avail. These fish do, however, like to prey on mullet, menhaden, and silversides. They will take small live baitfish, small crabs, or cut mullet. When shrimp are drifting near the top, seatrout are sometimes seen and heard as they gulp the prey with a plopping commotion. An angler can achieve the same effect with a popping plug, either used alone or with a bucktail trailing an inch or so behind it.

There is also good sport to be had from bridges and causeways by drifting a live shrimp, needlefish, or small mullet. But in very hot weather it is best to fish relatively deep holes at night on a moving tide. In general, the most productive tide stages and times of day are the same as for northern weakfish, but in pleasant spring or fall weather seatrout feed in shallower water. One can wade oyster beds, shrimp-rich flats, and the vicinity of mullet-gathering holes on a falling tide in water so shallow that it is possible to watch seatrout feeding and cast to them with bait, jigs, spoons, spinners, popping bugs, streamers, or plugs. The best plugs are silvery models that look like mullet or needlefish.

No solid evidence supports the contention that one part of the country breeds more polished sportsmen than other sections, so perhaps the southern adherence to very light tackle can be attributed to the shallow habitat of the fish. Though long casts are frequent, experienced anglers disdain anything heftier than a 6½-foot spinning rod with monofilament testing 8 pounds or a shorter baitcasting outfit for plugging with 10-pound test. It is in the South, too, that fly fishing for this sort of game has won the greatest favor. An 8½- or 9-foot bass-bugging rod is suitable, in summer with a weight-forward floating line and in winter with a sinking-tip line. A short leader tapered to a tippet of 12-pound strength is also suitable. When seatrout are popping at shrimp, popping bugs on no. 2 and 1/0 hooks will fool them. When they root about in grass, a better ploy is a small bucktail on a size 2 keel hook. Most of the time, however, the most appealing lures are shrimp flies or somewhat larger bucktails tied on 1/0 hooks with flashing strips of Mylar. Effective colors are pink, yellow, red and white, and green and white.

Index

Picture references are in italics

524/Index